Cosori Air Fryer Cookbook

Over 500 easy and healthy recipes for the Cosori Air Fryer, with a wide variety of delicious dishes to fry.

Tina Robinson

All Rights Reserved.

The content contained within this book may not be reproduced, duplicated, or transmitted without direct written permission from the author or the publisher. Under no circumstances will any blame or legal responsibility be held against the publisher, or author, for any damages, reparation, or monetary loss due to the information contained within this book, either directly or indirectly.

Legal Notice: This book is copyright protected. It is only for personal use. You cannot amend, distribute, sell, use, quote or paraphrase any part, or the content within this book, without the consent of the author or publisher.

Disclaimer Notice:

Please note the information contained within this document is for educational and entertainment purposes only. All effort has been executed to present accurate, up to date, reliable, complete information. No warranties of any kind are declared or implied. Readers acknowledge that the author is not engaged in the rendering of legal, financial, medical, or professional advice. The content within this book has been derived from various sources. Please consult a licensed professional before attempting any techniques outlined in this book. By reading this document, the reader agrees that under no circumstances is the author responsible for any losses, direct or indirect, that are incurred as a result of the use of the information contained within this document, including, but not limited to, errors, omissions, or inaccuracies.

CONTENTS

Introduction 10

Chapter 1 Getting Started with Your Cosori Air Fryer 11

What is a Cosori Air Fryer? 11
How & Why does it work? 12
How to Clean a Cosori Air Fryer? 12
How to maintenance Cosori Air Fryer? 13

Chapter 2 Bread And Breakfast Recipes 14

1......Green Egg Quiche 14
2......Healthy Granola 14
3......Banana-strawberry Cakecups 14
4......Tri-color Frittata 14
5......Easy Caprese Flatbread 15
6......Blueberry Pannenkoek (dutch Pancake) 15
7......Egg & Bacon Toasts 15
8......Chicken Scotch Eggs 15
9......Garlic Parmesan Bread Ring 15
10....Banana Muffins With Chocolate Chips 16
11....Mini Everything Bagels 16
12....Easy Corn Dog Cupcakes 16
13....Thai Turkey Sausage Patties 16
14....Parsley Egg Scramble With Cottage Cheese ... 17
15....Pesto Egg & Ham Sandwiches 17
16....Christmas Eggnog Bread 17
17....Cherry Beignets 17
18....Breakfast Burrito With Sausage 17
19....Peach Fritters 18
20....Western Frittata 18
21....Lime Muffins 19
22....Breakfast Frittata 19
23....Cheddar Cheese Biscuits 19
24....Breakfast Pot Pies 19
25....Carrot Orange Muffins 20
26....Cinnamon-coconut Doughnuts 20
27....Green Onion Pancakes 20
28....Mini Bacon Egg Quiches 21
29....Roasted Tomato And Cheddar Rolls 21
30....Vodka Basil Muffins With Strawberries 21
31....English Scones 21
32....Cream Cheese Deviled Eggs 22
33....Avocado Toasts With Poached Eggs 22
34....Huevos Rancheros 22
35....Chia Seed Banana Bread 22
36....Farmers Market Quiche 23
37....Blueberry French Toast Sticks 23
38....Orange Trail Oatmeal 23
39....Mediterranean Granola 23
40....Apple-cinnamon-walnut Muffins 24
41....Mascarpone Iced Cinnamon Rolls 24
42....Pepperoni Pizza Bread 24
43....Banana-blackberry Muffins 25
44....Broccoli Cornbread 25
45....Sweet-hot Pepperoni Pizza 25
46....Bacon, Broccoli And Swiss Cheese Bread Pudding 25
47....Honey Oatmeal 26
48....Ham And Cheddar Gritters 26
49....Egg And Sausage Crescent Rolls 26
50....Shakshuka Cups 26
51....French Toast Sticks 27
52....Walnut Pancake 27
53....Mini Pita Breads 27
54....Sugar-dusted Beignets 28
55....Apple & Turkey Breakfast Sausages 28
56....Cinnamon Pear Oat Muffins 28
57....Coconut & Peanut Rice Cereal 28
58....Lemon-blueberry Morning Bread 28
59....Herby Parmesan Pita 29
60....Crunchy Granola Muffins 29
61....Smooth Walnut-banana Loaf 29
62....Thyme Beef & Eggs 29
63....Chorizo Sausage & Cheese Balls 30

Chapter 3 Appetizers And Snacks Recipes 30

- 64....Seafood Egg Rolls 30
- 65....Fried Bananas 30
- 66....Grilled Cheese Sandwich Deluxe 30
- 67....Roasted Tomatillo Salsa 31
- 68....Fried Wontons 31
- 69....Artichoke-spinach Dip 31
- 70....Savory Sausage Balls 31
- 71....Poutine 32
- 72....Shrimp Egg Rolls 32
- 73....Plantain Chips 32
- 74....Zucchini Boats With Bacon 33
- 75....Antipasto-stuffed Cherry Tomatoes 33
- 76....Tomato & Garlic Roasted Potatoes 33
- 77....Cuban Sliders 33
- 78....Corn Dog Bites 33
- 79....Crispy Ravioli Bites 34
- 80....Onion Ring Nachos 34
- 81....String Bean Fries 34
- 82....Cheesy Pigs In A Blanket 35
- 83....Okra Chips 35
- 84....Rich Clam Spread 35
- 85....Avocado Fries, Vegan 35
- 86....Eggs In Avocado Halves 35
- 87....Root Vegetable Crisps 36
- 88....Balsamic Grape Dip 36
- 89....Red Potato Chips With Mexican Dip 36
- 90....Avocado Fries 36
- 91....Avocado Egg Rolls 37
- 92....Fried String Beans With Greek Sauce 37
- 93....Fried Peaches 37
- 94....Piri Piri Chicken Wings 37
- 95....Mozzarella En Carrozza With Puttanesca Sauce 38
- 96....Poppy Seed Mini Hot Dog Rolls 38
- 97....Hawaiian Ahi Tuna Bowls 38
- 98....Asian Five-spice Wings 39
- 99....Olive & Pepper Tapenade 39
- 100..Turkey Burger Sliders 39
- 101..Rumaki 39
- 102..Onion Puffs 39
- 103..Jalapeño Poppers 40
- 104..Cauliflower "tater" Tots 40
- 105..Honey-mustard Chicken Wings 40
- 106..Canadian-inspired Waffle Poutine 41
- 107..Mediterranean Potato Skins 41
- 108..Cinnamon Sweet Potato Fries 41
- 109..Spicy Sweet Potato Tater-tots 41
- 110..Crispy Tofu Bites 42
- 111..Russian Pierogi With Cheese Dip 42
- 112..Cajun-spiced Pickle Chips 42
- 113..Ranch Chips 42
- 114..Fried Dill Pickle Chips 42
- 115..Avocado Fries With Quick Salsa Fresca 43
- 116..Zucchini Fritters 43
- 117..Baba Ghanouj 43
- 118..Crab Rangoon Dip With Wonton Chips 44
- 119..Italian-style Fried Olives 44
- 120..Chinese-style Potstickers 44
- 121..Taquito Quesadillas 45
- 122..Garlic-herb Pita Chips 45
- 123..Turkey Spring Rolls 45
- 124..Breaded Mozzarella Sticks 45
- 125..Sweet Plantain Chips 45
- 126..Crab-stuffed Mushrooms 46
- 127..Paprika Onion Blossom 46
- 128..Crispy Curried Sweet Potato Fries 46
- 129..Sweet Chili Peanuts 46
- 130..Cheddar Stuffed Jalapeños 47
- 131..Vegetarian Fritters With Green Dip 47
- 132..Easy Crab Cakes 47
- 133..Spiced Roasted Pepitas 47
- 134..Fiery Sweet Chicken Wings 47
- 135..Classic Chicken Wings 48
- 136..Cheesy Potato Canapés With Bacon 48
- 137..Spiced Parsnip Chips 48
- 138..Cheesy Tortellini Bites 48

Chapter 4 Beef, pork & Lamb Recipes 49

139..Cheesy Mushroom-stuffed Pork Loins 49
140..Crispy Ham And Eggs 49
141..Wasabi-coated Pork Loin Chops 49
142..Mini Meatloaves With Pancetta 49
143..Wiener Schnitzel 50
144..Peppered Steak Bites 50
145..Crispy Pork Pork Escalopes 50
146..Citrus Pork Lettuce Wraps 50
147..French-style Steak Salad 50
148..Suwon Pork Meatballs 51
149..Tex-mex Beef Carnitas 51
150..Crispy Pierogi With Kielbasa And Onions 51
151..Kielbasa Sausage With Pierogies And Caramelized Onions 51
152..Easy Carnitas 52
153..Tuscan Chimichangas 52
154..Balsamic Beef & Veggie Skewers 52
155..Mongolian Beef 52
156..Lamb Meatballs With Quick Tomato Sauce 53
157..Spicy Hoisin Bbq Pork Chops 53
158..Beef Short Ribs 54
159..Blackberry Bbq Glazed Country-style Ribs 54
160..Crispy Lamb Shoulder Chops 54
161..Pork Chops With Cereal Crust 54
162..Kawaii Pork Roast 55
163..Provençal Grilled Rib-eye 55
164..Boneless Ribeyes 55
165..Kochukaru Pork Lettuce Cups 55
166..Orange Glazed Pork Tenderloin 55
167..Cal-mex Chimichangas 56
168..Tender Steak With Salsa Verde 56
169..Carne Asada 56
170..Leftover Roast Beef Risotto 56

171..Pork Schnitzel With Dill Sauce 57
172..T-bone Steak With Roasted Tomato, Corn And Asparagus Salsa 57
173..Lemon-garlic Strip Steak 57
174..Lemon Pork Escalopes 58
175..Authentic Country-style Pork Ribs 58
176..Asian-style Flank Steak 58
177..Indian Fry Bread Tacos 58
178..Classic Salisbury Steak Burgers 59
179..Sage Pork With Potatoes 59
180..Aromatic Pork Tenderloin 59
181..Basil Cheese & Ham Stromboli 59
182..Pork Cutlets With Almond-lemon Crust 59
183..French-style Pork Medallions 60
184..Creamy Horseradish Roast Beef 60
185..Skirt Steak Fajitas 60
186..Coffee-rubbed Pork Tenderloin 61
187..Original Köttbullar 61
188..Air-fried Roast Beef With Rosemary Roasted Potatoes 61
189..Sausage-cheese Calzone 61
190..Cinnamon-stick Kofta Skewers 62
191..Crispy Five-spice Pork Belly 62
192..Flank Steak With Chimichurri Sauce 63
193..Marinated Rib-eye Steak With Herb Roasted Mushrooms 63
194..Spiced Beef Empanadas 63
195..Calf's Liver 64
196..Paprika Fried Beef 64
197..Natchitoches Meat Pies 64
198..Pepperoni Bagel Pizzas 64
199..Stuffed Pork Chops 65
200..Pepper Steak 65
201..Lazy Mexican Meat Pizza 65
202..Easy-peasy Beef Sliders 65

Chapter 5 Poultry Recipes 66

- 203..Cal-mex Turkey Patties 66
- 204..Turkey Burgers 66
- 205..Air-fried Turkey Breast With Cherry Glaze 66
- 206..Sesame Orange Chicken 66
- 207..Turkey Scotch Eggs 67
- 208..Chicken Pigs In Blankets 67
- 209..Teriyaki Chicken Drumsticks 67
- 210..Buffalo Egg Rolls 68
- 211..Chicken Chimichangas 68
- 212..Moroccan-style Chicken Strips 68
- 213..Vip´s Club Sandwiches 69
- 214..Chicken Fried Steak With Gravy 69
- 215..Nacho Chicken Fries 69
- 216..Chicken Cordon Bleu 70
- 217..Daadi Chicken Salad 70
- 218..Crunchy Chicken Strips 70
- 219..Parmesan Chicken Meatloaf 70
- 220..Crispy Duck With Cherry Sauce 71
- 221..Turkey-hummus Wraps 71
- 222..Taquitos 71
- 223..Berry-glazed Turkey Breast 72
- 224..Buttermilk-fried Drumsticks 72
- 225..Spicy Black Bean Turkey Burgers With Cumin-avocado Spread 72
- 226..Maple Bacon Wrapped Chicken Breasts 73
- 227..Goat Cheese Stuffed Turkey Roulade 73
- 228..Fennel & Chicken Ratatouille 73
- 229..Spring Chicken Salad 73
- 230..Spinach And Feta Stuffed Chicken Breasts 74
- 231..Crispy "fried" Chicken 74
- 232..Peachy Chicken Chunks With Cherries 74
- 233..Spiced Mexican Stir-fried Chicken 74
- 234..Cornish Hens With Honey-lime Glaze 75
- 235..Buttery Chicken Legs 75
- 236..Sweet Nutty Chicken Breasts 75
- 237..Ranch Chicken Tortillas 75
- 238..Intense Buffalo Chicken Wings 75
- 239..Mushroom & Turkey Bread Pizza 76
- 240..Chicken Breasts Wrapped In Bacon 76
- 241..German Chicken Frikadellen 76
- 242..Cheesy Chicken-avocado Paninis 76
- 243..Indian-inspired Chicken Skewers 76
- 244..Party Buffalo Chicken Drumettes 77
- 245..Mumbai Chicken Nuggets 77
- 246..Greek Gyros With Chicken & Rice 77
- 247..Cantonese Chicken Drumsticks 77
- 248..Rich Turkey Burgers 78
- 249..Fancy Chicken Piccata 78
- 250..Tuscan Stuffed Chicken 78
- 251..Maewoon Chicken Legs 78
- 252..Indian Chicken Tandoori 78
- 253..Farmer´s Fried Chicken 79
- 254..Coconut Chicken With Apricot-ginger Sauce 79
- 255..Satay Chicken Skewers 79
- 256..Country Chicken Hoagies 80
- 257..Honey Lemon Thyme Glazed Cornish Hen 80
- 258..Chicken Thighs In Salsa Verde 80
- 259..Turkey Tenderloin With A Lemon Touch 80
- 260..Cheesy Chicken Tenders 80
- 261..Yogurt-marinated Chicken Legs 81
- 262..Cornflake Chicken Nuggets 81
- 263..Chicken Wellington 81
- 264..Asian-style Orange Chicken 81
- 265..Super-simple Herby Turkey 82

Chapter 6 Fish And Seafood Recipes 82

- 266..Cheesy Salmon-stuffed Avocados 82
- 267..Garlic-butter Lobster Tails 82
- 268..Creole Tilapia With Garlic Mayo 82
- 269..Easy Scallops With Lemon Butter 83
- 270..Crab Cakes 83
- 271..Fish Sticks For Grown-ups 83
- 272..Miso-rubbed Salmon Fillets 83
- 273..Salmon Puttanesca En Papillotte With Zucchini 84
- 274..Salmon Croquettes 84
- 275..Rich Salmon Burgers With Broccoli Slaw 84
- 276..Salty German-style Shrimp Pancakes 85
- 277..Crispy Fish Sandwiches 85
- 278..Fish Nuggets With Broccoli Dip 85
- 279..Horseradish Crusted Salmon 85

280..Collard Green & Cod Packets 86
281..Summer Sea Scallops 86
282..Cajun Flounder Fillets 86
283..Lightened-up Breaded Fish Filets 86
284..Shrimp Patties 86
285..Hot Calamari Rings 87
286..Mexican-style Salmon Stir-fry 87
287..Garlic-lemon Steamer Clams 87
288..King Prawns Al Ajillo 87
289..Old Bay Lobster Tails 87
290..Spiced Shrimp Empanadas 88
291..Sweet Potato–wrapped Shrimp 88
292..Mediterranean Salmon Cakes 88
293..Herb-rubbed Salmon With Avocado 88
294..Shrimp, Chorizo And Fingerling Potatoes 89
295..Quick Tuna Tacos 89
296..Crabmeat-stuffed Flounder 89
297..Sinaloa Fish Fajitas 89
298..Fish Cakes 90
299..Tilapia Al Pesto 90
300..Oyster Shrimp With Fried Rice 90
301..Caribbean Jerk Cod Fillets 90
302..Southern Shrimp With Cocktail Sauce 91
303..Saucy Shrimp 91
304..Parmesan Fish Bites 91
305..Cheese & Crab Stuffed Mushrooms 91
306..Shrimp Sliders With Avocado 92
307..Flounder Fillets 92
308..Piña Colada Shrimp 92
309..Fish Tacos With Jalapeño-lime Sauce 93
310..Smoked Paprika Cod Goujons 93
311..Coconut-shrimp Po' Boys 93
312..Tuna Nuggets In Hoisin Sauce 94
313..Curried Sweet-and-spicy Scallops 94
314..Asian-style Salmon Fillets 94

Chapter 7 Vegetarians Recipes 95

315..Black Bean Empanadas 95
316..Quinoa & Black Bean Stuffed Peppers 95
317..Sushi-style Deviled Eggs 95
318..Mushroom And Fried Onion Quesadilla 96
319..Cheesy Eggplant Rounds 96
320..Quinoa Green Pizza 96
321..Hearty Salad 96
322..Pineapple & Veggie Souvlaki 97
323..Roasted Vegetable Lasagna 97
324..Party Giant Nachos 97
325..Two-cheese Grilled Sandwiches 98
326..Vegetarian Shepherd´s Pie 98
327..Tandoori Paneer Naan Pizza 98
328..Mushroom Lasagna 99
329..Golden Breaded Mushrooms 99
330..Crunchy Rice Paper Samosas 99
331..Harissa Veggie Fries 99
332..Tropical Salsa 100
333..Rainbow Quinoa Patties 100
334..Stuffed Portobellos 100
335..Sweet Corn Bread 100
336..Cheddar-bean Flautas 101
337..Easy Zucchini Lasagna Roll-ups 101
338..Stuffed Zucchini Boats 101
339..Veggie Burgers 101
340..Curried Potato, Cauliflower And Pea Turnovers 102
341..Roasted Veggie Bowls 102
342..Lentil Burritos With Cilantro Chutney 102
343..Arancini With Marinara 103
344..Colorful Vegetable Medley 103
345..Cheese & Bean Burgers 103
346..Garlic Okra Chips 103
347..Spaghetti Squash And Kale Fritters With Pomodoro Sauce 104
348..Meatless Kimchi Bowls 104
349..Bell Pepper & Lentil Tacos 104
350..Falafels 105
351..Curried Cauliflower 105
352..Effortless Mac ´n´ Cheese 105
353..Tex-mex Potatoes With Avocado Dressing 105
354..Cheesy Veggie Frittata 105
355..Tofu & Spinach Lasagna 106
356..Spinach And Cheese Calzone 106
357..Honey Pear Chips 106
358..Crispy Apple Fries With Caramel Sauce 106
359..Spinach & Brie Frittata 106

360. Healthy Living Mushroom Enchiladas 107
361. Fried Potatoes With Bell Peppers 107
362. Spring Veggie Empanadas 107
363. Mexican Twice Air-fried Sweet Potatoes ... 108
364. Chicano Rice Bowls 108
365. Pine Nut Eggplant Dip 108
366. Garlicky Roasted Mushrooms 109
367. Mushroom, Zucchini And Black Bean Burgers 109
368. Roasted Vegetable Pita Pizza 109
369. Creamy Broccoli & Mushroom Casserole 109

Chapter 8 Vegetable Side Dishes Recipes 110

370. Speedy Baked Caprese With Avocado 110
371. Green Dip With Pine Nuts 110
372. Tuna Platter 110
373. Dijon Artichoke Hearts 110
374. Tofu & Broccoli Salad 110
375. Blistered Green Beans 111
376. Parmesan Asparagus 111
377. Okra 111
378. Latkes 111
379. Zucchini Fries 112
380. Herbed Zucchini Poppers 112
381. Sweet Roasted Pumpkin Rounds 112
382. Simple Zucchini Ribbons 112
383. Butternut Medallions With Honey Butter And Sage . 113
384. Steakhouse Baked Potatoes 113
385. Sesame Carrots And Sugar Snap Peas 113
386. Glazed Carrots 113
387. Creole Potato Wedges 114
388. Asiago Broccoli 114
389. Salt And Pepper Baked Potatoes 114
390. Stuffed Onions 114
391. Crispy Noodle Salad 115
392. Goat Cheese Stuffed Portobellos 115
393. Fried Pearl Onions With Balsamic Vinegar And Basil 115
394. Fried Eggplant Slices 115
395. Perfect Broccolini 116
396. Succulent Roasted Peppers 116
397. Cheesy Potato Pot 116
398. Simple Green Bake 116
399. Green Beans 117
400. Spiced Pumpkin Wedges 117
401. Jerk Rubbed Corn On The Cob 117
402. Summer Vegetables With Balsamic Drizzle, Goat Cheese And Basil 117
403. Ajillo Mushrooms 117
404. Curried Cauliflower With Cashews And Yogurt 118
405. Smooth & Silky Cauliflower Purée 118
406. Broccoli Au Gratin 118
407. Sticky Broccoli Florets 118
408. Roasted Brussels Sprouts 118
409. Almond-crusted Zucchini Fries 119
410. Roasted Fennel Salad 119
411. Basic Corn On The Cob 119
412. Hasselback Garlic-and-butter Potatoes 119
413. Beet Fries 120
414. Mom´s Potatoes Au Gratin 120
415. Honey-roasted Parsnips 120
416. Roasted Eggplant Halves With Herbed Ricotta .. 120
417. Tomato Candy 121
418. Hasselbacks 121
419. Fried Okra 121
420. Crispy Herbed Potatoes 121
421. Sriracha Green Beans 122
422. Parsnip Fries With Romesco Sauce 122
423. Lemony Green Bean Sautée 122
424. Roasted Broccoli And Red Bean Salad 122
425. Sea Salt Radishes 123
426. Balsamic Stuffed Mushrooms 123
427. Thyme Sweet Potato Wedges 123
428. Home Fries 123
429. Turkish Mutabal (eggplant Dip) 123
430. Curried Fruit 123
431. Pecorino Dill Muffins 124
432. Herb Roasted Jicama 124
433. Veggie Fritters 124
434. Dijon Roasted Purple Potatoes 124
435. Tasty Brussels Sprouts With Guanciale 124
436. Fried Cauliflowerwith Parmesan Lemon Dressing 125
437. Cheese-rice Stuffed Bell Peppers 125

Chapter 9 Desserts And Sweets Recipes ... 125

- 438..Nutty Cookies ... 125
- 439..Banana-almond Delights ... 125
- 440..Cinnamon Canned Biscuit Donuts ... 126
- 441..Cheese Blintzes ... 126
- 442..Sweet Potato Donut Holes ... 126
- 443..Honey-roasted Mixed Nuts ... 126
- 444..Nutty Banana Bread ... 127
- 445..Giant Buttery Chocolate Chip Cookie ... 127
- 446..Peanut Butter Cup Doughnut Holes ... 127
- 447..Maple Cinnamon Cheesecake ... 128
- 448..Giant Buttery Oatmeal Cookie ... 128
- 449..Fluffy Orange Cake ... 128
- 450..Sea-salted Caramel Cookie Cups ... 128
- 451..Homemade Chips Ahoy ... 129
- 452..Strawberry Pastry Rolls ... 129
- 453..Healthy Chickpea Cookies ... 129
- 454..Honeyed Tortilla Fritters ... 129
- 455..Mango Cobbler With Raspberries ... 130
- 456..Honey-pecan Yogurt Cake ... 130
- 457..Coconut Cream Roll-ups ... 130
- 458..Berry Streusel Cake ... 131
- 459..Orange Gooey Butter Cake ... 131
- 460..Mixed Berry Pie ... 131
- 461..Vanilla-strawberry Muffins ... 132
- 462..Brownies With White Chocolate ... 132
- 463..Giant Oatmeal–peanut Butter Cookie ... 132
- 464..Famous Chocolate Lava Cake ... 132
- 465..One-bowl Chocolate Buttermilk Cake ... 133
- 466..Apple & Blueberry Crumble ... 133
- 467..Baked Caramelized Peaches ... 133
- 468..Pear And Almond Biscotti Crumble ... 133
- 469..Dark Chocolate Cream Galette ... 134
- 470..Nutella Torte ... 134
- 471..British Bread Pudding ... 134
- 472..Rich Blueberry Biscuit Shortcakes ... 134
- 473..Apple Crisp ... 135
- 474..Fruity Oatmeal Crisp ... 135
- 475..Cheese & Honey Stuffed Figs ... 135
- 476..Air-fried Beignets ... 135
- 477..Fried Banana S'mores ... 136
- 478..Pumpkin Brownies ... 136
- 479..Strawberry Donuts ... 136
- 480..Mini Carrot Cakes ... 136
- 481..Spiced Fruit Skewers ... 137
- 482..Easy Churros ... 137
- 483..Sugared Pizza Dough Dippers With Raspberry Cream Cheese Dip ... 137
- 484..Banana Fritters ... 138
- 485..Mom´s Amaretto Cheesecake ... 138
- 486..Fried Pineapple Chunks ... 138
- 487..Blueberry Cheesecake Tartlets ... 138
- 488..Peanut Butter S'mores ... 139
- 489..Fried Cannoli Wontons ... 139
- 490..Oreo-coated Peanut Butter Cups ... 139
- 491..Chewy Coconut Cake ... 140
- 492..Chocolate Cake ... 140
- 493..Tortilla Fried Pies ... 140
- 494..Mango-chocolate Custard ... 140
- 495..Custard ... 141
- 496..Cherry Cheesecake Rolls ... 141
- 497..Chocolate Soufflés ... 141
- 498..Black And Blue Clafoutis ... 141
- 499..Fast Brownies ... 142
- 500..Caramel Blondies With Macadamia Nuts ... 142

RECIPES INDEX ... 143

Introduction

Whether you're an Cosori Air Fryer beginner or a veteran, you likely know that this mighty appliance has been revolutionizing kitchens everywhere for the past few years with no signs of slowing down. Cosori Air fryers continue to rise in popularity not only because they offer reduced cooking times and crispy food without all the oil and fat, but also because they can replace your oven, microwave, deep fryer, and dehydrator. All this saves you time, money, and precious counter space! Coriso Air frying makes it easy to feed your whole family healthy, irresistible meals !

Hi, my name is Tina Robinson. I am cookbook author and a Cosori Air Fryer recipe developer.I have been developing Cosori Air Fryer for 8 years.This is my third cookbook about Cosori Air Fryer. Thank you for choose my cookbook and start your Cosori Air Fryer journey with me!

This Cosori Air Fryer cookbook is suitable for both beginner and experienced users of the Cosori Air Fryer and has a wide variety of recipes for any taste. The recipes included are also easy to follow. Throughout this book you'll learn everything you need to know about using an Cosori air fryer, how to use your Cosiri Air Fryer , how to clean Cosiri Air Fryer, how to maintain Cosiri Air Fryer, as well as helpful ways to elevate your meals, even if you're completely new to cooking. So let's get air frying!

you'll find 600 easy, healthy, mouth-watering recipes for every occasion, from game day to Thanksgiving dinner, from breakfasts, lunches, and snacks to filling main courses and delectable desserts—all ready in less time than traditional cooking methods.

Along with delicious recipes, you'll find loads of kitchen hacks and flavoring suggestions to make cooking even more convenient and fitted to your preferences—there are so many ways to cut corners in the kitchen without cutting down on flavor!

In this book I will share the knowledge and experience to produce amazing meal with your Cosori air fryer. I never cut the concern when it comes to flavor ,but these are tricks I've learned over the years. I hope you're excited about the journey ahead.Welcome aboard. I'm thrilled to have you along!

Chapter 1 Getting Started with Your Cosori Air Fryer

What is a Cosori Air Fryer?

It is a counter top kitchen appliance that cooks similar to a convection oven but faster. It's hit the world with a bang and is making waves across borders.

It is particularly known for its ability to cook food to deep fried crispy perfection with little or no oil. It does this by its speedy air and heat circulation technology.

How & Why does it work?

The top section of an air fryer holds a heating mechanism and fan. You place the food in a fryer-style basket and when you turn it on, hot air rushes down and around the food. This rapid circulation makes the food crisp—much like deep-frying, but without the oil. It cooks food to crispy perfection. Thanks to its well aerated inner basket. It has a square basket which contains more than round baskets. Cooks food in less time than in the oven. I share more reasons further down in the pros & cons section of this guide.

How to Clean a Cosori Air Fryer?

1. Unplug the machine from the power outlet and wait for it to cool down.

2. Place a folded towel on top of a kitchen counter or table and put your air fryer on it.

3. Take off the top part of the machine that houses the air hole (the one that protects you from hot air).

4. Place another folded towel on top of the machine and unplug it again.

5. Put both parts on top of the machine that has been removed. This will protect them from dropping and damaging the machine during dishwasher washing.

6. Wash the Cosori air fryer parts in the dishwasher as usual.

7. Before you put them back together, make sure that all parts are clean and dry.

8. Put the top part of the air fryer back on and tighten screws to secure it in place.

9. Put in a small amount of vegetable oil (about 1 tablespoon) through the air hole that was covered by a metal door before you put the machine in a dishwasher for washing. This will protect the oils from spilling out during dishwasher washing.

10. Place the air fryer in the dishwasher and run it through a normal cycle.

11. When you're done, remove both parts of the machine, dry them in a towel, and plug in your Cosori air fryer once again.

12. Put them back together and make sure you put them back in place correctly this time.

How to maintenance Cosori Air Fryer?

Note:

Always clean the air fryer baskets and interior after every use.

Lining the outer basket with foil may make cleanup easier.

·Turn off and unplug the air fryer. Allow it to cool completely before cleaning. Pull out the baskets for faster cooling.

·Wipe the outside of the air fryer with a moist cloth, if necessary.

· The baskets are dishwasher safe. You can also wash the baskets with hot, soapy water and a non-abrasive sponge. Soak if necessary
Note: Baskets have a nonstick coating. Avoid metal utensils and abrasive cleaning materials.

·For stubborn grease:

1.In a small bowl, mix 2 tablespoons(30 mL) of baking soda and 1 tablespoon (15 mL) of water to form a spreadable paste.

2.Use a sponge to spread the paste on the baskets and scrub. Let the baskets sit for 15 minutes before rinsing.

3.Wash baskets with soap and water before using.

·Clean the inside of the air fryer with a slightly moist, non-abrasive sponge or cloth. Do not immerse in water.[Figure 6.1] Clean the heating coil, if needed, to remove food debris.

·Dry before using.
Note: Make sure that the heating coil is dry before turning on the air fryer.

Chapter 2 Bread And Breakfast Recipes

Green Egg Quiche

Servings: 4
Cooking Time: 30 Minutes
Ingredients:
- 1 cup broccoli florets
- 2 cups baby spinach
- 2 garlic cloves, minced
- ¼ tsp ground nutmeg
- 1 tbsp olive oil
- Salt and pepper to taste
- 4 eggs
- 2 scallions, chopped
- 1 red onion, chopped
- 1 tbsp sour cream
- ½ cup grated fontina cheese

Directions:
1. Preheat air fryer to 375°F. Combine broccoli, spinach, onion, garlic, nutmeg, olive oil, and salt in a medium bowl, tossing to coat. Arrange the broccoli in a single layer in the parchment-lined frying basket and cook for 5 minutes. Remove and set to the side.
2. Use the same medium bowl to whisk eggs, salt, pepper, scallions, and sour cream. Add the roasted broccoli and ¼ cup fontina cheese until all ingredients are well combined. Pour the mixture into a greased baking dish and top with cheese. Bake in the air fryer for 15-18 minutes until the center is set. Serve and enjoy.

Healthy Granola

Servings: 4
Cooking Time: 10 Minutes
Ingredients:
- ¼ cup chocolate hazelnut spread
- 1 cup chopped pecans
- 1 cup quick-cooking oats
- 1 tbsp chia seeds
- 1 tbsp flaxseed
- 1 tbsp sesame seeds
- 1 cup coconut shreds
- ¼ cup maple syrup
- 1 tbsp light brown sugar
- ½ tsp vanilla extract
- ¼ cup hazelnut flour
- 2 tbsp cocoa powder
- Salt to taste

Directions:
1. Preheat air fryer at 350ºF. Combine the pecans, oats, chia seeds, flaxseed, sesame seeds, coconut shreds, chocolate hazelnut spread, maple syrup, sugar, vanilla extract, hazelnut flour, cocoa powder, and salt in a bowl. Press mixture into a greased cake pan. Place cake pan in the frying basket and Bake for 5 minutes, stirring once. Let cool completely before crumbling. Store it into an airtight container up to 5 days.

Banana-strawberry Cakecups

Servings: 6
Cooking Time: 25 Minutes
Ingredients:
- ½ cup mashed bananas
- ¼ cup maple syrup
- ½ cup Greek yogurt
- 1 tsp vanilla extract
- 1 egg
- 1 ½ cups flour
- 1 tbsp cornstarch
- ½ tsp baking soda
- ½ tsp baking powder
- ½ tsp salt
- ½ cup strawberries, sliced

Directions:
1. Preheat air fryer to 360°F. Place the mashed bananas, maple syrup, yogurt, vanilla, and egg in a large bowl and mix until smooth. Sift in 1 ½ cups of the flour, baking soda, baking powder, and salt, then stir to combine.
2. In a small bowl, toss the strawberries with the cornstarch. Fold the mixture into the muffin batter. Divide the mixture evenly between greased muffin cups and place into the air frying basket. Bake for 12-15 minutes until golden brown on top and a toothpick inserted into the middle of one of the muffins comes out clean. Leave to cool for 5 minutes. Serve and enjoy!

Tri-color Frittata

Servings: 4
Cooking Time: 30 Minutes
Ingredients:
- 8 eggs, beaten
- 1 red bell pepper, diced
- Salt and pepper to taste
- 1 garlic clove, minced
- ½ tsp dried oregano
- ½ cup ricotta

Directions:
1. Preheat air fryer to 360°F. Place the beaten eggs, bell pepper, oregano, salt, black pepper, and garlic and mix well. Fold in ¼ cup half of ricotta cheese.
2. Pour the egg mixture into a greased cake pan and top with the remaining ricotta. Place into the air fryer and Bake for 18-20 minutes or until the eggs are set in the center. Let the frittata cool for 5 minutes. Serve sliced.

Easy Caprese Flatbread

Servings: 2
Cooking Time: 15 Minutes
Ingredients:
- 1 fresh mozzarella ball, sliced
- 1 flatbread
- 2 tsp olive oil
- ¼ garlic clove, minced
- 1 egg
- ⅛ tsp salt
- ¼ cup diced tomato
- 6 basil leaves
- ½ tsp dried oregano
- ½ tsp balsamic vinegar

Directions:
1. Preheat air fryer to 380°F. Lightly brush the top of the bread with olive oil, then top with garlic. Crack the egg into a small bowl and sprinkle with salt. Place the bread into the frying basket and gently pour the egg onto the top of the pita. Top with tomato, mozzarella, oregano and basil. Bake for 6 minutes. When ready, remove the pita pizza and drizzle with balsamic vinegar. Let it cool for 5 minutes. Slice and serve.

Blueberry Pannenkoek (dutch Pancake)

Servings: 4
Cooking Time: 30 Minutes
Ingredients:
- 3 eggs, beaten
- ½ cup buckwheat flour
- ½ cup milk
- ½ tsp vanilla
- 1 ½ cups blueberries, crushed
- 2 tbsp powdered sugar

Directions:
1. Preheat air fryer to 330°F. Mix together eggs, buckwheat flour, milk, and vanilla in a bowl. Pour the batter into a greased baking pan and add it to the fryer. Bake until the pancake is puffed and golden, 12-16 minutes. Remove the pan and flip the pancake over onto a plate. Add blueberries and powdered sugar as a topping and serve.

Egg & Bacon Toasts

Servings: 4
Cooking Time: 25 Minutes
Ingredients:
- 4 French bread slices, cut diagonally
- 1 + tsp butter
- 4 eggs
- 2 tbsp milk
- ½ tsp dried thyme
- Salt and pepper to taste
- 4 oz cooked bacon, crumbled
- 2/3 cup grated Colby cheese

Directions:
1. Preheat the air fryer to 350°F. Spray each slice of bread with oil and Bake in the frying basket for 2-3 minutes until light brown; set aside. Beat together the eggs, milk, thyme, salt, and pepper in a bowl and add the melted butter. Transfer to a 6-inch cake pan and place the pan into the fryer. Bake for 7-8 minutes, stirring once or until the eggs are set. Transfer the egg mixture into a bowl.
2. Top the bread slices with egg mixture, bacon, and cheese. Return to the fryer and Bake for 4-8 minutes or until the cheese melts and browns in spots. Serve.

Chicken Scotch Eggs

Servings: 4
Cooking Time: 25 Minutes
Ingredients:
- 1 lb ground chicken
- 2 tsp Dijon mustard
- 2 tsp grated yellow onion
- 1 tbsp chopped chives
- 1 tbsp chopped parsley
- ⅛ tsp ground nutmeg
- 1 lemon, zested
- Salt and pepper to taste
- 4 hard-boiled eggs, peeled
- 1 egg, beaten
- 1 cup bread crumbs
- 2 tsp olive oil

Directions:
1. Preheat air fryer to 350°F. In a bowl, mix the ground chicken, mustard, onion, chives, parsley, nutmeg, salt, lemon zest and pepper. Shape into 4 oval balls and form the balls evenly around the boiled eggs. Submerge them in the beaten egg and dip in the crumbs. Brush with olive oil. Place the scotch eggs in the frying basket and Air Fry for 14 minutes, flipping once. Serve hot.

Garlic Parmesan Bread Ring

Servings: 6
Cooking Time: 30 Minutes
Ingredients:
- ½ cup unsalted butter, melted
- ¼ teaspoon salt (omit if using salted butter)
- ¾ cup grated Parmesan cheese
- 3 to 4 cloves garlic, minced
- 1 tablespoon chopped fresh parsley
- 1 pound frozen bread dough, defrosted
- olive oil
- 1 egg, beaten

Directions:
1. Combine the melted butter, salt, Parmesan cheese, garlic and chopped parsley in a small bowl.
2. Roll the dough out into a rectangle that measures 8 inches by 17 inches. Spread the butter mixture over the dough, leaving a half-inch border un-buttered along one of the long edges. Roll the dough from one long edge to the other, ending with the un-buttered border. Pinch the seam shut tightly. Shape the log into

a circle sealing the ends together by pushing one end into the other and stretching the dough around it.

3. Cut out a circle of aluminum foil that is the same size as the air fryer basket. Brush the foil circle with oil and place an oven safe ramekin or glass in the center. Transfer the dough ring to the aluminum foil circle, around the ramekin. This will help you make sure the dough will fit in the basket and maintain its ring shape. Use kitchen shears to cut 8 slits around the outer edge of the dough ring halfway to the center. Brush the dough ring with egg wash.

4. Preheat the air fryer to 400°F for 4 minutes. When it has Preheated, brush the sides of the basket with oil and transfer the dough ring, foil circle and ramekin into the basket. Slide the drawer back into the air fryer, but do not turn the air fryer on. Let the dough rise inside the warm air fryer for 30 minutes.

5. After the bread has proofed in the air fryer for 30 minutes, set the temperature to 340°F and air-fry the bread ring for 15 minutes. Flip the bread over by inverting it onto a plate or cutting board and sliding it back into the air fryer basket. Air-fry for another 15 minutes. Let the bread cool for a few minutes before slicing the bread ring in between the slits and serving warm.

Banana Muffins With Chocolate Chips

Servings: 8
Cooking Time: 25 Minutes
Ingredients:
- 1 cup flour
- ½ tsp baking soda
- 1/3 cup brown sugar
- ¼ tsp salt
- 1/3 cup mashed banana
- ½ tsp vanilla extract
- 1 egg
- 1 tbsp vegetable oil
- ¼ cup chocolate chips
- 1 tbsp powdered sugar

Directions:
1. Preheat air fryer at 375°F. Combine dry ingredients in a bowl. In another bowl, mix wet ingredients. Pour wet ingredients into dry ingredients and gently toss to combine. Fold in chocolate chips. Do not overmix.
2. Spoon mixture into 8 greased silicone cupcake liners, place them in the frying basket, and Bake for 6-8 minutes. Let cool onto a cooling rack. Serve right away sprinkled with powdered sugar.

Mini Everything Bagels

Servings: 4
Cooking Time: 6 Minutes
Ingredients:
- 1 cup all-purpose flour
- 2 teaspoons baking powder
- ½ teaspoon salt
- 1 cup plain Greek yogurt
- 1 egg, whisked
- 1 teaspoon sesame seeds
- 1 teaspoon dehydrated onions
- ½ teaspoon poppy seeds
- ½ teaspoon garlic powder
- ½ teaspoon sea salt flakes

Directions:
1. In a large bowl, mix together the flour, baking powder, and salt. Make a well in the dough and add in the Greek yogurt. Mix with a spoon until a dough forms.
2. Place the dough onto a heavily floured surface and knead for 3 minutes. You may use up to 1 cup of additional flour as you knead the dough, if necessary.
3. Cut the dough into 8 pieces and roll each piece into a 6-inch, snakelike piece. Touch the ends of each piece together so it closes the circle and forms a bagel shape. Brush the tops of the bagels with the whisked egg.
4. In a small bowl, combine the sesame seeds, dehydrated onions, poppy seeds, garlic powder, and sea salt flakes. Sprinkle the seasoning on top of the bagels.
5. Preheat the air fryer to 360°F. Using a bench scraper or flat-edged spatula, carefully place the bagels into the air fryer basket. Spray the bagel tops with cooking spray. Air-fry the bagels for 6 minutes or until golden brown. Allow the bread to cool at least 10 minutes before slicing for serving.

Easy Corn Dog Cupcakes

Servings: 6
Cooking Time: 30 Minutes
Ingredients:
- 1 cup cornbread Mix
- 2 tsp granulated sugar
- Salt to taste
- 3/4 cup cream cheese
- 3 tbsp butter, melted
- 1 egg
- ¼ cup minced onions
- 1 tsp dried parsley
- 2 beef hot dogs, sliced and cut into half-moons

Directions:
1. Preheat air fryer at 350°F. Combine cornbread, sugar, and salt in a bowl. In another bowl, whisk cream cheese, parsley, butter, and egg. Pour wet ingredients to dry ingredients and toss to combine. Fold in onion and hot dog pieces. Transfer it into 8 greased silicone cupcake liners. Place it in the frying basket and Bake for 8-10 minutes. Serve right away.

Thai Turkey Sausage Patties

Servings: 4
Cooking Time: 30 Minutes
Ingredients:
- 12 oz turkey sausage
- 1 tsp onion powder
- 1 tsp dried coriander
- ¼ tsp Thai curry paste
- ¼ tsp red pepper flakes
- Salt and pepper to taste

Directions:
1. Preheat air fryer to 350°F. Place the sausage, onion, coriander, curry paste, red flakes, salt, and black pepper in a large bowl and mix well. Form into eight patties. Arrange the patties on the greased frying basket and Air Fry for 10 minutes, flipping once halfway through. Once the patties are cooked, transfer to a plate and serve hot.

Parsley Egg Scramble With Cottage Cheese

Servings: 2
Cooking Time: 15 Minutes
Ingredients:
- 1 tbsp cottage cheese, crumbled
- 4 eggs
- Salt and pepper to taste
- 2 tsp heavy cream
- 1 tbsp chopped parsley

Directions:
1. Preheat air fryer to 400°F. Grease a baking pan with olive oil. Beat the eggs, salt, and pepper in a bowl. Pour it into the pan, place the pan in the frying basket, and Air Fry for 5 minutes. Using a silicone spatula, stir in heavy cream, cottage cheese, and half of parsley and Air Fry for another 2 minutes. Scatter with parsley to serve.

Pesto Egg & Ham Sandwiches

Servings: 2
Cooking Time: 20 Minutes
Ingredients:
- 4 sandwich bread slices
- 2 tbsp butter, melted
- 4 eggs, scrambled
- 4 deli ham slices
- 2 Colby cheese slices
- 4 tsp basil pesto sauce
- ¼ tsp red chili flakes
- ¼ sliced avocado

Directions:
1. Preheat air fryer at 370°F. Brush 2 pieces of bread with half of the butter and place them, butter side down, into the frying basket. Divide eggs, chili flakes, sliced avocado, ham, and cheese on each bread slice.
2. Spread pesto on the remaining bread slices and place them, pesto side-down, onto the sandwiches. Brush the remaining butter on the tops of the sandwiches and Bake for 6 minutes, flipping once. Serve immediately.

Christmas Eggnog Bread

Servings: 6
Cooking Time: 18 Minutes
Ingredients:
- 1 cup flour, plus more for dusting
- ¼ cup sugar
- 1 teaspoon baking powder
- ¼ teaspoon salt
- ¼ teaspoon nutmeg
- ½ cup eggnog
- 1 egg yolk
- 1 tablespoon butter, plus 1 teaspoon, melted
- ¼ cup pecans
- ¼ cup chopped candied fruit (cherries, pineapple, or mixed fruits)
- cooking spray

Directions:
1. Preheat air fryer to 360°F.
2. In a medium bowl, stir together the flour, sugar, baking powder, salt, and nutmeg.
3. Add eggnog, egg yolk, and butter. Mix well but do not beat.
4. Stir in nuts and fruit.
5. Spray a 6 x 6-inch baking pan with cooking spray and dust with flour.
6. Spread batter into prepared pan and cook at 360°F for 18 minutes or until top is dark golden brown and bread starts to pull away from sides of pan.

Cherry Beignets

Servings: 4
Cooking Time: 25 Minutes
Ingredients:
- 2 tsp baking soda
- 1 ½ cups flour
- ¼ tsp salt
- 3 tbsp brown sugar
- 4 tsp chopped dried cherries
- ½ cup buttermilk
- 1 egg
- 3 tbsp melted lard

Directions:
1. Preheat air fryer to 330°F. Combine baking soda, flour, salt, and brown sugar in a bowl. Then stir in dried cherries. In a small bowl, beat together buttermilk and egg until smooth. Pour in with the dry ingredients and stir until just moistened.
2. On a floured work surface, pat the dough into a square. Divide it by cutting into 16 pieces. Lightly brush with melted lard. Arrange the squares in the frying basket, without overlapping. Air Fry until puffy and golden brown, 5-8 minutes. Serve.

Breakfast Burrito With Sausage

Servings: 6
Cooking Time: 35 Minutes
Ingredients:
- 2 tbsp olive oil
- Salt and pepper to taste
- 6 eggs, beaten
- ½ chopped red bell pepper
- ½ chopped green bell pepper
- 1 onion, finely chopped
- 8 oz chicken sausage
- ½ cup salsa

- 6 flour tortillas
- ½ cup grated cheddar

Directions:

1. Warm the olive oil in a skillet over medium heat. Add the eggs and stir-fry them for 2-3 minutes until scrambled. Season with salt and pepper and set aside.

2. Sauté the bell peppers and onion in the same skillet for 2-3 minutes until tender. Add and brown the chicken sausage, breaking into small pieces with a wooden spoon, about 4 minutes. Return the scrambled eggs and stir in the salsa. Remove the skillet from heat. Divide the mixture between the tortillas. Fold up the top and bottom edges, then roll to fully enclose the filling. Secure with toothpicks. Spritz with cooking spray.

3. Preheat air fryer to 400°F. Bake the burritos in the air fryer for 10 minutes, turning them once halfway through cooking until crisp. Garnish with cheddar cheese. Serve.

Peach Fritters

Servings: 8
Cooking Time: 6 Minutes

Ingredients:

- 1½ cups bread flour
- 1 teaspoon active dry yeast
- ¼ cup sugar
- ¼ teaspoon salt
- ½ cup warm milk
- ½ teaspoon vanilla extract
- 2 egg yolks
- 2 tablespoons melted butter
- 2 cups small diced peaches (fresh or frozen)
- 1 tablespoon butter
- 1 teaspoon ground cinnamon
- 1 to 2 tablespoons sugar
- Glaze
- ¾ cup powdered sugar
- 4 teaspoons milk

Directions:

1. Combine the flour, yeast, sugar and salt in a bowl. Add the milk, vanilla, egg yolks and melted butter and combine until the dough starts to come together. Transfer the dough to a floured surface and knead it by hand for 2 minutes. Shape the dough into a ball, place it in a large oiled bowl, cover with a clean kitchen towel and let the dough rise in a warm place for 1 to 1½ hours, or until the dough has doubled in size.

2. While the dough is rising, melt one tablespoon of butter in a medium saucepan on the stovetop. Add the diced peaches, cinnamon and sugar to taste. Cook the peaches for about 5 minutes, or until they soften. Set the peaches aside to cool.

3. When the dough has risen, transfer it to a floured surface and shape it into a 12-inch circle. Spread the peaches over half of the circle and fold the other half of the dough over the top. With a knife or a board scraper, score the dough by making slits in the dough in a diamond shape. Push the knife straight down into the dough and peaches, rather than slicing through. You should cut through the top layer of dough, but not the bottom. Roll the dough up into a log from one short end to the other. It should be roughly 8 inches long. Some of the peaches will be sticking out of the dough – don't worry, these are supposed to be a little random. Cut the log into 8 equal slices. Place the dough disks on a floured cookie sheet, cover with a clean kitchen towel and let rise in a warm place for 30 minutes.

4. Preheat the air fryer to 370°F.

5. Air-fry 2 or 3 fritters at a time at 370°F, for 3 minutes. Flip them over and continue to air-fry for another 2 to 3 minutes, until they are golden brown.

6. Combine the powdered sugar and milk together in a small bowl. Whisk vigorously until smooth. Allow the fritters to cool for at least 10 minutes and then brush the glaze over both the bottom and top of each one. Serve warm or at room temperature.

Western Frittata

Servings: 1
Cooking Time: 19 Minutes

Ingredients:

- ½ red or green bell pepper, cut into ½-inch chunks
- 1 teaspoon olive oil
- 3 eggs, beaten
- ¼ cup grated Cheddar cheese
- ¼ cup diced cooked ham
- salt and freshly ground black pepper, to taste
- 1 teaspoon butter
- 1 teaspoon chopped fresh parsley

Directions:

1. Preheat the air fryer to 400°F.

2. Toss the peppers with the olive oil and air-fry for 6 minutes, shaking the basket once or twice during the cooking process to redistribute the ingredients.

3. While the vegetables are cooking, beat the eggs well in a bowl, stir in the Cheddar cheese and ham, and season with salt and freshly ground black pepper. Add the air-fried peppers to this bowl when they have finished cooking.

4. Place a 6- or 7-inch non-stick metal cake pan into the air fryer basket with the butter using an aluminum sling to lower the pan into the basket. (Fold a piece of aluminum foil into a strip about 2-inches wide by 24-inches long.) Air-fry for 1 minute at 380°F to melt the butter. Remove the cake pan and rotate the pan to distribute the butter and grease the pan. Pour the egg mixture into the cake pan and return the pan to the air fryer, using the aluminum sling.

5. Air-fry at 380°F for 12 minutes, or until the frittata has puffed up and is lightly browned. Let the frittata sit in the air fryer for 5 minutes to cool to an edible temperature and set up. Remove the cake pan from the air fryer, sprinkle with parsley and serve immediately.

Lime Muffins

Servings: 6
Cooking Time: 30 Minutes
Ingredients:
- 1 ½ tbsp butter, softened
- 6 tbsp sugar
- 1 egg
- 1 egg white
- 1 tsp vanilla extract
- 1 tsp lime juice
- 1 lime, zested
- 5 oz Greek yogurt
- ¾ cup + 2 tbsp flour
- ¾ cup raspberries

Directions:
1. Beat butter and sugar in a mixer for 2 minutes at medium speed. In a separate bowl, whisk together the egg, egg white and vanilla. Pour into the mixer bowl, add lime juice and zest. Beat until combined. At a low speed, add yogurt then flour. Fold in the raspberries. Divide the mixture into 6 greased muffin cups using an ice cream scoop. The cups should be filled about ¾ of the way.
2. Preheat air fryer to 300°F. Put the muffins into the air fryer and Bake for 15 minutes until the tops are golden and a toothpick in the center comes out clean. Allow to cool before serving.

Breakfast Frittata

Servings: 2
Cooking Time: 25 Minutes
Ingredients:
- 4 cooked pancetta slices, chopped
- 5 eggs
- Salt and pepper to taste
- ½ leek, thinly sliced
- ½ cup grated cheddar cheese
- 1 tomato, sliced
- 1 cup iceberg lettuce, torn
- 2 tbsp milk

Directions:
1. Preheat air fryer to 320°F. Beat the eggs, milk, salt, and pepper in a bowl. Mix in pancetta and cheddar. Transfer to a greased with olive oil baking pan. Top with tomato slices and leek and place it in the frying basket. Bake for 14 minutes. Let cool for 5 minutes. Serve with lettuce.

Cheddar Cheese Biscuits

Servings: 8
Cooking Time: 22 Minutes
Ingredients:
- 2⅓ cups self-rising flour
- 2 tablespoons sugar
- ½ cup butter (1 stick), frozen for 15 minutes
- ½ cup grated Cheddar cheese, plus more to melt on top
- 1⅓ cups buttermilk
- 1 cup all-purpose flour, for shaping
- 1 tablespoon butter, melted

Directions:
1. Line a buttered 7-inch metal cake pan with parchment paper or a silicone liner.
2. Combine the flour and sugar in a large mixing bowl. Grate the butter into the flour. Add the grated cheese and stir to coat the cheese and butter with flour. Then add the buttermilk and stir just until you can no longer see streaks of flour. The dough should be quite wet.
3. Spread the all-purpose (not self-rising) flour out on a small cookie sheet. With a spoon, scoop 8 evenly sized balls of dough into the flour, making sure they don't touch each other. With floured hands, coat each dough ball with flour and toss them gently from hand to hand to shake off any excess flour. Place each floured dough ball into the prepared pan, right up next to the other. This will help the biscuits rise up, rather than spreading out.
4. Preheat the air fryer to 380°F.
5. Transfer the cake pan to the basket of the air fryer, lowering it into the basket using a sling made of aluminum foil (fold a piece of aluminum foil into a strip about 2-inches wide by 24-inches long). Let the ends of the aluminum foil sling hang across the cake pan before returning the basket to the air fryer.
6. Air-fry for 20 minutes. Check the biscuits a couple of times to make sure they are not getting too brown on top. If they are, re-arrange the aluminum foil strips to cover any brown parts. After 20 minutes, check the biscuits by inserting a toothpick into the center of the biscuits. It should come out clean. If it needs a little more time, continue to air-fry for a couple of extra minutes. Brush the tops of the biscuits with some melted butter and sprinkle a little more grated cheese on top if desired. Pop the basket back into the air fryer for another 2 minutes. Remove the cake pan from the air fryer using the aluminum sling. Let the biscuits cool for just a minute or two and then turn them out onto a plate and pull apart. Serve immediately.

Breakfast Pot Pies

Servings: 4
Cooking Time: 20 Minutes
Ingredients:
- 1 refrigerated pie crust
- ½ pound pork breakfast sausage
- ¼ cup diced onion
- 1 garlic clove, minced
- ½ teaspoon ground black pepper
- ¼ teaspoon salt
- 1 cup chopped bell peppers
- 1 cup roasted potatoes
- 2 cups milk
- 2 to 3 tablespoons all-purpose flour

Directions:
1. Flatten the store-bought pie crust out on an even surface. Cut 4 equal circles that are slightly larger than the circumference of ramekins (by about ¼ inch). Set aside.

2. In a medium pot, sauté the breakfast sausage with the onion, garlic, black pepper, and salt. When browned, add in the bell peppers and potatoes and cook an additional 3 to 4 minutes to soften the bell peppers. Remove from the heat and portion equally into the ramekins.

3. To the same pot (without washing it), add the milk. Heat over medium-high heat until boiling. Slowly reduce to a simmer and stir in the flour, 1 tablespoon at a time, until the gravy thickens and coats the back of a wooden spoon (about 5 minutes).

4. Remove from the heat and equally portion ½ cup of gravy into each ramekin on top of the sausage and potato mixture.

5. Place the circle pie crusts on top of the ramekins, lightly pressing them down on the perimeter of each ramekin with the prongs of a fork. Gently poke the prongs into the center top of the pie crust a few times to create holes for the steam to escape as the pie cooks.

6. Bake in the air fryer for 6 minutes (or until the tops are golden brown).

7. Remove and let cool 5 minutes before serving.

Carrot Orange Muffins

Servings: 12
Cooking Time: 12 Minutes
Ingredients:
- 1½ cups all-purpose flour
- ½ cup granulated sugar
- ½ teaspoon ground cinnamon
- 2 teaspoons baking powder
- ¼ teaspoon baking soda
- ½ teaspoon salt
- 2 large eggs
- ¼ cup vegetable oil
- ⅓ cup orange marmalade
- 2 cups grated carrots

Directions:
1. Preheat the air fryer to 320°F.
2. In a large bowl, whisk together the flour, sugar, cinnamon, baking powder, baking soda, and salt; set aside.
3. In a separate bowl, whisk together the eggs, vegetable oil, orange marmalade, and grated carrots.
4. Make a well in the dry ingredients; then pour the wet ingredients into the well of the dry ingredients. Using a rubber spatula, mix the ingredients for 1 minute or until slightly lumpy.
5. Using silicone muffin liners, fill 6 muffin liners two-thirds full.
6. Carefully place the muffin liners in the air fryer basket and bake for 12 minutes (or until the tops are browned and a toothpick inserted in the center comes out clean). Carefully remove the muffins from the basket and repeat with remaining batter.
7. Serve warm.

Cinnamon-coconut Doughnuts

Servings: 6
Cooking Time: 35 Minutes
Ingredients:
- 1 egg, beaten
- ¼ cup milk
- 2 tbsp safflower oil
- 1 ½ tsp vanilla
- ½ tsp lemon zest
- 1 ½ cups all-purpose flour
- ¾ cup coconut sugar
- 2 ½ tsp cinnamon
- ½ tsp ground nutmeg
- ¼ tsp salt
- ¾ tsp baking powder

Directions:
1. Preheat air fryer to 350°F. Add the egg, milk, oil, vanilla, and lemon zest. Stir well and set this wet mixture aside. In a different bowl, combine the flour, ½ cup coconut sugar, ½ teaspoon cinnamon, nutmeg, salt, and baking powder. Stir well. Add this mixture to the wet mix and blend. Pull off bits of the dough and roll into balls.

2. Place in the greased frying basket, leaving room between as they get bigger. Spray the tops with oil and Air Fry for 8-10 minutes, flipping once. During the last 2 minutes of frying, place 4 tbsp of coconut sugar and 2 tsp of cinnamon in a bowl and stir to combine. After frying, coat each donut by spraying with oil and toss in the cinnamon-sugar mix. Serve and enjoy!

Green Onion Pancakes

Servings: 4
Cooking Time: 8 Minutes
Ingredients:
- 2 cup all-purpose flour
- ½ teaspoon salt
- ¾ cup hot water
- 1 tablespoon vegetable oil
- 1 tablespoon butter, melted
- 2 cups finely chopped green onions
- 1 tablespoon black sesame seeds, for garnish

Directions:
1. In a large bowl, whisk together the flour and salt. Make a well in the center and pour in the hot water. Quickly stir the flour mixture together until a dough forms. Knead the dough for 5 minutes; then cover with a warm, wet towel and set aside for 30 minutes to rest.

2. In a small bowl, mix together the vegetable oil and melted butter.

3. On a floured surface, place the dough and cut it into 8 pieces. Working with 1 piece of dough at a time, use a rolling pin to roll out the dough until it's ¼ inch thick; then brush the surface with the oil and butter mixture and sprinkle with green onions. Next, fold the dough in half and then in half again. Roll out the dough again until it's ¼ inch thick and brush with the oil and butter mixture and green onions. Fold the dough in half and then in half again and roll out one last time until it's ¼ inch thick. Repeat this technique with all 8 pieces.

4. Meanwhile, preheat the air fryer to 400°F.

5. Place 1 or 2 pancakes into the air fryer basket (or as many as will fit in your fryer), and cook for 2 minutes or until crispy

and golden brown. Repeat until all the pancakes are cooked. Top with black sesame seeds for garnish, if desired.

Mini Bacon Egg Quiches

Servings:6
Cooking Time: 30 Minutes
Ingredients:
- 3 eggs
- 2 tbsp heavy cream
- ¼ tsp Dijon mustard
- Salt and pepper to taste
- 3 oz cooked bacon, crumbled
- ¼ cup grated cheddar

Directions:
1. Preheat air fryer to 350°F. Beat the eggs with salt and pepper in a bowl until fluffy. Stir in heavy cream, mustard, cooked bacon, and cheese. Divide the mixture between 6 greased muffin cups and place them in the frying basket. Bake for 8-10 minutes. Let cool slightly before serving.

Roasted Tomato And Cheddar Rolls

Servings: 12
Cooking Time: 55 Minutes
Ingredients:
- 4 Roma tomatoes
- ½ clove garlic, minced
- 1 tablespoon olive oil
- ¼ teaspoon dried thyme
- salt and freshly ground black pepper
- 4 cups all-purpose flour
- 1 teaspoon active dry yeast
- 2 teaspoons sugar
- 2 teaspoons salt
- 1 tablespoon olive oil
- 1 cup grated Cheddar cheese, plus more for sprinkling at the end
- 1½ cups water

Directions:
1. Cut the Roma tomatoes in half, remove the seeds with your fingers and transfer to a bowl. Add the garlic, olive oil, dried thyme, salt and freshly ground black pepper and toss well.
2. Preheat the air fryer to 390°F.
3. Place the tomatoes, cut side up in the air fryer basket and air-fry for 10 minutes. The tomatoes should just start to brown. Shake the basket to redistribute the tomatoes, and air-fry for another 5 to 10 minutes at 330°F until the tomatoes are no longer juicy. Let the tomatoes cool and then rough chop them.
4. Combine the flour, yeast, sugar and salt in the bowl of a stand mixer. Add the olive oil, chopped roasted tomatoes and Cheddar cheese to the flour mixture and start to mix using the dough hook attachment. As you're mixing, add 1¼ cups of the water, mixing until the dough comes together. Continue to knead the dough with the dough hook for another 10 minutes, adding enough water to the dough to get it to the right consistency.
5. Transfer the dough to an oiled bowl, cover with a clean kitchen towel and let it rest and rise until it has doubled in volume – about 1 to 2 hours. Then, divide the dough into 12 equal portions. Roll each portion of dough into a ball. Lightly coat each dough ball with oil and let the dough balls rest and rise a second time, covered lightly with plastic wrap for 45 minutes. (Alternately, you can place the rolls in the refrigerator overnight and take them out 2 hours before you bake them.)
6. Preheat the air fryer to 360°F.
7. Spray the dough balls and the air fryer basket with a little olive oil. Place three rolls at a time in the basket and bake for 10 minutes. Add a little grated Cheddar cheese on top of the rolls for the last 2 minutes of air frying for an attractive finish.

Vodka Basil Muffins With Strawberries

Servings:6
Cooking Time: 20 Minutes
Ingredients:
- ½ cup flour
- ½ cup granular sugar
- ½ tsp baking powder
- ⅛ tsp salt
- ½ cup chopped strawberries
- ¼ tsp vanilla extract
- 3 tbsp butter, melted
- 2 eggs
- ¼ tsp vodka
- 1 tbsp chopped basil

Directions:
1. Preheat air fryer to 375°F. Combine the dry ingredients in a bowl. Set aside. In another bowl, whisk the wet ingredients. Pour wet ingredients into the bowl with the dry ingredients and gently combine. Add basil and vodka to the batter. Do not overmix and spoon batter into six silicone cupcake liners lightly greased with olive oil. Place liners in the frying basket and Bake for 7 minutes. Let cool for 5 minutes onto a cooling rack before serving.

English Scones

Servings: 8
Cooking Time: 8 Minutes
Ingredients:
- 2 cups all-purpose flour
- 1 tablespoon baking powder
- ½ teaspoon salt
- 2 tablespoons sugar
- ¼ cup unsalted butter
- ⅔ cup plus 1 tablespoon whole milk, divided

Directions:
1. Preheat the air fryer to 380°F.
2. In a large bowl, whisk together the flour, baking powder, salt, and sugar. Using a pastry blender or your fingers, cut in the butter until pea-size crumbles appear. Make a well in the center and pour in ⅔ cup of the milk. Quickly mix the batter until a ball forms. Knead the dough 3 times.

3. Place the dough onto a floured surface and, using your hands or a rolling pin, flatten the dough until it's ¾ inch thick. Using a biscuit cutter or drinking glass, cut out 10 circles, reforming the dough and flattening as needed to use up the batter.
4. Brush the tops lightly with the remaining 1 tablespoon of milk.
5. Place the scones into the air fryer basket. Cook for 8 minutes or until golden brown and cooked in the center.

Cream Cheese Deviled Eggs

Servings: 4
Cooking Time: 20 Minutes
Ingredients:
- 2 cooked bacon slices, crumbled
- 4 whole eggs
- 2 tbsp mayonnaise
- 1 tsp yellow mustard
- ½ tsp dill pickle juice
- 1 tsp diced sweet pickles
- Salt and pepper to taste
- 2 tbsp cream cheese
- Parsley for sprinkling

Directions:
1. Preheat air fryer at 250°F. Place egg in the frying basket and Air Fry for 15 minutes. Then place them immediately into a bowl with ice and 1 cup of water to stop the cooking process. Let chill for 5 minutes, then carefully peel them. Cut egg in half lengthwise and spoon yolks into a bowl. Arrange the egg white halves on a plate.
2. Mash egg yolks with a fork. Stir in mayonnaise, mustard, pickle juice, diced pickles, salt, pepper and cream cheese. Pour 1 tbsp of the mixture into egg white halves, scatter with crumbled bacon and parsley and serve.

Avocado Toasts With Poached Eggs

Servings: 4
Cooking Time: 15 Minutes
Ingredients:
- 4 eggs
- Salt and pepper to taste
- 4 bread pieces, toasted
- 1 pitted avocado, sliced
- ½ tsp chili powder
- ½ tsp dried rosemary

Directions:
1. Preheat air fryer to 320°F. Crack 1 egg into each greased ramekin and season with salt and black pepper. Place the ramekins into the air frying basket. Bake for 6-8 minutes.
2. Scoop the flesh of the avocado into a small bowl. Season with salt, black pepper, chili powderp and rosemary. Using a fork, smash the avocado lightly. Spread the smashed avocado evenly over toasted bread slices. Remove the eggs from the air fryer and gently spoon one onto each slice of avocado toast. Serve and enjoy!

Huevos Rancheros

Servings: 4
Cooking Time: 45 Minutes + Cooling Time
Ingredients:
- 1 tbsp olive oil
- 20 cherry tomatoes, halved
- 2 chopped plum tomatoes
- ¼ cup tomato sauce
- 2 scallions, sliced
- 2 garlic cloves, minced
- 1 tsp honey
- ½ tsp salt
- ⅛ tsp cayenne pepper
- ¼ tsp grated nutmeg
- ¼ tsp paprika
- 4 eggs

Directions:
1. Preheat the air fryer to 370°F. Combine the olive oil, cherry tomatoes, plum tomatoes, tomato sauce, scallions, garlic, nutmeg, honey, salt, paprika and cayenne in a 7-inch springform pan that has been wrapped in foil to prevent leaks. Put the pan in the frying basket and
2. Bake the mix for 15-20 minutes, stirring twice until the tomatoes are soft. Mash some of the tomatoes in the pan with a fork, then stir them into the sauce. Also, break the eggs into the sauce, then return the pan to the fryer and Bake for 2 minutes. Remove the pan from the fryer and stir the eggs into the sauce, whisking them through the sauce. Don't mix in completely. Cook for 4-8 minutes more or until the eggs are set. Let cool, then serve.

Chia Seed Banana Bread

Servings: 6
Cooking Time: 35 Minutes
Ingredients:
- 2 bananas, mashed
- 2 tbsp sunflower oil
- 2 tbsp maple syrup
- ½ tsp vanilla
- ½ tbsp chia seeds
- ½ tbsp ground flaxseeds
- 1 cup pastry flour
- ¼ cup sugar
- ½ tsp cinnamon
- 1 orange, zested
- ¼ tsp salt
- ¼ tsp ground nutmeg
- ½ tsp baking powder

Directions:
1. Preheat air fryer to 350°F. Place the bananas, oil, maple syrup, vanilla, chia, and flaxseeds in a bowl and stir to combine. Add the flour, sugar, cinnamon, salt, nutmeg, baking powder, and orange zest. Stir to combine.
2. Pour the batter into a greased baking pan. Smooth the top with a rubber spatula and Bake for 25 minutes or until a knife

inserted in the center comes out clean. Remove and let cool for a minute, then cut into wedges and serve. Enjoy warm!

Farmers Market Quiche

Servings: 4
Cooking Time: 35 Minutes
Ingredients:
- 4 button mushrooms
- ¼ medium red bell pepper
- 1 teaspoon extra-virgin olive oil
- One 9-inch pie crust, at room temperature
- ¼ cup grated carrot
- ¼ cup chopped, fresh baby spinach leaves
- 3 eggs, whisked
- ¼ cup half-and-half
- ½ teaspoon thyme
- ½ teaspoon sea salt
- 2 ounces crumbled goat cheese or feta

Directions:
1. In a medium bowl, toss the mushrooms and bell pepper with extra-virgin olive oil; place into the air fryer basket. Set the temperature to 400°F for 8 minutes, stirring after 4 minutes. Remove from the air fryer, and roughly chop the mushrooms and bell peppers. Wipe the air fryer clean.
2. Prep a 7-inch oven-safe baking dish by spraying the bottom of the pan with cooking spray.
3. Place the pie crust into the baking dish; fold over and crimp the edges or use a fork to press to give the edges some shape.
4. In a medium bowl, mix together the mushrooms, bell peppers, carrots, spinach, and eggs. Stir in the half-and-half, thyme, and salt.
5. Pour the quiche mixture into the base of the pie shell. Top with crumbled cheese.
6. Place the quiche into the air fryer basket. Set the temperature to 325°F for 30 minutes.
7. When complete, turn the quiche halfway and cook an additional 5 minutes. Allow the quiche to rest 20 minutes prior to slicing and serving.

Blueberry French Toast Sticks

Servings: 4
Cooking Time: 20 Minutes
Ingredients:
- 3 bread slices, cut into strips
- 1 tbsp butter, melted
- 2 eggs
- 1 tbsp milk
- 1 tbsp sugar
- ½ tsp vanilla extract
- 1 cup fresh blueberries
- 1 tbsp lemon juice

Directions:
1. Preheat air fryer to 380°F. After laying the bread strips on a plate, sprinkle some melted butter over each piece. Whisk the eggs, milk, vanilla, and sugar, then dip the bread in the mix. Place on a wire rack to let the batter drip. Put the bread strips in the air fryer and Air Fry for 5-7 minutes. Use tongs to flip them once and cook until golden. With a fork, smash the blueberries and lemon juice together. Spoon the blueberries sauce over the French sticks. Serve immediately.

Orange Trail Oatmeal

Servings: 4
Cooking Time: 20 Minutes
Ingredients:
- 1 ½ cups quick-cooking oats
- 1/3 cup light brown sugar
- 1 egg
- 1 tsp orange zest
- 1 tbsp orange juice
- 2 tbsp whole milk
- 2 tbsp honey
- 2 tbsp butter, melted
- 2 tsp dried cranberries
- 1 tsp dried blueberries
- 1/8 tsp ground nutmeg
- Salt to taste
- ¼ cup pecan pieces

Directions:
1. Preheat air fryer at 325ºF. Combine the oats, sugar, egg, orange zest, orange juice, milk, honey, butter, dried cranberries, dried blueberries, nutmeg, salt, and pecan in a bowl. Press mixture into a greased cake pan. Place cake pan in the frying basket and Roast for 8 minutes. Let cool onto for 5 minutes before slicing. Serve.

Mediterranean Granola

Servings: 6
Cooking Time: 40 Minutes
Ingredients:
- 1 cup rolled oats
- ¼ cup dried cherries, diced
- ¼ cup almond slivers
- ¼ cup hazelnuts, chopped
- ¼ cup pepitas
- ¼ cup hemp hearts
- 3 tbsp honey
- 1 tbsp olive oil
- 1 tsp ground cinnamon
- ¼ tsp ground nutmeg
- ¼ tsp salt
- 2 tbsp dark chocolate chips
- 3 cups Greek yogurt

Directions:
1. Preheat air fryer to 260°F. Stir the oats, cherries, almonds, hazelnuts, pepitas, hemp hearts, 2 tbsp of honey, olive oil, cinnamon, nutmeg, and salt in a bowl, mixing well. Pour the mixture onto the parchment-lined frying basket and spread it into a single layer. Bake for 25-30 minutes, shaking twice. Let the granola cool completely. Stir in the chocolate chips. Divide

between 6 cups. Top with Greek yogurt and remaining honey to serve.

Apple-cinnamon-walnut Muffins

Servings: 8
Cooking Time: 11 Minutes
Ingredients:
- 1 cup flour
- ⅓ cup sugar
- 1 teaspoon baking powder
- ¼ teaspoon baking soda
- ¼ teaspoon salt
- 1 teaspoon cinnamon
- ¼ teaspoon ginger
- ¼ teaspoon nutmeg
- 1 egg
- 2 tablespoons pancake syrup, plus 2 teaspoons
- 2 tablespoons melted butter, plus 2 teaspoons
- ¾ cup unsweetened applesauce
- ½ teaspoon vanilla extract
- ¼ cup chopped walnuts
- ¼ cup diced apple
- 8 foil muffin cups, liners removed and sprayed with cooking spray

Directions:
1. Preheat air fryer to 330°F.
2. In a large bowl, stir together flour, sugar, baking powder, baking soda, salt, cinnamon, ginger, and nutmeg.
3. In a small bowl, beat egg until frothy. Add syrup, butter, applesauce, and vanilla and mix well.
4. Pour egg mixture into dry ingredients and stir just until moistened.
5. Gently stir in nuts and diced apple.
6. Divide batter among the 8 muffin cups.
7. Place 4 muffin cups in air fryer basket and cook at 330°F for 11minutes.
8. Repeat with remaining 4 muffins or until toothpick inserted in center comes out clean.

Mascarpone Iced Cinnamon Rolls

Servings: 6
Cooking Time: 40 Minutes
Ingredients:
- ¼ cup mascarpone cheese, softened
- 9 oz puff pastry sheet
- 3 tbsp light brown sugar
- 2 tsp ground cinnamon
- 2 tsp butter, melted
- ¼ tsp vanilla extract
- ¼ tsp salt
- 2 tbsp milk
- 1 tbsp lemon zest
- ¼ cup confectioners' sugar

Directions:

1. Preheat air fryer to 320°F. Mix the brown sugar and cinnamon in a small bowl. Unroll the pastry sheet on its paper and brush it with melted butter. Then sprinkle with cinnamon sugar. Roll up the dough tightly, then cut into rolls about 1-inch wide. Put into a greased baking pan with the spiral side showing. Put the pan into the air fryer and Bake until golden brown, 18-20 minutes. Set aside to cool for 5-10 minutes.
2. Meanwhile, add the mascarpone cheese, vanilla, and salt in a small bowl, whisking until smooth and creamy. Add the confectioners' sugar and continue whisking until fully blended. Pour and mix in 1 tsp of milk at a time until the glaze is pourable but still with some thickness. Spread the glaze over the warm cinnamon rolls and scatter with lemon zest. Serve and enjoy!

Pepperoni Pizza Bread

Servings: 4
Cooking Time: 15 Minutes
Ingredients:
- 7-inch round bread boule
- 2 cups grated mozzarella cheese
- 1 tablespoon dried oregano
- 1 cup pizza sauce
- 1 cup mini pepperoni or pepperoni slices, cut in quarters
- Pizza sauce for dipping (optional)

Directions:
1. Make 7 to 8 deep slices across the bread boule, leaving 1 inch of bread uncut at the bottom of every slice before you reach the cutting board. The slices should go about three quarters of the way through the boule and be about 2 inches apart from each other. Turn the bread boule 90 degrees and make 7 to 8 similar slices perpendicular to the first slices to form squares in the bread. Again, make sure you don't cut all the way through the bread.
2. Combine the mozzarella cheese and oregano in a small bowl.
3. Fill the slices in the bread with pizza sauce by gently spreading the bread apart and spooning the sauce in between the squares of bread. Top the sauce with the mozzarella cheese mixture and then the pepperoni. Do your very best to get the cheese and pepperoni in between the slices, rather than on top of the bread. Keep spreading the bread apart and stuffing the ingredients in, but be careful not to tear the bottom of the bread.
4. Preheat the air fryer to 320°F.
5. Transfer the bread boule to the air fryer basket and air-fry for 15 minutes, making sure the top doesn't get too dark. (It will just be the cheese on top that gets dark, so if you've done a good job of tucking the cheese in between the slices, this shouldn't be an issue.)
6. Carefully remove the bread from the basket with a spatula. Transfer it to a serving platter with more sauce to dip into if desired. Serve with a lot of napkins so that people can just pull the bread apart with their hands and enjoy!

Banana-blackberry Muffins

Servings: 6
Cooking Time: 20 Minutes
Ingredients:
- 1 ripe banana, mashed
- ½ cup milk
- 1 tsp apple cider vinegar
- 1 tsp vanilla extract
- 2 tbsp ground flaxseed
- 2 tbsp coconut sugar
- ¾ cup flour
- 1 tsp baking powder
- ½ tsp baking soda
- ¾ cup blackberries

Directions:
1. Preheat air fryer to 350°F. Place the banana in a bowl. Stir in milk, apple vinegar, vanilla extract, flaxseed, and coconut sugar until combined. In another bowl, combine flour, baking powder, and baking soda. Pour it into the banana mixture and toss to combine. Divide the batter between 6 muffin molds and top each with blackberries, pressing slightly. Bake for 16 minutes until golden brown and a toothpick comes out clean. Serve cooled.

Broccoli Cornbread

Servings: 6
Cooking Time: 18 Minutes
Ingredients:
- 1 cup frozen chopped broccoli, thawed and drained
- ¼ cup cottage cheese
- 1 egg, beaten
- 2 tablespoons minced onion
- 2 tablespoons melted butter
- ½ cup flour
- ½ cup yellow cornmeal
- 1 teaspoon baking powder
- ½ teaspoon salt
- ¼ cup milk, plus 2 tablespoons
- cooking spray

Directions:
1. Place thawed broccoli in colander and press with a spoon to squeeze out excess moisture.
2. Stir together all ingredients in a large bowl.
3. Spray 6 x 6-inch baking pan with cooking spray.
4. Spread batter in pan and cook at 330°F for 18 minutes or until cornbread is lightly browned and loaf starts to pull away from sides of pan.

Sweet-hot Pepperoni Pizza

Servings: 2
Cooking Time: 18 Minutes
Ingredients:
- 1 (6- to 8-ounce) pizza dough ball*
- olive oil
- ½ cup pizza sauce
- ¾ cup grated mozzarella cheese
- ½ cup thick sliced pepperoni
- ⅓ cup sliced pickled hot banana peppers
- ¼ teaspoon dried oregano
- 2 teaspoons honey

Directions:
1. Preheat the air fryer to 390°F.
2. Cut out a piece of aluminum foil the same size as the bottom of the air fryer basket. Brush the foil circle with olive oil. Shape the dough into a circle and place it on top of the foil. Dock the dough by piercing it several times with a fork. Brush the dough lightly with olive oil and transfer it into the air fryer basket with the foil on the bottom.
3. Air-fry the plain pizza dough for 6 minutes. Turn the dough over, remove the aluminum foil and brush again with olive oil. Air-fry for an additional 4 minutes.
4. Spread the pizza sauce on top of the dough and sprinkle the mozzarella cheese over the sauce. Top with the pepperoni, pepper slices and dried oregano. Lower the temperature of the air fryer to 350°F and cook for 8 minutes, until the cheese has melted and lightly browned. Transfer the pizza to a cutting board and drizzle with the honey. Slice and serve.

Bacon, Broccoli And Swiss Cheese Bread Pudding

Servings: 2
Cooking Time: 48 Minutes
Ingredients:
- ½ pound thick cut bacon, cut into ¼-inch pieces
- 3 cups brioche bread or rolls, cut into ½-inch cubes
- 3 eggs
- 1 cup milk
- ½ teaspoon salt
- freshly ground black pepper
- 1 cup frozen broccoli florets, thawed and chopped
- 1½ cups grated Swiss cheese

Directions:
1. Preheat the air fryer to 400°F.
2. Air-fry the bacon for 6 minutes until crispy, shaking the basket a few times while it cooks to help it cook evenly. Remove the bacon and set it aside on a paper towel.
3. Air-fry the brioche bread cubes for 2 minutes to dry and toast lightly. (If your brioche is a few days old and slightly stale, you can omit this step.)
4. Butter a 6- or 7-inch cake pan. Combine all the ingredients in a large bowl and toss well. Transfer the mixture to the buttered cake pan, cover with aluminum foil and refrigerate the bread pudding overnight, or for at least 8 hours.
5. Remove the casserole from the refrigerator an hour before you plan to cook, and let it sit on the countertop to come to room temperature.
6. Preheat the air fryer to 330°F. Transfer the covered cake pan, to the basket of the air fryer, lowering the dish into the basket using a sling made of aluminum foil (fold a piece of aluminum foil into a strip about 2-inches wide by 24-inches long). Fold the ends of the aluminum foil over the top of the

dish before returning the basket to the air fryer. Air-fry for 20 minutes. Remove the foil and air-fry for an additional 20 minutes. If the top starts to brown a little too much before the custard has set, simply return the foil to the pan. The bread pudding has cooked through when a skewer inserted into the center comes out clean.

Honey Oatmeal

Servings: 6
Cooking Time: 35 Minutes
Ingredients:
- 2 cups rolled oats
- 2 cups oat milk
- ¼ cup honey
- ½ cup Greek yogurt
- 1 tsp vanilla extract
- ½ tsp ground cinnamon
- ¼ tsp salt
- 1 ½ cups diced mango

Directions:
1. Preheat air fryer to 380°F. Stir together the oats, milk, honey, yogurt, vanilla, cinnamon, and salt in a large bowl until well combined. Fold in ¾ cup of the mango and then pour the mixture into a greased cake pan. Sprinkle the remaining manog across the top of the oatmeal mixture. Bake in the air fryer for 30 minutes. Leave to set and cool for 5 minutes. Serve and enjoy!

Ham And Cheddar Gritters

Servings: 6
Cooking Time: 12 Minutes
Ingredients:
- 4 cups water
- 1 cup quick-cooking grits
- ¼ teaspoon salt
- 2 tablespoons butter
- 2 cups grated Cheddar cheese, divided
- 1 cup finely diced ham
- 1 tablespoon chopped chives
- salt and freshly ground black pepper
- 1 egg, beaten
- 2 cups panko breadcrumbs
- vegetable oil

Directions:
1. Bring the water to a boil in a saucepan. Whisk in the grits and ¼ teaspoon of salt, and cook for 7 minutes until the grits are soft. Remove the pan from the heat and stir in the butter and 1 cup of the grated Cheddar cheese. Transfer the grits to a bowl and let them cool for just 10 to 15 minutes.
2. Stir the ham, chives and the rest of the cheese into the grits and season with salt and pepper to taste. Add the beaten egg and refrigerate the mixture for 30 minutes. (Try not to chill the grits much longer than 30 minutes, or the mixture will be too firm to shape into patties.)
3. While the grit mixture is chilling, make the country gravy and set it aside.
4. Place the panko breadcrumbs in a shallow dish. Measure out ¼-cup portions of the grits mixture and shape them into patties. Coat all sides of the patties with the panko breadcrumbs, patting them with your hands so the crumbs adhere to the patties. You should have about 16 patties. Spray both sides of the patties with oil.
5. Preheat the air fryer to 400°F.
6. In batches of 5 or 6, air-fry the fritters for 8 minutes. Using a flat spatula, flip the fritters over and air-fry for another 4 minutes.
7. Serve hot with country gravy.

Egg And Sausage Crescent Rolls

Servings: 8
Cooking Time: 11 Minutes
Ingredients:
- 5 large eggs
- ¼ teaspoon black pepper
- ¼ teaspoon salt
- 1 tablespoon milk
- ¼ cup shredded cheddar cheese
- One 8-ounce package refrigerated crescent rolls
- 4 tablespoon pesto sauce
- 8 fully cooked breakfast sausage links, defrosted

Directions:
1. Preheat the air fryer to 320°F.
2. In a medium bowl, crack the eggs and whisk with the pepper, salt, and milk. Pour into a frying pan over medium heat and scramble. Just before the eggs are done, turn off the heat and add in the cheese. Continue to cook until the cheese has melted and the eggs are finished (about 5 minutes total). Remove from the heat.
3. Remove the crescent rolls from the package and press them flat onto a clean surface lightly dusted with flour. Add 1½ teaspoons of pesto sauce across the center of each roll. Place equal portions of eggs across all 8 rolls. Then top each roll with a sausage link and roll the dough up tight so it resembles the crescent-roll shape.
4. Lightly spray your air fryer basket with olive oil mist and place the rolls on top. Bake for 6 minutes or until the tops of the rolls are lightly browned.
5. Remove and let cool 3 to 5 minutes before serving.

Shakshuka Cups

Servings: 4
Cooking Time: 25 Minutes
Ingredients:
- 2 tbsp tomato paste
- ½ cup chicken broth
- 4 tomatoes, diced
- 2 garlic cloves, minced
- ½ tsp dried oregano
- ½ tsp dried coriander
- ½ tsp dried basil
- ¼ tsp red pepper flakes
- ¼ tsp paprika

- 4 eggs
- Salt and pepper to taste
- 2 scallions, diced
- ½ cup grated cheddar cheese
- ½ cup Parmesan cheese
- 4 bread slices, toasted

Directions:
1. Preheat air fryer to 350°F. Combine the tomato paste, chicken broth, tomatoes, garlic, oregano, coriander, basil, red pepper flakes, and paprika. Pour the mixture evenly into greased ramekins. Bake in the air fryer for 5 minutes. Carefully remove the ramekins and crack one egg in each ramekin, then season with salt and pepper. Top with scallions, grated cheese, and Parmesan cheese. Return the ramekins to the frying basket and bake for 3-5 minutes until the eggs are set, and the cheese is melted. Serve with toasted bread immediately.

French Toast Sticks

Servings: 4
Cooking Time: 7 Minutes

Ingredients:
- 2 eggs
- ½ cup milk
- ⅛ teaspoon salt
- ½ teaspoon pure vanilla extract
- ¾ cup crushed cornflakes
- 6 slices sandwich bread, each slice cut into 4 strips
- oil for misting or cooking spray
- maple syrup or honey

Directions:
1. In a small bowl, beat together eggs, milk, salt, and vanilla.
2. Place crushed cornflakes on a plate or in a shallow dish.
3. Dip bread strips in egg mixture, shake off excess, and roll in cornflake crumbs.
4. Spray both sides of bread strips with oil.
5. Place bread strips in air fryer basket in single layer.
6. Cook at 390°F for 7 minutes or until they're dark golden brown.
7. Repeat steps 5 and 6 to cook remaining French toast sticks.
8. Serve with maple syrup or honey for dipping.

Walnut Pancake

Servings: 4
Cooking Time: 20 Minutes

Ingredients:
- 3 tablespoons butter, divided into thirds
- 1 cup flour
- 1½ teaspoons baking powder
- ¼ teaspoon salt
- 2 tablespoons sugar
- ¾ cup milk
- 1 egg, beaten
- 1 teaspoon pure vanilla extract
- ½ cup walnuts, roughly chopped
- maple syrup or fresh sliced fruit, for serving

Directions:
1. Place 1 tablespoon of the butter in air fryer baking pan. Cook at 330°F for 3 minutes to melt.
2. In a small dish or pan, melt the remaining 2 tablespoons of butter either in the microwave or on the stove.
3. In a medium bowl, stir together the flour, baking powder, salt, and sugar. Add milk, beaten egg, the 2 tablespoons of melted butter, and vanilla. Stir until combined but do not beat. Batter may be slightly lumpy.
4. Pour batter over the melted butter in air fryer baking pan. Sprinkle nuts evenly over top.
5. Cook for 20 minutes or until toothpick inserted in center comes out clean. Turn air fryer off, close the machine, and let pancake rest for 2 minutes.
6. Remove pancake from pan, slice, and serve with syrup or fresh fruit.

Mini Pita Breads

Servings: 8
Cooking Time: 6 Minutes

Ingredients:
- 2 teaspoons active dry yeast
- 1 tablespoon sugar
- 1¼ to 1½ cups warm water (90° - 110°F)
- 3¼ cups all-purpose flour
- 2 teaspoons salt
- 1 tablespoon olive oil, plus more for brushing
- kosher salt (optional)

Directions:
1. Dissolve the yeast, sugar and water in the bowl of a stand mixer. Let the mixture sit for 5 minutes to make sure the yeast is active – it should foam a little. (If there's no foaming, discard and start again with new yeast.) Combine the flour and salt in a bowl, and add it to the water, along with the olive oil. Mix with the dough hook until combined. Add a little more flour if needed to get the dough to pull away from the sides of the mixing bowl, or add a little more water if the dough seems too dry.
2. Knead the dough until it is smooth and elastic (about 8 minutes in the mixer or 15 minutes by hand). Transfer the dough to a lightly oiled bowl, cover and let it rise in a warm place until doubled in bulk. Divide the dough into 8 portions and roll each portion into a circle about 4-inches in diameter. Don't roll the balls too thin, or you won't get the pocket inside the pita.
3. Preheat the air fryer to 400°F.
4. Brush both sides of the dough with olive oil, and sprinkle with kosher salt if desired. Air-fry one at a time at 400°F for 6 minutes, flipping it over when there are two minutes left in the cooking time.

Sugar-dusted Beignets

Servings: 4
Cooking Time: 30 Minutes
Ingredients:
- 1 tsp fast active dry yeast
- 1/3 cup buttermilk
- 3 tbsp brown sugar
- 1 egg
- ½ tsp brandy
- 1 ½ cups flour
- 3 tbsp chopped dried plums
- 3 tbsp golden raisins
- 2 tbsp butter, melted
- 2 tbsp powdered sugar

Directions:
1. Combine the yeast with 3 tbsp of water and leave it until frothy, about 5 minutes. Add the buttermilk, brown sugar, brandy, and egg and stir. Add the flour and stir again. Use your hands to mix the plums and raisins into the dough. Leave the mix in the bowl for 15 minutes.
2. Preheat air fryer to 330°F. Shape the dough in a square, then slice it into 16 pieces. Make 16 balls, then drizzle butter over the balls. Put the balls in the air fryer in a single layer, making sure they don't touch. Air Fry for 5-8 minutes until they puff up and are golden. Repeat until all balls are cooked. Toss in powdered sugar and serve.

Apple & Turkey Breakfast Sausages

Servings: 4
Cooking Time: 15 Minutes
Ingredients:
- ½ tsp coriander seeds, crushed
- 1 tbsp chopped rosemary
- 1 tbsp chopped thyme
- Salt and pepper to taste
- 1 tsp fennel seeds, crushed
- ¾ tsp smoked paprika
- ½ tsp garlic powder
- ½ tsp shallot powder
- ⅛ tsp red pepper flakes
- 1 pound ground turkey
- ½ cup minced apples

Directions:
1. Combine all of the seasonings in a bowl. Add turkey and apple and blend seasonings in well with your hands. Form patties about 3 inches in diameter and ¼ inch thick.
2. Preheat air fryer to 400°F. Arrange patties in a single layer on the greased frying basket. Air Fry for 10 minutes, flipping once until brown and cooked through. Serve.

Cinnamon Pear Oat Muffins

Servings: 6
Cooking Time: 30 Minutes + Cooling Time
Ingredients:
- ½ cup apple sauce
- 1 large egg
- 1/3 cup brown sugar
- 2 tbsp butter, melted
- ½ cup milk
- 1 1/3 cups rolled oats
- 1 tsp ground cinnamon
- ½ tsp baking powder
- Pinch of salt
- ½ cup diced peeled pears

Directions:
1. Preheat the air fryer to 350°F. Place the apple sauce, egg, brown sugar, melted butter, and milk into a bowl and mix to combine. Stir in the oats, cinnamon, baking powder, and salt and mix well, then fold in the pears.
2. Grease 6 silicone muffin cups with baking spray, then spoon the batter in equal portions into the cups. Put the muffin cups in the frying basket and Bake for 13-18 minutes or until set. Leave to cool for 15 minutes. Serve.

Coconut & Peanut Rice Cereal

Servings: 4
Cooking Time: 15 Minutes
Ingredients:
- 4 cups rice cereal
- 1 cup coconut shreds
- 2 tbsp peanut butter
- 1 tsp vanilla extract
- ¼ cup honey
- 1 tbsp light brown sugar
- 2 tsp ground cinnamon
- ¼ cup hazelnut flour
- Salt to taste

Directions:
1. Preheat air fryer at 350°F. Combine the rice cereal, coconut shreds, peanut butter, vanilla extract, honey, brown sugar, cinnamon, hazelnut flour, and salt in a bowl. Press mixture into a greased cake pan. Place cake pan in the frying basket and Air Fry for 5 minutes, stirring once. Let cool completely for 10 minutes before crumbling. Store it into an airtight container up to 5 days.

Lemon-blueberry Morning Bread

Servings: 2
Cooking Time: 15 Minutes
Ingredients:
- ½ cup flour
- ¼ cup powdered sugar
- ½ tsp baking powder
- ⅛ tsp salt
- 2 tbsp butter, melted
- 1 egg
- ½ tsp gelatin
- ½ tsp vanilla extract
- 1 tsp lemon zest
- ½ cup blueberries

Directions:
1. Preheat air fryer to 300ºF. Mix the flour, sugar, baking powder, and salt in a bowl. In another bowl, whisk the butter, egg, gelatin, lemon zest, vanilla extract, and blueberries. Add egg mixture to flour mixture and stir until smooth. Spoon mixture into a pizza pan. Place pan in the frying basket and Bake for 10 minutes. Let sit for 5 minutes before slicing. Serve immediately.

Herby Parmesan Pita

Servings: 2
Cooking Time: 15 Minutes
Ingredients:
- 1 whole-wheat pita
- 2 tsp olive oil
- ¼ sweet onion, diced
- ¼ tsp garlic, minced
- 1 egg
- ¼ tsp dried tarragon
- ¼ tsp dried thyme
- ⅛ tsp salt
- 3 tsp grated Parmesan cheese

Directions:
1. Preheat air fryer to 380°F. Lightly brush the top of the pita with olive oil, then top with onion and garlic. Crack the egg into a small bowl and sprinkle it with tarragon, thyme, and salt. Place the pita in the frying basket and gently pour the egg onto the top of the pita. Sprinkle with cheese over the top. Bake for 6 minutes. Leave to cool for 5 minutes. Cut into pieces and serve.

Crunchy Granola Muffins

Servings: 4
Cooking Time: 15 Minutes
Ingredients:
- 1 cup walnut pieces
- 1 cup sunflower seeds
- 1 cup coconut flakes
- ¼ cup granulated sugar
- ⅛ cup coconut flour
- ⅛ cup pecan flour
- 2 tsp ground cinnamon
- 2 tbsp melted butter
- 2 tbsp almond butter
- ⅛ tsp salt

Directions:
1. Preheat air fryer to 300ºF. In a bowl, mix the walnuts, sunflower seeds, coconut flakes, sugar, coconut flour, pecan flour, cinnamon, butter, almond butter, and salt.
2. Spoon the mixture into an ungreased round 4-cup baking dish. Place it in the frying basket and Bake for 6 minutes, stirring once. Transfer to an airtight container, let cool for 10 minutes, then cover and store at room temperature until ready to serve.

Smooth Walnut-banana Loaf

Servings: 4
Cooking Time: 40 Minutes
Ingredients:
- 1/3 cup peanut butter, melted
- 2 tbsp butter, melted and cooled
- ¾ cup flour
- ½ tsp salt
- ¼ tsp baking soda
- 2 ripe bananas
- 2 eggs
- 1 tsp lemon juice
- ½ cup evaporated cane sugar
- ½ cup ground walnuts
- 1 tbsp blackstrap molasses
- 1 tsp vanilla extract

Directions:
1. Preheat air fryer to 310°F. Mix flour, salt, and baking soda in a small bowl. Mash together bananas and eggs in a large bowl, then stir in sugar, peanut butter, lemon juice, butter, walnuts, molasses, and vanilla. When it is well incorporated, stir in the flour mixture until just combined. Transfer the batter to a parchment-lined baking dish and make sure it is even. Bake in the air fryer for 30 to 35 minutes until a toothpick in the middle comes out clean, and the top is golden. Serve and enjoy.

Thyme Beef & Eggs

Servings: 1
Cooking Time: 25 Minutes
Ingredients:
- 2 tbsp butter
- 1 rosemary sprig
- 2 garlic cloves, pressed
- 8 oz sirloin steak
- Salt and pepper to taste
- ⅛ tsp cayenne pepper
- 2 eggs
- 1 tsp dried thyme

Directions:
1. Preheat air fryer to 400°F. On a clean cutting board, place butter and half of the rosemary spring in the center. Set aside. Season both sides of the steak with salt, black pepper, thyme, pressed garlic, and cayenne pepper. Transfer the steak to the frying basket and top with the other half of the rosemary sprig. Cook for 4 minutes, then flip the steak. Cook for another 3 minutes.
2. Remove the steak and set it on top of the butter and rosemary sprig on the cutter board. Tent with foil and let it rest. Grease ramekin and crack both eggs into it. Season with salt and pepper. Transfer the ramekin to the frying basket and bake for 4-5 minutes until the egg white is cooked and set. Remove the foil from the steak and slice. Serve with eggs and enjoy.

Chorizo Sausage & Cheese Balls

Servings: 4
Cooking Time: 25 Minutes
Ingredients:
- 1 egg white
- 1 lb chorizo ground sausage
- ¼ tsp smoked paprika
- 2 tbsp canned green chiles
- ¼ cup bread crumbs
- ¼ cup grated cheddar

Directions:
1. Preheat air fryer to 400°F. Mix all ingredients in a large bowl. Form into 16 balls. Put the sausage balls in the frying basket and Air Fry for 6 minutes. When done, shake the basket and cook for an additional 6 minutes. Transfer to a serving plate and serve.

Chapter 3 Appetizers And Snacks Recipes

Seafood Egg Rolls

Servings: 6
Cooking Time: 35 Minutes
Ingredients:
- 2 tbsp olive oil
- 1 shallot, chopped
- 2 garlic cloves, minced
- ½ cup shredded carrots
- 1 lb cooked shrimp, chopped
- 1 cup corn kernels
- 1/3 cup chopped cashews
- 1 tbsp soy sauce
- 2 tsp fish sauce
- 12 egg roll wrappers

Directions:
1. Preheat the air fryer to 400°F. Combine the olive oil, shallot, garlic, and carrots in a 6-inch. Put the pan in the frying basket and Air Fry for 3-5 minutes, stirring once. Remove the pan and put the veggies in a bowl. Add shrimp, corn, cashews, soy sauce, and fish sauce to the veggies and combine. Lay the egg roll wrappers on the clean work surface and brush the edges with water. Divide the filling equally and fill them, then brush the edges with water again. Roll up, folding in the side, enclosing the filling inside. Place 4 egg rolls in the basket and spray with cooking oil. Air Fry for 10-12 minutes, rotating once halfway through cooking until golden and crispy. Repeat with remaining rolls. Serve hot.

Fried Bananas

Servings: 4
Cooking Time: 8 Minutes
Ingredients:
- ½ cup panko breadcrumbs
- ½ cup sweetened coconut flakes
- ¼ cup sliced almonds
- ½ cup cornstarch
- 2 egg whites
- 1 tablespoon water
- 2 firm bananas
- oil for misting or cooking spray

Directions:
1. In food processor, combine panko, coconut, and almonds. Process to make small crumbs.
2. Place cornstarch in a shallow dish. In another shallow dish, beat together the egg whites and water until slightly foamy.
3. Preheat air fryer to 390°F.
4. Cut bananas in half crosswise. Cut each half in quarters lengthwise so you have 16 "sticks."
5. Dip banana sticks in cornstarch and tap to shake off excess. Then dip bananas in egg wash and roll in crumb mixture. Spray with oil.
6. Place bananas in air fryer basket in single layer and cook for 4minutes. If any spots have not browned, spritz with oil. Cook for 4 more minutes, until golden brown and crispy.
7. Repeat step 6 to cook remaining bananas.

Grilled Cheese Sandwich Deluxe

Servings: 4
Cooking Time: 6 Minutes
Ingredients:
- 8 ounces Brie
- 8 slices oat nut bread
- 1 large ripe pear, cored and cut into ½-inch-thick slices
- 2 tablespoons butter, melted

Directions:
1. Spread a quarter of the Brie on each of four slices of bread.
2. Top Brie with thick slices of pear, then the remaining 4 slices of bread.
3. Lightly brush both sides of each sandwich with melted butter.
4. Cooking 2 at a time, place sandwiches in air fryer basket and cook at 360°F for 6minutes or until cheese melts and outside looks golden brown.

Roasted Tomatillo Salsa

Servings: 4
Cooking Time: 35 Minutes + Cooling Time
Ingredients:
- 2 tbsp olive oil
- 1 serrano pepper
- 1 jalapeño pepper
- ¼ white onion
- 2 garlic cloves
- ¾ lb tomatillos
- 3 tbsp chopped cilantro
- ¼ tsp sugar
- Salt to taste

Directions:
1. Preheat air fryer to 400°F. Lightly drizzle the serrano, jalapeño, onion and garlic with some olive oil. Bake in the air fryer for 14 minutes, flipping them once until charred. Remove the peppers to a foil, wrap and let cool for 10 minutes. Put the rest of the veggies into a food processor. Lightly brush the tomatillos with the remaining olive oil. Cook in the air fryer for 10 minutes, flipping the tomatillos once until charred.
2. Transfer the tomatillos to your food processor. Unwrap the peppers. Peel off the skin and remove all of the seeds. Transfer to the food processor. Also, add cilantro, sugar, and salt. Pulse until coarsely chopped. Slowly add 5-6 tbsp of water until smooth and pureed. Serve.

Fried Wontons

Servings: 24
Cooking Time: 6 Minutes
Ingredients:
- 6 ounces Lean ground beef, pork, or turkey
- 1 tablespoon Regular or reduced-sodium soy sauce or tamari sauce
- 1½ teaspoons Minced garlic
- ¾ teaspoon Ground dried ginger
- ½ teaspoon Ground white pepper
- 24 Wonton wrappers (thawed, if necessary)
- Vegetable oil spray

Directions:
1. Preheat the air fryer to 350°F.
2. Stir the ground meat, soy or tamari sauce, garlic, ginger, and white pepper in a bowl until the spices are uniformly distributed in the mixture.
3. Set a small bowl of water on a clean, dry surface or next to a clean, dry cutting board. Set one wonton wrapper on the surface. Dip your clean finger in the water, then run it along the edges of the wrapper. Set 1 teaspoon of the ground meat mixture in the center of the wrapper. Fold it over, corner to corner, to create a filled triangle. Press to seal the edges, then pull the corners on the longest side up and together over the filling to create the classic wonton shape. Press the corners together to seal. Set aside and continue filling and making more filled wontons.
4. Generously coat the filled wontons on all sides with vegetable oil spray. Arrange them in the basket in one layer and air-fry for 6 minutes, shaking the basket gently at the 2- and 4-minute marks to rearrange the wontons (but always making sure they're still in one layer), until golden brown and crisp.
5. Pour the wontons in the basket onto a wire rack or even into a serving bowl. Cool for 2 or 3 minutes (but not much longer) and serve hot.

Artichoke-spinach Dip

Servings: 4
Cooking Time: 25 Minutes
Ingredients:
- 4 oz canned artichoke hearts, chopped
- ½ cup Greek yogurt
- ¼ cup cream cheese
- ½ cup spinach, chopped
- ½ red bell pepper, chopped
- 1 garlic clove, minced
- ½ tsp dried oregano
- 3 tsp grated Parmesan cheese

Directions:
1. Preheat air fryer to 340°F. Mix the yogurt and cream cheese. Add the artichoke, spinach, red bell pepper, garlic, and oregano, then put the mix in a pan and scatter Parmesan cheese on top. Put the pan in the frying basket and Bake for 9-14 minutes. The dip should be bubble and brown. Serve hot.

Savory Sausage Balls

Servings: 10
Cooking Time: 8 Minutes
Ingredients:
- 2 cups all-purpose flour
- 1 tablespoon baking powder
- ½ teaspoon garlic powder
- ¼ teaspoon onion powder
- ½ teaspoon salt
- 3 tablespoons milk
- 2½ cups grated pepper jack cheese
- 1 pound fresh sausage, casing removed

Directions:
1. Preheat the air fryer to 370°F.
2. In a large bowl, whisk together the flour, baking powder, garlic powder, onion powder, and salt. Add in the milk, grated cheese, and sausage.
3. Using a tablespoon, scoop out the sausage and roll it between your hands to form a rounded ball. You should end up with approximately 32 balls. Place them in the air fryer basket in a single layer and working in batches as necessary.
4. Cook for 8 minutes, or until the outer coating turns light brown.
5. Carefully remove, repeating with the remaining sausage balls.

Poutine

Servings: 2
Cooking Time: 25 Minutes
Ingredients:
- 2 russet potatoes, scrubbed and cut into ½-inch sticks
- 2 teaspoons vegetable oil
- 2 tablespoons butter
- ¼ onion, minced (about ¼ cup)
- 1 clove garlic, smashed
- ¼ teaspoon dried thyme
- 3 tablespoons flour
- 1 teaspoon tomato paste
- 1½ cups strong beef stock
- salt and lots of freshly ground black pepper
- a few dashes of Worcestershire sauce
- ⅔ cup chopped string cheese or cheese curds

Directions:
1. Bring a large saucepan of salted water to a boil on the stovetop while you peel and cut the potatoes. Blanch the potatoes in the boiling salted water for 4 minutes while you Preheat the air fryer to 400°F. Strain the potatoes and rinse them with cold water. Dry them well with a clean kitchen towel.
2. Toss the dried potato sticks gently with the oil and place them in the air fryer basket. Air-fry for 25 minutes, shaking the basket a few times while the fries cook to help them brown evenly.
3. While the fries are cooking, make the gravy. Melt the butter in a small saucepan over medium heat. Add the onion, garlic and thyme and cook for five minutes, until soft and just starting to brown. Stir in the flour and cook for another two minutes, stirring regularly. Finally, add the tomato paste and continue to cook for another minute or two. Whisk in the beef stock and bring the mixture to a boil to thicken. Season to taste with salt, lots of freshly ground black pepper and a few dashes of Worcestershire sauce. Keep the gravy warm.
4. As soon as the fries are done, season them with salt and transfer to a plate or basket. Top the fries with the cheese curds or string cheese, and pour the warm gravy over the top.

Shrimp Egg Rolls

Servings: 8
Cooking Time: 10 Minutes
Ingredients:
- 1 tablespoon vegetable oil
- ½ head green or savoy cabbage, finely shredded
- 1 cup shredded carrots
- 1 cup canned bean sprouts, drained
- 1 tablespoon soy sauce
- ½ teaspoon sugar
- 1 teaspoon sesame oil
- ¼ cup hoisin sauce
- freshly ground black pepper
- 1 pound cooked shrimp, diced
- ¼ cup scallions
- 8 egg roll wrappers
- vegetable oil
- duck sauce

Directions:
1. Preheat a large sauté pan over medium-high heat. Add the oil and cook the cabbage, carrots and bean sprouts until they start to wilt – about 3 minutes. Add the soy sauce, sugar, sesame oil, hoisin sauce and black pepper. Sauté for a few more minutes. Stir in the shrimp and scallions and cook until the vegetables are just tender. Transfer the mixture to a colander in a bowl to cool. Press or squeeze out any excess water from the filling so that you don't end up with soggy egg rolls.
2. To make the egg rolls, place the egg roll wrappers on a flat surface with one of the points facing towards you so they look like diamonds. Dividing the filling evenly between the eight wrappers, spoon the mixture onto the center of the egg roll wrappers. Spread the filling across the center of the wrappers from the left corner to the right corner, but leave 2 inches from each corner empty. Brush the empty sides of the wrapper with a little water. Fold the bottom corner of the wrapper tightly up over the filling, trying to avoid making any air pockets. Fold the left corner in toward the center and then the right corner toward the center. It should now look like an envelope. Tightly roll the egg roll from the bottom to the top open corner. Press to seal the egg roll together, brushing with a little extra water if need be. Repeat this technique with all 8 egg rolls.
3. Preheat the air fryer to 370°F.
4. Spray or brush all sides of the egg rolls with vegetable oil. Air-fry four egg rolls at a time for 10 minutes, turning them over halfway through the cooking time.
5. Serve hot with duck sauce or your favorite dipping sauce.

Plantain Chips

Servings: 2
Cooking Time: 14 Minutes
Ingredients:
- 1 large green plantain
- 2½ cups filtered water, divided
- 2 teaspoons sea salt, divided

Directions:
1. Slice the plantain into 1-inch pieces. Place the plantains into a large bowl, cover with 2 cups water and 1 teaspoon salt. Soak the plantains for 30 minutes; then remove and pat dry.
2. Preheat the air fryer to 390°F.
3. Place the plantain pieces into the air fryer basket, leaving space between the plantain rounds. Cook the plantains for 5 minutes, and carefully remove them from the air fryer basket.
4. Add the remaining water to a small bowl.
5. Using a small drinking glass, dip the bottom of the glass into the water and mash the warm plantains until they're ¼-inch thick. Return the plantains to the air fryer basket, sprinkle with the remaining sea salt, and spray lightly with cooking spray.
6. Cook for another 6 to 8 minutes, or until lightly golden brown edges appear.

Zucchini Boats With Bacon

Servings: 4
Cooking Time: 35 Minutes
Ingredients:
- 1 ¼ cups shredded Havarti cheese
- 3 bacon slices
- 2 large zucchini
- Salt and pepper to taste
- ¼ tsp garlic powder
- ¼ tsp sweet paprika
- 8 tsp buttermilk
- 2 tbsp chives, chopped

Directions:
1. Preheat air fryer to 350°F. Place the bacon in the frying basket and Air Fry it for 10 minutes, flipping once until crisp. Chop the bacon and set aside. Cut zucchini in half lengthwise and then crosswise so that you have 8 pieces. Scoop out the pulp. Sprinkle with salt, garlic, paprika, and black pepper. Place the zucchini skins in the greased frying basket. Air Fry until crisp-tender, 8-10 minutes. Remove the basket and add the Havarti inside each boat and top with bacon. Return stuffed boats to the air fryer and fry for 2 minutes or until the cheese has melted. Top with buttermilk and chives before serving immediately.

Antipasto-stuffed Cherry Tomatoes

Servings: 12
Cooking Time: 9 Minutes
Ingredients:
- 12 Large cherry tomatoes, preferably Campari tomatoes (about 1½ ounces each and the size of golf balls)
- ½ cup Seasoned Italian-style dried bread crumbs (gluten-free, if a concern)
- ¼ cup (about ¾ ounce) Finely grated Parmesan cheese
- ¼ cup Finely chopped pitted black olives
- ¼ cup Finely chopped marinated artichoke hearts
- 2 tablespoons Marinade from the artichokes
- 4 Sun-dried tomatoes (dry, not packed in oil), finely chopped
- Olive oil spray

Directions:
1. Preheat the air fryer to 400°F.
2. Cut the top off of each fresh tomato, exposing the seeds and pulp. (The tops can be saved for a snack, sprinkled with some kosher salt, to tide you over while the stuffed tomatoes cook.) Cut a very small slice off the bottom of each tomato (no cutting into the pulp) so it will stand up flat on your work surface. Use a melon baller to remove and discard the seeds and pulp from each tomato.
3. Mix the bread crumbs, cheese, olives, artichoke hearts, marinade, and sun-dried tomatoes in a bowl until well combined. Stuff this mixture into each prepared tomato, about 1½ tablespoons in each. Generously coat the tops of the tomatoes with olive oil spray.
4. Set the tomatoes stuffing side up in the basket. Air-fry undisturbed for 9 minutes, or until the stuffing has browned a bit and the tomatoes are blistered in places.
5. Remove the basket and cool the tomatoes in it for 5 minutes. Then use kitchen tongs to gently transfer the tomatoes to a serving platter.

Tomato & Garlic Roasted Potatoes

Servings: 4
Cooking Time: 25 Minutes
Ingredients:
- 16 cherry tomatoes, halved
- 6 red potatoes, cubed
- 3 garlic cloves, minced
- Salt and pepper to taste
- 1 tsp chopped chives
- 1 tbsp extra-virgin olive oil

Directions:
1. Preheat air fryer to 370°F. Combine cherry potatoes, garlic, salt, pepper, chives and olive oil in a resealable plastic bag. Seal and shake the bag. Put the potatoes in the greased frying basket and Roast for 10 minutes. Shake the basket, place the cherry tomatoes in, and cook for 10 more minutes. Allow to cool slightly and serve.

Cuban Sliders

Servings: 8
Cooking Time: 8 Minutes
Ingredients:
- 8 slices ciabatta bread, ¼-inch thick
- cooking spray
- 1 tablespoon brown mustard
- 6-8 ounces thin sliced leftover roast pork
- 4 ounces thin deli turkey
- ⅓ cup bread and butter pickle slices
- 2–3 ounces Pepper Jack cheese slices

Directions:
1. Spray one side of each slice of bread with butter or olive oil cooking spray.
2. Spread brown mustard on other side of each slice.
3. Layer pork roast, turkey, pickles, and cheese on 4 of the slices. Top with remaining slices.
4. Cook at 390°F for approximately 8minutes. The sandwiches should be golden brown.
5. Cut each slider in half to make 8 portions.

Corn Dog Bites

Servings: 3
Cooking Time: 12 Minutes
Ingredients:
- 3 cups Purchased cornbread stuffing mix
- ⅓ cup All-purpose flour
- 2 Large egg(s), well beaten
- 3 Hot dogs, cut into 2-inch pieces (vegetarian hot dogs, if preferred)
- Vegetable oil spray

Directions:
1. Preheat the air fryer to 375°F.
2. Put the cornbread stuffing mix in a food processor. Cover and pulse to grind into a mixture like fine bread crumbs.
3. Set up and fill three shallow soup plates or small pie plates on your counter: one for the flour, one for the egg(s), and one for the stuffing mix crumbs.
4. Dip a hot dog piece in the flour to coat it completely, then gently shake off any excess. Dip the hot dog piece into the egg(s) and gently roll it around to coat all surfaces, then pick it up and allow any excess egg to slip back into the rest. Set the hot dog piece in the stuffing mix crumbs and roll it gently to coat it evenly and well on all sides, even the ends. Set it aside on a cutting board and continue dipping and coating the remaining hot dog pieces.
5. Give the coated hot dog pieces a generous coating of vegetable oil spray on all sides, then set them in the basket in one layer with some space between them. Air-fry undisturbed for 10 minutes, or until golden brown and crunchy. (You'll need to add 2 minutes in the air fryer if the temperature is at 360°F.)
6. Use a nonstick-safe spatula, and perhaps a flatware fork for balance, to transfer the corn dog bites to a wire rack. Cool for 5 minutes before serving.

Crispy Ravioli Bites

Servings: 5
Cooking Time: 7 Minutes
Ingredients:
- ⅓ cup All-purpose flour
- 1 Large egg(s), well beaten
- ⅔ cup Seasoned Italian-style dried bread crumbs
- 10 ounces (about 20) Frozen mini ravioli, meat or cheese, thawed
- Olive oil spray

Directions:
1. Preheat the air fryer to 400°F.
2. Pour the flour into a medium bowl. Set up and fill two shallow soup plates or small pie plates on your counter: one with the beaten egg(s) and one with the bread crumbs.
3. Pour all the ravioli into the flour and toss well to coat. Pick up 1 ravioli, gently shake off any excess flour, and dip the ravioli in the egg(s), coating both sides. Let any excess egg slip back into the rest, then set the ravioli in the bread crumbs, turning it several times until lightly and evenly coated on all sides. Set aside on a cutting board and continue on with the remaining ravioli.
4. Lightly coat the ravioli on both sides with olive oil spray, then set them in the basket in as close to a single layer as you can. Some can lean up against the side of the basket. Air-fry for 7 minutes, tossing the basket at the 4-minute mark to rearrange the pieces, until brown and crisp.
5. Pour the contents of the basket onto a wire rack. Cool for 5 minutes before serving.

Onion Ring Nachos

Servings: 3
Cooking Time: 8 Minutes
Ingredients:
- ¾ pound Frozen breaded (not battered) onion rings (do not thaw)
- 1½ cups (about 6 ounces) Shredded Cheddar, Monterey Jack, or Swiss cheese, or a purchased Tex-Mex blend
- Up to 12 Pickled jalapeño rings

Directions:
1. Preheat the air fryer to 400°F.
2. When the machine is at temperature, spread the onion rings in the basket in a fairly even layer. Air-fry undisturbed for 6 minutes, or until crisp. Remove the basket from the machine.
3. Cut a circle of parchment paper to line a 6-inch round cake pan for a small air fryer, a 7-inch round cake pan for a medium air fryer, or an 8-inch round cake pan for a large machine.
4. Pour the onion rings into a fairly even layer in the cake pan, then sprinkle the cheese evenly over them. Dot with the jalapeño rings.
5. Set the pan in the basket and air-fry undisturbed for 2 minutes, until the cheese has melted and is bubbling.
6. Remove the pan from the basket. Cool for 5 minutes before serving.

String Bean Fries

Servings: 4
Cooking Time: 6 Minutes
Ingredients:
- ½ pound fresh string beans
- 2 eggs
- 4 teaspoons water
- ½ cup white flour
- ½ cup breadcrumbs
- ¼ teaspoon salt
- ¼ teaspoon ground black pepper
- ¼ teaspoon dry mustard (optional)
- oil for misting or cooking spray

Directions:
1. Preheat air fryer to 360°F.
2. Trim stem ends from string beans, wash, and pat dry.
3. In a shallow dish, beat eggs and water together until well blended.
4. Place flour in a second shallow dish.
5. In a third shallow dish, stir together the breadcrumbs, salt, pepper, and dry mustard if using.
6. Dip each string bean in egg mixture, flour, egg mixture again, then breadcrumbs.
7. When you finish coating all the string beans, open air fryer and place them in basket.
8. Cook for 3minutes.
9. Stop and mist string beans with oil or cooking spray.
10. Cook for 3 moreminutes or until string beans are crispy and nicely browned.

Cheesy Pigs In A Blanket

Servings: 4
Cooking Time: 7 Minutes
Ingredients:
- 24 cocktail size smoked sausages
- 6 slices deli-sliced Cheddar cheese, each cut into 8 rectangular pieces
- 1 (8-ounce) tube refrigerated crescent roll dough
- ketchup or mustard for dipping

Directions:
1. Unroll the crescent roll dough into one large sheet. If your crescent roll dough has perforated seams, pinch or roll all the perforated seams together. Cut the large sheet of dough into 4 rectangles. Then cut each rectangle into 6 pieces by making one slice lengthwise in the middle and 2 slices horizontally. You should have 24 pieces of dough.
2. Make a deep slit lengthwise down the center of the cocktail sausage. Stuff two pieces of cheese into the slit in the sausage. Roll one piece of crescent dough around the stuffed cocktail sausage leaving the ends of the sausage exposed. Pinch the seam together. Repeat with the remaining sausages.
3. Preheat the air fryer to 350°F.
4. Air-fry in 2 batches, placing the sausages seam side down in the basket. Air-fry for 7 minutes. Serve hot with ketchup or your favorite mustard for dipping.

Okra Chips

Servings: 4
Cooking Time: 16 Minutes
Ingredients:
- 1¼ pounds Thin fresh okra pods, cut into 1-inch pieces
- 1½ tablespoons Vegetable or canola oil
- ¾ teaspoon Coarse sea salt or kosher salt

Directions:
1. Preheat the air fryer to 400°F.
2. Toss the okra, oil, and salt in a large bowl until the pieces are well and evenly coated.
3. When the machine is at temperature, pour the contents of the bowl into the basket. Air-fry, tossing several times, for 16 minutes, or until crisp and quite brown (maybe even a little blackened on the thin bits).
4. Pour the contents of the basket onto a wire rack. Cool for a couple of minutes before serving.

Rich Clam Spread

Servings: 6
Cooking Time: 40 Minutes
Ingredients:
- 2 cans chopped clams in clam juice
- 1/3 cup panko bread crumbs
- 1 garlic clove, minced
- 1 tbsp olive oil
- 1 tbsp lemon juice
- ¼ tsp hot sauce
- 1 tsp Worcestershire sauce
- ½ tsp shallot powder
- ¼ tsp dried dill
- Salt and pepper to taste
- ½ tsp sweet paprika
- 4 tsp grated Parmesan cheese
- 2 celery stalks, chopped

Directions:
1. Completely drain one can of clams. Add them to a bowl along with the entire can of clams, breadcrumbs, garlic, olive oil, lemon juice, Worcestershire sauce, hot sauce, shallot powder, dill, pepper, salt, paprika, and 2 tbsp Parmesan. Combine well and set aside for 10 minutes. After that time, put the mixture in a greased baking dish.
2. Preheat air fryer to 325°F. Put the dish in the air fryer and Bake for 10 minutes. Sprinkle the remaining paprika and Parmesan, and continue to cook until golden brown on top, 8-10 minutes. Serve hot along with celery sticks.

Avocado Fries, Vegan

Servings: 4
Cooking Time: 10 Minutes
Ingredients:
- ¼ cup almond or coconut milk
- 1 tablespoon lime juice
- ⅛ teaspoon hot sauce
- 2 tablespoons flour
- ¾ cup panko breadcrumbs
- ¼ cup cornmeal
- ¼ teaspoon salt
- 1 large avocado
- oil for misting or cooking spray

Directions:
1. In a small bowl, whisk together the almond or coconut milk, lime juice, and hot sauce.
2. Place flour on a sheet of wax paper.
3. Mix panko, cornmeal, and salt and place on another sheet of wax paper.
4. Split avocado in half and remove pit. Peel or use a spoon to lift avocado halves out of the skin.
5. Cut avocado lengthwise into ½-inch slices. Dip each in flour, then milk mixture, then roll in panko mixture.
6. Mist with oil or cooking spray and cook at 390°F for 10 minutes, until crust is brown and crispy.

Eggs In Avocado Halves

Servings: 3
Cooking Time: 23 Minutes
Ingredients:
- 3 Hass avocados, halved and pitted but not peeled
- 6 Medium eggs
- Vegetable oil spray
- 3 tablespoons Heavy or light cream (not fat-free cream)
- To taste Table salt
- To taste Ground black pepper

Directions:
1. Preheat the air fryer to 350°F.

2. Slice a small amount off the (skin) side of each avocado half so it can sit stable, without rocking. Lightly coat the skin of the avocado half (the side that will now sit stable) with vegetable oil spray.
3. Arrange the avocado halves open side up on a cutting board, then crack an egg into the indentation in each where the pit had been. If any white overflows the avocado half, wipe that bit of white off the cut edge of the avocado before proceeding.
4. Remove the basket (or its attachment) from the machine and set the filled avocado halves in it in one layer. Return it to the machine without pushing it in. Drizzle each avocado half with about 1½ teaspoons cream, a little salt, and a little ground black pepper.
5. Air-fry undisturbed for 10 minutes for a soft-set yolk, or air-fry for 13 minutes for more-set eggs.
6. Use a nonstick-safe spatula and a flatware fork for balance to transfer the avocado halves to serving plates. Cool a minute or two before serving.

Root Vegetable Crisps

Servings: 4
Cooking Time: 8 Minutes
Ingredients:
- 1 small taro root, peeled and washed
- 1 small yucca root, peeled and washed
- 1 small purple sweet potato, washed
- 2 cups filtered water
- 2 teaspoons extra-virgin olive oil
- ½ teaspoon salt

Directions:
1. Using a mandolin, slice the taro root, yucca root, and purple sweet potato into ⅛-inch slices.
2. Add the water to a large bowl. Add the sliced vegetables and soak for at least 30 minutes.
3. Preheat the air fryer to 370°F.
4. Drain the water and pat the vegetables dry with a paper towel or kitchen cloth. Toss the vegetables with the olive oil and sprinkle with salt. Liberally spray the air fryer basket with olive oil mist.
5. Place the vegetables into the air fryer basket, making sure not to overlap the pieces.
6. Cook for 8 minutes, shaking the basket every 2 minutes, until the outer edges start to turn up and the vegetables start to brown. Remove from the basket and serve warm. Repeat with the remaining vegetable slices until all are cooked.

Balsamic Grape Dip

Servings: 6
Cooking Time: 25 Minutes
Ingredients:
- 2 cups seedless red grapes
- 1 tbsp balsamic vinegar
- 1 tbsp honey
- 1 cup Greek yogurt
- 2 tbsp milk
- 2 tbsp minced fresh basil

Directions:

1. Preheat air fryer to 380°F. Add the grapes and balsamic vinegar to the frying basket, then pour honey over and toss to coat. Roast for 8-12 minutes, shriveling the grapes, and take them out of the air fryer. Mix the milk and yogurt together, then gently stir in the grapes and basil. Serve and enjoy!

Red Potato Chips With Mexican Dip

Servings: 6
Cooking Time: 35 Minutes
Ingredients:
- 1 tsp smoked paprika
- 1 tbsp lemon juice
- 10 purple red potatoes
- 1 tsp olive oil
- 2 tsp minced thyme
- ⅛ tsp cayenne pepper
- Sea salt to taste
- 1 cup Greek yogurt
- 2 chipotle chiles, minced
- 2 tbsp adobo sauce

Directions:
1. Preheat air fryer to 400°F. Cut the potatoes lengthwise in thin strips and put them in a bowl. Spray olive oil all over them and toss until the strips are evenly coated. Add the potatoes to the frying basket and Air Fry for 9-14 minutes. Use a metal spoon to mix them up at around minute 5. Mix the yogurt, chipotle chiles, adobo sauce, paprika, and lemon juice in a bowl, then put it in the refrigerator. When cooking is finished, put the potatoes on a large plate and toss thyme, cayenne pepper, and sea salt on top. Serve with this Mexican dip. Enjoy!

Avocado Fries

Servings: 8
Cooking Time: 8 Minutes
Ingredients:
- 2 medium avocados, firm but ripe
- 1 large egg
- ½ teaspoon garlic powder
- ¼ teaspoon cayenne pepper
- ¼ teaspoon salt
- ¾ cup almond flour
- ½ cup finely grated Parmesan cheese
- ½ cup gluten-free breadcrumbs

Directions:
1. Preheat the air fryer to 370°F.
2. Rinse the outside of the avocado with water. Slice the avocado in half, slice it in half again, and then slice it in half once more to get 8 slices. Remove the outer skin. Repeat for the other avocado. Set the avocado slices aside.
3. In a small bowl, whisk the egg, garlic powder, cayenne pepper, and salt in a small bowl. Set aside.
4. In a separate bowl, pour the almond flour.
5. In a third bowl, mix the Parmesan cheese and breadcrumbs.
6. Carefully roll the avocado slices in the almond flour, then dip them in the egg wash, and coat them in the cheese and breadcrumb topping. Repeat until all 16 fries are coated.

7. Liberally spray the air fryer basket with olive oil spray and place the avocado fries into the basket, leaving a little space around the sides between fries. Depending on the size of your air fryer, you may need to cook these in batches.
8. Cook fries for 8 minutes, or until the outer coating turns light brown.
9. Carefully remove, repeat with remaining slices, and then serve warm.

Avocado Egg Rolls

Servings: 8
Cooking Time: 8 Minutes
Ingredients:
- 8 full-size egg roll wrappers
- 1 medium avocado, sliced into 8 pieces
- 1 cup cooked black beans, divided
- ½ cup mild salsa, divided
- ½ cup shredded Mexican cheese, divided
- ⅓ cup filtered water, divided
- ½ cup sour cream
- 1 teaspoon chipotle hot sauce

Directions:
1. Preheat the air fryer to 400°F.
2. Place the egg roll wrapper on a flat surface and place 1 strip of avocado down in the center.
3. Top the avocado with 2 tablespoons of black beans, 1 tablespoon of salsa, and 1 tablespoon of shredded cheese.
4. Place two of your fingers into the water, and then moisten the four outside edges of the egg roll wrapper with water (so the outer edges will secure shut).
5. Fold the bottom corner up, covering the filling. Then secure the sides over the top, remembering to lightly moisten them so they stick. Tightly roll the egg roll up and moisten the final flap of the wrapper and firmly press it into the egg roll to secure it shut.
6. Repeat Steps 2–5 until all 8 egg rolls are complete.
7. When ready to cook, spray the air fryer basket with olive oil spray and place the egg rolls into the basket. Depending on the size and type of air fryer you have, you may need to do this in two sets.
8. Cook for 4 minutes, flip, and then cook the remaining 4 minutes.
9. Repeat until all the egg rolls are cooked. Meanwhile, mix the sour cream with the hot sauce to serve as a dipping sauce.
10. Serve warm.

Fried String Beans With Greek Sauce

Servings: 4
Cooking Time: 10 Minutes
Ingredients:
- 1 egg
- 1 tbsp flour
- ¼ tsp paprika
- ½ tsp garlic powder
- Salt to taste
- ¼ cup bread crumbs
- ¼ lemon zest
- ½ lb whole string beans
- ½ cup Greek yogurt
- 1 tbsp lemon juice
- ⅛ tsp cayenne pepper

Directions:
1. Preheat air fryer to 380°F. Whisk the egg and 2 tbsp of water in a bowl until frothy. Sift the flour, paprika, garlic powder, and salt in another bowl, then stir in the bread crumbs. Dip each string bean into the egg mixture, then roll into the bread crumb mixture. Put the string beans in a single layer in the greased frying basket. Air Fry them for 5 minutes until the breading is golden brown. Stir the yogurt, lemon juice and zest, salt, and cayenne in a small bowl. Serve the bean fries with lemon-yogurt sauce.

Fried Peaches

Servings: 4
Cooking Time: 8 Minutes
Ingredients:
- 2 egg whites
- 1 tablespoon water
- ¼ cup sliced almonds
- 2 tablespoons brown sugar
- ½ teaspoon almond extract
- 1 cup crisp rice cereal
- 2 medium, very firm peaches, peeled and pitted
- ¼ cup cornstarch
- oil for misting or cooking spray

Directions:
1. Preheat air fryer to 390°F.
2. Beat together egg whites and water in a shallow dish.
3. In a food processor, combine the almonds, brown sugar, and almond extract. Process until ingredients combine well and the nuts are finely chopped.
4. Add cereal and pulse just until cereal crushes. Pour crumb mixture into a shallow dish or onto a plate.
5. Cut each peach into eighths and place in a plastic bag or container with lid. Add cornstarch, seal, and shake to coat.
6. Remove peach slices from bag or container, tapping them hard to shake off the excess cornstarch. Dip in egg wash and roll in crumbs. Spray with oil.
7. Place in air fryer basket and cook for 5minutes. Shake basket, separate any that have stuck together, and spritz a little oil on any spots that aren't browning.
8. Cook for 3 minutes longer, until golden brown and crispy.

Piri Piri Chicken Wings

Servings: 4
Cooking Time: 45 Minutes
Ingredients:
- 1 cup crushed cracker crumbs
- 1 tbsp sweet paprika
- 1 tbsp smoked paprika
- 1 tbsp Piri Piri seasoning
- 1 tsp sea salt

- 2 tsp onion powder
- 1 tsp garlic powder
- 2 lb chicken drumettes
- 2 tbsp olive oil

Directions:
1. Preheat the air fryer to 380°F. Combine the cracker crumbs, paprikas, Piri Piri seasoning, sea salt, onion and garlic powders in a bowl and mix well. Pour into a screw-top glass jar and set aside. Put the drumettes in a large bowl, drizzle with the olive oil, and toss to coat. Sprinkle 1/3 cup of the breading mix over the meat and press the mix into the drumettes. Put half the drumettes in the frying basket and Air Fry for 20-25 minutes, shaking the basket once until golden and crisp. Serve hot.

Mozzarella En Carrozza With Puttanesca Sauce

Servings: 6
Cooking Time: 8 Minutes
Ingredients:
- Puttanesca Sauce
- 2 teaspoons olive oil
- 1 anchovy, chopped (optional)
- 2 cloves garlic, minced
- 1 (14-ounce) can petite diced tomatoes
- ½ cup chicken stock or water
- ⅓ cup Kalamata olives, chopped
- 2 tablespoons capers
- ½ teaspoon dried oregano
- ¼ teaspoon crushed red pepper flakes
- salt and freshly ground black pepper
- 1 tablespoon fresh parsley, chopped
- 8 slices of thinly sliced white bread (Pepperidge Farm®)
- 8 ounces mozzarella cheese, cut into ¼-inch slices
- ½ cup all-purpose flour
- 3 eggs, beaten
- 1½ cups seasoned panko breadcrumbs
- ½ teaspoon garlic powder
- ½ teaspoon salt
- freshly ground black pepper
- olive oil, in a spray bottle

Directions:
1. Start by making the puttanesca sauce. Heat the olive oil in a medium saucepan on the stovetop. Add the anchovies (if using, and I really think you should!) and garlic and sauté for 3 minutes, or until the anchovies have "melted" into the oil. Add the tomatoes, chicken stock, olives, capers, oregano and crushed red pepper flakes and simmer the sauce for 20 minutes. Season with salt and freshly ground black pepper and stir in the fresh parsley.
2. Cut the crusts off the slices of bread. Place four slices of the bread on a cutting board. Divide the cheese between the four slices of bread. Top the cheese with the remaining four slices of bread to make little sandwiches and cut each sandwich into 4 triangles.
3. Set up a dredging station using three shallow dishes. Place the flour in the first shallow dish, the eggs in the second dish and in the third dish, combine the panko breadcrumbs, garlic powder, salt and black pepper. Dredge each little triangle in the flour first (you might think this is redundant, but it helps to get the coating to adhere to the edges of the sandwiches) and then dip them into the egg, making sure both the sides and the edges are coated. Let the excess egg drip off and then press the triangles into the breadcrumb mixture, pressing the crumbs on with your hands so they adhere. Place the coated triangles in the freezer for 2 hours, until the cheese is frozen.
4. Preheat the air fryer to 390°F. Spray all sides of the mozzarella triangles with oil and transfer a single layer of triangles to the air fryer basket. Air-fry in batches at 390°F for 5 minutes. Turn the triangles over and air-fry for an additional 3 minutes.
5. Serve mozzarella triangles immediately with the warm puttanesca sauce.

Poppy Seed Mini Hot Dog Rolls

Servings: 4
Cooking Time: 25 Minutes
Ingredients:
- 8 small mini hot dogs
- 8 pastry dough sheets
- 1 tbsp vegetable oil
- 1 tbsp poppy seeds

Directions:
1. Preheat the air fryer to 350°F. Roll the mini hot dogs into a pastry dough sheet, wrapping them snugly. Brush the rolls with vegetable oil on all sides. Arrange them on the frying basket and sprinkle poppy seeds on top. Bake for 15 minutes until the pastry crust is golden brown. Serve.

Hawaiian Ahi Tuna Bowls

Servings: 4
Cooking Time: 20 Minutes
Ingredients:
- 8 oz sushi-grade tuna steaks, cubed
- ½ peeled cucumber, diced
- 12 wonton wrappers
- ¾ cup dried beans
- 2 tbsp soy sauce
- 1 tsp toasted sesame oil
- ½ tsp Sriracha sauce
- 1 chili, minced
- 2 oz avocado, cubed
- ¼ cup sliced scallions
- 1 tbsp toasted sesame seeds

Directions:
1. Make wonton bowls by placing each wonton wrapper in a foil-lined baking cup. Press gently in the middle and against the sides. Use a light coating of cooking spray. Spoon a heaping tbsp of dried beans into the wonton cup.
2. Preheat air fryer to 280°F. Place the cups in a single layer on the frying basket. Bake until brown and crispy, 9-11 minutes.

Using tongs, carefully remove the cups and allow them to cool slightly. Remove the beans and place the cups to the side. In a bowl, whisk together the chili, soy sauce, sesame oil, and sriracha. Toss in tuna, cucumber, avocado, and scallions. Place 2 heaping tbsp of the tuna mixture into each wonton cup. Top with sesame seeds and serve immediately.

Asian Five-spice Wings

Servings: 4
Cooking Time: 15 Minutes
Ingredients:
- 2 pounds chicken wings
- ½ cup Asian-style salad dressing
- 2 tablespoons Chinese five-spice powder

Directions:
1. Cut off wing tips and discard or freeze for stock. Cut remaining wing pieces in two at the joint.
2. Place wing pieces in a large sealable plastic bag. Pour in the Asian dressing, seal bag, and massage the marinade into the wings until well coated. Refrigerate for at least an hour.
3. Remove wings from bag, drain off excess marinade, and place wings in air fryer basket.
4. Cook at 360°F for 15minutes or until juices run clear. About halfway through cooking time, shake the basket or stir wings for more even cooking.
5. Transfer cooked wings to plate in a single layer. Sprinkle half of the Chinese five-spice powder on the wings, turn, and sprinkle other side with remaining seasoning.

Olive & Pepper Tapenade

Servings: 4
Cooking Time: 10 Minutes
Ingredients:
- 1 red bell pepper
- 3 tbsp olive oil
- ½ cup black olives, chopped
- 1 garlic clove, minced
- ½ tsp dried oregano
- 1 tbsp white wine juice

Directions:
1. Preheat air fryer to 380°F. Lightly brush the outside of the bell pepper with some olive oil and put it in the frying basket. Roast for 5 minutes. Combine the remaining olive oil with olives, garlic, oregano, and white wine in a bowl. Remove the red pepper from the air fryer, then gently slice off the stem and discard the seeds. Chop into small pieces. Add the chopped pepper to the olive mixture and stir all together until combined. Serve and enjoy!

Turkey Burger Sliders

Servings: 8
Cooking Time: 7 Minutes
Ingredients:
- 1 pound ground turkey
- ¼ teaspoon curry powder
- 1 teaspoon Hoisin sauce
- ½ teaspoon salt
- 8 slider buns
- ½ cup slivered red onions
- ½ cup slivered green or red bell pepper
- ½ cup fresh chopped pineapple (or pineapple tidbits from kids' fruit cups, drained)
- light cream cheese, softened

Directions:
1. Combine turkey, curry powder, Hoisin sauce, and salt and mix together well.
2. Shape turkey mixture into 8 small patties.
3. Place patties in air fryer basket and cook at 360°F for 7minutes, until patties are well done and juices run clear.
4. Place each patty on the bottom half of a slider bun and top with onions, peppers, and pineapple. Spread the remaining bun halves with cream cheese to taste, place on top, and serve.

Rumaki

Servings: 24
Cooking Time: 12 Minutes
Ingredients:
- 10 ounces raw chicken livers
- 1 can sliced water chestnuts, drained
- ¼ cup low-sodium teriyaki sauce
- 12 slices turkey bacon
- toothpicks

Directions:
1. Cut livers into 1½-inch pieces, trimming out tough veins as you slice.
2. Place livers, water chestnuts, and teriyaki sauce in small container with lid. If needed, add another tablespoon of teriyaki sauce to make sure livers are covered. Refrigerate for 1 hour.
3. When ready to cook, cut bacon slices in half crosswise.
4. Wrap 1 piece of liver and 1 slice of water chestnut in each bacon strip. Secure with toothpick.
5. When you have wrapped half of the livers, place them in the air fryer basket in a single layer.
6. Cook at 390°F for 12 minutes, until liver is done and bacon is crispy.
7. While first batch cooks, wrap the remaining livers. Repeat step 6 to cook your second batch.

Onion Puffs

Servings: 14
Cooking Time: 8 Minutes
Ingredients:
- Vegetable oil spray
- ¾ cup Chopped yellow or white onion
- ½ cup Seasoned Italian-style panko bread crumbs
- 4½ tablespoons All-purpose flour
- 4½ tablespoons Whole, low-fat, or fat-free milk
- 1½ tablespoons Yellow cornmeal
- 1¼ teaspoons Granulated white sugar
- ½ teaspoon Baking powder
- ¼ teaspoon Table salt

Directions:

1. Cut or tear a piece of aluminum foil so that it lines the air fryer's basket with a ½-inch space on each of its four sides. Lightly coat the foil with vegetable oil spray, then set the foil sprayed side up inside the basket.
2. Preheat the air fryer to 400°F.
3. Stir the onion, bread crumbs, flour, milk, cornmeal, sugar, baking powder, and salt in a bowl to form a thick batter.
4. Remove the basket from the machine. Drop the onion batter by 2-tablespoon measures onto the foil, spacing the mounds evenly across its surface. Return the basket to the machine and air-fry undisturbed for 4 minutes.
5. Remove the basket from the machine. Lightly coat the puffs with vegetable oil spray. Use kitchen tongs to pick up a corner of the foil, then gently pull it out of the basket, letting the puffs slip onto the basket directly. Return the basket to the machine and continue air-frying undisturbed for 8 minutes, or until brown and crunchy.
6. Use kitchen tongs to transfer the puffs to a wire rack or a serving platter. Cool for 5 minutes before serving.

Jalapeño Poppers

Servings: 18
Cooking Time: 5 Minutes
Ingredients:
- ½ pound jalapeño peppers
- ¼ cup cornstarch
- 1 egg
- 1 tablespoon lime juice
- ¼ cup plain breadcrumbs
- ¼ cup panko breadcrumbs
- ½ teaspoon salt
- oil for misting or cooking spray
- Filling
- 4 ounces cream cheese
- 1 teaspoon grated lime zest
- ¼ teaspoon chile powder
- ⅛ teaspoon garlic powder
- ¼ teaspoon salt

Directions:
1. Combine all filling ingredients in small bowl and mix well. Refrigerate while preparing peppers.
2. Cut jalapeños into ½-inch lengthwise slices. Use a small, sharp knife to remove seeds and veins.
3. a. For mild appetizers, discard seeds and veins.
4. b. For hot appetizers, finely chop seeds and veins. Stir a small amount into filling, taste, and continue adding a little at a time until filling is as hot as you like.
5. Stuff each pepper slice with filling.
6. Place cornstarch in a shallow dish.
7. In another shallow dish, beat together egg and lime juice.
8. Place breadcrumbs and salt in a third shallow dish and stir together.
9. Dip each pepper slice in cornstarch, shake off excess, then dip in egg mixture.
10. Roll in breadcrumbs, pressing to make coating stick.
11. Place pepper slices on a plate in single layer and freeze them for 30 minutes.
12. Preheat air fryer to 390°F.
13. Spray frozen peppers with oil or cooking spray. Place in air fryer basket in a single layer and cook for 5 minutes.

Cauliflower "tater" Tots

Servings: 6
Cooking Time: 10 Minutes
Ingredients:
- 1 head of cauliflower
- 2 eggs
- ¼ cup all-purpose flour*
- ½ cup grated Parmesan cheese
- 1 teaspoon salt
- freshly ground black pepper
- vegetable or olive oil, in a spray bottle

Directions:
1. Grate the head of cauliflower with a box grater or finely chop it in a food processor. You should have about 3½ cups. Place the chopped cauliflower in the center of a clean kitchen towel and twist the towel tightly to squeeze all the water out of the cauliflower. (This can be done in two batches to make it easier to drain all the water from the cauliflower.)
2. Place the squeezed cauliflower in a large bowl. Add the eggs, flour, Parmesan cheese, salt and freshly ground black pepper. Shape the cauliflower into small cylinders or "tater tot" shapes, rolling roughly one tablespoon of the mixture at a time. Place the tots on a cookie sheet lined with paper towel to absorb any residual moisture. Spray the cauliflower tots all over with oil.
3. Preheat the air fryer to 400°F.
4. Air-fry the tots at 400°F, one layer at a time for 10 minutes, turning them over for the last few minutes of the cooking process for even browning. Season with salt and black pepper. Serve hot with your favorite dipping sauce.

Honey-mustard Chicken Wings

Servings: 2
Cooking Time: 14 Minutes
Ingredients:
- 2 pounds chicken wings
- salt and freshly ground black pepper
- 2 tablespoons butter
- ¼ cup honey
- ¼ cup spicy brown mustard
- pinch ground cayenne pepper
- 2 teaspoons Worcestershire sauce

Directions:
1. Prepare the chicken wings by cutting off the wing tips and discarding (or freezing for chicken stock). Divide the drumettes from the wingettes by cutting through the joint. Place the chicken wing pieces in a large bowl.
2. Preheat the air fryer to 400°F.

3. Season the wings with salt and freshly ground black pepper and air-fry the wings in two batches for 10 minutes per batch, shaking the basket half way through the cooking process.

4. While the wings are air-frying, combine the remaining ingredients in a small saucepan over low heat.

5. When both batches are done, toss all the wings with the honey-mustard sauce and toss them all back into the basket for another 4 minutes to heat through and finish cooking. Give the basket a good shake part way through the cooking process to redistribute the wings. Remove the wings from the air fryer and serve.

Canadian-inspired Waffle Poutine

Servings: 4
Cooking Time: 30 Minutes
Ingredients:
- 1 cup frozen waffle cut fries
- 2 tsp olive oil
- 1 red bell pepper, chopped
- 2 green onions, sliced
- 1 cup grated mozzarella
- ½ cup beef gravy

Directions:
1. Preheat air fryer to 380°F. Toss the waffle fries with olive oil, then place in the frying basket. Air Fry for about 10-12 minutes, shake the basket once until crisp and lightly golden. Take the fries out of the basket and place in a baking pan. Top with peppers, green onions, and mozzarella cheese. Cook until the vegetables are tender, about 3 minutes. Remove the pan from the fryer and drizzle beef gravy over all of the fries and vegetables. Heat the gravy through for about 2 minutes, then serve.

Mediterranean Potato Skins

Servings: 4
Cooking Time: 50 Minutes
Ingredients:
- 2 russet potatoes
- 3 tbsp olive oil
- Salt and pepper to taste
- 2 tbsp rosemary, chopped
- 10 Kalamata olives, diced
- ¼ cup crumbled feta
- 2 tbsp chopped dill

Directions:
1. Preheat air fryer to 380°F. Poke 2-3 holes in the potatoes with a fork. Drizzle them with some olive oil and sprinkle with salt. Put the potatoes into the frying basket and Bake for 30 minutes. When the potatoes are ready, remove them from the fryer and slice in half. Scoop out the flesh of the potatoes with a spoon, leaving a ½-inch layer of potato inside the skins, and set the skins aside.

2. Combine the scooped potato middles with the remaining olive oil, salt, black pepper, and rosemary in a medium bowl. Mix until well combined. Spoon the potato filling into the potato skins, spreading it evenly over them. Top with olives, dill and feta. Put the loaded potato skins back into the air fryer and Bake for 15 minutes. Enjoy!

Cinnamon Sweet Potato Fries

Servings: 5
Cooking Time: 30 Minutes
Ingredients:
- 3 sweet potatoes
- 2 tsp butter, melted
- 1 tsp cinnamon
- Salt and pepper to taste

Directions:
1. Preheat air fryer to 400°F. Peel the potatoes and slice them thinly crosswise. Transfer the slices to a large bowl. Toss with butter, cinnamon, salt, and pepper until fully coated. Place half of the slices into the air fryer. Stacking is ok. Air Fry for 10 minutes. Shake the basket, and cook for another 10-12 minutes until crispy. Serve hot.

Spicy Sweet Potato Tater-tots

Servings: 6
Cooking Time: 10 Minutes
Ingredients:
- 6 cups filtered water
- 2 medium sweet potatoes, peeled and cut in half
- 1 teaspoon garlic powder
- ½ teaspoon black pepper, divided
- ½ teaspoon salt, divided
- 1 cup panko breadcrumbs
- 1 teaspoon blackened seasoning

Directions:
1. In a large stovetop pot, bring the water to a boil. Add the sweet potatoes and let boil about 10 minutes, until a metal fork prong can be inserted but the potatoes still have a slight give (not completely mashed).

2. Carefully remove the potatoes from the pot and let cool.

3. When you're able to touch them, grate the potatoes into a large bowl. Mix the garlic powder, ¼ teaspoon of the black pepper, and ¼ teaspoon of the salt into the potatoes. Place the mixture in the refrigerator and let set at least 45 minutes (if you're leaving them longer than 45 minutes, cover the bowl).

4. Before assembling, mix the breadcrumbs and blackened seasoning in a small bowl.

5. Remove the sweet potatoes from the refrigerator and preheat the air fryer to 400°F.

6. Assemble the tater-tots by using a teaspoon to portion batter evenly and form into a tater-tot shape. Roll each tater-tot in the breadcrumb mixture. Then carefully place the tater-tots in the air fryer basket. Be sure that you've liberally sprayed the air fryer basket with an olive oil mist. Repeat until tater-tots fill the basket without touching one another. You'll need to do multiple batches, depending on the size of your air fryer.

7. Cook the tater-tots for 3 to 6 minutes, flip, and cook another 3 to 6 minutes.

8. Remove from the air fryer carefully and keep warm until ready to serve.

Crispy Tofu Bites

Servings: 4
Cooking Time: 20 Minutes
Ingredients:
- 1 pound Extra firm unflavored tofu
- Vegetable oil spray

Directions:
1. Wrap the piece of tofu in a triple layer of paper towels. Place it on a wooden cutting board and set a large pot on top of it to press out excess moisture. Set aside for 10 minutes.
2. Preheat the air fryer to 400°F.
3. Remove the pot and unwrap the tofu. Cut it into 1-inch cubes. Place these in a bowl and coat them generously with vegetable oil spray. Toss gently, then spray generously again before tossing, until all are glistening.
4. Gently pour the tofu pieces into the basket, spread them into as close to one layer as possible, and air-fry for 20 minutes, using kitchen tongs to gently rearrange the pieces at the 7- and 14-minute marks, until light brown and crisp.
5. Gently pour the tofu pieces onto a wire rack. Cool for 5 minutes before serving warm.

Russian Pierogi With Cheese Dip

Servings: 6
Cooking Time: 20 Minutes
Ingredients:
- 1 package frozen pierogi
- 1 cup sour cream
- 1 tbsp fresh lemon juice
- ½ chopped red bell pepper
- 3 spring onions, chopped
- ½ cup shredded carrot
- 1 tsp dried rosemary

Directions:
1. Preheat the air fryer to 400°F. Mix the sour cream and lemon juice in a bowl, then add the bell pepper, spring onions, carrot, and rosemary and mix well. Set the dip aside. Put as many frozen pierogi as will fit in the frying basket in a single layer and spray with cooking oil. Air Fry for 11-14 minutes, rotating pierogis once until golden. Repeat with the remaining pierogi. Serve with the dip.

Cajun-spiced Pickle Chips

Servings: 4
Cooking Time: 20 Minutes
Ingredients:
- 16 oz canned pickle slices
- ½ cup flour
- 2 tbsp cornmeal
- 3 tsp Cajun seasoning
- 1 tbsp dried parsley
- 1 egg, beaten
- ¼ tsp hot sauce
- ½ cup buttermilk
- 3 tbsp light mayonnaise
- 3 tbsp chopped chives
- ⅛ tsp garlic powder
- ⅛ tsp onion powder
- Salt and pepper to taste

Directions:
1. Preheat air fryer to 350°F. Mix flour, cornmeal, Cajun seasoning, and parsley in a bowl. Put the beaten egg in a small bowl nearby. One at a time, dip a pickle slice in the egg, then roll in the crumb mixture. Gently press the crumbs, so they stick to the pickle. Place the chips in the greased frying basket and Air Fry for 7-9 minutes, flipping once until golden and crispy. In a bowl, whisk hot sauce, buttermilk, mayonnaise, chives, garlic and onion powder, salt, and pepper. Serve with pickles.

Ranch Chips

Servings: 2
Cooking Time: 30 Minutes
Ingredients:
- 1 tsp dry ranch seasoning
- Salt and pepper to taste
- 2 cups sliced potatoes
- 2 tsp olive oil
- ¼ cup white wine vinegar

Directions:
1. Preheat air fryer at 400°F. In a bowl, combine ranch mix, salt, and pepper. Reserve ½ tsp for garnish. In another bowl, mix sliced fingerling potatoes with the vinegar and stir around. Let soak in the vinegar water for at least thirty minutes then drain the potatoes and pat them dry.
2. Place potato chips and spread with olive oil until coated. Sprinkle with the ranch mixture and toss to coat. Place potato chips in the frying basket and Air Fry for 16 minutes, shaking 4 times. Transfer it into a bowl. Sprinkle with the reserved mixture and let sit for 15 minutes. Serve immediately.

Fried Dill Pickle Chips

Servings: 4
Cooking Time: 12 Minutes
Ingredients:
- 1 cup All-purpose flour or tapioca flour
- 1 Large egg white(s)
- 1 tablespoon Brine from a jar of dill pickles
- 1 cup Seasoned Italian-style dried bread crumbs (gluten-free, if a concern)
- 2 Large dill pickle(s) (8 to 10 inches long), cut into ½-inch-thick rounds
- Vegetable oil spray

Directions:
1. Preheat the air fryer to 400°F.
2. Set up and fill three shallow soup plates or small pie plates on your counter: one for the flour, one for the egg white(s) whisked with the pickle brine, and one for the bread crumbs.
3. Set a pickle round in the flour and turn it to coat all sides, even the edge. Gently shake off the excess flour, then dip the round into the egg-white mixture and turn to coat both sides

and the edge. Let any excess egg white mixture slip back into the rest, then set the round in the bread crumbs and turn it to coat both sides as well as the edge. Set aside on a cutting board and soldier on, dipping and coating the remaining rounds. Lightly coat the coated rounds on both sides with vegetable oil spray.

4. Set the pickle rounds in the basket in one layer. Air-fry undisturbed for 7 minutes, or until golden brown and crunchy. Cool in the basket for a few minutes before using kitchen tongs to transfer the (still hot) rounds to a serving platter.

Avocado Fries With Quick Salsa Fresca

Servings: 4
Cooking Time: 6 Minutes
Ingredients:
- ½ cup flour*
- 2 teaspoons salt
- 2 eggs, lightly beaten
- 1 cup panko breadcrumbs*
- ⅛ teaspoon cayenne pepper
- ¼ teaspoon smoked paprika (optional)
- 2 large avocados, just ripe
- vegetable oil, in a spray bottle
- Quick Salsa Fresca
- 1 cup cherry tomatoes
- 1 tablespoon-sized chunk of shallot or red onion
- 2 teaspoons fresh lime juice
- 1 teaspoon chopped fresh cilantro or parsley
- salt and freshly ground black pepper

Directions:
1. Set up a dredging station with three shallow dishes. Place the flour and salt in the first shallow dish. Place the eggs into the second dish. Combine the breadcrumbs, cayenne pepper and paprika (if using) in the third dish.
2. Preheat the air fryer to 400°F.
3. Cut the avocado in half around the pit and separate the two sides. Slice the avocados into long strips while still in their skin. Run a spoon around the slices, separating them from the avocado skin. Try to keep the slices whole, but don't worry if they break – you can still coat and air-fry the pieces.
4. Coat the avocado slices by dredging them first in the flour, then the egg and then the breadcrumbs, pressing the crumbs on gently with your hands. Set the coated avocado fries on a tray and spray them on all sides with vegetable oil.
5. Air-fry the avocado fries, one layer at a time, at 400°F for 6 minutes, turning them over halfway through the cooking time and spraying lightly again if necessary. When the fries are nicely browned on all sides, season with salt and remove.
6. While the avocado fries are air-frying, make the salsa fresca by combining everything in a food processor. Pulse several times until the salsa is a chunky purée. Serve the fries warm with the salsa on the side for dipping.

Zucchini Fritters

Servings: 8
Cooking Time: 10 Minutes

Ingredients:
- 2 cups grated zucchini
- ½ teaspoon sea salt
- 1 egg
- ½ teaspoon garlic powder
- ¼ teaspoon onion powder
- ¼ cup grated Parmesan cheese
- ½ cup all-purpose flour
- ¼ teaspoon baking powder
- ½ cup Greek yogurt or sour cream
- ½ lime, juiced
- ¼ cup chopped cilantro
- ¼ teaspoon ground cumin
- ¼ teaspoon salt

Directions:
1. Preheat the air fryer to 360°F.
2. In a large colander, place a kitchen towel. Inside the towel, place the grated zucchini and sprinkle the sea salt over the top. Let the zucchini sit for 5 minutes; then, using the towel, squeeze dry the zucchini.
3. In a medium bowl, mix together the egg, garlic powder, onion powder, Parmesan cheese, flour, and baking powder. Add in the grated zucchini, and stir until completely combined.
4. Pierce a piece of parchment paper with a fork 4 to 6 times. Place the parchment paper into the air fryer basket. Using a tablespoon, place 6 to 8 heaping tablespoons of fritter batter onto the parchment paper. Spray the fritters with cooking spray and cook for 5 minutes, turn the fritters over, and cook another 5 minutes.
5. Meanwhile, while the fritters are cooking, make the sauce. In a small bowl, whisk together the Greek yogurt or sour cream, lime juice, cilantro, cumin, and salt.
6. Repeat Steps 2–4 with the remaining batter.

Baba Ghanouj

Servings: 2
Cooking Time: 40 Minutes
Ingredients:
- 2 Small (12-ounce) purple Italian eggplant(s)
- ¼ cup Olive oil
- ¼ cup Tahini
- ½ teaspoon Ground black pepper
- ¼ teaspoon Onion powder
- ¼ teaspoon Mild smoked paprika (optional)
- Up to 1 teaspoon Table salt

Directions:
1. Preheat the air fryer to 400°F.
2. Prick the eggplant(s) on all sides with a fork. When the machine is at temperature, set the eggplant(s) in the basket in one layer. Air-fry undisturbed for 40 minutes, or until blackened and soft.
3. Remove the basket from the machine. Cool the eggplant(s) in the basket for 20 minutes.
4. Use a nonstick-safe spatula, and perhaps a flatware tablespoon for balance, to gently transfer the eggplant(s) to a

bowl. The juices will run out. Make sure the bowl is close to the basket. Split the eggplant(s) open.

5. Scrape the soft insides of half an eggplant into a food processor. Repeat with the remaining piece(s). Add any juices from the bowl to the eggplant in the food processor, but discard the skins and stems.

6. Add the olive oil, tahini, pepper, onion powder, and smoked paprika (if using). Add about half the salt, then cover and process until smooth, stopping the machine at least once to scrape down the inside of the canister. Check the spread for salt and add more as needed. Scrape the baba ghanouj into a bowl and serve warm, or set aside at room temperature for up to 2 hours, or cover and store in the refrigerator for up to 4 days.

Crab Rangoon Dip With Wonton Chips

Servings: 6
Cooking Time: 18 Minutes
Ingredients:
- Wonton Chips:
- 1 (12-ounce) package wonton wrappers
- vegetable oil
- sea salt
- Crab Rangoon Dip:
- 8 ounces cream cheese, softened
- ¾ cup sour cream
- 1 teaspoon Worcestershire sauce
- 1½ teaspoons soy sauce
- 1 teaspoon sesame oil
- ⅛ teaspoon ground cayenne pepper
- ¼ teaspoon salt
- freshly ground black pepper
- 8 ounces cooked crabmeat
- 1 cup grated white Cheddar cheese
- ⅓ cup chopped scallions
- paprika (for garnish)

Directions:
1. Cut the wonton wrappers in half diagonally to form triangles. Working in batches, lay the wonton triangles on a flat surface and brush or spray both sides with vegetable oil.
2. Preheat the air fryer to 370°F.
3. Place about 10 to 12 wonton triangles in the air fryer basket, letting them overlap slightly. Air-fry for just 2 minutes, shaking the basket halfway through the cooking time. Transfer the wonton chips to a large bowl and season immediately with sea salt. (You'll hear the chips start to spin around in the air fryer when they are almost done.) Repeat with the rest of wontons (keeping those fishing hands at bay!).
4. To make the dip, combine the cream cheese, sour cream, Worcestershire sauce, soy sauce, sesame oil, cayenne pepper, salt, and freshly ground black pepper in a bowl. Mix well and then fold in the crabmeat, Cheddar cheese, and scallions.
5. Transfer the dip to a 7-inch ceramic baking pan or shallow casserole dish. Sprinkle paprika on top and cover the dish with aluminum foil. Lower the dish into the air fryer basket using a sling made of aluminum foil (fold a piece of aluminum foil into a strip about 2-inches wide by 24-inches long). Air-fry for 11 minutes. Remove the aluminum foil and air-fry for another 5 minutes to finish cooking and brown the top. Serve hot with the wonton chips.

Italian-style Fried Olives

Servings: 4
Cooking Time: 25 Minutes
Ingredients:
- 1 jar pitted green olives
- ½ cup all-purpose flour
- Salt and pepper to taste
- 1 tsp Italian seasoning
- ½ cup bread crumbs
- 1 egg

Directions:
1. Preheat air fryer to 400°F. Set out three small bowls. In the first, mix flour, Italian seasoning, salt and pepper. In the bowl, beat the egg. In the third bowl, add bread crumbs. Dip the olives in the flour, then the egg, then in the crumbs. When all of the olives are breaded, place them in the greased frying basket and Air Fry for 6 minutes. Turn them and cook for another 2 minutes or until brown and crispy. Serve chilled.

Chinese-style Potstickers

Servings: 6
Cooking Time: 30 Minutes
Ingredients:
- 1 cup shredded Chinese cabbage
- ¼ cup chopped shiitake mushrooms
- ¼ cup grated carrots
- 2 tbsp minced chives
- 2 garlic cloves, minced
- 2 tsp grated fresh ginger
- 12 dumpling wrappers
- 2 tsp sesame oil

Directions:
1. Preheat air fryer to 370°F. Toss the Chinese cabbage, shiitake mushrooms, carrots, chives, garlic, and ginger in a baking pan and stir. Place the pan in the fryer and Bake for 3-6 minutes. Put a dumpling wrapper on a clean workspace, then top with a tablespoon of the veggie mix.
2. Fold the wrapper in half to form a half-circle and use water to seal the edges. Repeat with remaining wrappers and filling. Brush the potstickers with sesame oil and arrange them on the frying basket. Air Fry for 5 minutes until the bottoms should are golden brown. Take the pan out, add 1 tbsp of water, and put it back in the fryer to Air Fry for 4-6 minutes longer. Serve hot.

Taquito Quesadillas

Servings: 4
Cooking Time: 35 Minutes
Ingredients:
- 8 tbsp Mexican blend shredded cheese
- 8 soft corn tortillas
- 2 tsp olive oil
- ¼ cup chopped cilantro

Directions:
1. Preheat air fryer at 350°F. Spread cheese and coriander over 4 tortillas; top each with the remaining tortillas and brush the tops lightly with oil. Place quesadillas in the frying basket and Air Fry for 6 minutes. Serve warm.

Garlic-herb Pita Chips

Servings: 4
Cooking Time: 6 Minutes
Ingredients:
- ¼ teaspoon dried basil
- ¼ teaspoon marjoram
- ¼ teaspoon ground oregano
- ¼ teaspoon garlic powder
- ¼ teaspoon ground thyme
- ¼ teaspoon salt
- 2 whole 6-inch pitas, whole grain or white
- oil for misting or cooking spray

Directions:
1. Mix all seasonings together.
2. Cut each pita half into 4 wedges. Break apart wedges at the fold.
3. Mist one side of pita wedges with oil. Sprinkle with half of seasoning mix.
4. Turn pita wedges over, mist the other side with oil, and sprinkle with remaining seasonings.
5. Place pita wedges in air fryer basket and cook at 330°F for 2minutes.
6. Shake basket and cook for 2minutes longer. Shake again, and if needed cook for 2 moreminutes, until crisp. Watch carefully because at this point they will cook very quickly.

Turkey Spring Rolls

Servings: 4
Cooking Time: 20 Minutes
Ingredients:
- 1 lb turkey breast, grilled, cut into chunks
- 1 celery stalk, julienned
- 1 carrot, grated
- 1 tsp fresh ginger, minced
- 1 tsp sugar
- 1 tsp chicken stock powder
- 1 egg
- 1 tsp corn starch
- 6 spring roll wrappers

Directions:
1. Preheat the air fryer to 360°F. Mix the turkey, celery, carrot, ginger, sugar, and chicken stock powder in a large bowl. Combine thoroughly and set aside. In another bowl, beat the egg, and stir in the cornstarch. On a clean surface, spoon the turkey filling into each spring roll, roll up and seal the seams with the egg-cornstarch mixture. Put each roll in the greased frying basket and Air Fry for 7-8 minutes, flipping once until golden brown. Serve hot.

Breaded Mozzarella Sticks

Servings: 6
Cooking Time: 25 Minutes
Ingredients:
- 2 tbsp flour
- 1 egg
- 1 tbsp milk
- ½ cup bread crumbs
- ¼ tsp salt
- ¼ tsp Italian seasoning
- 10 mozzarella sticks
- 2 tsp olive oil
- ½ cup warm marinara sauce

Directions:
1. Place the flour in a bowl. In another bowl, beat the egg and milk. In a third bowl, combine the crumbs, salt, and Italian seasoning. Cut the mozzarella sticks into thirds. Roll each piece in flour, then dredge in egg mixture, and finally roll in breadcrumb mixture. Shake off the excess between each step. Place them in the freezer for 10 minutes.
2. Preheat air fryer to 400°F. Place mozzarella sticks in the frying basket and Air Fry for 5 minutes, shake twice and brush with olive oil. Serve the mozzarella sticks immediately with marinara sauce.

Sweet Plantain Chips

Servings: 4
Cooking Time: 11 Minutes
Ingredients:
- 2 Very ripe plantain(s), peeled and sliced into 1-inch pieces
- Vegetable oil spray
- 3 tablespoons Maple syrup
- For garnishing Coarse sea salt or kosher salt

Directions:
1. Pour about ½ cup water into the bottom of your air fryer basket or into a metal tray on a lower rack in some models. Preheat the air fryer to 400°F.
2. Put the plantain pieces in a bowl, coat them with vegetable oil spray, and toss gently, spraying at least one more time and tossing repeatedly, until the pieces are well coated.
3. When the machine is at temperature, arrange the plantain pieces in the basket in one layer. Air-fry undisturbed for 5 minutes.
4. Remove the basket from the machine and spray the back of a metal spatula with vegetable oil spray. Use the spatula to press down on the plantain pieces, spraying it again as needed, to flatten the pieces to about half their original height. Brush the plantain pieces with maple syrup, then return the basket to

the machine and continue air-frying undisturbed for 6 minutes, or until the plantain pieces are soft and caramelized.

5. Use kitchen tongs to transfer the pieces to a serving platter. Sprinkle the pieces with salt and cool for a couple of minutes before serving. Or cool to room temperature before serving, about 1 hour.

Crab-stuffed Mushrooms

Servings: 4
Cooking Time: 20 Minutes
Ingredients:
- ½ cup shredded mozzarella cheese
- 8 portobello mushrooms
- 1 tbsp olive oil
- ¼ tsp salt
- 3 oz lump crabmeat
- 3 tsp grated Parmesan cheese
- ¼ cup panko bread crumbs
- 1 tbsp ground walnuts
- 3 tsp mayonnaise
- 2 tbsp chopped chives
- 1 egg, beaten
- 1 garlic clove, minced
- ¼ tsp seafood seasoning
- 1 tbsp chopped cilantro

Directions:
1. Clean the mushrooms with a damp paper towel. Remove stems and chop them finely. Set aside. Take the mushroom caps and brush with oil before sprinkling with salt. Combine the remaining ingredients, excluding mozzarella, in a bowl. Spoon crab filling mixture into each mushroom cap. Top each cap with mozzarella and press down so that it may stick to the filling.
2. Preheat air fryer to 360°F. Place the stuffed mushrooms in the greased frying basket. Bake 8-10 minutes until the mushrooms are soft and the mozzarella is golden. Serve.

Paprika Onion Blossom

Servings: 4
Cooking Time: 35 Minutes + Cooling Time
Ingredients:
- 1 large onion
- 1 ½ cups flour
- 1 tsp garlic powder
- 1 tsp paprika
- ½ tsp bell pepper powder
- Salt and pepper to taste
- 2 eggs
- 1 cup milk

Directions:
1. Remove the tip of the onion but leave the root base intact. Peel the onion to the root and remove skin. Place the onion cut-side down on a cutting board. Starting ½-inch down from the root, cut down to the bottom. Repeat until the onion is divided into quarters. Starting ½-inch down from the root, repeat the cuts in between the first cuts. Repeat this process in between the cuts until you have 16 cuts in the onion. Flip the onion onto the root and carefully spread the inner layers. Set aside.
2. In a bowl, add flour, garlic, paprika, bell pepper, salt, and pepper, then stir. In another large bowl, whisk eggs and milk. Place the onion in the flour bowl and cover with flour mixture. Transfer the onion into the egg mixture and coat completely with either a spoon or basting brush. Return the onion to the flour bowl and cover completely. Take a sheet of foil and wrap the onion with the foil. Freeze for 45 minutes.
3. Preheat air fryer to 400°F. Remove the onion from the foil and place in the greased frying basket. Air Fry for 10 minutes. Lightly spray the onion with cooking oil, then cook for another 10-15 minutes. Serve immediately.

Crispy Curried Sweet Potato Fries

Servings: 4
Cooking Time: 20 Minutes
Ingredients:
- ½ cup sour cream
- ½ cup peach chutney
- 3 tsp curry powder
- 2 sweet potatoes, julienned
- 1 tbsp olive oil
- Salt and pepper to taste

Directions:
1. Preheat air fryer to 390°F. Mix together sour cream, peach chutney, and 1 ½ tsp curry powder in a small bowl. Set aside. In a medium bowl, add sweet potatoes, olive oil, the rest of the curry powder, salt, and pepper. Toss to coat. Place the potatoes in the frying basket. Bake for about 6 minutes, then shake the basket once. Cook for an additional 4-6 minutes or until the potatoes are golden and crispy. Serve the fries hot in a basket along with the chutney sauce for dipping.

Sweet Chili Peanuts

Servings: 6
Cooking Time: 5 Minutes
Ingredients:
- 2 cups (10 ounces) Shelled raw peanuts
- 2 tablespoons Granulated white sugar
- 2 teaspoons Hot red pepper sauce, such as Cholula or Tabasco (gluten-free, if a concern)

Directions:
1. Preheat the air fryer to 400°F.
2. Toss the peanuts, sugar, and hot pepper sauce in a bowl until the peanuts are well coated.
3. When the machine is at temperature, pour the peanuts into the basket, spreading them into one layer as much as you can. Air-fry undisturbed for 3 minutes.
4. Shake the basket to rearrange the peanuts. Continue air-frying for 2 minutes more, shaking and stirring the peanuts every 30 seconds, until golden brown.
5. Pour the peanuts onto a large lipped baking sheet. Spread them into one layer and cool for 5 minutes before serving.

Cheddar Stuffed Jalapeños

Servings: 5
Cooking Time: 15 Minutes
Ingredients:
- 10 jalapeño peppers
- 6 oz ricotta cheese
- ¼ cup grated cheddar
- 2 tbsp bread crumbs

Directions:
1. Preheat air fryer to 340°F. Cut jalapeños in half lengthwise. Clean out the seeds and membrane. Set aside. Microwave ricotta cheese in a small bowl for 15 seconds to soften. Stir in cheddar cheese to combine. Stuff each jalapeño half with the cheese mixture. Top the poppers with bread crumbs. Place in air fryer and lightly spray with cooking oil. Bake for 5-6 minutes. Serve warm.

Vegetarian Fritters With Green Dip

Servings: 6
Cooking Time: 40 Minutes
Ingredients:
- ½ cup grated carrots
- ½ cup grated zucchini
- ¼ cup minced yellow onion
- 1 garlic clove, minced
- 1 large egg
- ¼ cup flour
- ¼ cup bread crumbs
- Salt and pepper to taste
- ½ tsp ground cumin
- ½ avocado, peeled and pitted
- ½ cup plain Greek yogurt
- 1 tsp lime juice
- 1 tbsp white vinegar
- ¼ cup chopped cilantro

Directions:
1. Preheat air fryer to 375°F. Combine carrots, zucchini, onion, garlic, egg, flour, bread crumbs, salt, pepper, and cumin in a large bowl. Scoop out 12 equal portions of the vegetables and form them into patties. Arrange the patties on the greased basket. Air Fry for 5 minutes, then flip the patties. Air Fry for another 5 minutes. Check if the fritters are golden and cooked through. If more time is needed, cook for another 3-5 minutes.
2. While the fritters are cooking, prepare the avocado sauce. Mash the avocado in a small bowl to the desired texture. Stir in yogurt, white vinegar, chopped cilantro, lime juice, and salt. When the fritter is done, transfer to a serving plate along with the avocado sauce for dipping. Serve warm and enjoy.

Easy Crab Cakes

Servings: 4
Cooking Time: 20 Minutes
Ingredients:
- 1 cup lump crab meat
- 2 green onions, minced
- 3 garlic cloves, minced
- ½ lime, juiced
- 2 tbsp mayonnaise
- 2 eggs, beaten
- 1 tsp fresh grated ginger
- ½ tsp allspice
- ½ cup breadcrumbs
- 2 tsp oyster sauce
- 2 tsp spicy mustard
- Pinch of black pepper

Directions:
1. Preheat air fryer to 350°F. Place the crab meat, lime juice, mayonnaise, onions, garlic, ginger, oyster sauce, mustard, allspice, and black pepper in a large mixing bowl. Stir thoroughly until all the ingredients are evenly combined.
2. Form the mixture into patties. Dip the patties into the beaten eggs, and then roll in the breadcrumbs, coating thoroughly on all sides. Place the coated cakes in the lined frying basket and Air Fry for 5 minutes. Flip the cakes over and cook for another 5 minutes until golden brown and crispy on the outside and tantalizingly juicy on the inside. Serve hot.

Spiced Roasted Pepitas

Servings: 4
Cooking Time: 25 Minutes
Ingredients:
- 2 cups pumpkin seeds
- 1 tbsp butter, melted
- Salt and pepper to taste
- ½ tsp shallot powder
- ½ tsp smoked paprika
- ½ tsp dried parsley
- ½ tsp garlic powder
- ¼ tsp dried chives
- ¼ tsp dry mustard
- ¼ tsp celery seed

Directions:
1. Preheat air fryer to 325°F. Combine the pumpkin seeds, butter, and salt in a bowl. Place the seed mixture in the frying basket and Roast for 13 minutes, turning once. Transfer to a medium serving bowl. Stir in shallot powder, paprika, parsley, garlic powder, chives, dry mustard, celery seed, and black pepper. Serve right away.

Fiery Sweet Chicken Wings

Servings: 4
Cooking Time: 30 Minutes
Ingredients:
- 8 chicken wings
- 1 tbsp olive oil
- 3 tbsp brown sugar
- 2 tbsp maple syrup
- ½ cup apple cider vinegar
- ½ tsp Aleppo pepper flakes
- Salt to taste

Directions:
1. Preheat air fryer to 390°F. Toss the wings with olive oil in a bowl. Bake in the air fryer for 20 minutes, shaking the basket twice. While the chicken is cooking, whisk together sugar, maple syrup, vinegar, Aleppo pepper flakes, and salt in a small bowl. Transfer the wings to a baking pan, then pour the sauce over the wings. Toss well to coat. Cook in the air fryer until the wings are glazed, or for another 5 minutes. Serve hot.

Classic Chicken Wings

Servings: 8
Cooking Time: 20 Minutes
Ingredients:
- 16 chicken wings
- ¼ cup all-purpose flour
- ¼ teaspoon garlic powder
- ¼ teaspoon paprika
- ½ teaspoon salt
- ½ teaspoon black pepper
- ¼ cup butter
- ½ cup hot sauce
- ½ teaspoon Worcestershire sauce
- 2 ounces crumbled blue cheese, for garnish

Directions:
1. Preheat the air fryer to 380°F.
2. Pat the chicken wings dry with paper towels.
3. In a medium bowl, mix together the flour, garlic powder, paprika, salt, and pepper. Toss the chicken wings with the flour mixture, dusting off any excess.
4. Place the chicken wings in the air fryer basket, making sure that the chicken wings aren't touching. Cook the chicken wings for 10 minutes, turn over, and cook another 5 minutes. Raise the temperature to 400°F and continue crisping the chicken wings for an additional 3 to 5 minutes.
5. Meanwhile, in a microwave-safe bowl, melt the butter and hot sauce for 1 to 2 minutes in the microwave. Remove from the microwave and stir in the Worcestershire sauce.
6. When the chicken wings have cooked, immediately transfer the chicken wings into the hot sauce mixture. Serve the coated chicken wings on a plate, and top with crumbled blue cheese.

Cheesy Potato Canapés With Bacon

Servings: 4
Cooking Time: 35 Minutes
Ingredients:
- 4 bacon slices
- 4 russet potatoes, sliced
- 1 tbsp olive oil
- 1 tsp mustard powder
- Salt and pepper to taste
- 1 cup grated cheddar
- 2 tsp chopped chives
- 2 tsp chopped scallions

Directions:
1. Cook bacon in a skillet for 5 minutes over medium heat. Drain on a paper towel and crumble. Set aside. Add the potatoes to a large bowl and coat them with olive oil, mustard powder, salt and pepper.
2. Preheat air fryer to 400°F. Place the potatoes in the greased frying basket. Air Fry for 10 minutes. Shake the basket and cook for another 5-8 minutes or until potatoes are cooked through and edges are crisp. Transfer the potato bites to a serving dish. Serve warm topped with cheese, bacon, chives, and scallions.

Spiced Parsnip Chips

Servings: 2
Cooking Time: 35 Minutes
Ingredients:
- ½ tsp smoked paprika
- ¼ tsp chili powder
- ¼ tsp garlic powder
- ⅛ tsp onion powder
- ⅛ tsp cayenne pepper
- ⅛ tsp granulated sugar
- 1 tsp salt
- 1 parsnip, cut into chips
- 2 tsp olive oil

Directions:
1. Preheat air fryer to 400ºF. Mix all spices in a bowl and reserve. In another bowl, combine parsnip chips, olive oil, and salt. Place parsnip chips in the lightly greased frying basket and Air Fry for 12 minutes, shaking once. Transfer the chips to a bowl, toss in seasoning mix, and let sit for 15 minutes before serving.

Cheesy Tortellini Bites

Servings: 8
Cooking Time: 10 Minutes
Ingredients:
- 1 large egg
- ½ teaspoon black pepper
- ½ teaspoon garlic powder
- 1 teaspoon Italian seasoning
- 12 ounces frozen cheese tortellini
- ½ cup panko breadcrumbs

Directions:
1. Preheat the air fryer to 380°F.
2. Spray the air fryer basket with an olive-oil-based spray.
3. In a medium bowl, whisk the egg with the pepper, garlic powder, and Italian seasoning.
4. Dip the tortellini in the egg batter and then coat with the breadcrumbs. Place each tortellini in the basket, trying not to overlap them. You may need to cook in batches to ensure the even crisp all around.
5. Bake for 5 minutes, shake the basket, and bake another 5 minutes.
6. Remove and let cool 5 minutes. Serve with marinara sauce, ranch, or your favorite dressing.

Chapter 4 Beef, pork & Lamb Recipes

Cheesy Mushroom-stuffed Pork Loins

Servings: 3
Cooking Time: 30 Minutes
Ingredients:
- ¾ cup diced mushrooms
- 2 tsp olive oil
- 1 shallot, diced
- Salt and pepper to taste
- 3 center-cut pork loins
- 6 Gruyère cheese slices

Directions:
1. Warm the olive oil in a skillet over medium heat. Add in shallot and mushrooms and stir-fry for 3 minutes. Sprinkle with salt and pepper and cook for 1 minute.
2. Preheat air fryer to 350ºF. Cut a pocket into each pork loin and set aside. Stuff an even amount of mushroom mixture into each chop pocket and top with 2 Gruyere cheese slices into each pocket. Place the pork in the lightly greased frying basket and Air Fry for 11 minutes cooked through and the cheese has melted. Let sit onto a cutting board for 5 minutes before serving.

Crispy Ham And Eggs

Servings: 3
Cooking Time: 9 Minutes
Ingredients:
- 2 cups Rice-puff cereal, such as Rice Krispies
- ¼ cup Maple syrup
- ½ pound ¼- to ½-inch-thick ham steak (gluten-free, if a concern)
- 1 tablespoon Unsalted butter
- 3 Large eggs
- ⅛ teaspoon Table salt
- ⅛ teaspoon Ground black pepper

Directions:
1. Preheat the air fryer to 400°F.
2. Pour the cereal into a food processor, cover, and process until finely ground. Pour the ground cereal into a shallow soup plate or a small pie plate.
3. Smear the maple syrup on both sides of the ham, then set the ham into the ground cereal. Turn a few times, pressing gently, until evenly coated.
4. Set the ham steak in the basket and air-fry undisturbed for 5 minutes, or until browned.
5. Meanwhile, melt the butter in a medium or large nonstick skillet set over medium heat. Crack the eggs into the skillet and cook until the whites are set and the yolks are hot, about 3 minutes (or 4 minutes for a more set yolk.) Season with the salt and pepper.
6. When the ham is ready, transfer it to a serving platter, then slip the eggs from the skillet on top of it. Divide into portions to serve.

Wasabi-coated Pork Loin Chops

Servings: 3
Cooking Time: 14 Minutes
Ingredients:
- 1½ cups Wasabi peas
- ¼ cup Plain panko bread crumbs
- 1 Large egg white(s)
- 2 tablespoons Water
- 3 5- to 6-ounce boneless center-cut pork loin chops (about ½ inch thick)

Directions:
1. Preheat the air fryer to 375°F.
2. Put the wasabi peas in a food processor. Cover and process until finely ground, about like panko bread crumbs. Add the bread crumbs and pulse a few times to blend.
3. Set up and fill two shallow soup plates or small pie plates on your counter: one for the egg white(s), whisked with the water until uniform; and one for the wasabi pea mixture.
4. Dip a pork chop in the egg white mixture, coating the chop on both sides as well as around the edge. Allow any excess egg white mixture to slip back into the rest, then set the chop in the wasabi pea mixture. Press gently and turn it several times to coat evenly on both sides and around the edge. Set aside, then dip and coat the remaining chop(s).
5. Set the chops in the basket with as much air space between them as possible. Air-fry, turning once at the 6-minute mark, for 12 minutes, or until the chops are crisp and browned and an instant-read meat thermometer inserted into the center of a chop registers 145°F. If the machine is at 360°F, you may need to add 2 minutes to the cooking time.
6. Use kitchen tongs to transfer the chops to a wire rack. Cool for a couple of minutes before serving.

Mini Meatloaves With Pancetta

Servings: 4
Cooking Time: 40 Minutes
Ingredients:
- ¼ cup grated Parmesan
- 1/3 cup quick-cooking oats
- 2 tbsp milk
- 3 tbsp ketchup
- 3 tbsp Dijon mustard
- 1 egg
- 1 tsp dried oregano
- Salt and pepper to taste
- 1 lb lean ground beef
- 4 pancetta slices, uncooked

Directions:
1. Preheat the air fryer to 375°F. Combine the oats, milk, 1 tbsp of ketchup, 1 tbsp of mustard, the egg, oregano, Parmesan cheese, salt, and pepper, and mix. Add the beef and mix with your hands, then form 4 mini loaves. Wrap each mini loaf with pancetta, covering the meat.

2. Combine the remaining ketchup and mustard and set aside. Line the frying basket with foil and poke holes in it, then set the loaves in the basket. Brush with the ketchup/mustard mix. Bake for 17-22 minutes or until cooked and golden. Serve and enjoy!

Wiener Schnitzel

Servings: 4
Cooking Time: 14 Minutes
Ingredients:
- 4 thin boneless pork loin chops
- 2 tablespoons lemon juice
- ½ cup flour
- 1 teaspoon salt
- ¼ teaspoon marjoram
- 1 cup plain breadcrumbs
- 2 eggs, beaten
- oil for misting or cooking spray

Directions:
1. Rub the lemon juice into all sides of pork chops.
2. Mix together the flour, salt, and marjoram.
3. Place flour mixture on a sheet of wax paper.
4. Place breadcrumbs on another sheet of wax paper.
5. Roll pork chops in flour, dip in beaten eggs, then roll in breadcrumbs. Mist all sides with oil or cooking spray.
6. Spray air fryer basket with nonstick cooking spray and place pork chops in basket.
7. Cook at 390°F for 7minutes. Turn, mist again, and cook for another 7 minutes, until well done. Serve with lemon wedges.

Peppered Steak Bites

Servings: 4
Cooking Time: 14 Minutes
Ingredients:
- 1 pound sirloin steak, cut into 1-inch cubes
- ½ teaspoon coarse sea salt
- 1 teaspoon coarse black pepper
- 2 teaspoons Worcestershire sauce
- ½ teaspoon garlic powder
- ¼ teaspoon red pepper flakes
- ¼ cup chopped parsley

Directions:
1. Preheat the air fryer to 390°F.
2. In a large bowl, place the steak cubes and toss with the salt, pepper, Worcestershire sauce, garlic powder, and red pepper flakes.
3. Pour the steak into the air fryer basket and cook for 10 to 14 minutes, depending on how well done you prefer your bites. Starting at the 8-minute mark, toss the steak bites every 2 minutes to check for doneness.
4. When the steak is cooked, remove it from the basket to a serving bowl and top with the chopped parsley. Allow the steak to rest for 5 minutes before serving.

Crispy Pork Pork Escalopes

Servings: 4
Cooking Time: 20 Minutes
Ingredients:
- 4 pork loin steaks
- Salt and pepper to taste
- ¼ cup flour
- 2 tbsp bread crumbs

Directions:
1. Preheat air fryer to 380°F. Season pork with salt and pepper. In one shallow bowl, add flour. In another, add bread crumbs. Dip the steaks first in the flour, then in the crumbs. Place them in the fryer and spray with oil. Bake for 12-14 minutes, flipping once until crisp. Serve.

Citrus Pork Lettuce Wraps

Servings:4
Cooking Time: 35 Minutes
Ingredients:
- Salt and white pepper to taste
- 1 tbsp cornstarch
- 1 tbsp red wine vinegar
- 2 tbsp orange marmalade
- 1 tsp pulp-free orange juice
- 2 tsp olive oil
- ¼ tsp chili pepper
- ¼ tsp ground ginger
- 1 lb pork loin, cubed
- 8 iceberg lettuce leaves

Directions:
1. Create a slurry by whisking cornstarch and 1 tbsp of water in a bowl. Set aside. Place a small saucepan over medium heat. Add the red wine vinegar, orange marmalade, orange juice, olive oil, chili pepper, and ginger and cook for 3 minutes, stirring continuously. Mix in the slurry and simmer for 1 more minute. Turn the heat off and let it thicken, about3 minutes.
2. Preheat air fryer to 350ºF. Sprinkle the pork with salt and white pepper. Place them in the greased frying basket and Air Fry for 8-10 minutes until cooked through and browned, turning once. Transfer pork cubes to a bowl with the sauce and toss to coat. Serve in lettuce leaves.

French-style Steak Salad

Servings: 4
Cooking Time: 25 Minutes
Ingredients:
- 1 cup sliced strawberries
- 4 tbsp crumbled blue cheese
- ¼ cup olive oil
- Salt and pepper to taste
- 1 flank steak
- ¼cup balsamic vinaigrette
- 1 tbsp Dijon mustard
- 2 tbsp lemon juice
- 8 cups baby arugula
- ½ red onion, sliced
- 4 tbsp pecan pieces
- 4 tbsp sunflower seeds

- 1 sliced kiwi
- 1 sliced orange

Directions:

1. In a bowl, whisk olive oil, salt, lemon juice and pepper. Toss in flank steak and let marinate covered in the fridge for 30 minutes up to overnight. Preheat air fryer at 325ºF. Place flank steak in the greased frying basket and Bake for 18-20 minutes until rare, flipping once. Let rest for 5 minutes before slicing thinly against the grain.

2. In a salad bowl, whisk balsamic vinaigrette and mustard. Stir in arugula, salt, and pepper. Divide between 4 serving bowls. Top each salad with blue cheese, onion, pecan, sunflower seeds, strawberries, kiwi, orange and sliced steak. Serve immediately.

Suwon Pork Meatballs

Servings: 4
Cooking Time: 30 Minutes
Ingredients:

- 1 lb ground pork
- 1 egg
- 1 tsp cumin
- 1 tbsp gochujang
- 1 tsp tamari
- ¼ tsp ground ginger
- ¼ cup bread crumbs
- 1 scallion, sliced
- 4 tbsp plum jam
- 1 tsp toasted sesame seeds

Directions:

1. Preheat air fryer at 350ºF. In a bowl, combine all ingredients, except scallion greens, sesame seeds and plum jam. Form mixture into meatballs. Place meatballs in the greased frying basket and Air Fry for 8 minutes, flipping once. Garnish with scallion greens, plum jam and toasted sesame seeds to serve.

Tex-mex Beef Carnitas

Servings: 4
Cooking Time: 30 Minutes
Ingredients:

- 1 ¼ lb flank steak, cut into strips
- 1 ½ cups grated Colby cheese
- Salt and pepper to taste
- 2 tbsp lime juice
- 4 garlic cloves, minced
- 2 tsp chipotle powder
- 1 red bell pepper, sliced
- 1 yellow bell pepper, sliced
- 1 tbsp chili oil
- ½ cup salsa
- 8 corn tortillas

Directions:

1. Preheat the air fryer to 400°F. Lay the strips in a bowl and sprinkle with salt, pepper, lime juice, garlic, and chipotle powder. Toss well and let marinate. In the frying basket, combine the bell peppers and chili oil and toss.

2. Air Fry for 6 minutes or until crispy but tender. Drain the steak and discard the liquid. Lay the steak in the basket on top of the peppers and fry for 7-9 minutes more until browned. Divide the strips among tortillas and top with pepper strips, salsa, and cheese. Fold and serve.

Crispy Pierogi With Kielbasa And Onions

Servings: 3
Cooking Time: 20 Minutes
Ingredients:

- 6 Frozen potato and cheese pierogi, thawed (about 12 pierogi to 1 pound)
- ½ pound Smoked kielbasa, sliced into ½-inch-thick rounds
- ¾ cup Very roughly chopped sweet onion, preferably Vidalia
- Vegetable oil spray

Directions:

1. Preheat the air fryer to 375°F.
2. Put the pierogi, kielbasa rounds, and onion in a large bowl. Coat them with vegetable oil spray, toss well, spray again, and toss until everything is glistening.
3. When the machine is at temperature, dump the contents of the bowl it into the basket. (Items may be leaning against each other and even on top of each other.) Air-fry, tossing and rearranging everything twice so that all covered surfaces get exposed, for 20 minutes, or until the sausages have begun to brown and the pierogi are crisp.
4. Pour the contents of the basket onto a serving platter. Wait a minute or two just to take make sure nothing's searing hot before serving.

Kielbasa Sausage With Pierogies And Caramelized Onions

Servings: 3
Cooking Time: 30 Minutes
Ingredients:

- 1 Vidalia or sweet onion, sliced
- olive oil
- salt and freshly ground black pepper
- 2 tablespoons butter, cut into small cubes
- 1 teaspoon sugar
- 1 pound light Polish kielbasa sausage, cut into 2-inch chunks
- 1 (13-ounce) package frozen mini pierogies
- 2 teaspoons vegetable or olive oil
- chopped scallions

Directions:

1. Preheat the air fryer to 400°F.
2. Toss the sliced onions with a little olive oil, salt and pepper and transfer them to the air fryer basket. Dot the onions with pieces of butter and air-fry at 400°F for 2 minutes. Then sprinkle the sugar over the onions and stir. Pour any melted butter from the bottom of the air fryer drawer over the onions

(do this over the sink – some of the butter will spill through the basket). Continue to air-fry for another 13 minutes, stirring or shaking the basket every few minutes to cook the onions evenly.

3. Add the kielbasa chunks to the onions and toss. Air-fry for another 5 minutes, shaking the basket halfway through the cooking time. Transfer the kielbasa and onions to a bowl and cover with aluminum foil to keep warm.

4. Toss the frozen pierogies with the vegetable or olive oil and transfer them to the air fryer basket. Air-fry at 400°F for 8 minutes, shaking the basket twice during the cooking time.

5. When the pierogies have finished cooking, return the kielbasa and onions to the air fryer and gently toss with the pierogies. Air-fry for 2 more minutes and then transfer everything to a serving platter. Garnish with the chopped scallions and serve hot with the spicy sour cream sauce below.

6. Kielbasa Sausage with Pierogies and Caramelized Onions

Easy Carnitas

Servings: 3
Cooking Time: 25 Minutes
Ingredients:
- 1½ pounds Boneless country-style pork ribs, cut into 2-inch pieces
- ¼ cup Orange juice
- 2 tablespoons Brine from a jar of pickles, any type, even pickled jalapeño rings (gluten-free, if a concern)
- 2 teaspoons Minced garlic
- 2 teaspoons Minced fresh oregano leaves
- ¾ teaspoon Ground cumin
- ¾ teaspoon Table salt
- ¾ teaspoon Ground black pepper

Directions:
1. Mix the country-style pork rib pieces, orange juice, pickle brine, garlic, oregano, cumin, salt, and pepper in a large bowl. Cover and refrigerate for at least 2 hours or up to 10 hours, stirring the mixture occasionally.
2. Preheat the air fryer to 400°F. Set the rib pieces in their bowl on the counter as the machine heats.
3. Use kitchen tongs to transfer the rib pieces to the basket, arranging them in one layer. Some may touch. Air-fry for 25 minutes, turning and rearranging the pieces at the 10- and 20-minute marks to make sure all surfaces have been exposed to the air currents, until browned and sizzling.
4. Use clean kitchen tongs to transfer the rib pieces to a wire rack. Cool for a couple of minutes before serving.

Tuscan Chimichangas

Servings: 2
Cooking Time: 8 Minutes
Ingredients:
- ¼ pound Thinly sliced deli ham, chopped
- 1 cup Drained and rinsed canned white beans
- ½ cup (about 2 ounces) Shredded semi-firm mozzarella
- ¼ cup Chopped sun-dried tomatoes
- ¼ cup Bottled Italian salad dressing, vinaigrette type
- 2 Burrito-size (12-inch) flour tortilla(s)
- Olive oil spray

Directions:
1. Preheat the air fryer to 375°F.
2. Mix the ham, beans, cheese, tomatoes, and salad dressing in a bowl.
3. Lay a tortilla on a clean, dry work surface. Put all of the ham mixture in a narrow oval in the middle of the tortilla, if making one burrito; or half of this mixture, if making two. Fold the parts of the tortilla that are closest to the ends of the filling oval up and over the filling, then roll the tortilla tightly closed, but don't press down hard. Generously coat the tortilla with olive oil spray. Make a second filled tortilla, if necessary.
4. Set the filled tortilla(s) seam side down in the basket, with at least ½ inch between them, if making two. Air-fry undisturbed for 8 minutes, or until crisp and lightly browned.
5. Use kitchen tongs and a nonstick-safe spatula to transfer the chimichanga(s) to a wire rack. Cool for 5 minutes before serving.

Balsamic Beef & Veggie Skewers

Servings: 4
Cooking Time: 25 Minutes
Ingredients:
- 2 tbsp balsamic vinegar
- 2 tsp olive oil
- ½ tsp dried oregano
- Salt and pepper to taste
- ¾ lb round steak, cubed
- 1 red bell pepper, sliced
- 1 yellow bell pepper, sliced
- 1 cup cherry tomatoes

Directions:
1. Preheat air fryer to 390°F. Put the balsamic vinegar, olive oil, oregano, salt, and black pepper in a bowl and stir. Toss the steak in and allow to marinate for 10 minutes. Poke 8 metal skewers through the beef, bell peppers, and cherry tomatoes, alternating ingredients as you go. Place the skewers in the air fryer and Air Fry for 5-7 minutes, turning once until the beef is golden and cooked through and the veggies are tender. Serve and enjoy!

Mongolian Beef

Servings: 4
Cooking Time: 15 Minutes
Ingredients:
- 1½ pounds flank steak, thinly sliced
- on the bias into ¼-inch strips
- Marinade
- 2 tablespoons soy sauce*
- 1 clove garlic, smashed
- big pinch crushed red pepper flakes
- Sauce
- 1 tablespoon vegetable oil
- 2 cloves garlic, minced
- 1 tablespoon finely grated fresh ginger
- 3 dried red chili peppers

- ¾ cup soy sauce*
- ¾ cup chicken stock
- 5 to 6 tablespoons brown sugar (depending on how sweet you want the sauce)
- ½ cup cornstarch, divided
- 1 bunch scallions, sliced into 2-inch pieces

Directions:
1. Marinate the beef in the soy sauce, garlic and red pepper flakes for one hour.
2. In the meantime, make the sauce. Preheat a small saucepan over medium heat on the stovetop. Add the oil, garlic, ginger and dried chili peppers and sauté for just a minute or two. Add the soy sauce, chicken stock and brown sugar and continue to simmer for a few minutes. Dissolve 3 tablespoons of cornstarch in 3 tablespoons of water and stir this into the saucepan. Stir the sauce over medium heat until it thickens. Set this aside.
3. Preheat the air fryer to 400°F.
4. Remove the beef from the marinade and transfer it to a zipper sealable plastic bag with the remaining cornstarch. Shake it around to completely coat the beef and transfer the coated strips of beef to a baking sheet or plate, shaking off any excess cornstarch. Spray the strips with vegetable oil on all sides and transfer them to the air fryer basket.
5. Air-fry at 400°F for 15 minutes, shaking the basket to toss and rotate the beef strips throughout the cooking process. Add the scallions for the last 4 minutes of the cooking. Transfer the hot beef strips and scallions to a bowl and toss with the sauce (warmed on the stovetop if necessary), coating all the beef strips with the sauce. Serve warm over white rice.

Lamb Meatballs With Quick Tomato Sauce

Servings: 4
Cooking Time: 8 Minutes
Ingredients:
- ½ small onion, finely diced
- 1 clove garlic, minced
- 1 pound ground lamb
- 2 tablespoons fresh parsley, finely chopped (plus more for garnish)
- 2 teaspoons fresh oregano, finely chopped
- 2 tablespoons milk
- 1 egg yolk
- salt and freshly ground black pepper
- ½ cup crumbled feta cheese, for garnish
- Tomato Sauce:
- 2 tablespoons butter
- 1 clove garlic, smashed
- pinch crushed red pepper flakes
- ¼ teaspoon ground cinnamon
- 1 (28-ounce) can crushed tomatoes
- salt, to taste

Directions:
1. Combine all ingredients for the meatballs in a large bowl and mix just until everything is combined. Shape the mixture into 1½-inch balls or shape the meat between two spoons to make quenelles (little three-sided footballs).
2. Preheat the air fryer to 400°F.
3. While the air fryer is Preheating, start the quick tomato sauce. Place the butter, garlic and red pepper flakes in a sauté pan and heat over medium heat on the stovetop. Let the garlic sizzle a little, but before the butter starts to brown, add the cinnamon and tomatoes. Bring to a simmer and simmer for 15 minutes. Season to taste with salt (but not too much as the feta that you will be sprinkling on at the end will be salty).
4. Brush the bottom of the air fryer basket with a little oil and transfer the meatballs to the air fryer basket in one layer, air-frying in batches if necessary.
5. Air-fry at 400°F for 8 minutes, giving the basket a shake once during the cooking process to turn the meatballs over.
6. To serve, spoon a pool of the tomato sauce onto plates and add the meatballs in a decorative manner. Sprinkle the feta cheese on top and garnish with more fresh parsley. Serve immediately.

Spicy Hoisin Bbq Pork Chops

Servings: 2
Cooking Time: 12 Minutes
Ingredients:
- 3 tablespoons hoisin sauce
- ¼ cup honey
- 1 tablespoon soy sauce
- 3 tablespoons rice vinegar
- 2 tablespoons brown sugar
- 1½ teaspoons grated fresh ginger
- 1 to 2 teaspoons Sriracha sauce, to taste
- 2 to 3 bone-in center cut pork chops, 1-inch thick (about 1¼ pounds)
- chopped scallions, for garnish

Directions:
1. Combine the hoisin sauce, honey, soy sauce, rice vinegar, brown sugar, ginger, and Sriracha sauce in a small saucepan. Whisk the ingredients together and bring the mixture to a boil over medium-high heat on the stovetop. Reduce the heat and simmer the sauce until it has reduced in volume and thickened slightly – about 10 minutes.
2. Preheat the air fryer to 400°F.
3. Place the pork chops into the air fryer basket and pour half the hoisin BBQ sauce over the top. Air-fry for 6 minutes. Then, flip the chops over, pour the remaining hoisin BBQ sauce on top and air-fry for 6 more minutes, depending on the thickness of the pork chops. The internal temperature of the pork chops should be 155°F when tested with an instant read thermometer.
4. Let the pork chops rest for 5 minutes before serving. You can spoon a little of the sauce from the bottom drawer of the air fryer over the top if desired. Sprinkle with chopped scallions and serve.

Beef Short Ribs

Servings: 4
Cooking Time: 20 Minutes
Ingredients:
- 2 tablespoons soy sauce
- 1 tablespoon sesame oil
- 2 tablespoons brown sugar
- 1 teaspoon ground ginger
- 2 garlic cloves, crushed
- 1 pound beef short ribs

Directions:
1. In a small bowl, mix together the soy sauce, sesame oil, brown sugar, and ginger. Transfer the mixture to a large resealable plastic bag, and place the garlic cloves and short ribs into the bag. Secure and place in the refrigerator for an hour (or overnight).
2. When you're ready to prepare the dish, preheat the air fryer to 330°F.
3. Liberally spray the air fryer basket with olive oil mist and set the beef short ribs in the basket.
4. Cook for 10 minutes, flip the short ribs, and then cook another 10 minutes.
5. Remove the short ribs from the air fryer basket, loosely cover with aluminum foil, and let them rest. The short ribs will continue to cook after they're removed from the basket. Check the internal temperature after 5 minutes to make sure it reached 145°F if you prefer a well-done meat. If it didn't reach 145°F and you would like it to be cooked longer, you can put it back into the air fryer basket at 330°F for another 3 minutes.
6. Remove from the basket and let it rest, covered with aluminum foil, for 5 minutes. Serve immediately.

Blackberry Bbq Glazed Country-style Ribs

Servings: 2
Cooking Time: 40 Minutes
Ingredients:
- ½ cup + 2 tablespoons sherry or Madeira wine, divided
- 1 pound boneless country-style pork ribs
- salt and freshly ground black pepper
- 1 tablespoon Chinese 5-spice powder
- ¼ cup blackberry preserves
- ¼ cup hoisin sauce*
- 1 clove garlic, minced
- 1 generous tablespoon grated fresh ginger
- 2 scallions, chopped
- 1 tablespoon sesame seeds, toasted

Directions:
1. Preheat the air fryer to 330°F and pour ½ cup of the sherry into the bottom of the air fryer drawer.
2. Season the ribs with salt, pepper and the 5-spice powder.
3. Air-fry the ribs at 330°F for 20 minutes, turning them over halfway through the cooking time.
4. While the ribs are cooking, make the sauce. Combine the remaining sherry, blackberry preserves, hoisin sauce, garlic and ginger in a small saucepan. Bring to a simmer on the stovetop for a few minutes, until the sauce thickens.
5. When the time is up on the air fryer, turn the ribs over, pour a little sauce on the ribs and air-fry for another 10 minutes at 330°F. Turn the ribs over again, pour on more of the sauce and air-fry at 330°F for a final 10 minutes.
6. Let the ribs rest for at least 5 minutes before serving them warm with a little more glaze brushed on and the scallions and sesame seeds sprinkled on top.

Crispy Lamb Shoulder Chops

Servings: 3
Cooking Time: 28 Minutes
Ingredients:
- ¾ cup All-purpose flour or gluten-free all-purpose flour
- 2 teaspoons Mild paprika
- 2 teaspoons Table salt
- 1½ teaspoons Garlic powder
- 1½ teaspoons Dried sage leaves
- 3 6-ounce bone-in lamb shoulder chops, any excess fat trimmed
- Olive oil spray

Directions:
1. Whisk the flour, paprika, salt, garlic powder, and sage in a large bowl until the mixture is of a uniform color. Add the chops and toss well to coat. Transfer them to a cutting board.
2. Preheat the air fryer to 375°F.
3. When the machine is at temperature, again dredge the chops one by one in the flour mixture. Lightly coat both sides of each chop with olive oil spray before putting it in the basket. Continue on with the remaining chop(s), leaving air space between them in the basket.
4. Air-fry, turning once, for 25 minutes, or until the chops are well browned and tender when pierced with the point of a paring knife. If the machine is at 360°F, you may need to add up to 3 minutes to the cooking time.
5. Use kitchen tongs to transfer the chops to a wire rack. Cool for 5 minutes before serving.

Pork Chops With Cereal Crust

Servings: 2
Cooking Time: 20 Minutes
Ingredients:
- ¼ cup grated Parmesan
- 1 egg
- 1 tbsp Dijon mustard
- ¼ cup crushed bran cereal
- ¼ tsp black pepper
- ¼ tsp cumin powder
- ¼ tsp nutmeg
- 1 tsp horseradish powder
- 2 pork chops

Directions:
1. Preheat air fryer at 350ºF. Whisk egg and mustard in a bowl. In another bowl, combine Parmesan cheese, cumin powder, nutmeg, horseradish powder, bran cereal, and black

pepper. Dip pork chops in the egg mixture, then dredge them in the cheese mixture. Place pork chops in the frying basket and Air Fry for 12 minutes, tossing once. Let rest onto a cutting board for 5 minutes. Serve.

Kawaii Pork Roast

Servings: 6
Cooking Time: 50 Minutes
Ingredients:
- Salt and white pepper to taste
- 2 tbsp soy sauce
- 2 tbsp honey
- 1 tbsp sesame oil
- ¼ tsp ground ginger
- 1 tsp oregano
- 2 cloves garlic, minced
- 1 boneless pork loin

Directions:
1. Preheat air fryer at 350°F. Mix all ingredients in a bowl. Massage mixture into all sides of pork loin. Place pork loin in the greased frying basket and Roast for 40 minutes, flipping once. Let rest onto a cutting board for 5 minutes before slicing. Serve right away.

Provençal Grilled Rib-eye

Servings: 4
Cooking Time: 25 Minutes
Ingredients:
- 4 ribeye steaks
- 1 tbsp herbs de Provence
- Salt and pepper to taste

Directions:
1. Preheat air fryer to 360°F. Season the steaks with herbs, salt and pepper. Place them in the greased frying basket and cook for 8-12 minutes, flipping once. Use a thermometer to check for doneness and adjust time as needed. Let the steak rest for a few minutes and serve.

Boneless Ribeyes

Servings: 2
Cooking Time: 10-15 Minutes
Ingredients:
- 2 8-ounce boneless ribeye steaks
- 4 teaspoons Worcestershire sauce
- ½ teaspoon garlic powder
- pepper
- 4 teaspoons extra virgin olive oil
- salt

Directions:
1. Season steaks on both sides with Worcestershire sauce. Use the back of a spoon to spread evenly.
2. Sprinkle both sides of steaks with garlic powder and coarsely ground black pepper to taste.
3. Drizzle both sides of steaks with olive oil, again using the back of a spoon to spread evenly over surfaces.
4. Allow steaks to marinate for 30minutes.
5. Place both steaks in air fryer basket and cook at 390°F for 5minutes.
6. Turn steaks over and cook until done:
7. Medium rare: additional 5 minutes
8. Medium: additional 7 minutes
9. Well done: additional 10 minutes
10. Remove steaks from air fryer basket and let sit 5minutes. Salt to taste and serve.

Kochukaru Pork Lettuce Cups

Servings: 4
Cooking Time: 25 Minutes
Ingredients:
- 1 tsp kochukaru (chili pepper flakes)
- 12 baby romaine lettuce leaves
- 1 lb pork tenderloin, sliced
- Salt and pepper to taste
- 3 scallions, chopped
- 3 garlic cloves, crushed
- ¼ cup soy sauce
- 2 tbsp gochujang
- ½ tbsp light brown sugar
- ½ tbsp honey
- 1 tbsp grated fresh ginger
- 2 tbsp rice vinegar
- 1 tsp toasted sesame oil
- 2 ¼ cups cooked brown rice
- ½ tbsp sesame seeds
- 2 spring onions, sliced

Directions:
1. Mix the scallions, garlic, soy sauce, kochukaru, honey, brown sugar, and ginger in a small bowl. Mix well. Place the pork in a large bowl. Season with salt and pepper. Pour the marinade over the pork, tossing the meat in the marinade until coated. Cover the bowl with plastic wrap and allow to marinate overnight. When ready to cook,
2. Preheat air fryer to 400°F. Remove the pork from the bowl and discard the marinade. Place the pork in the greased frying basket and Air Fry for 10 minutes, flipping once until browned and cooked through. Meanwhile, prepare the gochujang sauce. Mix the gochujang, rice vinegar, and sesame oil until smooth. To make the cup, add 3 tbsp of brown rice on the lettuce leaf. Place a slice of pork on top, drizzle a tsp of gochujang sauce and sprinkle with some sesame seeds and spring onions. Wrap the lettuce over the mixture similar to a burrito. Serve warm.

Orange Glazed Pork Tenderloin

Servings: 3
Cooking Time: 23 Minutes
Ingredients:
- 2 tablespoons brown sugar
- 2 teaspoons cornstarch
- 2 teaspoons Dijon mustard
- ½ cup orange juice
- ½ teaspoon soy sauce*
- 2 teaspoons grated fresh ginger

- ¼ cup white wine
- zest of 1 orange
- 1 pound pork tenderloin
- salt and freshly ground black pepper
- oranges, halved (for garnish)
- fresh parsley or other green herb (for garnish)

Directions:
1. Combine the brown sugar, cornstarch, Dijon mustard, orange juice, soy sauce, ginger, white wine and orange zest in a small saucepan and bring the mixture to a boil on the stovetop. Lower the heat and simmer while you cook the pork tenderloin or until the sauce has thickened.
2. Preheat the air fryer to 370°F.
3. Season all sides of the pork tenderloin with salt and freshly ground black pepper. Transfer the tenderloin to the air fryer basket, bending the pork into a wide "U" shape if necessary to fit in the basket. Air-fry at 370°F for 20 to 23 minutes, or until the internal temperature reaches 145°F. Flip the tenderloin over halfway through the cooking process and baste with the sauce.
4. Transfer the tenderloin to a cutting board and let it rest for 5 minutes. Slice the pork at a slight angle and serve immediately with orange halves and fresh herbs to dress it up. Drizzle any remaining glaze over the top.

Cal-mex Chimichangas

Servings: 4
Cooking Time: 30 Minutes
Ingredients:
- 1 can diced tomatoes with chiles
- 1 cup shredded cheddar
- ½ cup chopped onions
- 2 garlic cloves, minced
- 1 lb ground beef
- 2 tbsp taco seasoning
- Salt and pepper to taste
- 4 flour tortillas
- ½ cup Pico de Gallo

Directions:
1. Warm the olive oil in a skillet over medium heat and stir-fry the onion and garlic for 3 minutes or until fragrant. Add ground beef, taco seasoning, salt and pepper. Stir and break up the beef with a spoon. Cook for 3-4 minutes or until it is browned. Stir in diced tomatoes with chiles. Scoop ½ cup of beef onto each tortilla. Form chimichangas by folding the sides of the tortilla into the middle, then roll up from the bottom. Use a toothpick to secure the chimichanga.
2. Preheat air fryer to 400°F. Lightly spray the chimichangas with cooking oil. Place the first batch in the fryer and Bake for 8 minutes. Transfer to a serving dish and top with shredded cheese and pico de gallo.

Tender Steak With Salsa Verde

Servings:4
Cooking Time: 20 Minutes
Ingredients:
- 1 flank steak, halved
- 1 ½ cups salsa verde
- ½ tsp black pepper

Directions:
1. Toss steak and 1 cup of salsa verde in a bowl and refrigerate covered for 2 hours. Preheat air fryer to 400°F. Add steaks to the lightly greased frying basket and Air Fry for 10-12 minutes or until you reach your desired doneness, flipping once. Let sit onto a cutting board for 5 minutes. Thinly slice against the grain and divide between 4 plates. Spoon over the remaining salsa verde and serve sprinkled with black pepper to serve.

Carne Asada

Servings: 4
Cooking Time: 15 Minutes
Ingredients:
- 4 cloves garlic, minced
- 3 chipotle peppers in adobo, chopped
- ⅓ cup chopped fresh parsley
- ⅓ cup chopped fresh oregano
- 1 teaspoon ground cumin seed
- juice of 2 limes
- ⅓ cup olive oil
- 1 to 1½ pounds flank steak (depending on your appetites)
- salt
- tortillas and guacamole (optional – for serving)

Directions:
1. Make the marinade: Combine the garlic, chipotle, parsley, oregano, cumin, lime juice and olive oil in a non-reactive bowl. Coat the flank steak with the marinade and let it marinate for 30 minutes to 8 hours. (Don't leave the steak out of refrigeration for longer than 2 hours, however.)
2. Preheat the air fryer to 390°F.
3. Remove the steak from the marinade and place it in the air fryer basket. Season the steak with salt and air-fry for 15 minutes, turning the steak over halfway through the cooking time and seasoning again with salt. This should cook the steak to medium. Add or subtract two minutes for medium-well or medium-rare.
4. Remember to let the steak rest before slicing the meat against the grain. Serve with warm tortillas, guacamole and a fresh salsa like the Tomato-Corn Salsa below.

Leftover Roast Beef Risotto

Servings: 4
Cooking Time: 30 Minutes
Ingredients:
- ½ chopped red bell pepper
- ½ chopped cooked roast beef
- 3 tbsp grated Parmesan
- 2 tsp butter, melted
- 1 shallot, finely chopped
- 3 garlic cloves, minced
- ¾ cup short-grain rice
- 1¼ cups beef broth

Directions:

1. Preheat air fryer to 390°F. Add the melted butter, shallot, garlic, and red bell pepper to a baking pan and stir to combine. Air Fry for 2 minutes, or until the vegetables are crisp-tender. Remove from the air fryer and stir in the rice, broth, and roast beef. Put the cooking pan back into the fryer and Bake for 18-22 minutes, stirring once during cooking until the rice is al dente and the beef is cooked through. Sprinkle with Parmesan and serve.

Pork Schnitzel With Dill Sauce

Servings: 4
Cooking Time: 4 Minutes
Ingredients:
- 6 boneless, center cut pork chops (about 1½ pounds)
- ½ cup flour
- 1½ teaspoons salt
- freshly ground black pepper
- 2 eggs
- ½ cup milk
- 1½ cups toasted fine breadcrumbs
- 1 teaspoon paprika
- 3 tablespoons butter, melted
- 2 tablespoons vegetable or olive oil
- lemon wedges
- Dill Sauce:
- 1 cup chicken stock
- 1½ tablespoons cornstarch
- ⅓ cup sour cream
- 1½ tablespoons chopped fresh dill
- salt and pepper

Directions:
1. Trim the excess fat from the pork chops and pound each chop with a meat mallet between two pieces of plastic wrap until they are ½-inch thick.
2. Set up a dredging station. Combine the flour, salt, and black pepper in a shallow dish. Whisk the eggs and milk together in a second shallow dish. Finally, combine the breadcrumbs and paprika in a third shallow dish.
3. Dip each flattened pork chop in the flour. Shake off the excess flour and dip each chop into the egg mixture. Finally dip them into the breadcrumbs and press the breadcrumbs onto the meat firmly. Place each finished chop on a baking sheet until they are all coated.
4. Preheat the air fryer to 400°F.
5. Combine the melted butter and the oil in a small bowl and lightly brush both sides of the coated pork chops. Do not brush the chops too heavily or the breading will not be as crispy.
6. Air-fry one schnitzel at a time for 4 minutes, turning it over halfway through the cooking time. Hold the cooked schnitzels warm on a baking pan in a 170°F oven while you finish air-frying the rest.
7. While the schnitzels are cooking, whisk the chicken stock and cornstarch together in a small saucepan over medium-high heat on the stovetop. Bring the mixture to a boil and simmer for 2 minutes. Remove the saucepan from heat and whisk in the sour cream. Add the chopped fresh dill and season with salt and pepper.
8. Transfer the pork schnitzel to a platter and serve with dill sauce and lemon wedges. For a traditional meal, serve this along side some egg noodles, spätzle or German potato salad.

T-bone Steak With Roasted Tomato, Corn And Asparagus Salsa

Servings: 2
Cooking Time: 15-20 Minutes
Ingredients:
- 1 (20-ounce) T-bone steak
- salt and freshly ground black pepper
- Salsa
- 1½ cups cherry tomatoes
- ¾ cup corn kernels (fresh, or frozen and thawed)
- 1½ cups sliced asparagus (1-inch slices) (about ½ bunch)
- 1 tablespoon + 1 teaspoon olive oil, divided
- salt and freshly ground black pepper
- 1½ teaspoons red wine vinegar
- 3 tablespoons chopped fresh basil
- 1 tablespoon chopped fresh chives

Directions:
1. Preheat the air fryer to 400°F.
2. Season the steak with salt and pepper and air-fry at 400°F for 10 minutes (medium-rare), 12 minutes (medium), or 15 minutes (well-done), flipping the steak once halfway through the cooking time.
3. In the meantime, toss the tomatoes, corn and asparagus in a bowl with a teaspoon or so of olive oil, salt and freshly ground black pepper.
4. When the steak has finished cooking, remove it to a cutting board, tent loosely with foil and let it rest. Transfer the vegetables to the air fryer and air-fry at 400°F for 5 minutes, shaking the basket once or twice during the cooking process. Transfer the cooked vegetables back into the bowl and toss with the red wine vinegar, remaining olive oil and fresh herbs.
5. To serve, slice the steak on the bias and serve with some of the salsa on top.

Lemon-garlic Strip Steak

Servings: 2
Cooking Time: 15 Minutes
Ingredients:
- 3 cloves garlic, minced
- 1 tbsp lemon juice
- 1 tbsp olive oil
- Salt and pepper to taste
- 1 tbsp chopped parsley
- ½ tsp chopped rosemary
- ½ tsp chopped sage
- 1 strip steak

Directions:
1. In a small bowl, whisk all ingredients. Brush mixture over strip steak and let marinate covered in the fridge for 30 minutes.

Preheat air fryer at 400ºF. Place strip steak in the greased frying basket and Bake for 8 minutes until rare, turning once. Let rest onto a cutting board for 5 minutes before serving.

Lemon Pork Escalopes

Servings: 4
Cooking Time: 45 Minutes
Ingredients:
- 4 pork loin chops
- 1 cup breadcrumbs
- 2 eggs, beaten
- Salt and pepper to taste
- ½ tbsp thyme, chopped
- ½ tsp smoked paprika
- ½ tsp ground cumin
- 1 lemon, zested

Directions:
1. Preheat air fryer to 350ºF. Mix the breadcrumbs, thyme, smoked paprika, cumin, lemon zest, salt, and pepper in a bowl. Add the pork chops and toss to coat. Dip in the beaten eggs, then dip again into the dry ingredients. Place the coated chops in the greased frying basket and Air Fry for 16-18 minutes, turning once. Serve and enjoy!

Authentic Country-style Pork Ribs

Servings: 4
Cooking Time: 50 Minutes
Ingredients:
- 1 tsp smoked paprika
- 1 tsp garlic powder
- 1 tbsp honey
- 1 tbsp BBQ sauce
- 1 onion, cut into rings
- Salt and pepper to taste
- 2 tbsp olive oil
- 2 lb country-style pork ribs

Directions:
1. Preheat air fryer at 350ºF. Mix all seasonings in a bowl. Massage olive oil into pork ribs and sprinkle with spice mixture. Place pork ribs in the greased frying basket and Air Fry for 40 minutes, flipping every 10 minutes. Serve.

Asian-style Flank Steak

Servings: 4
Cooking Time: 25 Minutes
Ingredients:
- 1 lb flank steak, cut into strips
- 4 tbsp cornstarch
- Black pepper to taste
- 1 tbsp grated ginger
- 3 garlic cloves, minced
- 2/3 cup beef stock
- 2 tbsp soy sauce
- 2 tbsp light brown sugar
- 2 scallions, chopped
- 1 tbsp sesame seeds

Directions:
1. Preheat the air fryer to 400ºF. Sprinkle the beef with 3 tbsp of cornstarch and pepper, then toss to coat. Line the frying basket with round parchment paper with holes poked in it. Add the steak and spray with cooking oil. Bake or 8-12 minutes, shaking after 5 minutes until the beef is browned. Remove from the fryer and set aside. Combine the remaining cornstarch, ginger, garlic, beef stock, soy sauce, sugar, and scallions in a bowl and put it in the frying basket. Bake for 5-8 minutes, stirring after 3 minutes until the sauce is thick and glossy. Plate the beef, pour the sauce over, toss, and sprinkle with sesame seeds to serve.

Indian Fry Bread Tacos

Servings: 4
Cooking Time: 20 Minutes
Ingredients:
- 1 cup all-purpose flour
- 1½ teaspoons salt, divided
- 1½ teaspoons baking powder
- ¼ cup milk
- ¼ cup warm water
- ½ pound lean ground beef
- One 14.5-ounce can pinto beans, drained and rinsed
- 1 tablespoon taco seasoning
- ½ cup shredded cheddar cheese
- 2 cups shredded lettuce
- ¼ cup black olives, chopped
- 1 Roma tomato, diced
- 1 avocado, diced
- 1 lime

Directions:
1. In a large bowl, whisk together the flour, 1 teaspoon of salt, and baking powder. Make a well in the center and add in the milk and water. Form a ball and gently knead the dough four times. Cover the bowl with a damp towel, and set aside.
2. Preheat the air fryer to 380ºF.
3. In a medium bowl, mix together the ground beef, beans, and taco seasoning. Crumble the meat mixture into the air fryer basket and cook for 5 minutes; toss the meat and cook an additional 2 to 3 minutes, or until cooked fully. Place the cooked meat in a bowl for taco assembly; season with the remaining ½ teaspoon salt as desired.
4. On a floured surface, place the dough. Cut the dough into 4 equal parts. Using a rolling pin, roll out each piece of dough to 5 inches in diameter. Spray the dough with cooking spray and place in the air fryer basket, working in batches as needed. Cook for 3 minutes, flip over, spray with cooking spray, and cook for an additional 1 to 3 minutes, until golden and puffy.
5. To assemble, place the fry breads on a serving platter. Equally divide the meat and bean mixture on top of the fry bread. Divide the cheese, lettuce, olives, tomatoes, and avocado among the four tacos. Squeeze lime over the top prior to serving.

Classic Salisbury Steak Burgers

Servings: 4
Cooking Time: 35 Minutes
Ingredients:
- ¼ cup bread crumbs
- 2 tbsp beef broth
- 1 tbsp cooking sherry
- 1 tbsp ketchup
- 1 tbsp Dijon mustard
- 2 tsp Worcestershire sauce
- ½ tsp onion powder
- ½ tsp garlic powder
- 1 lb ground beef
- 1 cup sliced mushrooms
- 1 tbsp butter
- 4 buns, split and toasted

Directions:
1. Preheat the air fryer to 375°F. Combine the bread crumbs, broth, cooking sherry, ketchup, mustard, Worcestershire sauce, garlic and onion powder and mix well. Add the beef and mix with hands, then form into 4 patties and refrigerate while preparing the mushrooms. Mix the mushrooms and butter in a 6-inch pan. Place the pan in the air fryer and Bake for 8-10 minutes, stirring once until the mushrooms are brown and tender. Remove and set aside. Line the frying basket with round parchment paper and punch holes in it. Lay the burgers in a single layer and cook for 11-14 minutes or until cooked through. Put the burgers on the bun bottoms, top with the mushrooms, then the bun tops.

Sage Pork With Potatoes

Servings: 4
Cooking Time: 30 Minutes
Ingredients:
- 2 cups potatoes
- 2 tsp olive oil
- 1 lb pork tenderloin, cubed
- 1 onion, chopped
- 1 red bell pepper, chopped
- 2 garlic cloves, minced
- ½ tsp dried sage
- ½ tsp fennel seeds, crushed
- 2 tbsp chicken broth

Directions:
1. Preheat air fryer to 370°F. Add the potatoes and olive oil to a bowl and toss to coat. Transfer them to the frying basket and Air Fry for 15 minutes. Remove the bowl. Add the pork, onion, red bell pepper, garlic, sage, and fennel seeds, to the potatoes, add chicken broth and stir gently. Return the bowl to the frying basket and cook for 10 minutes. Be sure to shake the basket at least once. The pork should be cooked through and the potatoes soft and crispy. Serve immediately.

Aromatic Pork Tenderloin

Servings: 6
Cooking Time: 65 Minutes
Ingredients:
- 1 pork tenderloin
- 2 tbsp olive oil
- 2 garlic cloves, minced
- 1 tsp dried sage
- 1 tsp dried marjoram
- 1 tsp dried thyme
- 1 tsp paprika
- Salt and pepper to taste

Directions:
1. Preheat air fryer to 360°F. Drizzle oil over the tenderloin, then rub garlic, sage, marjoram, thyme, paprika, salt and pepper all over. Place the tenderloin in the greased frying basket and Bake for 45 minutes. Flip the pork and cook for another 15 minutes. Check the temperature for doneness. Let the cooked tenderloin rest for 10 minutes before slicing. Serve and enjoy!

Basil Cheese & Ham Stromboli

Servings: 6
Cooking Time: 30 Minutes
Ingredients:
- 1 can refrigerated pizza dough
- ½ cup shredded mozzarella
- ½ red bell pepper, sliced
- 2 tsp all-purpose flour
- 6 Havarti cheese slices
- 12 deli ham slices
- ½ tsp dried basil
- 1 tsp garlic powder
- ½ tsp oregano
- Black pepper to taste

Directions:
1. Preheat air fryer to 400°F. Flour a flat work surface and roll out the pizza dough. Use a knife to cut into 6 equal-sized rectangles. On each rectangle, add 1 slice of Havarti, 1 tbsp of mozzarella, 2 slices of ham, and some red pepper slices. Season with basil, garlic, oregano, and black pepper. Fold one side of the dough over the filling to the opposite side. Press the edges with the back of a fork to seal them. Place one batch of stromboli in the fryer and lightly spray with cooking oil. Air Fry for 10 minutes. Serve and enjoy!

Pork Cutlets With Almond-lemon Crust

Servings: 3
Cooking Time: 14 Minutes
Ingredients:
- ¾ cup Almond flour
- ¾ cup Plain dried bread crumbs (gluten-free, if a concern)
- 1½ teaspoons Finely grated lemon zest
- 1¼ teaspoons Table salt
- ¾ teaspoon Garlic powder
- ¾ teaspoon Dried oregano
- 1 Large egg white(s)

- 2 tablespoons Water
- 3 6-ounce center-cut boneless pork loin chops (about ¾ inch thick)
- Olive oil spray

Directions:
1. Preheat the air fryer to 375°F.
2. Mix the almond flour, bread crumbs, lemon zest, salt, garlic powder, and dried oregano in a large bowl until well combined.
3. Whisk the egg white(s) and water in a shallow soup plate or small pie plate until uniform.
4. Dip a chop in the egg white mixture, turning it to coat all sides, even the ends. Let any excess egg white mixture slip back into the rest, then set it in the almond flour mixture. Turn it several times, pressing gently to coat it evenly. Generously coat the chop with olive oil spray, then set aside to dip and coat the remaining chop(s).
5. Set the chops in the basket with as much air space between them as possible. Air-fry undisturbed for 12 minutes, or until browned and crunchy. You may need to add 2 minutes to the cooking time if the machine is at 360°F.
6. Use kitchen tongs to transfer the chops to a wire rack. Cool for a few minutes before serving.

French-style Pork Medallions

Servings: 4
Cooking Time: 25 Minutes
Ingredients:
- 1 lb pork medallions
- Salt and pepper to taste
- ½ tsp dried marjoram
- 2 tbsp butter
- 1 tbsp olive oil
- 1 tsp garlic powder
- 1 shallot, diced
- 1 cup chicken stock
- 2 tbsp Dijon mustard
- 2 tbsp grainy mustard
- 1/3 cup heavy cream

Directions:
1. Preheat the air fryer to 350°F. Pound the pork medallions with a rolling pin to about ¼ inch thickness. Rub them with salt, pepper, garlic, and marjoram. Place into the greased frying basket and Bake for 7 minutes or until almost done. Remove and wipe the basket clean. Combine the butter, olive oil, shallot, and stock in a baking pan, and set it in the frying basket. Bake for 5 minutes or until the shallot is crispy and tender. Add the mustard and heavy cream and cook for 4 more minutes or until the mix starts to thicken. Then add the pork to the sauce and cook for 5 more minutes, or until the sauce simmers. Remove and serve warm.

Creamy Horseradish Roast Beef

Servings: 6
Cooking Time: 65 Minutes + Chilling Time
Ingredients:
- 1 topside roast, tied
- Salt to taste
- 1 tsp butter, melted
- 2 tbsp Dijon mustard
- 3 tbsp prepared horseradish
- 1 garlic clove, minced
- 2/3 cup buttermilk
- 2 tsp red wine
- 1 tbsp minced chives
- Salt and pepper to taste

Directions:
1. Preheat air fryer to 320°F. Mix salt, butter, half of the mustard, 1 tsp of horseradish, and garlic until blended. Rub all over the roast. Bake the roast in the air fryer for 30-35 minutes, flipping once until browned. Transfer to a cutting board and cover with foil. Let rest for 15 minutes.
2. In a bowl, mix buttermilk, horseradish, remaining mustard, chives, wine, salt, and pepper until smooth. Refrigerate. When ready to serve, carve the roast into thin slices and serve with horseradish cream on the side.

Skirt Steak Fajitas

Servings: 4
Cooking Time: 30 Minutes
Ingredients:
- 2 tablespoons olive oil
- ¼ cup lime juice
- 1 clove garlic, minced
- ½ teaspoon ground cumin
- ½ teaspoon hot sauce
- ½ teaspoon salt
- 2 tablespoons chopped fresh cilantro
- 1 pound skirt steak
- 1 onion, sliced
- 1 teaspoon chili powder
- 1 red pepper, sliced
- 1 green pepper, sliced
- salt and freshly ground black pepper
- 8 flour tortillas
- shredded lettuce, crumbled Queso Fresco (or grated Cheddar cheese), sliced black olives, diced tomatoes, sour cream and guacamole for serving

Directions:
1. Combine the olive oil, lime juice, garlic, cumin, hot sauce, salt and cilantro in a shallow dish. Add the skirt steak and turn it over several times to coat all sides. Pierce the steak with a needle-style meat tenderizer or paring knife. Marinate the steak in the refrigerator for at least 3 hours, or overnight. When you are ready to cook, remove the steak from the refrigerator and let it sit at room temperature for 30 minutes.
2. Preheat the air fryer to 400°F.
3. Toss the onion slices with the chili powder and a little olive oil and transfer them to the air fryer basket. Air-fry at 400°F for 5 minutes. Add the red and green peppers to the air fryer basket with the onions, season with salt and pepper and

air-fry for 8 more minutes, until the onions and peppers are soft. Transfer the vegetables to a dish and cover with aluminum foil to keep warm.

4. Place the skirt steak in the air fryer basket and pour the marinade over the top. Air-fry at 400°F for 12 minutes. Flip the steak over and air-fry at 400°F for an additional 5 minutes. (The time needed for your steak will depend on the thickness of the skirt steak. 17 minutes should bring your steak to roughly medium.) Transfer the cooked steak to a cutting board and let the steak rest for a few minutes. If the peppers and onions need to be heated, return them to the air fryer for just 1 to 2 minutes.

5. Thinly slice the steak at an angle, cutting against the grain of the steak. Serve the steak with the onions and peppers, the warm tortillas and the fajita toppings on the side so that everyone can make their own fajita.

Coffee-rubbed Pork Tenderloin

Servings: 4
Cooking Time: 30 Minutes
Ingredients:
- 1 tbsp packed brown sugar
- 2 tsp espresso powder
- 1 tsp bell pepper powder
- ½ tsp dried parsley
- 1 tbsp honey
- ½ tbsp lemon juice
- 2 tsp olive oil
- 1 pound pork tenderloin

Directions:
1. Preheat air fryer to 400°F. Toss the brown sugar, espresso powder, bell pepper powder, and parsley in a bowl and mix together. Add the honey, lemon juice, and olive oil, then stir well. Smear the pork with the mix, then allow to marinate for 10 minutes before putting it in the air fryer. Roast for 9-11 minutes until the pork is cooked through. Slice before serving.

Original Köttbullar

Servings: 4
Cooking Time: 30 Minutes
Ingredients:
- 1 lb ground beef
- 1 small onion, chopped
- 1 clove garlic, minced
- 1/3 cup bread crumbs
- 1 egg, beaten
- Salt and pepper to taste
- 1 cup beef broth
- 1/3 cup heavy cream
- 2 tbsp flour

Directions:
1. Preheat air fryer to 370°F. Combine beef, onion, garlic, crumbs, egg, salt and pepper in a bowl. Scoop 2 tbsp of mixture and form meatballs with hands. Place the meatballs in the greased frying basket. Bake for 14 minutes.
2. Meanwhile, stir-fry beef broth and heavy cream in a saucepan over medium heat for 2 minutes; stir in flour. Cover and simmer for 4 minutes or until the sauce thicken. Transfer meatballs to a serving dish and drizzle with sauce. Serve and enjoy!

Air-fried Roast Beef With Rosemary Roasted Potatoes

Servings: 8
Cooking Time: 60 Minutes
Ingredients:
- 1 (5-pound) top sirloin roast
- salt and freshly ground black pepper
- 1 teaspoon dried thyme
- 2 pounds red potatoes, halved or quartered
- 2 teaspoons olive oil
- 1 teaspoon very finely chopped fresh rosemary, plus more for garnish

Directions:
1. Start by making sure your roast will fit into the air fryer basket without touching the top element. Trim it if you have to in order to get it to fit nicely in your air fryer. (You can always save the trimmings for another use, like a beef sandwich.)
2. Preheat the air fryer to 360°F.
3. Season the beef all over with salt, pepper and thyme. Transfer the seasoned roast to the air fryer basket.
4. Air-fry at 360°F for 20 minutes. Turn the roast over and continue to air-fry at 360°F for another 20 minutes.
5. Toss the potatoes with the olive oil, salt, pepper and fresh rosemary. Turn the roast over again in the air fryer basket and toss the potatoes in around the sides of the roast. Air-fry the roast and potatoes at 360°F for another 20 minutes. Check the internal temperature of the roast with an instant-read thermometer, and continue to roast until the beef is 5° lower than your desired degree of doneness. (Rare – 130°F, Medium – 150°F, Well done – 170°F.) Let the roast rest for 5 to 10 minutes before slicing and serving. While the roast is resting, continue to air-fry the potatoes if desired for extra browning and crispiness.
6. Slice the roast and serve with the potatoes, adding a little more fresh rosemary if desired.

Sausage-cheese Calzone

Servings: 8
Cooking Time: 8 Minutes
Ingredients:
- Crust
- 2 cups white wheat flour, plus more for kneading and rolling
- 1 package (¼ ounce) RapidRise yeast
- 1 teaspoon salt
- ½ teaspoon dried basil
- 1 cup warm water (115°F to 125°F)
- 2 teaspoons olive oil
- Filling
- ¼ pound Italian sausage
- ½ cup ricotta cheese
- 4 ounces mozzarella cheese, shredded

- ¼ cup grated Parmesan cheese
- oil for misting or cooking spray
- marinara sauce for serving

Directions:
1. Crumble Italian sausage into air fryer baking pan and cook at 390°F for 5minutes. Stir, breaking apart, and cook for 3 to 4minutes, until well done. Remove and set aside on paper towels to drain.
2. To make dough, combine flour, yeast, salt, and basil. Add warm water and oil and stir until a soft dough forms. Turn out onto lightly floured board and knead for 3 or 4minutes. Let dough rest for 10minutes.
3. To make filling, combine the three cheeses in a medium bowl and mix well. Stir in the cooked sausage.
4. Cut dough into 8 pieces.
5. Working with 4 pieces of the dough, press each into a circle about 5 inches in diameter. Top each dough circle with 2 heaping tablespoons of filling. Fold over to create a half-moon shape and press edges firmly together. Be sure that edges are firmly sealed to prevent leakage. Spray both sides with oil or cooking spray.
6. Place 4 calzones in air fryer basket and cook at 360°F for 5minutes. Mist with oil and cook for 3 minutes, until crust is done and nicely browned.
7. While the first batch is cooking, press out the remaining dough, fill, and shape into calzones.
8. Spray both sides with oil and cook for 5minutes. If needed, mist with oil and continue cooking for 3 minutes longer. This second batch will cook a little faster than the first because your air fryer is already hot.
9. Serve with marinara sauce on the side for dipping.

Cinnamon-stick Kofta Skewers

Servings: 8
Cooking Time: 15 Minutes
Ingredients:
- 1 pound Lean ground beef
- ½ teaspoon Ground cumin
- ½ teaspoon Onion powder
- ½ teaspoon Ground dried turmeric
- ½ teaspoon Ground cinnamon
- ½ teaspoon Table salt
- Up to a ⅛ teaspoon Cayenne
- 8 3½- to 4-inch-long cinnamon sticks (see the headnote)
- Vegetable oil spray

Directions:
1. Preheat the air fryer to 375°F.
2. Gently mix the ground beef, cumin, onion powder, turmeric, cinnamon, salt, and cayenne in a bowl until the meat is evenly mixed with the spices. (Clean, dry hands work best!) Divide this mixture into 2-ounce portions, each about the size of a golf ball.
3. Wrap one portion of the meat mixture around a cinnamon stick, using about three-quarters of the length of the stick, covering one end but leaving a little "handle" of cinnamon stick protruding from the other end. Set aside and continue making more kofta skewers.
4. Generously coat the formed kofta skewers on all sides with vegetable oil spray. Set them in the basket with as much air space between them as possible. Air-fry undisturbed for 13 minutes, or until browned and cooked through. If the machine is at 360°F, you may need to add 2 minutes to the cooking time.
5. Use a nonstick-safe spatula, and perhaps kitchen tongs for balance, to gently transfer the kofta skewers to a wire rack. Cool for at least 5 minutes or up to 20 minutes before serving.

Crispy Five-spice Pork Belly

Servings: 6
Cooking Time: 60-75 Minutes
Ingredients:
- 1½ pounds Pork belly with skin
- 3 tablespoons Shaoxing (Chinese cooking rice wine), dry sherry, or white grape juice
- 1½ teaspoons Granulated white sugar
- ¾ teaspoon Five-spice powder (see the headnote)
- 1¼ cups Coarse sea salt or kosher salt

Directions:
1. Preheat the air fryer to 350°F.
2. Set the pork belly skin side up on a cutting board. Use a meat fork to make dozens and dozens of tiny holes all across the surface of the skin. You can hardly make too many holes. These will allow the skin to bubble up and keep it from becoming hard as it roasts.
3. Turn the pork belly over so that one of its longer sides faces you. Make four evenly spaced vertical slits in the meat. The slits should go about halfway into the meat toward the fat.
4. Mix the Shaoxing or its substitute, sugar, and five-spice powder in a small bowl until the sugar dissolves. Massage this mixture across the meat and into the cuts.
5. Turn the pork belly over again. Blot dry any moisture on the skin. Make a double-thickness aluminum foil tray by setting two 10-inch-long pieces of foil on top of another. Set the pork belly skin side up in the center of this tray. Fold the sides of the tray up toward the pork, crimping the foil as you work to make a high-sided case all around the pork belly. Seal the foil to the meat on all sides so that only the skin is exposed.
6. Pour the salt onto the skin and pat it down and in place to create a crust. Pick up the foil tray with the pork in it and set it in the basket.
7. Air-fry undisturbed for 35 minutes for a small batch, 45 minutes for a medium batch, or 50 minutes for a large batch.
8. Remove the foil tray with the pork belly still in it. Warning: The foil tray is full of scalding-hot fat. Discard the fat in the tray (not down the drain!), as well as the tray itself. Transfer the pork belly to a cutting board.
9. Raise the air fryer temperature to 375°F (or 380°F or 390°F, if one of these is the closest setting). Brush the salt crust off the pork, removing any visible salt from the sides of the meat, too.
10. When the machine is at temperature, return the pork belly skin side up to the basket. Air-fry undisturbed for 25 minutes, or until crisp and very well browned. If the machine is at 390°F,

you may be able to shave 5 minutes off the cooking time so that the skin doesn't blacken.

11. Use a nonstick-safe spatula, and perhaps a silicone baking mitt, to transfer the pork belly to a wire rack. Cool for 10 minutes before serving.

Flank Steak With Chimichurri Sauce

Servings: 4
Cooking Time: 25 Minutes + Chilling Time
Ingredients:
- For Marinade
- 2/3 cup olive oil
- 1 tbsp Dijon mustard
- 1 orange, juiced and zested
- 1 lime, juiced and zested
- 1/3 cup tamari sauce
- 2 tbsp red wine vinegar
- 4 cloves garlic, minced
- 1 flank steak
- For Chimichurri Sauce
- 2 red jalapeños, minced
- 1 cup Italian parsley leaves
- ¼ cup cilantro leaves
- ¼ cup oregano leaves
- ¼ cup olive oil
- ½ onion, diced
- 4 cloves garlic, minced
- 2 tbsp lime juice
- 2 tsp lime zest
- 2 tbsp red wine vinegar
- ½ tsp ground cumin
- ½ tsp salt

Directions:
1. Whisk all the marinade ingredients in a large bowl. Toss in flank steak and let marinate covered for at least 1 hour. In a food processor, blend parsley, cilantro, oregano, red jalapeños, olive oil, onion, garlic, lime juice, lime zest, vinegar, cumin, and salt until you reach your desired consistency. Let chill in the fridge until ready to use.
2. Preheat air fryer at 325°F. Place flank steak in the greased frying basket and Bake for 18-20 minutes until rare, turning once. Let rest onto a cutting board for 5 minutes before slicing thinly against the grain. Serve with chimichurri sauce on the side.

Marinated Rib-eye Steak With Herb Roasted Mushrooms

Servings: 2
Cooking Time: 10-15 Minutes
Ingredients:
- 2 tablespoons Worcestershire sauce
- ¼ cup red wine
- 2 (8-ounce) boneless rib-eye steaks
- coarsely ground black pepper
- 8 ounces baby bella (cremini) mushrooms, stems trimmed and caps halved
- 2 tablespoons olive oil
- 1 teaspoon dried parsley
- 1 teaspoon fresh thyme leaves
- salt and freshly ground black pepper
- chopped fresh chives or parsley

Directions:
1. Combine the Worcestershire sauce and red wine in a shallow baking dish. Add the steaks to the marinade, pierce them several times with the tines of a fork or a meat tenderizer and season them generously with the coarsely ground black pepper. Flip the steaks over and pierce the other side in a similar fashion, seasoning again with the coarsely ground black pepper. Marinate the steaks for 2 hours.
2. Preheat the air fryer to 400°F.
3. Toss the mushrooms in a bowl with the olive oil, dried parsley, thyme, salt and freshly ground black pepper. Transfer the steaks from the marinade to the air fryer basket, season with salt and scatter the mushrooms on top.
4. Air-fry the steaks for 10 minutes for medium-rare, 12 minutes for medium, or 15 minutes for well-done, flipping the steaks once halfway through the cooking time.
5. Serve the steaks and mushrooms together with the chives or parsley sprinkled on top. A good steak sauce or some horseradish would be a nice accompaniment.

Spiced Beef Empanadas

Servings: 4
Cooking Time: 35 Minutes
Ingredients:
- 2 tbsp olive oil
- 6 oz ground beef
- 1 shallot, diced
- ½ tsp ground cumin
- ½ tsp nutmeg
- ½ tsp ground cloves
- 1 pinch of brown sugar
- 2 tsp red chili powder
- 4 empanada dough shells

Directions:
1. Preheat air fryer to 350°F. Warm the olive oil in a saucepan over medium heat. Crumble and cook the ground beef for 4-5 minutes. Add in the shallot, cumin, nutmeg, chili powder, and clove and stir-fry for 3 minutes. Kill the heat and let the mixture cool slightly. Divide the beef mixture between the empanada shells. Fold the empanada shells over and use a fork to seal the edges. Sprinkle brown sugar over. Place the empanadas in the foil-lined frying basket and Bake for 15 minutes. Halfway through, flip the empanadas. Cook them until golden. Serve and enjoy!

Calf's Liver

Servings: 4
Cooking Time: 5 Minutes
Ingredients:
- 1 pound sliced calf's liver
- salt and pepper
- 2 eggs
- 2 tablespoons milk
- ½ cup whole wheat flour
- 1½ cups panko breadcrumbs
- ½ cup plain breadcrumbs
- ½ teaspoon salt
- ¼ teaspoon pepper
- oil for misting or cooking spray

Directions:
1. Cut liver slices crosswise into strips about ½-inch wide. Sprinkle with salt and pepper to taste.
2. Beat together egg and milk in a shallow dish.
3. Place wheat flour in a second shallow dish.
4. In a third shallow dish, mix together panko, plain breadcrumbs, ½ teaspoon salt, and ¼ teaspoon pepper.
5. Preheat air fryer to 390°F.
6. Dip liver strips in flour, egg wash, and then breadcrumbs, pressing in coating slightly to make crumbs stick.
7. Cooking half the liver at a time, place strips in air fryer basket in a single layer, close but not touching. Cook at 390°F for 5 minutes or until done to your preference.
8. Repeat step 7 to cook remaining liver.

Paprika Fried Beef

Servings: 4
Cooking Time: 30 Minutes
Ingredients:
- Celery salt to taste
- 4 beef cube steaks
- ½ cup milk
- 1 cup flour
- 2 tsp paprika
- 1 egg
- 1 cup bread crumbs
- 2 tbsp olive oil

Directions:
1. Preheat air fryer to 350°F. Place the cube steaks in a zipper sealed bag or between two sheets of cling wrap. Gently pound the steaks until they are slightly thinner. Set aside. In a bowl, mix together milk, flour, paprika, celery salt, and egg until just combined. In a separate bowl, mix together the crumbs and olive oil. Take the steaks and dip them into the buttermilk batter, shake off some of the excess, and return to a plate for 5 minutes. Next, dip the steaks in the bread crumbs, patting the crumbs into both sides. Air Fry the steaks until the crust is crispy and brown, 12-16 minutes. Serve warm.

Natchitoches Meat Pies

Servings: 8
Cooking Time: 12 Minutes
Ingredients:
- Filling
- ½ pound lean ground beef
- ¼ cup finely chopped onion
- ¼ cup finely chopped green bell pepper
- ⅛ teaspoon salt
- ½ teaspoon garlic powder
- ½ teaspoon red pepper flakes
- 1 tablespoon low sodium Worcestershire sauce
- Crust
- 2 cups self-rising flour
- ¼ cup butter, finely diced
- 1 cup milk
- Egg Wash
- 1 egg
- 1 tablespoon water or milk
- oil for misting or cooking spray

Directions:
1. Mix all filling ingredients well and shape into 4 small patties.
2. Cook patties in air fryer basket at 390°F for 10 to 12minutes or until well done.
3. Place patties in large bowl and use fork and knife to crumble meat into very small pieces. Set aside.
4. To make the crust, use a pastry blender or fork to cut the butter into the flour until well mixed. Add milk and stir until dough stiffens.
5. Divide dough into 8 equal portions.
6. On a lightly floured surface, roll each portion of dough into a circle. The circle should be thin and about 5 inches in diameter, but don't worry about getting a perfect shape. Uneven circles result in a rustic look that many people prefer.
7. Spoon 2 tablespoons of meat filling onto each dough circle.
8. Brush egg wash all the way around the edge of dough circle, about ½-inch deep.
9. Fold each circle in half and press dough with tines of a dinner fork to seal the edges all the way around.
10. Brush tops of sealed meat pies with egg wash.
11. Cook filled pies in a single layer in air fryer basket at 360°F for 4minutes. Spray tops with oil or cooking spray, turn pies over, and spray bottoms with oil or cooking spray. Cook for an additional 2minutes.
12. Repeat previous step to cook remaining pies.

Pepperoni Bagel Pizzas

Servings: 4
Cooking Time: 20 Minutes
Ingredients:
- 2 bagels, halved horizontally
- 2 cups shredded mozzarella
- ¼ cup grated Parmesan
- 1 cup passata
- 1/3 cup sliced pepperoni
- 2 scallions, chopped

- 2 tbsp minced fresh chives
- 1tsp red chili flakes

Directions:
1. Preheat the air fryer to 375°F. Put the bagel halves, cut side up, in the frying basket. Bake for 2-3 minutes until golden. Remove and top them with passata, pepperoni, scallions, and cheeses. Put the bagels topping-side up to the frying basket and cook for 8-12 more minutes or until the bagels are hot and the cheese has melted and is bubbling. Top with the chives and chili flakes and serve.

Stuffed Pork Chops

Servings: 4
Cooking Time: 12 Minutes
Ingredients:
- 4 boneless pork chops
- ½ teaspoon salt
- ½ teaspoon black pepper
- ¼ teaspoon paprika
- 1 cup frozen spinach, defrosted and squeezed dry
- 2 cloves garlic, minced
- 2 ounces cream cheese
- ¼ cup grated Parmesan cheese
- 1 tablespoon extra-virgin olive oil

Directions:
1. Pat the pork chops with a paper towel. Make a slit in the side of each pork chop to create a pouch.
2. Season the pork chops with the salt, pepper, and paprika.
3. In a small bowl, mix together the spinach, garlic, cream cheese, and Parmesan cheese.
4. Divide the mixture into fourths and stuff the pork chop pouches. Secure the pouches with toothpicks.
5. Preheat the air fryer to 400°F.
6. Place the stuffed pork chops in the air fryer basket and spray liberally with cooking spray. Cook for 6 minutes, flip and coat with more cooking spray, and cook another 6 minutes. Check to make sure the meat is cooked to an internal temperature of 145°F. Cook the pork chops in batches, as needed.

Pepper Steak

Servings: 4
Cooking Time: 30 Minutes
Ingredients:
- 2 tablespoons cornstarch
- 1 tablespoon sugar
- ¾ cup beef broth
- ¼ cup hoisin sauce
- 3 tablespoons soy sauce
- 1 teaspoon sesame oil
- ½ teaspoon freshly ground black pepper
- 1½ pounds boneless New York strip steaks, sliced into ½-inch strips
- 1 onion, sliced
- 3 small bell peppers, red, yellow and green, sliced

Directions:
1. Whisk the cornstarch and sugar together in a large bowl to break up any lumps in the cornstarch. Add the beef broth and whisk until combined and smooth. Stir in the hoisin sauce, soy sauce, sesame oil and freshly ground black pepper. Add the beef, onion and peppers, and toss to coat. Marinate the beef and vegetables at room temperature for 30 minutes, stirring a few times to keep meat and vegetables coated.
2. Preheat the air fryer to 350°F.
3. Transfer the beef, onion, and peppers to the air fryer basket with tongs, reserving the marinade. Air-fry the beef and vegetables for 30 minutes, stirring well two or three times during the cooking process.
4. While the beef is air-frying, bring the reserved marinade to a simmer in a small saucepan over medium heat on the stovetop. Simmer for 5 minutes until the sauce thickens.
5. When the steak and vegetables have finished cooking, transfer them to a serving platter. Pour the hot sauce over the pepper steak and serve with white rice.

Lazy Mexican Meat Pizza

Servings: 4
Cooking Time: 35 Minutes
Ingredients:
- 1 ¼ cups canned refried beans
- 2 cups shredded cheddar
- ½ cup chopped cilantro
- 2/3 cup salsa
- 1 red bell pepper, chopped
- 1 sliced jalapeño
- 1 pizza crust
- 16 meatballs, halved

Directions:
1. Preheat the air fryer to 375°F. Combine the refried beans, salsa, jalapeño, and bell pepper in a bowl and spread on the pizza crust. Top with meatball halves and sprinkle with cheddar cheese. Put the pizza in the greased frying basket and Bake for 7-10 minutes until hot and the cheese is brown. Sprinkle with the fresh cilantro and serve.

Easy-peasy Beef Sliders

Servings:4
Cooking Time: 25 Minutes
Ingredients:
- 1 lb ground beef
- ¼ tsp cumin
- ¼ tsp mustard power
- 1/3 cup grated yellow onion
- ½ tsp smoked paprika
- Salt and pepper to taste

Directions:
1. Preheat air fryer to 350°F. Combine the ground beef, cumin, mustard, onion, paprika, salt, and black pepper in a bowl. Form mixture into 8 patties and make a slight indentation in the middle of each. Place beef patties in the greased frying basket and Air Fry for 8-10 minutes, flipping once. Serve right away and enjoy!

Chapter 5 Poultry Recipes

Cal-mex Turkey Patties

Servings: 4
Cooking Time: 30 Minutes
Ingredients:
- 1/3 cup crushed corn tortilla chips
- 1/3 cup grated American cheese
- 1 egg, beaten
- ¼ cup salsa
- Salt and pepper to taste
- 1 lb ground turkey
- 1 tbsp olive oil
- 1 tsp chili powder

Directions:
1. Preheat air fryer to 330°F. Mix together egg, tortilla chips, salsa, cheese, salt, and pepper in a bowl. Using your hands, add the ground turkey and mix gently until just combined. Divide the meat into 4 equal portions and shape into patties about ½ inch thick. Brush the patties with olive oil and sprinkle with chili powder. Air Fry the patties for 14-16 minutes, flipping once until cooked through and golden. Serve and enjoy!

Turkey Burgers

Servings: 4
Cooking Time: 13 Minutes
Ingredients:
- 1 pound ground turkey
- ¼ cup diced red onion
- 1 tablespoon grilled chicken seasoning
- ½ teaspoon dried parsley
- ½ teaspoon salt
- 4 slices provolone cheese
- 4 whole-grain sandwich buns
- Suggested toppings: lettuce, sliced tomatoes, dill pickles, and mustard

Directions:
1. Combine the turkey, onion, chicken seasoning, parsley, and salt and mix well.
2. Shape into 4 patties.
3. Cook at 360°F for 11 minutes or until turkey is well done and juices run clear.
4. Top each burger with a slice of cheese and cook 2 minutes to melt.
5. Serve on buns with your favorite toppings.

Air-fried Turkey Breast With Cherry Glaze

Servings: 6
Cooking Time: 54 Minutes
Ingredients:
- 1 (5-pound) turkey breast
- 2 teaspoons olive oil
- 1 teaspoon dried thyme
- ½ teaspoon dried sage
- 1 teaspoon salt
- ½ teaspoon freshly ground black pepper
- ½ cup cherry preserves
- 1 tablespoon chopped fresh thyme leaves
- 1 teaspoon soy sauce*
- freshly ground black pepper

Directions:
1. All turkeys are built differently, so depending on the turkey breast and how your butcher has prepared it, you may need to trim the bottom of the ribs in order to get the turkey to sit upright in the air fryer basket without touching the heating element. The key to this recipe is getting the right size turkey breast. Once you've managed that, the rest is easy, so make sure your turkey breast fits into the air fryer basket before you Preheat the air fryer.
2. Preheat the air fryer to 350°F.
3. Brush the turkey breast all over with the olive oil. Combine the thyme, sage, salt and pepper and rub the outside of the turkey breast with the spice mixture.
4. Transfer the seasoned turkey breast to the air fryer basket, breast side up, and air-fry at 350°F for 25 minutes. Turn the turkey breast on its side and air-fry for another 12 minutes. Turn the turkey breast on the opposite side and air-fry for 12 more minutes. The internal temperature of the turkey breast should reach 165°F when fully cooked.
5. While the turkey is air-frying, make the glaze by combining the cherry preserves, fresh thyme, soy sauce and pepper in a small bowl. When the cooking time is up, return the turkey breast to an upright position and brush the glaze all over the turkey. Air-fry for a final 5 minutes, until the skin is nicely browned and crispy. Let the turkey rest, loosely tented with foil, for at least 5 minutes before slicing and serving.

Sesame Orange Chicken

Servings: 2
Cooking Time: 9 Minutes
Ingredients:
- 1 pound boneless, skinless chicken breasts, cut into cubes
- salt and freshly ground black pepper
- ¼ cup cornstarch
- 2 eggs, beaten
- 1½ cups panko breadcrumbs
- vegetable or peanut oil, in a spray bottle
- 12 ounces orange marmalade
- 1 tablespoon soy sauce
- 1 teaspoon minced ginger
- 2 tablespoons hoisin sauce
- 1 tablespoon sesame oil
- sesame seeds, toasted

Directions:

1. Season the chicken pieces with salt and pepper. Set up a dredging station. Put the cornstarch in a zipper-sealable plastic bag. Place the beaten eggs in a bowl and put the panko breadcrumbs in a shallow dish. Transfer the seasoned chicken to the bag with the cornstarch and shake well to completely coat the chicken on all sides. Remove the chicken from the bag, shaking off any excess cornstarch and dip the pieces into the egg. Let any excess egg drip from the chicken and transfer into the breadcrumbs, pressing the crumbs onto the chicken pieces with your hands. Spray the chicken pieces with vegetable or peanut oil.
2. Preheat the air fryer to 400°F.
3. Combine the orange marmalade, soy sauce, ginger, hoisin sauce and sesame oil in a saucepan. Bring the mixture to a boil on the stovetop, lower the heat and simmer for 10 minutes, until the sauce has thickened. Set aside and keep warm.
4. Transfer the coated chicken to the air fryer basket and air-fry at 400°F for 9 minutes, shaking the basket a few times during the cooking process to help the chicken cook evenly.
5. Right before serving, toss the browned chicken pieces with the sesame orange sauce. Serve over white rice with steamed broccoli. Sprinkle the sesame seeds on top.

Turkey Scotch Eggs

Servings: 4
Cooking Time: 30 Minutes
Ingredients:
- 1 ½ lb ground turkey
- 1 tbsp ground cumin
- 1 tsp ground coriander
- 2 garlic cloves, minced
- 3 raw eggs
- 1 ½ cups bread crumbs
- 6 hard-cooked eggs, peeled
- ½ cup flour

Directions:
1. Preheat air fryer to 370°F. Place the ground turkey, cumin, coriander, garlic, one egg, and ½ cup of bread crumbs in a large bowl and mix until well incorporated.
2. Divide into 6 equal portions, then flatten each into long ovals. Set aside. In a shallow bowl, beat the remaining raw eggs. In another shallow bowl, add flour. Do the same with another plate for bread crumbs. Roll each cooked egg in flour, then wrap with one oval of chicken sausage until completely covered.
3. Roll again in flour, then coat in the beaten egg before rolling in bread crumbs. Arrange the eggs in the greased frying basket. Air Fry for 12-14 minutes, flipping once until the sausage is cooked and the eggs are brown. Serve.

Chicken Pigs In Blankets

Servings: 4
Cooking Time: 40 Minutes
Ingredients:
- 8 chicken drumsticks, boneless, skinless
- 2 tbsp light brown sugar
- 2 tbsp ketchup
- 1 tbsp grainy mustard
- 8 smoked bacon slices
- 1 tsp chopped fresh sage

Directions:
1. Preheat the air fryer to 350°F. Mix brown sugar, sage, ketchup, and mustard in a bowl and brush the chicken with it. Wrap slices of bacon around the drumsticks and brush with the remaining mix. Line the frying basket with round parchment paper with holes. Set 4 drumsticks on the paper, add a raised rack and set the other drumsticks on it. Bake for 25-35 minutes, moving the bottom drumsticks to the top, top to the bottom, and flipping at about 14-16 minutes. Sprinkle with sage and serve.

Teriyaki Chicken Drumsticks

Servings: 2
Cooking Time: 17 Minutes
Ingredients:
- 2 tablespoons soy sauce*
- ¼ cup dry sherry
- 1 tablespoon brown sugar
- 2 tablespoons water
- 1 tablespoon rice wine vinegar
- 1 clove garlic, crushed
- 1-inch fresh ginger, peeled and sliced
- pinch crushed red pepper flakes
- 4 to 6 bone-in, skin-on chicken drumsticks
- 1 tablespoon cornstarch
- fresh cilantro leaves

Directions:
1. Make the marinade by combining the soy sauce, dry sherry, brown sugar, water, rice vinegar, garlic, ginger and crushed red pepper flakes. Pour the marinade over the chicken legs, cover and let the chicken marinate for 1 to 4 hours in the refrigerator.
2. Preheat the air fryer to 380°F.
3. Transfer the chicken from the marinade to the air fryer basket, transferring any extra marinade to a small saucepan. Air-fry at 380°F for 8 minutes. Flip the chicken over and continue to air-fry for another 6 minutes, watching to make sure it doesn't brown too much.
4. While the chicken is cooking, bring the reserved marinade to a simmer on the stovetop. Dissolve the cornstarch in 2 tablespoons of water and stir this into the saucepan. Bring to a boil to thicken the sauce. Remove the garlic clove and slices of ginger from the sauce and set aside.
5. When the time is up on the air fryer, brush the thickened sauce on the chicken and air-fry for 3 more minutes. Remove the chicken from the air fryer and brush with the remaining sauce.
6. Serve over rice and sprinkle the cilantro leaves on top.

Buffalo Egg Rolls

Servings: 8
Cooking Time: 9 Minutes Per Batch
Ingredients:
- 1 teaspoon water
- 1 tablespoon cornstarch
- 1 egg
- 2½ cups cooked chicken, diced or shredded (see opposite page)
- ⅓ cup chopped green onion
- ⅓ cup diced celery
- ⅓ cup buffalo wing sauce
- 8 egg roll wraps
- oil for misting or cooking spray
- Blue Cheese Dip
- 3 ounces cream cheese, softened
- ⅓ cup blue cheese, crumbled
- 1 teaspoon Worcestershire sauce
- ¼ teaspoon garlic powder
- ¼ cup buttermilk (or sour cream)

Directions:
1. Mix water and cornstarch in a small bowl until dissolved. Add egg, beat well, and set aside.
2. In a medium size bowl, mix together chicken, green onion, celery, and buffalo wing sauce.
3. Divide chicken mixture evenly among 8 egg roll wraps, spooning ½ inch from one edge.
4. Moisten all edges of each wrap with beaten egg wash.
5. Fold the short ends over filling, then roll up tightly and press to seal edges.
6. Brush outside of wraps with egg wash, then spritz with oil or cooking spray.
7. Place 4 egg rolls in air fryer basket.
8. Cook at 390°F for 9 minutes or until outside is brown and crispy.
9. While the rolls are cooking, prepare the Blue Cheese Dip. With a fork, mash together cream cheese and blue cheese.
10. Stir in remaining ingredients.
11. Dip should be just thick enough to slightly cling to egg rolls. If too thick, stir in buttermilk or milk 1 tablespoon at a time until you reach the desired consistency.
12. Cook remaining 4 egg rolls as in steps 7 and 8.
13. Serve while hot with Blue Cheese Dip, more buffalo wing sauce, or both.

Chicken Chimichangas

Servings: 4
Cooking Time: 10 Minutes
Ingredients:
- 2 cups cooked chicken, shredded
- 2 tablespoons chopped green chiles
- ½ teaspoon oregano
- ½ teaspoon cumin
- ½ teaspoon onion powder
- ¼ teaspoon garlic powder
- salt and pepper
- 8 flour tortillas (6- or 7-inch diameter)
- oil for misting or cooking spray
- Chimichanga Sauce
- 2 tablespoons butter
- 2 tablespoons flour
- 1 cup chicken broth
- ¼ cup light sour cream
- ¼ teaspoon salt
- 2 ounces Pepper Jack or Monterey Jack cheese, shredded

Directions:
1. Make the sauce by melting butter in a saucepan over medium-low heat. Stir in flour until smooth and slightly bubbly. Gradually add broth, stirring constantly until smooth. Cook and stir 1 minute, until the mixture slightly thickens. Remove from heat and stir in sour cream and salt. Set aside.
2. In a medium bowl, mix together the chicken, chiles, oregano, cumin, onion powder, garlic, salt, and pepper. Stir in 3 to 4 tablespoons of the sauce, using just enough to make the filling moist but not soupy.
3. Divide filling among the 8 tortillas. Place filling down the center of tortilla, stopping about 1 inch from edges. Fold one side of tortilla over filling, fold the two sides in, and then roll up. Mist all sides with oil or cooking spray.
4. Place chimichangas in air fryer basket seam side down. To fit more into the basket, you can stand them on their sides with the seams against the sides of the basket.
5. Cook at 360°F for 10 minutes or until heated through and crispy brown outside.
6. Add the shredded cheese to the remaining sauce. Stir over low heat, warming just until the cheese melts. Don't boil or sour cream may curdle.
7. Drizzle the sauce over the chimichangas.

Moroccan-style Chicken Strips

Servings: 4
Cooking Time: 30 Minutes
Ingredients:
- 4 chicken breasts, cut into strips
- 2 tsp olive oil
- 2 tbsp cornstarch
- 3 garlic cloves, minced
- ½ cup chicken broth
- ¼ cup lemon juice
- 1 tbsp honey
- ½ tsp ras el hanout
- 1 cup cooked couscous

Directions:
1. Preheat air fryer to 400°F. Mix the chicken and olive oil in a bowl, then add the cornstarch. Stir to coat. Add the garlic and transfer to a baking pan. Put the pan in the fryer. Bake for 10 minutes. Stir at least once during cooking.
2. When done, pour in the chicken broth, lemon juice, honey, and ras el hanout. Bake for an additional 6-9 minutes or until the sauce is thick and the chicken cooked through with no pink showing. Serve with couscous.

Vip's Club Sandwiches

Servings: 4
Cooking Time: 50 Minutes
Ingredients:
- 1 cup buttermilk
- 1 egg
- 1 cup bread crumbs
- 1 tsp garlic powder
- Salt and pepper to taste
- 4 chicken cutlets
- 3 tbsp butter, melted
- 4 hamburger buns
- 4 tbsp mayonnaise
- 4 tsp yellow mustard
- 8 dill pickle chips
- 4 pieces iceberg lettuce
- ½ sliced avocado
- 4 slices cooked bacon
- 8 vine-ripe tomato slices
- 1 tsp chia seeds

Directions:
1. Preheat air fryer at 400°F. Beat the buttermilk and egg in a bowl. In another bowl, combine breadcrumbs, garlic powder, salt, and black pepper. Dip chicken cutlets in the egg mixture, then dredge them in the breadcrumbs mixture. Brush chicken cutlets lightly with melted butter on both sides, place them in the greased frying basket, and Air Fry for 18-20 minutes. Spread the mayonnaise on the top buns and mustard on the bottom buns. Add chicken onto bottom buns and top with pickles, lettuce, chia seeds, avocado, bacon, and tomato. Cover with the top buns. Serve and enjoy!

Chicken Fried Steak With Gravy

Servings: 4
Cooking Time: 10 Minutes Per Batch
Ingredients:
- ½ cup flour
- 2 teaspoons salt, divided
- freshly ground black pepper
- ¼ teaspoon garlic powder
- 1 cup buttermilk
- 1 cup fine breadcrumbs
- 4 tenderized top round steaks (about 6 to 8 ounces each; ½-inch thick)
- vegetable or canola oil
- For the Gravy:
- 2 tablespoons butter or bacon drippings
- ¼ onion, minced (about ¼ cup)
- 1 clove garlic, smashed
- ¼ teaspoon dried thyme
- 3 tablespoons flour
- 1 cup milk
- salt and lots of freshly ground black pepper
- a few dashes of Worcestershire sauce

Directions:
1. Set up a dredging station. Combine the flour, 1 teaspoon of salt, black pepper and garlic powder in a shallow bowl. Pour the buttermilk into a second shallow bowl. Finally, put the breadcrumbs and 1 teaspoon of salt in a third shallow bowl.
2. Dip the tenderized steaks into the flour, then the buttermilk, and then the breadcrumb mixture, pressing the crumbs onto the steak. Place them on a baking sheet and spray both sides generously with vegetable or canola oil.
3. Preheat the air fryer to 400°F.
4. Transfer the steaks to the air fryer basket, two at a time, and air-fry for 10 minutes, flipping the steaks over halfway through the cooking time. This will cook your steaks to medium. If you want the steaks cooked a little more or less, add or subtract a minute or two. Hold the first batch of steaks warm in a 170°F oven while you cook the second batch.
5. While the steaks are cooking, make the gravy. Melt the butter in a small saucepan over medium heat on the stovetop. Add the onion, garlic and thyme and cook for five minutes, until the onion is soft and just starting to brown. Stir in the flour and cook for another five minutes, stirring regularly, until the mixture starts to brown. Whisk in the milk and bring the mixture to a boil to thicken. Season to taste with salt, lots of freshly ground black pepper and a few dashes of Worcestershire sauce.
6. Plate the chicken fried steaks with mashed potatoes and vegetables and serve the gravy at the table to pour over the top.

Nacho Chicken Fries

Servings: 4
Cooking Time: 7 Minutes
Ingredients:
- 1 pound chicken tenders
- salt
- ¼ cup flour
- 2 eggs
- ¾ cup panko breadcrumbs
- ¾ cup crushed organic nacho cheese tortilla chips
- oil for misting or cooking spray
- Seasoning Mix
- 1 tablespoon chili powder
- 1 teaspoon ground cumin
- ½ teaspoon garlic powder
- ½ teaspoon onion powder

Directions:
1. Stir together all seasonings in a small cup and set aside.
2. Cut chicken tenders in half crosswise, then cut into strips no wider than about ½ inch.
3. Preheat air fryer to 390°F.
4. Salt chicken to taste. Place strips in large bowl and sprinkle with 1 tablespoon of the seasoning mix. Stir well to distribute seasonings.
5. Add flour to chicken and stir well to coat all sides.
6. Beat eggs together in a shallow dish.
7. In a second shallow dish, combine the panko, crushed chips, and the remaining 2 teaspoons of seasoning mix.

8. Dip chicken strips in eggs, then roll in crumbs. Mist with oil or cooking spray.
9. Chicken strips will cook best if done in two batches. They can be crowded and overlapping a little but not stacked in double or triple layers.
10. Cook for 4 minutes. Shake basket, mist with oil, and cook 3 more minutes, until chicken juices run clear and outside is crispy.
11. Repeat step 10 to cook remaining chicken fries.

Chicken Cordon Bleu

Servings: 2
Cooking Time: 16 Minutes
Ingredients:
- 2 boneless, skinless chicken breasts
- ¼ teaspoon salt
- 2 teaspoons Dijon mustard
- 2 ounces deli ham
- 2 ounces Swiss, fontina, or Gruyère cheese
- ⅓ cup all-purpose flour
- 1 egg
- ½ cup breadcrumbs

Directions:
1. Pat the chicken breasts with a paper towel. Season the chicken with the salt. Pound the chicken breasts to 1½ inches thick. Create a pouch by slicing the side of each chicken breast. Spread 1 teaspoon Dijon mustard inside the pouch of each chicken breast. Wrap a 1-ounce slice of ham around a 1-ounce slice of cheese and place into the pouch. Repeat with the remaining ham and cheese.
2. In a medium bowl, place the flour.
3. In a second bowl, whisk the egg.
4. In a third bowl, place the breadcrumbs.
5. Dredge the chicken in the flour and shake off the excess. Next, dip the chicken into the egg and then in the breadcrumbs. Set the chicken on a plate and repeat with the remaining chicken piece.
6. Preheat the air fryer to 360°F.
7. Place the chicken in the air fryer basket and spray liberally with cooking spray. Cook for 8 minutes, turn the chicken breasts over, and liberally spray with cooking spray again; cook another 6 minutes. Once golden brown, check for an internal temperature of 165°F.

Daadi Chicken Salad

Servings: 2
Cooking Time: 30 Minutes
Ingredients:
- ½ cup chopped golden raisins
- 1 Granny Smith apple, grated
- 2 chicken breasts
- Salt and pepper to taste
- ¾ cup mayonnaise
- 1 tbsp lime juice
- 1 tsp curry powder
- ½ sliced avocado
- 1 scallion, minced
- 2 tbsp chopped pecans
- 1 tsp poppy seeds

Directions:
1. Preheat air fryer at 350°F. Sprinkle chicken breasts with salt and pepper, place them in the greased frying basket, and Air Fry for 8-10 minutes, tossing once. Let rest for 5 minutes before cutting. In a salad bowl, combine chopped chicken, mayonnaise, lime juice, curry powder, raisins, apple, avocado, scallion, and pecans. Let sit covered in the fridge until ready to eat. Before serve sprinkled with the poppy seeds.

Crunchy Chicken Strips

Servings: 4
Cooking Time: 40 Minutes
Ingredients:
- 1 chicken breast, sliced into strips
- 1 tbsp grated Parmesan cheese
- 1 cup breadcrumbs
- 1 tbsp chicken seasoning
- 2 eggs, beaten
- Salt and pepper to taste

Directions:
1. Preheat air fryer to 350°F. Mix the breadcrumbs, Parmesan cheese, chicken seasoning, salt, and pepper in a mixing bowl. Coat the chicken with the crumb mixture, then dip in the beaten eggs. Finally, coat again with the dry ingredients. Arrange the coated chicken pieces on the greased frying basket and Air Fry for 15 minutes. Turn over halfway through cooking and cook for another 15 minutes. Serve immediately.

Parmesan Chicken Meatloaf

Servings: 4
Cooking Time: 45 Minutes
Ingredients:
- 1 ½ tsp evaporated cane sugar
- 1 lb ground chicken
- 4 garlic cloves, minced
- 2 tbsp grated Parmesan
- ¼ cup heavy cream
- ¼ cup minced onion
- 2 tbsp chopped basil
- 2 tbsp chopped parsley
- Salt and pepper to taste
- ½ tsp onion powder
- ½ cup bread crumbs
- ¼ tsp red pepper flakes
- 1 egg
- 1 cup tomato sauce
- ½ tsp garlic powder
- ½ tsp dried thyme
- ½ tsp dried oregano
- 1 tbsp coconut aminos

Directions:

1. Preheat air fryer to 400°F. Combine chicken, garlic, minced onion, oregano, thyme, basil, salt, pepper, onion powder, Parmesan cheese, red pepper flakes, bread crumbs, egg, and cream in a large bowl. Transfer the chicken mixture to a prepared baking dish. Stir together tomato sauce, garlic powder, coconut aminos, and sugar in a small bowl. Spread over the meatloaf. Loosely cover with foil. Place the pan in the frying basket and bake for 15 minutes. Take the foil off and bake for another 15 minutes. Allow resting for 10 minutes before slicing. Serve sprinkled with parsley.

Crispy Duck With Cherry Sauce

Servings: 2
Cooking Time: 33 Minutes
Ingredients:
- 1 whole duck (up to 5 pounds), split in half, back and rib bones removed
- 1 teaspoon olive oil
- salt and freshly ground black pepper
- Cherry Sauce:
- 1 tablespoon butter
- 1 shallot, minced
- ½ cup sherry
- ¾ cup cherry preserves 1 cup chicken stock
- 1 teaspoon white wine vinegar
- 1 teaspoon fresh thyme leaves
- salt and freshly ground black pepper

Directions:
1. Preheat the air fryer to 400°F.
2. Trim some of the fat from the duck. Rub olive oil on the duck and season with salt and pepper. Place the duck halves in the air fryer basket, breast side up and facing the center of the basket.
3. Air-fry the duck for 20 minutes. Turn the duck over and air-fry for another 6 minutes.
4. While duck is air-frying, make the cherry sauce. Melt the butter in a large sauté pan. Add the shallot and sauté until it is just starting to brown – about 2 to 3 minutes. Add the sherry and deglaze the pan by scraping up any brown bits from the bottom of the pan. Simmer the liquid for a few minutes, until it has reduced by half. Add the cherry preserves, chicken stock and white wine vinegar. Whisk well to combine all the ingredients. Simmer the sauce until it thickens and coats the back of a spoon – about 5 to 7 minutes. Season with salt and pepper and stir in the fresh thyme leaves.
5. When the air fryer timer goes off, spoon some cherry sauce over the duck and continue to air-fry at 400°F for 4 more minutes. Then, turn the duck halves back over so that the breast side is facing up. Spoon more cherry sauce over the top of the duck, covering the skin completely. Air-fry for 3 more minutes and then remove the duck to a plate to rest for a few minutes.
6. Serve the duck in halves, or cut each piece in half again for a smaller serving. Spoon any additional sauce over the duck or serve it on the side.

Turkey-hummus Wraps

Servings: 4
Cooking Time: 7 Minutes Per Batch
Ingredients:
- 4 large whole wheat wraps
- ½ cup hummus
- 16 thin slices deli turkey
- 8 slices provolone cheese
- 1 cup fresh baby spinach (or more to taste)

Directions:
1. To assemble, place 2 tablespoons of hummus on each wrap and spread to within about a half inch from edges. Top with 4 slices of turkey and 2 slices of provolone. Finish with ¼ cup of baby spinach—or pile on as much as you like.
2. Roll up each wrap. You don't need to fold or seal the ends.
3. Place 2 wraps in air fryer basket, seam side down.
4. Cook at 360°F for 4minutes to warm filling and melt cheese. If you like, you can continue cooking for 3 more minutes, until the wrap is slightly crispy.
5. Repeat step 4 to cook remaining wraps.

Taquitos

Servings: 12
Cooking Time: 6 Minutes Per Batch
Ingredients:
- 1 teaspoon butter
- 2 tablespoons chopped green onions
- 1 cup cooked chicken, shredded
- 2 tablespoons chopped green chiles
- 2 ounces Pepper Jack cheese, shredded
- 4 tablespoons salsa
- ½ teaspoon lime juice
- ¼ teaspoon cumin
- ½ teaspoon chile powder
- ⅛ teaspoon garlic powder
- 12 corn tortillas
- oil for misting or cooking spray

Directions:
1. Melt butter in a saucepan over medium heat. Add green onions and sauté a minute or two, until tender.
2. Remove from heat and stir in the chicken, green chiles, cheese, salsa, lime juice, and seasonings.
3. Preheat air fryer to 390°F.
4. To soften refrigerated tortillas, wrap in damp paper towels and microwave for 30 to 60 seconds, until slightly warmed.
5. Remove one tortilla at a time, keeping others covered with the damp paper towels. Place a heaping tablespoon of filling into tortilla, roll up and secure with toothpick. Spray all sides with oil or cooking spray.
6. Place taquitos in air fryer basket, either in a single layer or stacked. To stack, leave plenty of space between taquitos and alternate the direction of the layers, 4 on the bottom lengthwise, then 4 more on top crosswise.
7. Cook for 6minutes or until brown and crispy.
8. Repeat steps 6 and 7 to cook remaining taquitos.
9. Serve hot with guacamole, sour cream, salsa or all three!

Berry-glazed Turkey Breast

Servings: 4
Cooking Time: 1 Hour 25 Minutes
Ingredients:
- 1 bone-in, skin-on turkey breast
- 1 tbsp olive oil
- Salt and pepper to taste
- 1 cup raspberries
- 1 cup chopped strawberries
- 2 tbsp balsamic vinegar
- 2 tbsp butter, melted
- 1 tbsp honey mustard
- 1 tsp dried rosemary

Directions:
1. Preheat the air fryer to 350°F. Lay the turkey breast skin-side up in the frying basket, brush with the oil, and sprinkle with salt and pepper. Bake for 55-65 minutes, flipping twice. Meanwhile, mix the berries, vinegar, melted butter, rosemary and honey mustard in a blender and blend until smooth. Turn the turkey skin-side up inside the fryer and brush with half of the berry mix. Bake for 5 more minutes. Put the remaining berry mix in a small saucepan and simmer for 3-4 minutes while the turkey cooks. When the turkey is done, let it stand for 10 minutes, then carve. Serve with the remaining glaze.

Buttermilk-fried Drumsticks

Servings: 2
Cooking Time: 25 Minutes
Ingredients:
- 1 egg
- ½ cup buttermilk
- ¾ cup self-rising flour
- ¾ cup seasoned panko breadcrumbs
- 1 teaspoon salt
- ¼ teaspoon ground black pepper (to mix into coating)
- 4 chicken drumsticks, skin on
- oil for misting or cooking spray

Directions:
1. Beat together egg and buttermilk in shallow dish.
2. In a second shallow dish, combine the flour, panko crumbs, salt, and pepper.
3. Sprinkle chicken legs with additional salt and pepper to taste.
4. Dip legs in buttermilk mixture, then roll in panko mixture, pressing in crumbs to make coating stick. Mist with oil or cooking spray.
5. Spray air fryer basket with cooking spray.
6. Cook drumsticks at 360°F for 10minutes. Turn pieces over and cook an additional 10minutes.
7. Turn pieces to check for browning. If you have any white spots that haven't begun to brown, spritz them with oil or cooking spray. Continue cooking for 5 more minutes or until crust is golden brown and juices run clear. Larger, meatier drumsticks will take longer to cook than small ones.

Spicy Black Bean Turkey Burgers With Cumin-avocado Spread

Servings: 2
Cooking Time: 20 Minutes
Ingredients:
- 1 cup canned black beans, drained and rinsed
- ¾ pound lean ground turkey
- 2 tablespoons minced red onion
- 1 Jalapeño pepper, seeded and minced
- 2 tablespoons plain breadcrumbs
- ½ teaspoon chili powder
- ¼ teaspoon cayenne pepper
- salt, to taste
- olive or vegetable oil
- 2 slices pepper jack cheese
- toasted burger rolls, sliced tomatoes, lettuce leaves
- Cumin-Avocado Spread:
- 1 ripe avocado
- juice of 1 lime
- 1 teaspoon ground cumin
- ½ teaspoon salt
- 1 tablespoon chopped fresh cilantro
- freshly ground black pepper

Directions:
1. Place the black beans in a large bowl and smash them slightly with the back of a fork. Add the ground turkey, red onion, Jalapeño pepper, breadcrumbs, chili powder and cayenne pepper. Season with salt. Mix with your hands to combine all the ingredients and then shape them into 2 patties. Brush both sides of the burger patties with a little olive or vegetable oil.
2. Preheat the air fryer to 380°F.
3. Transfer the burgers to the air fryer basket and air-fry for 20 minutes, flipping them over halfway through the cooking process. Top the burgers with the pepper jack cheese (securing the slices to the burgers with a toothpick) for the last 2 minutes of the cooking process.
4. While the burgers are cooking, make the cumin avocado spread. Place the avocado, lime juice, cumin and salt in food processor and process until smooth. (For a chunkier spread, you can mash this by hand in a bowl.) Stir in the cilantro and season with freshly ground black pepper. Chill the spread until you are ready to serve.
5. When the burgers have finished cooking, remove them from the air fryer and let them rest on a plate, covered gently with aluminum foil. Brush a little olive oil on the insides of the burger rolls. Place the rolls, cut side up, into the air fryer basket and air-fry at 400°F for 1 minute to toast and warm them.
6. Spread the cumin-avocado spread on the rolls and build your burgers with lettuce and sliced tomatoes and any other ingredient you like. Serve warm with a side of sweet potato fries.

Maple Bacon Wrapped Chicken Breasts

Servings: 2
Cooking Time: 18 Minutes
Ingredients:
- 2 (6-ounce) boneless, skinless chicken breasts
- 2 tablespoons maple syrup, divided
- freshly ground black pepper
- 6 slices thick-sliced bacon
- fresh celery or parsley leaves
- Ranch Dressing:
- ¼ cup mayonnaise
- ¼ cup buttermilk
- ¼ cup Greek yogurt
- 1 tablespoon chopped fresh chives
- 1 tablespoon chopped fresh parsley
- 1 tablespoon chopped fresh dill
- 1 tablespoon lemon juice
- salt and freshly ground black pepper

Directions:
1. Brush the chicken breasts with half the maple syrup and season with freshly ground black pepper. Wrap three slices of bacon around each chicken breast, securing the ends with toothpicks.
2. Preheat the air fryer to 380°F.
3. Air-fry the chicken for 6 minutes. Then turn the chicken breasts over, pour more maple syrup on top and air-fry for another 6 minutes. Turn the chicken breasts one more time, brush the remaining maple syrup all over and continue to air-fry for a final 6 minutes.
4. While the chicken is cooking, prepare the dressing by combining all the dressing ingredients together in a bowl.
5. When the chicken has finished cooking, remove the toothpicks and serve each breast with a little dressing drizzled over each one. Scatter lots of fresh celery or parsley leaves on top.

Goat Cheese Stuffed Turkey Roulade

Servings: 4
Cooking Time: 55 Minutes
Ingredients:
- 1 boneless turkey breast, skinless
- Salt and pepper to taste
- 4 oz goat cheese
- 1 tbsp marjoram
- 1 tbsp sage
- 2 garlic cloves, minced
- 2 tbsp olive oil
- 2 tbsp chopped cilantro

Directions:
1. Preheat air fryer to 380°F. Butterfly the turkey breast with a sharp knife and season with salt and pepper. Mix together the goat cheese, marjoram, sage, and garlic in a bowl. Spread the cheese mixture over the turkey breast, then roll it up tightly, tucking the ends underneath.
2. Put the turkey breast roulade onto a piece of aluminum foil, wrap it up, and place it into the air fryer. Bake for 30 minutes. Turn the turkey breast, brush the top with oil, and then continue to cook for another 10-15 minutes. Slice and serve sprinkled with cilantro.

Fennel & Chicken Ratatouille

Servings: 4
Cooking Time: 30 Minutes
Ingredients:
- 1 lb boneless, skinless chicken thighs, cubed
- 2 tbsp grated Parmesan cheese
- 1 eggplant, cubed
- 1 zucchini, cubed
- 1 bell pepper, diced
- 1 fennel bulb, sliced
- 1 tsp salt
- 1 tsp Italian seasoning
- 2 tbsp olive oil
- 1 can diced tomatoes
- 1 tsp pasta sauce
- 2 tbsp basil leaves

Directions:
1. Preheat air fryer to 400ºF. Mix the chicken, eggplant, zucchini, bell pepper, fennel, salt, Italian seasoning, and oil in a bowl. Place the chicken mixture in the frying basket and Air Fry for 7 minutes. Transfer it to a cake pan. Mix in tomatoes along with juices and pasta sauce. Air Fry for 8 minutes. Scatter with Parmesan and basil. Serve.

Spring Chicken Salad

Servings: 4
Cooking Time: 25 Minutes
Ingredients:
- 3 chicken breasts, cubed
- 1 small red onion, sliced
- 1 red bell pepper, sliced
- 1 cup green beans, sliced
- 2 tbsp ranch salad dressing
- 2 tbsp lemon juice
- ½ tsp dried basil
- 10 oz spring mix

Directions:
1. Preheat air fryer to 400°F. Put the chicken, red onion, red bell pepper, and green beans in the frying basket and Roast for 10-13 minutes until the chicken is cooked through. Shake the basket at least once while cooking. As the chicken is cooking, combine the ranch dressing, lemon juice, and basil. When the chicken is done, remove it and along with the veggies to a bowl and pour the dressing over. Stir to coat. Serve with spring mix.

Spinach And Feta Stuffed Chicken Breasts

Servings: 4
Cooking Time: 27 Minutes
Ingredients:
- 1 (10-ounce) package frozen spinach, thawed and drained well
- 1 cup feta cheese, crumbled
- ½ teaspoon freshly ground black pepper
- 4 boneless chicken breasts
- salt and freshly ground black pepper
- 1 tablespoon olive oil

Directions:
1. Prepare the filling. Squeeze out as much liquid as possible from the thawed spinach. Rough chop the spinach and transfer it to a mixing bowl with the feta cheese and the freshly ground black pepper.
2. Prepare the chicken breast. Place the chicken breast on a cutting board and press down on the chicken breast with one hand to keep it stabilized. Make an incision about 1-inch long in the fattest side of the breast. Move the knife up and down inside the chicken breast, without poking through either the top or the bottom, or the other side of the breast. The inside pocket should be about 3-inches long, but the opening should only be about 1-inch wide. If this is too difficult, you can make the incision longer, but you will have to be more careful when cooking the chicken breast since this will expose more of the stuffing.
3. Once you have prepared the chicken breasts, use your fingers to stuff the filling into each pocket, spreading the mixture down as far as you can.
4. Preheat the air fryer to 380°F.
5. Lightly brush or spray the air fryer basket and the chicken breasts with olive oil. Transfer two of the stuffed chicken breasts to the air fryer. Air-fry for 12 minutes, turning the chicken breasts over halfway through the cooking time. Remove the chicken to a resting plate and air-fry the second two breasts for 12 minutes. Return the first batch of chicken to the air fryer with the second batch and air-fry for 3 more minutes. When the chicken is cooked, an instant read thermometer should register 165°F in the thickest part of the chicken, as well as in the stuffing.
6. Remove the chicken breasts and let them rest on a cutting board for 2 to 3 minutes. Slice the chicken on the bias and serve with the slices fanned out.

Crispy "fried" Chicken

Servings: 4
Cooking Time: 14 Minutes
Ingredients:
- ¾ cup all-purpose flour
- ½ teaspoon paprika
- ¼ teaspoon black pepper
- ¼ teaspoon salt
- 2 large eggs
- 1½ cups panko breadcrumbs
- 1 pound boneless, skinless chicken tenders

Directions:
1. Preheat the air fryer to 400°F.
2. In a shallow bowl, mix the flour with the paprika, pepper, and salt.
3. In a separate bowl, whisk the eggs; set aside.
4. In a third bowl, place the breadcrumbs.
5. Liberally spray the air fryer basket with olive oil spray.
6. Pat the chicken tenders dry with a paper towel. Dredge the tenders one at a time in the flour, then dip them in the egg, and toss them in the breadcrumb coating. Repeat until all tenders are coated.
7. Set each tender in the air fryer, leaving room on each side of the tender to allow for flipping.
8. When the basket is full, cook 4 to 7 minutes, flip, and cook another 4 to 7 minutes.
9. Remove the tenders and let cool 5 minutes before serving. Repeat until all tenders are cooked.

Peachy Chicken Chunks With Cherries

Servings: 4
Cooking Time: 16 Minutes
Ingredients:
- ⅓ cup peach preserves
- 1 teaspoon ground rosemary
- ½ teaspoon black pepper
- ½ teaspoon salt
- ½ teaspoon marjoram
- 1 teaspoon light olive oil
- 1 pound boneless chicken breasts, cut in 1½-inch chunks
- oil for misting or cooking spray
- 10-ounce package frozen unsweetened dark cherries, thawed and drained

Directions:
1. In a medium bowl, mix together peach preserves, rosemary, pepper, salt, marjoram, and olive oil.
2. Stir in chicken chunks and toss to coat well with the preserve mixture.
3. Spray air fryer basket with oil or cooking spray and lay chicken chunks in basket.
4. Cook at 390°F for 7minutes. Stir. Cook for 8 more minutes or until chicken juices run clear.
5. When chicken has cooked through, scatter the cherries over and cook for additional minute to heat cherries.

Spiced Mexican Stir-fried Chicken

Servings: 4
Cooking Time: 30 Minutes
Ingredients:
- 1 lb chicken breasts, cubed
- 2 green onions, chopped
- 1 red bell pepper, chopped
- 1 jalapeño pepper, minced
- 2 tsp olive oil
- 2/3 cup canned black beans
- ½ cup salsa

- 2 tsp Mexican chili powder

Directions:
1. Preheat air fryer to 400°F. Combine the chicken, green onions, bell pepper, jalapeño, and olive oil in a bowl. Transfer to a bowl to the frying basket and Air Fry for 10 minutes, stirring once during cooking. When done, stir in the black beans, salsa, and chili powder. Air Fry for 7-10 minutes or until cooked through. Serve.

Cornish Hens With Honey-lime Glaze

Servings: 2
Cooking Time: 30 Minutes
Ingredients:
- 1 Cornish game hen (1½–2 pounds)
- 1 tablespoon honey
- 1 tablespoon lime juice
- 1 teaspoon poultry seasoning
- salt and pepper
- cooking spray

Directions:
1. To split the hen into halves, cut through breast bone and down one side of the backbone.
2. Mix the honey, lime juice, and poultry seasoning together and brush or rub onto all sides of the hen. Season to taste with salt and pepper.
3. Spray air fryer basket with cooking spray and place hen halves in the basket, skin-side down.
4. Cook at 330°F for 30 minutes. Hen will be done when juices run clear when pierced at leg joint with a fork. Let hen rest for 5 to 10minutes before cutting.

Buttery Chicken Legs

Servings:4
Cooking Time: 50 Minutes
Ingredients:
- 1 tsp baking powder
- 1 tsp dried mustard
- 1 tsp smoked paprika
- 1 tsp garlic powder
- 1 tsp dried thyme
- Salt and pepper to taste
- 1 ½ lb chicken legs
- 3 tbsp butter, melted

Directions:
1. Preheat air fryer to 370°F. Combine all ingredients, except for butter, in a bowl until coated. Place the chicken legs in the greased frying basket. Air Fry for 18 minutes, flipping once and brushing with melted butter on both sides. Let chill onto a serving plate for 5 minutes before serving.

Sweet Nutty Chicken Breasts

Servings:4
Cooking Time: 30 Minutes
Ingredients:
- 2 chicken breasts, halved lengthwise
- ¼ cup honey mustard
- ¼ cup chopped pecans
- 1 tbsp olive oil
- 1 tbsp parsley, chopped

Directions:
1. Preheat air fryer to 350°F. Brush chicken breasts with honey mustard and olive oil on all sides. Place the pecans in a bowl. Add and coat the chicken breasts. Place the breasts in the greased frying basket and Air Fry for 25 minutes, turning once. Let chill onto a serving plate for 5 minutes. Sprinkle with parsley and serve.

Ranch Chicken Tortillas

Servings: 4
Cooking Time: 35 Minutes
Ingredients:
- 2 chicken breasts
- 1 tbsp Ranch seasoning
- 1 tbsp taco seasoning
- 1 cup flour
- 1 egg
- ½ cup bread crumbs
- 4 flour tortillas
- 1 ½ cups shredded lettuce
- 3 tbsp ranch dressing
- 2 tbsp cilantro, chopped

Directions:
1. Preheat air fryer to 370°F. Slice the chicken breasts into cutlets by cutting in half horizontally on a cutting board. Rub with ranch and taco seasonings. In one shallow bowl, add flour. In another shallow bowl, beat the egg. In the third shallow bowl, add bread crumbs.
2. Lightly spray the air fryer basket with cooking oil. First, dip the cutlet in the flour, dredge in egg, and then finish by coating with bread crumbs. Place the cutlets in the fryer and Bake for 6-8 minutes. Flip them and cook further for 4 minutes until crisp. Allow the chicken to cook for a few minutes, then cut into strips. Divide into 4 equal portions along with shredded lettuce, ranch dressing, cilantro and tortillas. Serve and enjoy!

Intense Buffalo Chicken Wings

Servings: 2
Cooking Time: 40 Minutes
Ingredients:
- 8 chicken wings
- ½ cup melted butter
- 2 tbsp Tabasco sauce
- ½ tbsp lemon juice
- 1 tbsp Worcestershire sauce
- 2 tsp cayenne pepper
- 1 tsp garlic powder
- 1 tsp lemon zest
- Salt and pepper to taste

Directions:
1. Preheat air fryer to 350°F. Place the melted butter, Tabasco, lemon juice, Worcestershire sauce, cayenne, garlic powder, lemon zest, salt, and pepper in a bowl and stir to combine. Dip

the chicken wings into the mixture, coating thoroughly. Lay the coated chicken wings on the foil-lined frying basket in an even layer. Air Fry for 16-18 minutes. Shake the basket several times during cooking until the chicken wings are crispy brown. Serve.

Mushroom & Turkey Bread Pizza

Servings: 4
Cooking Time: 35 Minutes
Ingredients:
- 10 cooked turkey sausages, sliced
- 1 cup shredded mozzarella cheese
- 1 cup shredded Cheddar cheese
- 1 French loaf bread
- 2 tbsp butter, softened
- 1 tsp garlic powder
- 1 1/3 cups marinara sauce
- 1 tsp Italian seasoning
- 2 scallions, chopped
- 1 cup mushrooms, sliced

Directions:
1. Preheat the air fryer to 370°F. Cut the bread in half crosswise, then split each half horizontally. Combine butter and garlic powder, then spread on the cut sides of the bread. Bake the halves in the fryer for 3-5 minutes or until the leaves start to brown. Set the toasted bread on a work surface and spread marinara sauce over the top. Sprinkle the Italian seasoning, then top with sausages, scallions, mushrooms, and cheeses. Set the pizzas in the air fryer and Bake for 8-12 minutes or until the cheese is melted and starting to brown. Serve hot.

Chicken Breasts Wrapped In Bacon

Servings: 4
Cooking Time: 35 Minutes
Ingredients:
- ¼ cup mayonnaise
- ¼ cup sour cream
- 3 tbsp ketchup
- 1 tbsp yellow mustard
- 1 tbsp light brown sugar
- 1 lb chicken tenders
- 1 tsp dried parsley
- 8 bacon slices

Directions:
1. Preheat the air fryer to 370°F. Combine the mayonnaise, sour cream, ketchup, mustard, and brown sugar in a bowl and mix well, then set aside. Sprinkle the chicken with the parsley and wrap each one in a slice of bacon. Put the wrapped chicken in the frying basket in a single layer and Air Fry for 18-20 minutes, flipping once until the bacon is crisp. Serve with sauce.

German Chicken Frikadellen

Servings: 6
Cooking Time: 20 Minutes
Ingredients:
- 1 lb ground chicken
- 1 egg
- ¾ cup bread crumbs
- ¼ cup diced onions
- 1 grated carrot
- 1 tsp yellow mustard
- Salt and pepper to taste
- ¼ cup chopped parsley

Directions:
1. Preheat air fryer at 350ºF. In a bowl, combine the ground chicken, egg, crumbs, onions, carrot, parsley, salt, and pepper. Mix well with your hands. Form mixture into meatballs. Place them in the frying basket and Air Fry for 8-10 minutes, tossing once until golden. Serve right away.

Cheesy Chicken-avocado Paninis

Servings: 2
Cooking Time: 25 Minutes
Ingredients:
- 2 tbsp mayonnaise
- 4 tsp yellow mustard
- 4 sandwich bread slices
- 4 oz sliced deli chicken ham
- 2 oz sliced provolone cheese
- 2 oz sliced mozzarella
- 1 avocado, sliced
- 1 tomato, sliced
- Salt and pepper to taste
- 1 tsp sesame seeds
- 2 tbsp butter, melted

Directions:
1. Preheat air fryer at 350ºF. Rub mayonnaise and mustard on the inside of each bread slice. Top 2 bread slices with chicken ham, provolone and mozzarella cheese, avocado, sesame seeds, and tomato slices. Season with salt and pepper. Then, close sandwiches with the remaining bread slices. Brush the top and bottom of each sandwich lightly with melted butter. Place sandwiches in the frying basket and Bake for 6 minutes, flipping once. Serve.

Indian-inspired Chicken Skewers

Servings: 4
Cooking Time: 40 Minutes + Chilling Time
Ingredients:
- 1 lb boneless, skinless chicken thighs, cubed
- 1 red onion, diced
- 1 tbsp grated ginger
- 2 tbsp lime juice
- 1 cup canned coconut milk
- 2 tbsp tomato paste
- 2 tbsp olive oil
- 1 tbsp ground cumin
- 1 tbsp ground coriander
- 1 tsp cayenne pepper
- 1 tsp ground turmeric
- ½ tsp red chili powder
- ¼ tsp curry powder

- 2 tsp salt
- 2 tbsp chopped cilantro

Directions:
1. Toss red onion, ginger, lime juice, coconut milk, tomato paste, olive oil, cumin, coriander, cayenne pepper, turmeric, chili powder, curry powder, salt, and chicken until fully coated. Let chill in the fridge for 2 hours.
2. Preheat air fryer to 350°F. Thread chicken onto 8 skewers and place them on a kebab rack. Place rack in the frying basket and Air Fry for 12 minutes. Discard marinade. Garnish with cilantro to serve.

Party Buffalo Chicken Drumettes

Servings: 6
Cooking Time: 30 Minutes
Ingredients:
- 16 chicken drumettes
- 1 tsp garlic powder
- 1 tbsp chicken seasoning
- Black pepper to taste
- ¼ cup Buffalo wings sauce
- 2 spring onions, sliced

Directions:
1. Preheat air fryer to 400°F. Sprinkle garlic, chicken seasoning, and black pepper on the drumettes. Place them in the fryer and spray with cooking oil. Air Fry for 10 minutes, shaking the basket once. Transfer the drumettes to a large bowl. Drizzle with Buffalo wing sauce and toss to coat. Place in the fryer and Fry for 7-8 minutes, until crispy. Allow to cool slightly. Top with spring onions and serve warm.

Mumbai Chicken Nuggets

Servings: 4
Cooking Time: 30 Minutes
Ingredients:
- 1 lb boneless, skinless chicken breasts
- 4 tsp curry powder
- Salt and pepper to taste
- 1 egg, beaten
- 2 tbsp sesame oil
- 1 cup panko bread crumbs
- ½ cup coconut yogurt
- 1/3 cup mango chutney
- ¼ cup mayonnaise

Directions:
1. Preheat the air fryer to 400°F. Cube the chicken into 1-inch pieces and sprinkle with 3 tsp of curry powder, salt, and pepper; toss to coat. Beat together the egg and sesame oil in a shallow bowl and scatter the panko onto a separate plate. Dip the chicken in the egg, then in the panko, and press to coat. Lay the coated nuggets on a wire rack as you work. Set the nuggets in the greased frying basket and Air Fry for 7-10 minutes, rearranging once halfway through cooking. While the nuggets are cooking, combine the yogurt, chutney, mayonnaise, and the remaining teaspoon of curry powder in a small bowl. Serve the nuggets with the dipping sauce.

Greek Gyros With Chicken & Rice

Servings: 4
Cooking Time: 25 Minutes
Ingredients:
- 1 lb chicken breasts, cubed
- ¼ cup cream cheese
- 2 tbsp olive oil
- 1 tsp dried oregano
- 1 tsp ground cumin
- 1 tsp ground cinnamon
- ¼ tsp ground nutmeg
- Salt and pepper to taste
- ¼ tsp ground turmeric
- 2 cups cooked rice
- 1 cup Tzatziki sauce

Directions:
1. Preheat air fryer to 380°F. Put all ingredients in a bowl and mix together until the chicken is coated well. Spread the chicken mixture in the frying basket, then Bake for 10 minutes. Stir the chicken mixture and Bake for an additional 5 minutes. Serve with rice and tzatziki sauce.

Cantonese Chicken Drumsticks

Servings: 4
Cooking Time: 30 Minutes
Ingredients:
- 3 tbsp lime juice
- 3 tbsp oyster sauce
- 6 chicken drumsticks
- 1 tbsp peanut oil
- 3 tbsp honey
- 3 tbsp brown sugar
- 2 tbsp ketchup
- ¼ cup pineapple juice

Directions:
1. Preheat air fryer to 350°F. Drizzle some lime juice and oyster sauce on the drumsticks. Transfer to the frying basket and drizzle with peanut oil. Shake the basket to coat. Bake for 18 minutes until the drumsticks are almost done.
2. Meanwhile, combine the rest of the lime juice and the oyster sauce along with the honey, sugar, ketchup and pineapple juice in a 6-inch metal bowl. When the chicken is done, transfer to the bowl and coat the chicken with the sauce. Put the metal bowl in the basket and cook for 5-7 minutes, turning halfway, until golden and cooked through. Serve and enjoy!

Rich Turkey Burgers

Servings: 4
Cooking Time: 30 Minutes
Ingredients:
- 2 tbsp finely grated Emmental
- 1/3 cup minced onions
- ¼ cup grated carrots
- 2 garlic cloves, minced
- 2 tsp olive oil
- 1 tsp dried marjoram
- 1 egg
- 1 lb ground turkey

Directions:
1. Preheat air fryer to 400°F. Mix the onions, carrots, garlic, olive oil, marjoram, Emmental, and egg in a bowl, then add the ground turkey. Use your hands to mix the ingredients together. Form the mixture into 4 patties. Set them in the air fryer and Air Fry for 18-20 minutes, flipping once until cooked through and golden. Serve.

Fancy Chicken Piccata

Servings: 4
Cooking Time: 30 Minutes
Ingredients:
- 1 lb chicken breasts, cut into cutlets
- Salt and pepper to taste
- 2 egg whites
- 2/3 cup bread crumbs
- 1 tsp Italian seasoning
- 1 tbsp whipped butter
- ½ cup chicken broth
- ½ onion powder
- ¼ cup fino sherry
- Juice of 1 lemon
- 1 tbsp capers, drained
- 1 lemon, sliced
- 2 tbsp chopped parsley

Directions:
1. Preheat air fryer to 370°F. Place the cutlets between two sheets of parchment paper. Pound to a ¼-inch thickness and season with salt and pepper. Beat egg whites with 1 tsp of water in a bowl. Put the bread crumbs, Parmesan cheese, onion powder, and Italian seasoning in a second bowl. Dip the cutlet in the egg bowl, and then in the crumb mix. Put the cutlets in the greased frying basket. Air Fry for 6 minutes, flipping once until crispy and golden.
2. Melt butter in a skillet. Stir in broth, sherry, lemon juice, lemon halves, and black pepper. Bring to a boil over high heat until the sauce is reduced by half, 4 minutes. Remove from heat. Pick out the lemon rinds and discard them. Stir in capers. Plate a cutlet, spoon some sauce over and garnish with lemon sleeves and parsley to serve.

Tuscan Stuffed Chicken

Servings: 4
Cooking Time: 30 Minutes
Ingredients:
- 1/3 cup ricotta cheese
- 1 cup Tuscan kale, chopped
- 4 chicken breasts
- 1 tbsp chicken seasoning
- Salt and pepper to taste
- 1 tsp paprika

Directions:
1. Preheat air fryer to 370°F. Soften the ricotta cheese in a microwave-safe bowl for 15 seconds. Combine in a bowl along with Tuscan kale. Set aside. Cut 4-5 slits in the top of each chicken breast about ¾ of the way down. Season with chicken seasoning, salt, and pepper.
2. Place the chicken with the slits facing up in the greased frying basket. Lightly spray the chicken with oil. Bake for 6-8 minutes. Slide-out and stuff the cream cheese mixture into the chicken slits. Sprinkle ½ tsp of paprika and cook for another 3 minutes. Serve and enjoy!

Maewoon Chicken Legs

Servings: 4
Cooking Time: 30 Minutes + Chilling Time
Ingredients:
- 4 scallions, sliced, whites and greens separated
- ¼ cup tamari
- 2 tbsp sesame oil
- 1 tsp sesame seeds
- ¼ cup honey
- 2 tbsp gochujang
- 2 tbsp ketchup
- 4 cloves garlic, minced
- ½ tsp ground ginger
- Salt and pepper to taste
- 1 tbsp parsley
- 1 ½ lb chicken legs

Directions:
1. Whisk all ingredients, except chicken and scallion greens, in a bowl. Reserve ¼ cup of marinade. Toss chicken legs in the remaining marinade and chill for 30 minutes.
2. Preheat air fryer at 400°F. Place chicken legs in the greased frying basket and Air Fry for 10 minutes. Turn chicken. Cook for 8 more minutes. Let sit in a serving dish for 5 minutes. Coat the cooked chicken with the reserved marinade and scatter with scallion greens, sesame seeds and parsley to serve.

Indian Chicken Tandoori

Servings: 2
Cooking Time: 35 Minutes
Ingredients:
- 2 chicken breasts, cubed
- ½ cup hung curd
- 1 tsp turmeric powder
- 1 tsp red chili powder
- 1 tsp chaat masala powder
- Pinch of salt

Directions:
1. Preheat air fryer to 350°F. Mix the hung curd, turmeric, red chili powder, chaat masala powder, and salt in a mixing bowl. Stir until the mixture is free of lumps. Coat the chicken with the mixture, cover, and refrigerate for 30 minutes to marinate. Place the marinated chicken chunks in a baking pan and drizzle with the remaining marinade. Bake for 25 minutes until the chicken is juicy and spiced. Serve warm.

Farmer's Fried Chicken

Servings: 4
Cooking Time: 55 Minutes
Ingredients:
- 3 lb whole chicken, cut into breasts, drumsticks, and thighs
- 2 cups flour
- 4 tsp salt
- 4 tsp dried basil
- 4 tsp dried thyme
- 2 tsp dried shallot powder
- 2 tsp smoked paprika
- 1 tsp mustard powder
- 1 tsp celery salt
- 1 cup kefir
- ¼ cup honey

Directions:
1. Preheat the air fryer to 370°F. Combine the flour, salt, basil, thyme, shallot, paprika, mustard powder, and celery salt in a bowl. Pour into a glass jar. Mix the kefir and honey in a large bowl and add the chicken, stir to coat. Marinate for 15 minutes at room temperature. Remove the chicken from the kefir mixture; discard the rest. Put 2/3 cup of the flour mix onto a plate and dip the chicken. Shake gently and put on a wire rack for 10 minutes. Line the frying basket with round parchment paper with holes punched in it. Place the chicken in a single layer and spray with cooking oil. Air Fry for 18-25 minutes, flipping once around minute 10. Serve hot.

Coconut Chicken With Apricot-ginger Sauce

Servings: 4
Cooking Time: 8 Minutes Per Batch
Ingredients:
- 1½ pounds boneless, skinless chicken tenders, cut in large chunks (about 1¼ inches)
- salt and pepper
- ½ cup cornstarch
- 2 eggs
- 1 tablespoon milk
- 3 cups shredded coconut (see below)
- oil for misting or cooking spray
- Apricot-Ginger Sauce
- ½ cup apricot preserves
- 2 tablespoons white vinegar
- ¼ teaspoon ground ginger
- ¼ teaspoon low-sodium soy sauce
- 2 teaspoons white or yellow onion, grated or finely minced

Directions:
1. Mix all ingredients for the Apricot-Ginger Sauce well and let sit for flavors to blend while you cook the chicken.
2. Season chicken chunks with salt and pepper to taste.
3. Place cornstarch in a shallow dish.
4. In another shallow dish, beat together eggs and milk.
5. Place coconut in a third shallow dish. (If also using panko breadcrumbs, as suggested below, stir them to mix well.)
6. Spray air fryer basket with oil or cooking spray.
7. Dip each chicken chunk into cornstarch, shake off excess, and dip in egg mixture.
8. Shake off excess egg mixture and roll lightly in coconut or coconut mixture. Spray with oil.
9. Place coated chicken chunks in air fryer basket in a single layer, close together but without sides touching.
10. Cook at 360°F for 4minutes, stop, and turn chunks over.
11. Cook an additional 4 minutes or until chicken is done inside and coating is crispy brown.
12. Repeat steps 9 through 11 to cook remaining chicken chunks.

Satay Chicken Skewers

Servings: 4
Cooking Time: 35 Minutes
Ingredients:
- 2 chicken breasts, cut into strips
- 1 ½ tbsp Thai red curry paste
- ¼ cup peanut butter
- 1 tbsp maple syrup
- 1 tbsp tamari
- 1 tbsp lime juice
- 2 tsp chopped onions
- ¼ tsp minced ginger
- 1 clove garlic, minced
- 1 cup coconut milk
- 1 tsp fish sauce
- 1 tbsp chopped cilantro

Directions:
1. Mix the peanut butter, maple syrup, tamari, lime juice, ¼ tsp of sriracha, onions, ginger, garlic, and 2 tbsp of water in a bowl. Reserve 1 tbsp of the sauce. Set aside. Combine the reserved peanut sauce, fish sauce, coconut milk, Thai red curry paste, cilantro and chicken strips in a bowl and let marinate in the fridge for 15 minutes.
2. Preheat air fryer at 350ºF. Thread chicken strips onto skewers and place them on a kebab rack. Place rack in the frying basket and Air Fry for 12 minutes. Serve with previously prepared peanut sauce on the side.

Country Chicken Hoagies

Servings: 2
Cooking Time: 30 Minutes
Ingredients:
- ¼ cup button mushrooms, sliced
- 1 hoagie bun, halved
- 1 chicken breast, cubed
- ½ white onion, sliced
- 1 cup bell pepper strips
- 2 cheddar cheese slices

Directions:
1. Preheat air fryer to 320°F. Place the chicken pieces, onions, bell pepper strips, and mushroom slices on one side of the frying basket. Lay the hoagie bun halves, crusty side up and soft side down, on the other half of the air fryer. Bake for 10 minutes. Flip the hoagie buns and cover with cheddar cheese. Stir the chicken and vegetables. Cook for another 6 minutes until the cheese is melted and the chicken is juicy on the inside and crispy on the outside. Place the cheesy hoagie halves on a serving plate and cover one half with the chicken and veggies. Close with the other cheesy hoagie half. Serve.

Honey Lemon Thyme Glazed Cornish Hen

Servings: 2
Cooking Time: 20 Minutes
Ingredients:
- 1 (2-pound) Cornish game hen, split in half
- olive oil
- salt and freshly ground black pepper
- ¼ teaspoon dried thyme
- ¼ cup honey
- 1 tablespoon lemon zest
- juice of 1 lemon
- 1½ teaspoons chopped fresh thyme leaves
- ½ teaspoon soy sauce
- freshly ground black pepper

Directions:
1. Split the game hen in half by cutting down each side of the backbone and then cutting through the breast. Brush or spray both halves of the game hen with the olive oil and then season with the salt, pepper and dried thyme.
2. Preheat the air fryer to 390°F.
3. Place the game hen, skin side down, into the air fryer and air-fry for 5 minutes. Turn the hen halves over and air-fry for 10 minutes.
4. While the hen is cooking, combine the honey, lemon zest and juice, fresh thyme, soy sauce and pepper in a small bowl.
5. When the air fryer timer rings, brush the honey glaze onto the game hen and continue to air-fry for another 3 to 5 minutes, just until the hen is nicely glazed, browned and has an internal temperature of 165°F.
6. Let the hen rest for 5 minutes and serve warm.

Chicken Thighs In Salsa Verde

Servings: 4
Cooking Time: 35 Minutes
Ingredients:
- 4 boneless, skinless chicken thighs
- 1 cup salsa verde
- 1 tsp mashed garlic

Directions:
1. Preheat air fryer at 350°F. Add chicken thighs to a cake pan and cover with salsa verde and mashed garlic. Place cake pan in the frying basket and Bake for 30 minutes. Let rest for 5 minutes before serving.

Turkey Tenderloin With A Lemon Touch

Servings: 4
Cooking Time: 45 Minutes
Ingredients:
- 1 lb boneless, skinless turkey breast tenderloin
- Salt and pepper to taste
- ½ tsp garlic powder
- ½ tsp chili powder
- ½ tsp dried thyme
- 1 lemon, juiced
- 1 tbsp chopped cilantro

Directions:
1. Preheat air fryer to 350°F. Dry the turkey completely with a paper towel, then season with salt, pepper, garlic powder, chili powder, and thyme. Place the turkey in the frying basket. Squeeze the lemon juice over the turkey and bake for 10 minutes. Turn the turkey and bake for another 10 to 15 minutes. Allow to rest for 10 minutes before slicing. Serve sprinkled with cilantro and enjoy.

Cheesy Chicken Tenders

Servings: 4
Cooking Time: 25 Minutes
Ingredients:
- 1 cup grated Parmesan cheese
- ¼ cup grated cheddar
- 1 ¼ lb chicken tenders
- 1 egg, beaten
- 2 tbsp milk
- Salt and pepper to taste
- ½ tsp garlic powder
- 1 tsp dried thyme
- ¼ tsp shallot powder

Directions:
1. Preheat the air fryer to 400°F. Stir the egg and milk until combined. Mix the salt, pepper, garlic, thyme, shallot, cheddar cheese, and Parmesan cheese on a plate. Dip the chicken in the egg mix, then in the cheese mix, and press to coat. Lay the tenders in the frying basket in a single layer. Add a raised rack to cook more at one time. Spray all with oil and Bake for 12-16 minutes, flipping once halfway through cooking. Serve hot.

Yogurt-marinated Chicken Legs

Servings: 4
Cooking Time: 50 Minutes
Ingredients:
- 1 cup Greek yogurt
- 1 tbsp Dijon mustard
- 1 tsp smoked paprika
- 1 tbsp crushed red pepper
- 1 tsp garlic powder
- 1 tsp dried oregano
- 1 tsp dried thyme
- 1 teaspoon ground cumin
- ¼ cup lemon juice
- Salt and pepper to taste
- 1 ½ lb chicken legs
- 3 tbsp butter, melted

Directions:
1. Combine all ingredients, except chicken and butter, in a bowl. Fold in chicken legs and toss until coated. Let sit covered in the fridge for 60 minutes up to overnight.
2. Preheat air fryer at 375ºF. Shake excess marinade from chicken; place them in the greased frying basket and Air Fry for 18 minutes, brush melted butter and flip once. Let chill for 5 minutes before serving.

Cornflake Chicken Nuggets

Servings: 4
Cooking Time: 25 Minutes
Ingredients:
- 1 egg white
- 1 tbsp lemon juice
- ½ tsp dried basil
- ½ tsp ground paprika
- 1 lb chicken breast fingers
- ½ cup ground cornflakes
- 2 slices bread, crumbled

Directions:
1. Preheat air fryer to 400ºF. Whisk the egg white, lemon juice, basil, and paprika, then add the chicken and stir. Combine the cornflakes and breadcrumbs on a plate, then put the chicken fingers in the mix to coat. Put the nuggets in the frying basket and Air Fry for 10-13 minutes, turning halfway through, until golden, crisp and cooked through. Serve hot!

Chicken Wellington

Servings: 2
Cooking Time: 31 Minutes
Ingredients:
- 2 (5-ounce) boneless, skinless chicken breasts
- ½ cup White Worcestershire sauce
- 3 tablespoons butter
- ½ cup finely diced onion (about ½ onion)
- 8 ounces button mushrooms, finely chopped
- ¼ cup chicken stock
- 2 tablespoons White Worcestershire sauce (or white wine)
- salt and freshly ground black pepper
- 1 tablespoon chopped fresh tarragon
- 2 sheets puff pastry, thawed
- 1 egg, beaten
- vegetable oil

Directions:
1. Place the chicken breasts in a shallow dish. Pour the White Worcestershire sauce over the chicken coating both sides and marinate for 30 minutes.
2. While the chicken is marinating, melt the butter in a large skillet over medium-high heat on the stovetop. Add the onion and sauté for a few minutes, until it starts to soften. Add the mushrooms and sauté for 5 minutes until the vegetables are brown and soft. Deglaze the skillet with the chicken stock, scraping up any bits from the bottom of the pan. Add the White Worcestershire sauce and simmer for 3 minutes until the mixture reduces and starts to thicken. Season with salt and freshly ground black pepper. Remove the mushroom mixture from the heat and stir in the fresh tarragon. Let the mushroom mixture cool.
3. Preheat the air fryer to 360°F.
4. Remove the chicken from the marinade and transfer it to the air fryer basket. Tuck the small end of the chicken breast under the thicker part to shape it into a circle rather than an oval. Pour the marinade over the chicken and air-fry for 10 minutes.
5. Roll out the puff pastry and cut out two 6-inch squares. Brush the perimeter of each square with the egg wash. Place half of the mushroom mixture in the center of each puff pastry square. Place the chicken breasts, top side down on the mushroom mixture. Starting with one corner of puff pastry and working in one direction, pull the pastry up over the chicken to enclose it and press the ends of the pastry together in the middle. Brush the pastry with the egg wash to seal the edges. Turn the Wellingtons over and set aside.
6. To make a decorative design with the remaining puff pastry, cut out four 10-inch strips. For each Wellington, twist two of the strips together, place them over the chicken breast wrapped in puff pastry, and tuck the ends underneath to seal it. Brush the entire top and sides of the Wellingtons with the egg wash.
7. Preheat the air fryer to 350°F.
8. Spray or brush the air fryer basket with vegetable oil. Air-fry the chicken Wellingtons for 13 minutes. Carefully turn the Wellingtons over. Air-fry for another 8 minutes. Transfer to serving plates, light a candle and enjoy!

Asian-style Orange Chicken

Servings: 4
Cooking Time: 25 Minutes
Ingredients:
- 1 lb chicken breasts, cubed
- Salt and pepper to taste
- 6 tbsp cornstarch
- 1 cup orange juice
- ¼ cup orange marmalade
- ¼ cup ketchup
- ½ tsp ground ginger

- 2 tbsp soy sauce
- 1 1/3 cups edamame beans

Directions:
1. Preheat the air fryer to 375°F. Sprinkle the cubes with salt and pepper. Coat with 4 tbsp of cornstarch and set aside on a wire rack. Mix the orange juice, marmalade, ketchup, ginger, soy sauce, and the remaining cornstarch in a cake pan, then stir in the beans. Set the pan in the frying basket and Bake for 5-8 minutes, stirring once during cooking until the sauce is thick and bubbling. Remove from the fryer and set aside. Put the chicken in the frying basket and fry for 10-12 minutes, shaking the basket once. Stir the chicken into the sauce and beans in the pan. Return to the fryer and reheat for 2 minutes.

Super-simple Herby Turkey

Servings: 4
Cooking Time: 35 Minutes

Ingredients:
- 2 turkey tenderloins
- 2 tbsp olive oil
- Salt and pepper to taste
- 2 tbsp minced rosemary
- 1 tbsp minced thyme
- 1 tbsp minced sage

Directions:
1. Preheat the air fryer to 350°F. Brush the tenderloins with olive oil and sprinkle with salt and pepper. Mix rosemary, thyme, and sage, then rub the seasoning onto the meat. Put the tenderloins in the frying basket and Bake for 22-27 minutes, flipping once until cooked through. Lay the turkey on a serving plate, cover with foil, and let stand for 5 minutes. Slice before serving.

Chapter 6 Fish And Seafood Recipes

Cheesy Salmon-stuffed Avocados

Servings: 2
Cooking Time: 20 Minutes

Ingredients:
- ¼ cup apple cider vinegar
- 1 tsp granular sugar
- ¼ cup sliced red onions
- 2 oz cream cheese, softened
- 1 tbsp capers
- 2 halved avocados, pitted
- 4 oz smoked salmon
- ¼ tsp dried dill
- 2 cherry tomatoes, halved
- 1 tbsp cilantro, chopped

Directions:
1. Warm apple vinegar and sugar in a saucepan over medium heat and simmer for 4 minutes until boiling. Add in onion and turn the heat off. Let sit until ready to use. Drain before using. In a small bowl, combine cream cheese and capers. Let chill in the fridge until ready to use.
2. Preheat air fryer to 350ºF. Place avocado halves, cut sides-up, in the frying basket, and Air Fry for 4 minutes. Transfer avocado halves to 2 plates. Top with cream cheese mixture, smoked salmon, dill, red onions, tomato halves and cilantro. Serve immediately.

Garlic-butter Lobster Tails

Servings: 2
Cooking Time: 20 Minutes

Ingredients:
- 2 lobster tails
- 1 tbsp butter, melted
- ½ tsp Old Bay Seasoning
- ½ tsp garlic powder
- 1 tbsp chopped parsley
- 2 lemon wedges

Directions:
1. Preheat air fryer to 400ºF. Using kitchen shears, cut down the middle of each lobster tail on the softer side. Carefully run your finger between the lobster meat and the shell to loosen the meat. Place lobster tails in the frying basket, cut sides up, and Air Fry for 4 minutes. Rub with butter, garlic powder and Old Bay seasoning and cook for 4 more minutes. Garnish with parsley and lemon wedges. Serve and enjoy!

Creole Tilapia With Garlic Mayo

Servings: 4
Cooking Time: 20 Minutes

Ingredients:
- 4 tilapia fillets
- 2 tbsp olive oil
- 1 tsp paprika
- 1 tsp garlic powder
- 1 tsp dried basil
- ½ tsp Creole seasoning
- ½ tsp chili powder
- 2 garlic cloves, minced
- 1 tbsp mayonnaise
- 1 tsp olive oil
- ½ lemon, juiced

- Salt and pepper to taste

Directions:
1. Preheat air fryer to 400°F. Coat the tilapia with some olive oil, then season with paprika, garlic powder, basil, and Creole seasoning. Bake in the greased frying basket for 15 minutes, flipping once during cooking.
2. While the fish is cooking, whisk together garlic, mayonnaise, olive oil, lemon juice, chili powder, salt and pepper in a bowl. Serve the cooked fish with the aioli.

Easy Scallops With Lemon Butter

Servings: 3
Cooking Time: 4 Minutes

Ingredients:
- 1 tablespoon Olive oil
- 2 teaspoons Minced garlic
- 1 teaspoon Finely grated lemon zest
- ½ teaspoon Red pepper flakes
- ¼ teaspoon Table salt
- 1 pound Sea scallops
- 3 tablespoons Butter, melted
- 1½ tablespoons Lemon juice

Directions:
1. Preheat the air fryer to 400°F.
2. Gently stir the olive oil, garlic, lemon zest, red pepper flakes, and salt in a bowl. Add the scallops and stir very gently until they are evenly and well coated.
3. When the machine is at temperature, arrange the scallops in a single layer in the basket. Some may touch. Air-fry undisturbed for 4 minutes, or until the scallops are opaque and firm.
4. While the scallops cook, stir the melted butter and lemon juice in a serving bowl. When the scallops are ready, pour them from the basket into this bowl. Toss well before serving.

Crab Cakes

Servings: 2
Cooking Time: 10 Minutes

Ingredients:
- 1 teaspoon butter
- ⅓ cup finely diced onion
- ⅓ cup finely diced celery
- ¼ cup mayonnaise
- 1 teaspoon Dijon mustard
- 1 egg
- pinch ground cayenne pepper
- 1 teaspoon salt
- freshly ground black pepper
- 16 ounces lump crabmeat
- ½ cup + 2 tablespoons panko breadcrumbs, divided

Directions:
1. Melt the butter in a skillet over medium heat. Sauté the onion and celery until it starts to soften, but not brown – about 4 minutes. Transfer the cooked vegetables to a large bowl. Add the mayonnaise, Dijon mustard, egg, cayenne pepper, salt and freshly ground black pepper to the bowl. Gently fold in the lump crabmeat and 2 tablespoons of panko breadcrumbs. Stir carefully so you don't break up all the crab pieces.
2. Preheat the air fryer to 400°F.
3. Place the remaining panko breadcrumbs in a shallow dish. Divide the crab mixture into 4 portions and shape each portion into a round patty. Dredge the crab patties in the breadcrumbs, coating both sides as well as the edges with the crumbs.
4. Air-fry the crab cakes for 5 minutes. Using a flat spatula, gently turn the cakes over and air-fry for another 5 minutes. Serve the crab cakes with tartar sauce or cocktail sauce, or dress it up with the suggestion below.

Fish Sticks For Grown-ups

Servings: 4
Cooking Time: 6 Minutes

Ingredients:
- 1 pound fish fillets
- ½ teaspoon hot sauce
- 1 tablespoon coarse brown mustard
- 1 teaspoon Worcestershire sauce
- salt
- Crumb Coating
- ¾ cup panko breadcrumbs
- ¼ cup stone-ground cornmeal
- ¼ teaspoon salt
- oil for misting or cooking spray

Directions:
1. Cut fish fillets crosswise into slices 1-inch wide.
2. Mix the hot sauce, mustard, and Worcestershire sauce together to make a paste and rub on all sides of the fish. Season to taste with salt.
3. Mix crumb coating ingredients together and spread on a sheet of wax paper.
4. Roll the fish fillets in the crumb mixture.
5. Spray all sides with olive oil or cooking spray and place in air fryer basket in a single layer.
6. Cook at 390°F for 6 minutes, until fish flakes easily.

Miso-rubbed Salmon Fillets

Servings: 3
Cooking Time: 5 Minutes

Ingredients:
- ¼ cup White (shiro) miso paste (usually made from rice and soy beans)
- 1½ tablespoons Mirin or a substitute (see here)
- 2½ teaspoons Unseasoned rice vinegar (see here)
- Vegetable oil spray
- 3 6-ounce skin-on salmon fillets (for more information, see here)

Directions:
1. Preheat the air fryer to 400°F.
2. Mix the miso, mirin, and vinegar in a small bowl until uniform.
3. Remove the basket from the machine. Generously spray the skin side of each fillet. Pick them up one by one with a nonstick-safe spatula and set them in the basket skin side down

with as much air space between them as possible. Coat the top of each fillet with the miso mixture, dividing it evenly between them.
4. Return the basket to the machine. Air-fry undisturbed for 5 minutes, or until lightly browned and firm.
5. Use a nonstick-safe spatula to transfer the fillets to serving plates. Cool for only a minute or so before serving.

Salmon Puttanesca En Papillotte With Zucchini

Servings: 2
Cooking Time: 17 Minutes
Ingredients:
- 1 small zucchini, sliced into ¼-inch thick half moons
- 1 teaspoon olive oil
- salt and freshly ground black pepper
- 2 (5-ounce) salmon fillets
- 1 beefsteak tomato, chopped (about 1 cup)
- 1 tablespoon capers, rinsed
- 10 black olives, pitted and sliced
- 2 tablespoons dry vermouth or white wine 2 tablespoons butter
- ¼ cup chopped fresh basil, chopped

Directions:
1. Preheat the air fryer to 400°F.
2. Toss the zucchini with the olive oil, salt and freshly ground black pepper. Transfer the zucchini into the air fryer basket and air-fry for 5 minutes, shaking the basket once or twice during the cooking process.
3. Cut out 2 large rectangles of parchment paper – about 13-inches by 15-inches each. Divide the air-fried zucchini between the two pieces of parchment paper, placing the vegetables in the center of each rectangle.
4. Place a fillet of salmon on each pile of zucchini. Season the fish very well with salt and pepper. Toss the tomato, capers, olives and vermouth (or white wine) together in a bowl. Divide the tomato mixture between the two fish packages, placing it on top of the fish fillets and pouring any juice out of the bowl onto the fish. Top each fillet with a tablespoon of butter.
5. Fold up each parchment square. Bring two edges together and fold them over a few times, leaving some space above the fish. Twist the open sides together and upwards so they can serve as handles for the packet, but don't let them extend beyond the top of the air fryer basket.
6. Place the two packages into the air fryer and air-fry at 400°F for 12 minutes. The packages should be puffed up and slightly browned when fully cooked. Once cooked, let the fish sit in the parchment for 2 minutes.
7. Serve the fish in the parchment paper, or if desired, remove the parchment paper before serving. Garnish with a little fresh basil.

Salmon Croquettes

Servings: 4
Cooking Time: 8 Minutes
Ingredients:
- 1 tablespoon oil
- ½ cup breadcrumbs
- 1 14.75-ounce can salmon, drained and all skin and fat removed
- 1 egg, beaten
- ⅓ cup coarsely crushed saltine crackers (about 8 crackers)
- ½ teaspoon Old Bay Seasoning
- ½ teaspoon onion powder
- ½ teaspoon Worcestershire sauce

Directions:
1. Preheat air fryer to 390°F.
2. In a shallow dish, mix oil and breadcrumbs until crumbly.
3. In a large bowl, combine the salmon, egg, cracker crumbs, Old Bay, onion powder, and Worcestershire. Mix well and shape into 8 small patties about ½-inch thick.
4. Gently dip each patty into breadcrumb mixture and turn to coat well on all sides.
5. Cook at 390°F for 8minutes or until outside is crispy and browned.

Rich Salmon Burgers With Broccoli Slaw

Servings: 4
Cooking Time: 25 Minutes
Ingredients:
- 1 lb salmon fillets
- 1 egg
- ¼ cup dill, chopped
- 1 cup bread crumbs
- Salt to taste
- ½ tsp cayenne pepper
- 1 lime, zested
- 1 tsp fish sauce
- 4 buns
- 3 cups chopped broccoli
- ½ cup shredded carrots
- ¼ cup sunflower seeds
- 2 garlic cloves, minced
- 1 cup Greek yogurt

Directions:
1. Preheat air fryer to 360°F. Blitz the salmon fillets in your food processor until they are finely chopped. Remove to a large bowl and add egg, dill, bread crumbs, salt, and cayenne. Stir to combine. Form the mixture into 4 patties. Put them into the frying basket and Bake for 10 minutes, flipping once. Combine broccoli, carrots, sunflower seeds, garlic, salt, lime, fish sauce, and Greek yogurt in a bowl. Serve the salmon burgers onto buns with broccoli slaw. Enjoy!

Salty German-style Shrimp Pancakes

Servings: 4
Cooking Time: 15 Minutes
Ingredients:
- 1 tbsp butter
- 3 eggs, beaten
- ½ cup flour
- ½ cup milk
- ⅛ tsp salt
- 1 cup salsa
- 1 cup cooked shrimp, minced
- 2 tbsp cilantro, chopped

Directions:
1. Preheat air fryer to 390°F. Mix the eggs, flour, milk, and salt in a bowl until frothy. Pour the batter into a greased baking pan and place in the air fryer. Bake for 15 minutes or until the pancake is puffed and golden. Flip the pancake onto a plate. Mix salsa, shrimp, and cilantro. Top the pancake and serve.

Crispy Fish Sandwiches

Servings: 4
Cooking Time: 25 Minutes
Ingredients:
- ½ cup torn iceberg lettuce
- ½ cup mayonnaise
- 1 tbsp Dijon mustard
- ½ cup diced dill pickles
- 1 tsp capers
- 1 tsp tarragon
- 1 tsp dill
- Salt and pepper to taste
- 1/3 cup flour
- 2 tbsp cornstarch
- 1 tsp smoked paprika
- ¼ cup milk
- 1 egg
- ½ cup bread crumbs
- 4 cod fillets, cut in half
- 1 vine-ripe tomato, sliced
- 4 hamburger buns

Directions:
1. Mix the mayonnaise, mustard, pickles, capers, tarragon, dill, salt, and pepper in a small bowl and let the resulting tartare sauce chill covered in the fridge until ready to use. Preheat air fryer at 375°F. In a bowl, mix the flour, cornstarch, paprika, and salt. In another bowl, beat the milk and egg and in a third bowl, add the breadcrumbs. Roll the cod in the flour mixture, shake off excess flour. Then, dip in the egg, shake off excess egg. Finally, dredge in the breadcrumbs mixture. Place fish pieces in the greased frying basket and Air Fry for 6 minutes, flipping once. Add cooked fish, lettuce, tomato slices, and tartar sauce to each bottom bun and top with the top bun. Serve.

Fish Nuggets With Broccoli Dip

Servings: 4
Cooking Time: 40 Minutes
Ingredients:
- 1 lb cod fillets, cut into chunks
- 1 ½ cups broccoli florets
- ¼ cup grated Parmesan
- 3 garlic cloves, peeled
- 3 tbsp sour cream
- 2 tbsp lemon juice
- 2 tbsp olive oil
- 2 egg whites
- 1 cup panko bread crumbs
- 1 tsp dried dill
- Salt and pepper to taste

Directions:
1. Preheat the air fryer to 400°F. Put the broccoli and garlic in the greased frying basket and Air Fry for 5-7 minutes or until tender. Remove to a blender and add sour cream, lemon juice, olive oil, and ½ tsp of salt and process until smooth. Set the sauce aside. Beat the egg whites until frothy in a shallow bowl. On a plate, combine the panko, Parmesan, dill, pepper, and the remaining ½ tsp of salt. Dip the cod fillets in the egg whites, then the breadcrumbs, pressing to coat. Put half the cubes in the frying basket and spray with cooking oil. Air Fry for 6-8 minutes or until the fish is cooked through. Serve the fish with the sauce and enjoy!

Horseradish Crusted Salmon

Servings: 2
Cooking Time: 14 Minutes
Ingredients:
- 2 (5-ounce) salmon fillets
- salt and freshly ground black pepper
- 2 teaspoons Dijon mustard
- ½ cup panko breadcrumbs*
- 2 tablespoons prepared horseradish
- ½ teaspoon finely chopped lemon zest
- 1 tablespoon olive oil
- 1 tablespoon chopped fresh parsley

Directions:
1. Preheat the air fryer to 360°F.
2. Season the salmon with salt and freshly ground black pepper. Then spread the Dijon mustard on the salmon, coating the entire surface.
3. Combine the breadcrumbs, horseradish, lemon zest and olive oil in a small bowl. Spread the mixture over the top of the salmon and press down lightly with your hands, adhering it to the salmon using the mustard as "glue".
4. Transfer the salmon to the air fryer basket and air-fry at 360°F for 14 minutes (depending on how thick your fillet is) or until the fish feels firm to the touch. Sprinkle with the parsley.

Collard Green & Cod Packets

Servings: 4
Cooking Time: 20 Minutes
Ingredients:
- 2 cups collard greens, chopped
- 1 tsp salt
- ½ tsp dried rosemary
- ½ tsp dried thyme
- ½ tsp garlic powder
- 4 cod fillets
- 1 shallot, thinly sliced
- ¼ cup olive oil
- 1 lemon, juiced

Directions:
1. Preheat air fryer to 380°F. Mix together the salt, rosemary, thyme, and garlic powder in a small bowl. Rub the spice mixture onto the cod fillets. Divide the fish fillets among 4 sheets of foil. Top with shallot slices and collard greens. Drizzle with olive oil and lemon juice. Fold and seal the sides of the foil packets and then place them into the frying basket. Steam in the fryer for 11-13 minutes until the cod is cooked through. Serve and enjoy!

Summer Sea Scallops

Servings: 4
Cooking Time: 30 Minutes
Ingredients:
- 1 cup asparagus
- 1 cup peas
- 1 cup chopped broccoli
- 2 tsp olive oil
- ½ tsp dried oregano
- 12 oz sea scallops

Directions:
1. Preheat air fryer to 400°F. Add the asparagus, peas, and broccoli to a bowl and mix with olive oil. Put the bowl in the fryer and Air Fry for 4-6 minutes until crispy and soft. Take the veggies out and add the herbs; let sit. Add the scallops to the fryer and Air Fry for 4-5 minutes until the scallops are springy to the touch. Serve immediately with the vegetables. Enjoy!

Cajun Flounder Fillets

Servings: 2
Cooking Time: 5 Minutes
Ingredients:
- 2 4-ounce skinless flounder fillet(s)
- 2 teaspoons Peanut oil
- 1 teaspoon Purchased or homemade Cajun dried seasoning blend (see the headnote)

Directions:
1. Preheat the air fryer to 400°F.
2. Oil the fillet(s) by drizzling on the peanut oil, then gently rubbing in the oil with your clean, dry fingers. Sprinkle the seasoning blend evenly over both sides of the fillet(s).
3. When the machine is at temperature, set the fillet(s) in the basket. If working with more than one fillet, they should not touch, although they may be quite close together, depending on the basket's size. Air-fry undisturbed for 5 minutes, or until lightly browned and cooked through.
4. Use a nonstick-safe spatula to transfer the fillets to a serving platter or plate(s). Serve at once.

Lightened-up Breaded Fish Filets

Servings: 4
Cooking Time: 10 Minutes
Ingredients:
- ½ cup all-purpose flour
- ½ teaspoon cayenne pepper
- 1 teaspoon garlic powder
- ½ teaspoon black pepper
- ¼ teaspoon salt
- 2 eggs, whisked
- 1½ cups panko breadcrumbs
- 1 pound boneless white fish filets
- 1 cup tartar sauce
- 1 lemon, sliced into wedges

Directions:
1. In a medium bowl, mix the flour, cayenne pepper, garlic powder, pepper, and salt.
2. In a shallow dish, place the eggs.
3. In a third dish, place the breadcrumbs.
4. Cover the fish in the flour, dip them in the egg, and coat them with panko. Repeat until all fish are covered in the breading.
5. Liberally spray the metal trivet that fits inside the air fryer basket with olive oil mist. Place the fish onto the trivet, leaving space between the filets to flip. Cook for 5 minutes, flip the fish, and cook another 5 minutes. Repeat until all the fish is cooked.
6. Serve warm with tartar sauce and lemon wedges.

Shrimp Patties

Servings: 4
Cooking Time: 10 Minutes
Ingredients:
- ½ pound shelled and deveined raw shrimp
- ¼ cup chopped red bell pepper
- ¼ cup chopped green onion
- ¼ cup chopped celery
- 2 cups cooked sushi rice
- ½ teaspoon garlic powder
- ½ teaspoon Old Bay Seasoning
- ½ teaspoon salt
- 2 teaspoons Worcestershire sauce
- ½ cup plain breadcrumbs
- oil for misting or cooking spray

Directions:
1. Finely chop the shrimp. You can do this in a food processor, but it takes only a few pulses. Be careful not to overprocess into mush.
2. Place shrimp in a large bowl and add all other ingredients except the breadcrumbs and oil. Stir until well combined.
3. Preheat air fryer to 390°F.

4. Shape shrimp mixture into 8 patties, no more than ½-inch thick. Roll patties in breadcrumbs and mist with oil or cooking spray.
5. Place 4 shrimp patties in air fryer basket and cook at 390°F for 10 minutes, until shrimp cooks through and outside is crispy.
6. Repeat step 5 to cook remaining shrimp patties.

Hot Calamari Rings

Servings: 4
Cooking Time: 25 Minutes
Ingredients:
- ½ cup all-purpose flour
- 2 tsp hot chili powder
- 2 eggs
- 1 tbsp milk
- 1 cup bread crumbs
- Salt and pepper to taste
- 1 lb calamari rings
- 1 lime, quartered
- ½ cup aioli sauce

Directions:
1. Preheat air fryer at 400°F. In a shallow bowl, add flour and hot chili powder. In another bowl, mix the eggs and milk. In a third bowl, mix the breadcrumbs, salt and pepper. Dip calamari rings in flour mix first, then in eggs mix and shake off excess. Then, roll ring through breadcrumb mixture. Place calamari rings in the greased frying basket and Air Fry for 4 minutes, tossing once. Squeeze lime quarters over calamari. Serve with aioli sauce.

Mexican-style Salmon Stir-fry

Servings: 4
Cooking Time: 30 Minutes
Ingredients:
- 12 oz salmon fillets, cubed
- 1 red bell pepper, chopped
- 1 red onion, chopped
- 1 jalapeño pepper, minced
- ¼ cup salsa
- 2 tbsp tomato juice
- 2 tsp peanut oil
- 1 tsp chili powder
- 2 tbsp cilantro, chopped

Directions:
1. Preheat air fryer to 360°F. Mix salmon, bell pepper, onion, jalapeño, salsa, tomato juice, peanut oil, and chili powder in a bowl and put it into the air fryer. Air Fry for 12-14 minutes until the salmon is firm and the veggies are crispy and soft, stirring once. Serve topped with cilantro.

Garlic-lemon Steamer Clams

Servings: 2
Cooking Time: 30 Minutes
Ingredients:
- 25 Manila clams, scrubbed
- 2 tbsp butter, melted
- 1 garlic clove, minced
- 2 lemon wedges

Directions:
1. Add the clams to a large bowl filled with water and let sit for 10 minutes. Drain. Pour more water and let sit for 10 more minutes. Drain. Preheat air fryer to 350°F. Place clams in the basket and Air Fry for 7 minutes. Discard any clams that don´t open. Remove clams from shells and place them into a large serving dish. Drizzle with melted butter and garlic and squeeze lemon on top. Serve.

King Prawns Al Ajillo

Servings: 4
Cooking Time: 15 Minutes
Ingredients:
- 1 ¼ lb peeled king prawns, deveined
- ½ cup grated Parmesan
- 1 tbsp olive oil
- 1 tbsp lemon juice
- ½ tsp garlic powder
- 2 garlic cloves, minced

Directions:
1. Preheat the air fryer to 350°F. In a large bowl, add the prawns and sprinkle with olive oil, lemon juice, and garlic powder. Toss in the minced garlic and Parmesan, then toss to coat. Put the prawns in the frying basket and Air Fry for 10-15 minutes or until the prawns cook through. Shake the basket once while cooking. Serve immediately.

Old Bay Lobster Tails

Servings: 2
Cooking Time: 20 Minutes
Ingredients:
- ¼ cup green onions, sliced
- 2 uncooked lobster tails
- 1 tbsp butter, melted
- ½ tsp Old Bay Seasoning
- 1 tbsp chopped parsley
- 1 tsp dried sage
- 1 tsp dried thyme
- 1 garlic clove, chopped
- 1 tbsp basil paste
- 2 lemon wedges

Directions:
1. Preheat air fryer at 400°F. Using kitchen shears, cut down the middle of each lobster tail on the softer side. Carefully run your finger between lobster meat and shell to loosen the meat. Place lobster tails, cut side-up, in the frying basket and Air Fry for 4 minutes. Brush the tail meat with butter and season with old bay seasoning, sage, thyme, garlic, green onions, basil paste and cook for another 4 minutes. Scatter with parsley and serve with lemon wedges. Enjoy!

Spiced Shrimp Empanadas

Servings: 5
Cooking Time: 30 Minutes
Ingredients:
- ½ lb peeled and deveined shrimp, chopped
- 2 tbsp diced red bell peppers
- 1 shallot, minced
- 1 scallion, chopped
- 2 garlic cloves, minced
- 2 tbsp chopped cilantro
- ½ tbsp lemon juice
- ¼ tsp sweet paprika
- ⅛ tsp salt
- ⅛ tsp red pepper flakes
- ¼ tsp ground nutmeg
- 1 large egg, beaten
- 10 empanada discs

Directions:
1. Combine all ingredients, except the egg and empanada discs, in a bowl. Toss to coat. Beat the 1 egg with 1 tsp of water in a small bowl until blended. Set aside.
2. On your work board, place one empanada disc. Add 2 tbsp of shrimp mixture in the middle. Brush the edges of the disc with the egg mixture. Fold the disc in half and seal the edges. Crimp with a fork by pressing around the edges. Brush the tops with the egg mixture. Preheat air fryer to 380°F. Put the empanadas in the greased frying basket and Air Fry for 9 minutes, flipping once until golden and crispy. Serve hot.

Sweet Potato–wrapped Shrimp

Servings: 3
Cooking Time: 6 Minutes
Ingredients:
- 24 Long spiralized sweet potato strands
- Olive oil spray
- ¼ teaspoon Garlic powder
- ¼ teaspoon Table salt
- Up to a ⅛ teaspoon Cayenne
- 12 Large shrimp (20–25 per pound), peeled and deveined

Directions:
1. Preheat the air fryer to 400°F.
2. Lay the spiralized sweet potato strands on a large swath of paper towels and straighten out the strands to long ropes. Coat them with olive oil spray, then sprinkle them with the garlic powder, salt, and cayenne.
3. Pick up 2 strands and wrap them around the center of a shrimp, with the ends tucked under what now becomes the bottom side of the shrimp. Continue wrapping the remainder of the shrimp.
4. Set the shrimp bottom side down in the basket with as much air space between them as possible. Air-fry undisturbed for 6 minutes, or until the sweet potato strands are crisp and the shrimp are pink and firm.
5. Use kitchen tongs to transfer the shrimp to a wire rack. Cool for only a minute or two before serving.

Mediterranean Salmon Cakes

Servings: 4
Cooking Time: 30 Minutes
Ingredients:
- ¼ cup heavy cream
- 5 tbsp mayonnaise
- 2 cloves garlic, minced
- ¼ tsp caper juice
- 2 tsp lemon juice
- 1 tbsp capers
- 1 can salmon
- 2 tsp lemon zest
- 1 egg
- ¼ minced red bell peppers
- ½ cup flour
- ⅛ tsp salt
- 2 tbsp sliced green olives

Directions:
1. Combine heavy cream, 2 tbsp of mayonnaise, garlic, caper juices, capers, and lemon juice in a bowl. Place the resulting caper sauce in the fridge until ready to use.
2. Preheat air fryer to 400°F. Combine canned salmon, lemon zest, egg, remaining mayo, bell peppers, flour, and salt in a bowl. Form into 8 patties. Place the patties in the greased frying basket and Air Fry for 10 minutes, turning once. Let rest for 5 minutes before drizzling with lemon sauce. Garnish with green olives to serve.

Herb-rubbed Salmon With Avocado

Servings: 4
Cooking Time: 30 Minutes
Ingredients:
- 1 tbsp sweet paprika
- ½ tsp cayenne pepper
- 1 tsp garlic powder
- 1 tsp dried oregano
- ½ tsp dried coriander
- 1 tsp dried thyme
- ½ tsp dried dill
- Salt and pepper to taste
- 4 wild salmon fillets
- 2 tbsp chopped red onion
- 1½ tbsp fresh lemon juice
- 1 tsp olive oil
- 2 tbsp cilantro, chopped
- 1 avocado, diced

Directions:
1. Mix paprika, cayenne, garlic powder, oregano, thyme, dill, coriander, salt, and pepper in a small bowl. Spray and rub cooking oil on both sides of the fish, then cover with the spices. Add red onion, lemon juice, olive oil, cilantro, salt, and pepper in a bowl. Set aside for 5 minutes, then carefully add avocado.
2. Preheat air fryer to 400°F. Place the salmon skin-side down in the greased frying basket and Bake for 5-7 minutes or until

the fish flakes easily with a fork. Transfer to a plate and top with the avocado salsa.

Shrimp, Chorizo And Fingerling Potatoes

Servings: 4
Cooking Time: 16 Minutes
Ingredients:
- ½ red onion, chopped into 1-inch chunks
- 8 fingerling potatoes, sliced into 1-inch slices or halved lengthwise
- 1 teaspoon olive oil
- salt and freshly ground black pepper
- 8 ounces raw chorizo sausage, sliced into 1-inch chunks
- 16 raw large shrimp, peeled, deveined and tails removed
- 1 lime
- ¼ cup chopped fresh cilantro
- chopped orange zest (optional)

Directions:
1. Preheat the air fryer to 380°F.
2. Combine the red onion and potato chunks in a bowl and toss with the olive oil, salt and freshly ground black pepper.
3. Transfer the vegetables to the air fryer basket and air-fry for 6 minutes, shaking the basket a few times during the cooking process.
4. Add the chorizo chunks and continue to air-fry for another 5 minutes.
5. Add the shrimp, season with salt and continue to air-fry, shaking the basket every once in a while, for another 5 minutes.
6. Transfer the tossed shrimp, chorizo and potato to a bowl and squeeze some lime juice over the top to taste. Toss in the fresh cilantro, orange zest and a drizzle of olive oil, and season again to taste.
7. Serve with a fresh green salad.

Quick Tuna Tacos

Servings: 4
Cooking Time: 20 Minutes
Ingredients:
- 2 cups torn romaine lettuce
- 1 lb fresh tuna steak, cubed
- 1 tbsp grated fresh ginger
- 2 garlic cloves, minced
- ½ tsp toasted sesame oil
- 4 tortillas
- ¼ cup mild salsa
- 1 red bell pepper, sliced

Directions:
1. Preheat air fryer to 390°F. Combine the tuna, ginger, garlic, and sesame oil in a bowl and allow to marinate for 10 minutes. Lay the marinated tuna in the fryer and Grill for 4-7 minutes. Serve right away with tortillas, mild salsa, lettuce, and bell pepper for delicious tacos.

Crabmeat-stuffed Flounder

Servings: 3
Cooking Time: 12 Minutes
Ingredients:
- 4½ ounces Purchased backfin or claw crabmeat, picked over for bits of shell and cartilage
- 6 Saltine crackers, crushed into fine crumbs
- 2 tablespoons plus 1 teaspoon Regular or low-fat mayonnaise (not fat-free)
- ¾ teaspoon Yellow prepared mustard
- 1½ teaspoons Worcestershire sauce
- ⅛ teaspoon Celery salt
- 3 5- to 6-ounce skinless flounder fillets
- Vegetable oil spray
- Mild paprika

Directions:
1. Preheat the air fryer to 400°F.
2. Gently mix the crabmeat, crushed saltines, mayonnaise, mustard, Worcestershire sauce, and celery salt in a bowl until well combined.
3. Generously coat the flat side of a fillet with vegetable oil spray. Set the fillet sprayed side down on your work surface. Cut the fillet in half widthwise, then cut one of the halves in half lengthwise. Set a scant ⅓ cup of the crabmeat mixture on top of the undivided half of the fish fillet, mounding the mixture to make an oval that somewhat fits the shape of the fillet with at least a ¼-inch border of fillet beyond the filling all around.
4. Take the two thin divided quarters (that is, the halves of the half) and lay them lengthwise over the filling, overlapping at each end and leaving a little space in the middle where the filling peeks through. Coat the top of the stuffed flounder piece with vegetable oil spray, then sprinkle paprika over the stuffed flounder fillet. Set aside and use the remaining fillet(s) to make more stuffed flounder "packets," repeating steps 3 and
5. Use a nonstick-safe spatula to transfer the stuffed flounder fillets to the basket. Leave as much space between them as possible. Air-fry undisturbed for 12 minutes, or until lightly brown and firm (but not hard).
6. Use that same spatula, plus perhaps another one, to transfer the fillets to a serving platter or plates. Cool for a minute or two, then serve hot.

Sinaloa Fish Fajitas

Servings: 4
Cooking Time: 30 Minutes
Ingredients:
- 1 lemon, thinly sliced
- 16 oz red snapper filets
- 1 tbsp olive oil
- 1 tbsp cayenne pepper
- ½ tsp salt
- 2 cups shredded coleslaw
- 1 carrot, shredded
- 2 tbsp orange juice
- ½ cup salsa
- 4 flour tortillas
- ½ cup sour cream

- 2 avocados, sliced

Directions:
1. Preheat the air fryer to 350°F. Lay the lemon slices at the bottom of the basket. Drizzle the fillets with olive oil and sprinkle with cayenne pepper and salt. Lay the fillets on top of the lemons and Bake for 6-9 minutes or until the fish easily flakes. While the fish cooks, toss the coleslaw, carrot, orange juice, and salsa in a bowl. When the fish is done, remove it and cover. Toss the lemons. Air Fry the tortillas for 2-3 minutes to warm up. Add the fish to the tortillas and top with a cabbage mix, sour cream, and avocados. Serve and enjoy!

Fish Cakes

Servings: 4
Cooking Time: 10 Minutes
Ingredients:
- ¾ cup mashed potatoes (about 1 large russet potato)
- 12 ounces cod or other white fish
- salt and pepper
- oil for misting or cooking spray
- 1 large egg
- ¼ cup potato starch
- ½ cup panko breadcrumbs
- 1 tablespoon fresh chopped chives
- 2 tablespoons minced onion

Directions:
1. Peel potatoes, cut into cubes, and cook on stovetop till soft.
2. Salt and pepper raw fish to taste. Mist with oil or cooking spray, and cook in air fryer at 360°F for 6 to 8minutes, until fish flakes easily. If fish is crowded, rearrange halfway through cooking to ensure all pieces cook evenly.
3. Transfer fish to a plate and break apart to cool.
4. Beat egg in a shallow dish.
5. Place potato starch in another shallow dish, and panko crumbs in a third dish.
6. When potatoes are done, drain in colander and rinse with cold water.
7. In a large bowl, mash the potatoes and stir in the chives and onion. Add salt and pepper to taste, then stir in the fish.
8. If needed, stir in a tablespoon of the beaten egg to help bind the mixture.
9. Shape into 8 small, fat patties. Dust lightly with potato starch, dip in egg, and roll in panko crumbs. Spray both sides with oil or cooking spray.
10. Cook at 360°F for 10 minutes, until golden brown and crispy.

Tilapia Al Pesto

Servings:4
Cooking Time: 25 Minutes
Ingredients:
- 4 tilapia fillets
- 1 egg
- 2 tbsp buttermilk
- 1 cup crushed cornflakes
- Salt and pepper to taste
- 4 tsp pesto
- 2 tbsp butter, melted
- 4 lemon wedges

Directions:
1. Preheat air fryer to 350°F. Whisk egg and buttermilk in a bowl. In another bowl, combine cornflakes, salt, and pepper. Spread 1 tsp of pesto on each tilapia fillet, then tightly roll the fillet from one short end to the other. Secure with a toothpick. Dip each fillet in the egg mixture and dredge in the cornflake mixture. Place fillets in the greased frying basket, drizzle with melted butter, and Air Fry for 6 minutes. Let rest onto a serving dish for 5 minutes before removing the toothpicks. Serve with lemon wedges.

Oyster Shrimp With Fried Rice

Servings: 4
Cooking Time: 40 Minutes
Ingredients:
- 1 lb peeled shrimp, deveined
- 1 shallot, chopped
- 2 garlic cloves, minced
- 1 tbsp olive oil
- 1 tbsp butter
- 2 eggs, beaten
- 2 cups cooked rice
- 1 cup baby peas
- 2 tbsp fish sauce
- 1 tbsp oyster sauce

Directions:
1. Preheat the air fryer to 370°F. Combine the shrimp, shallot, garlic, and olive oil in a cake pan. Put the cake pan in the air fryer and Bake the shrimp for 5-7 minutes, stirring once until shrimp are no pinker. Remove into a bowl, and set aside. Put the butter in the hot cake pan to melt. Add the eggs and return to the fryer. Bake for 4-6 minutes, stirring once until the eggs are set. Remove the eggs from the pan and set aside.
2. Add the rice, peas, oyster sauce, and fish sauce to the pan and return it to the fryer. Bake for 12-15 minutes, stirring once halfway through. Pour in the shrimp and eggs and stir. Cook for 2-3 more minutes until everything is hot.

Caribbean Jerk Cod Fillets

Servings:2
Cooking Time: 20 Minutes
Ingredients:
- ¼ cup chopped cooked shrimp
- ¼ cup diced mango
- 1 tomato, diced
- 2 tbsp diced red onion
- 1 tbsp chopped parsley
- ¼ tsp ginger powder
- 2 tsp lime juice
- Salt and pepper to taste
- 2 cod fillets
- 2 tsp Jerk seasoning

Directions:

1. In a bowl, combine the shrimp, mango, tomato, red onion, parsley, ginger powder, lime juice, salt, and black pepper. Let chill the salsa in the fridge until ready to use.
2. Preheat air fryer to 350ºF. Sprinkle cod fillets with Jerk seasoning. Place them in the greased frying basket and Air Fry for 10 minutes or until the cod is opaque and flakes easily with a fork. Divide between 2 medium plates. Serve topped with the Caribbean salsa.

Southern Shrimp With Cocktail Sauce

Servings: 2
Cooking Time: 20 Minutes
Ingredients:
- ½ lb raw shrimp, tail on, deveined and shelled
- 1 cup ketchup
- 2 tbsp prepared horseradish
- 1 tbsp lemon juice
- ½ tsp Worcestershire sauce
- 1/8 tsp chili powder
- Salt and pepper to taste
- 1/3 cup flour
- 2 tbsp cornstarch
- ¼ cup milk
- 1 egg
- ½ cup bread crumbs
- 1 tbsp Cajun seasoning
- 1 lemon, cut into pieces

Directions:
1. In a small bowl, whisk the ketchup, horseradish, lemon juice, Worcestershire sauce, chili powder, salt, and pepper. Let chill covered in the fridge until ready to use. Preheat air fryer at 375ºF. In a bowl, mix the flour, cornstarch, and salt. In another bowl, beat the milk and egg and in a third bowl, combine breadcrumbs and Cajun seasoning.
2. Roll the shrimp in the flour mixture, shake off excess flour. Then, dip in the egg, shake off excess egg. Finally, dredge in the breadcrumbs mixture. Place shrimp in the greased frying basket and Air Fry for 8 minutes, flipping once. Serve with cocktail sauce and lemon slices.

Saucy Shrimp

Servings: 4
Cooking Time: 30 Minutes
Ingredients:
- 1 lb peeled shrimp, deveined
- ½ cup grated coconut
- ¼ cup bread crumbs
- ¼ cup flour
- ¼ tsp smoked paprika
- Salt and pepper to taste
- 1 egg
- 2 tbsp maple syrup
- ½ tsp rice vinegar
- 1 tbsp hot sauce
- 1/8 tsp red pepper flakes
- ¼ cup orange juice
- 1 tsp cornstarch
- ½ cup banana ketchup
- 1 lemon, sliced

Directions:
1. Preheat air fryer to 350ºF. Combine coconut, bread crumbs, flour, paprika, black pepper, and salt in a bowl. In a separate bowl, whisk egg and 1 teaspoon water. Dip one shrimp into the egg bowl and shake off excess drips. Dip the shrimp in the bread crumb mixture and coat it completely. Continue the process for all of the shrimp. Arrange the shrimp on the greased frying basket. Air Fry for 5 minutes, then use tongs to flip the shrimp. Cook for another 2-3 minutes.
2. To make the sauce, add maple syrup, banana ketchup, hot sauce, vinegar, and red pepper flakes in a small saucepan over medium heat. Make a slurry in a small bowl with orange juice and cornstarch. Stir in slurry and continue stirring. Bring the sauce to a boil and cook for 5 minutes. When the sauce begins to thicken, remove from heat and allow to sit for 5 minutes. Serve shrimp warm along with sauce and lemon slices on the side.

Parmesan Fish Bites

Servings: 2
Cooking Time: 30 Minutes
Ingredients:
- 1 haddock fillet, cut into bite-sized pieces
- 1 tbsp shredded cheddar
- 2 tbsp shredded Parmesan
- 2 eggs, beaten
- ½ cup breadcrumbs
- Salt and pepper to taste
- ½ cup mayoracha sauce

Directions:
1. Preheat air fryer to 350°F. Dip the strips in the beaten eggs. Place the bread crumbs, Parmesan, cheddar, salt and pepper in a bowl and mix well. Coat the fish strips in the dry mixture and place them on the foil-lined frying basket. Air Fry for 14-16 minutes. Halfway through the cooking time, shake the basket. When the cooking time is over, the fish will be cooked through and crust golden brown. Serve with mayoracha sauce (mixed mayo with sriracha) for dipping and enjoy!

Cheese & Crab Stuffed Mushrooms

Servings: 2
Cooking Time: 30 Minutes
Ingredients:
- 6 oz lump crabmeat, shells discarded
- 6 oz mascarpone cheese, softened
- 2 jalapeño peppers, minced
- ¼ cup diced red onions
- 2 tsp grated Parmesan cheese
- 2 portobello mushroom caps
- 2 tbsp butter, divided
- ½ tsp prepared horseradish
- ¼ tsp Worcestershire sauce

- ¼ tsp smoked paprika
- Salt and pepper to taste
- ¼ cup bread crumbs

Directions:

1. Melt 1 tbsp of butter in a skillet over heat for 30 seconds. Add in onion and cook for 3 minutes until tender. Stir in mascarpone cheese, Parmesan cheese, horseradish, jalapeño peppers, Worcestershire sauce, paprika, salt and pepper and cook for 2 minutes until smooth. Fold in crabmeat. Spoon mixture into mushroom caps. Set aside.
2. Preheat air fryer at 350°F. Microwave the remaining butter until melted. Stir in breadcrumbs. Scatter over stuffed mushrooms. Place mushrooms in the greased frying basket and Bake for 8 minutes. Serve immediately.

Shrimp Sliders With Avocado

Servings: 4
Cooking Time: 10 Minutes

Ingredients:

- 16 raw jumbo shrimp, peeled, deveined and tails removed (about 1 pound)
- 1 rib celery, finely chopped
- 2 carrots, grated (about ½ cup) 2 teaspoons lemon juice
- 2 teaspoons Dijon mustard
- ¼ cup chopped fresh basil or parsley
- ½ cup breadcrumbs
- ½ teaspoon salt
- freshly ground black pepper
- vegetable or olive oil, in a spray bottle
- 8 slider buns
- mayonnaise
- butter lettuce
- 2 avocados, sliced and peeled

Directions:

1. Put the shrimp into a food processor and pulse it a few times to rough chop the shrimp. Remove three quarters of the shrimp and transfer it to a bowl. Continue to process the remaining shrimp in the food processor until it is a smooth purée. Transfer the purée to the bowl with the chopped shrimp.
2. Add the celery, carrots, lemon juice, mustard, basil, breadcrumbs, salt and pepper to the bowl and combine well.
3. Preheat the air fryer to 380°F.
4. While the air fryer Preheats, shape the shrimp mixture into 8 patties. Spray both sides of the patties with oil and transfer one layer of patties to the air fryer basket. Air-fry for 10 minutes, flipping the patties over halfway through the cooking time.
5. Prepare the slider rolls by toasting them and spreading a little mayonnaise on both halves. Place a piece of butter lettuce on the bottom bun, top with the shrimp slider and then finish with the avocado slices on top. Pop the top half of the bun on top and enjoy!

Flounder Fillets

Servings: 4
Cooking Time: 8 Minutes

Ingredients:

- 1 egg white
- 1 tablespoon water
- 1 cup panko breadcrumbs
- 2 tablespoons extra-light virgin olive oil
- 4 4-ounce flounder fillets
- salt and pepper
- oil for misting or cooking spray

Directions:

1. Preheat air fryer to 390°F.
2. Beat together egg white and water in shallow dish.
3. In another shallow dish, mix panko crumbs and oil until well combined and crumbly (best done by hand).
4. Season flounder fillets with salt and pepper to taste. Dip each fillet into egg mixture and then roll in panko crumbs, pressing in crumbs so that fish is nicely coated.
5. Spray air fryer basket with nonstick cooking spray and add fillets. Cook at 390°F for 3minutes.
6. Spray fish fillets but do not turn. Cook 5 minutes longer or until golden brown and crispy. Using a spatula, carefully remove fish from basket and serve.

Piña Colada Shrimp

Servings: 4
Cooking Time: 25 Minutes

Ingredients:

- 1 lb large shrimp, deveined and shelled
- 1 can crushed pineapple
- ½ cup sour cream
- ¼ cup pineapple preserves
- 2 egg whites
- 1 tbsp dark rum
- 2/3 cup cornstarch
- 2/3 cup sweetened coconut
- 1 cup panko bread crumbs

Directions:

1. Preheat air fryer to 400°F. Drain the crushed pineapple and reserve the juice. Next, transfer the pineapple to a small bowl and mix with sour cream and preserves. Set aside. In a shallow bowl, beat egg whites with 1 tbsp of the reserved pineapple juice and rum. On a separate plate, add the cornstarch. On another plate, stir together coconut and bread crumbs. Coat the shrimp with the cornstarch. Then, dip the shrimp into the egg white mixture. Shake off drips and then coat with the coconut mixture. Place the shrimp in the greased frying basket. Air Fry until crispy and golden, 7 minutes. Serve warm.

Fish Tacos With Jalapeño-lime Sauce

Servings: 4
Cooking Time: 7 Minutes
Ingredients:
- Fish Tacos
- 1 pound fish fillets
- ¼ teaspoon cumin
- ¼ teaspoon coriander
- ⅛ teaspoon ground red pepper
- 1 tablespoon lime zest
- ¼ teaspoon smoked paprika
- 1 teaspoon oil
- cooking spray
- 6–8 corn or flour tortillas (6-inch size)
- Jalapeño-Lime Sauce
- ½ cup sour cream
- 1 tablespoon lime juice
- ¼ teaspoon grated lime zest
- ½ teaspoon minced jalapeño (flesh only)
- ¼ teaspoon cumin
- Napa Cabbage Garnish
- 1 cup shredded Napa cabbage
- ¼ cup slivered red or green bell pepper
- ¼ cup slivered onion

Directions:
1. Slice the fish fillets into strips approximately ½-inch thick.
2. Put the strips into a sealable plastic bag along with the cumin, coriander, red pepper, lime zest, smoked paprika, and oil. Massage seasonings into the fish until evenly distributed.
3. Spray air fryer basket with nonstick cooking spray and place seasoned fish inside.
4. Cook at 390°F for approximately 5minutes. Shake basket to distribute fish. Cook an additional 2 minutes, until fish flakes easily.
5. While the fish is cooking, prepare the Jalapeño-Lime Sauce by mixing the sour cream, lime juice, lime zest, jalapeño, and cumin together to make a smooth sauce. Set aside.
6. Mix the cabbage, bell pepper, and onion together and set aside.
7. To warm refrigerated tortillas, wrap in damp paper towels and microwave for 30 to 60 seconds.
8. To serve, spoon some of fish into a warm tortilla. Add one or two tablespoons Napa Cabbage Garnish and drizzle with Jalapeño-Lime Sauce.

Smoked Paprika Cod Goujons

Servings: 2
Cooking Time: 30 Minutes
Ingredients:
- 1 cod fillet, cut into chunks
- 2 eggs, beaten
- ¼ cup breadcrumbs
- ¼ cup rice flour
- 1 lemon, juiced
- ½ tbsp garlic powder
- 1 tsp smoked paprika
- Salt and pepper to taste

Directions:
1. Preheat air fryer to 350°F. In a bowl, stir the beaten eggs and lemon juice thoroughly. Dip the cod chunks in the mixture. In another bowl, mix the bread crumbs, rice flour, garlic powder, smoked paprika, salt, and pepper.
2. Coat the cod with the crumb mixture. Transfer the coated cod to the greased frying basket. Air Fry for 14-16 minutes until the fish goujons are cooked through and their crust is golden, brown, and delicious. Toss the basket two or three times during the cooking time. Serve.

Coconut-shrimp Po' Boys

Servings: 4
Cooking Time: 5 Minutes
Ingredients:
- ½ cup cornstarch
- 2 eggs
- 2 tablespoons milk
- ¾ cup shredded coconut
- ½ cup panko breadcrumbs
- 1 pound (31–35 count) shrimp, peeled and deveined
- Old Bay Seasoning
- oil for misting or cooking spray
- 2 large hoagie rolls
- honey mustard or light mayonnaise
- 1½ cups shredded lettuce
- 1 large tomato, thinly sliced

Directions:
1. Place cornstarch in a shallow dish or plate.
2. In another shallow dish, beat together eggs and milk.
3. In a third dish mix the coconut and panko crumbs.
4. Sprinkle shrimp with Old Bay Seasoning to taste.
5. Dip shrimp in cornstarch to coat lightly, dip in egg mixture, shake off excess, and roll in coconut mixture to coat well.
6. Spray both sides of coated shrimp with oil or cooking spray.
7. Cook half the shrimp in a single layer at 390°F for 5minutes.
8. Repeat to cook remaining shrimp.
9. To Assemble
10. Split each hoagie lengthwise, leaving one long edge intact.
11. Place in air fryer basket and cook at 390°F for 1 to 2minutes or until heated through.
12. Remove buns, break apart, and place on 4 plates, cut side up.
13. Spread with honey mustard and/or mayonnaise.
14. Top with shredded lettuce, tomato slices, and coconut shrimp.

Tuna Nuggets In Hoisin Sauce

Servings: 4
Cooking Time: 7 Minutes
Ingredients:
- ½ cup hoisin sauce
- 2 tablespoons rice wine vinegar
- 2 teaspoons sesame oil
- 1 teaspoon garlic powder
- 2 teaspoons dried lemongrass
- ¼ teaspoon red pepper flakes
- ½ small onion, quartered and thinly sliced
- 8 ounces fresh tuna, cut into 1-inch cubes
- cooking spray
- 3 cups cooked jasmine rice

Directions:
1. Mix the hoisin sauce, vinegar, sesame oil, and seasonings together.
2. Stir in the onions and tuna nuggets.
3. Spray air fryer baking pan with nonstick spray and pour in tuna mixture.
4. Cook at 390°F for 3minutes. Stir gently.
5. Cook 2minutes and stir again, checking for doneness. Tuna should be barely cooked through, just beginning to flake and still very moist. If necessary, continue cooking and stirring in 1-minute intervals until done.
6. Serve warm over hot jasmine rice.

Curried Sweet-and-spicy Scallops

Servings:3
Cooking Time: 5 Minutes
Ingredients:
- 6 tablespoons Thai sweet chili sauce
- 2 cups (from about 5 cups cereal) Crushed Rice Krispies or other rice-puff cereal
- 2 teaspoons Yellow curry powder, purchased or homemade (see here)
- 1 pound Sea scallops
- Vegetable oil spray

Directions:
1. Preheat the air fryer to 400°F.
2. Set up and fill two shallow soup plates or small pie plates on your counter: one for the chili sauce and one for crumbs, mixed with the curry powder.
3. Dip a scallop into the chili sauce, coating it on all sides. Set it in the cereal mixture and turn several times to coat evenly. Gently shake off any excess and set the scallop on a cutting board. Continue dipping and coating the remaining scallops. Coat them all on all sides with the vegetable oil spray.
4. Set the scallops in the basket with as much air space between them as possible. Air-fry undisturbed for 5 minutes, or until lightly browned and crunchy.
5. Remove the basket. Set aside for 2 minutes to let the coating set up. Then gently pour the contents of the basket onto a platter and serve at once.

Asian-style Salmon Fillets

Servings: 4
Cooking Time: 15 Minutes
Ingredients:
- 1 tbsp sesame oil
- 2 tbsp miso paste
- 2 tbsp tamari
- 2 tbsp soy sauce
- 2 tbsp dark brown sugar
- ½ tsp garlic powder
- ½ tsp ginger powder
- 4 salmon fillets
- 4 cups cooked brown rice
- 4 lemon slices

Directions:
1. Preheat air fryer at 375ºF. In a bowl, combine all ingredients, except for salmon and cooked rice. Add 1/3 of the marinade to a shallow dish, submerge salmon fillets and let marinate covered in the fridge for 10 minutes. Reserve the remaining marinade. Place salmon fillets, skin side up, in the greased frying basket and Air Fry for 6-8 minutes, turning once, and brush with the reserved marinade. Divide cooked rice into serving dishes and top each with a salmon fillet. Pour the remaining marinade on top and serve with lemon slices on the side.

Chapter 7 Vegetarians Recipes

Black Bean Empanadas

Servings: 12
Cooking Time: 35 Minutes
Ingredients:
- 1½ cups all-purpose flour
- 1 cup whole-wheat flour
- 1 teaspoon salt
- ½ cup cold unsalted butter
- 1 egg
- ½ cup milk
- One 14.5-ounce can black beans, drained and rinsed
- ¼ cup chopped cilantro
- 1 cup shredded purple cabbage
- 1 cup shredded Monterey jack cheese
- ¼ cup salsa

Directions:
1. In a food processor, place the all-purpose flour, whole-wheat flour, salt, and butter into processor and process for 2 minutes, scraping down the sides of the food processor every 30 seconds. Add in the egg and blend for 30 seconds. Using the pulse button, add in the milk 1 tablespoon at a time, or until dough is moist enough to handle and be rolled into a ball. Let the dough rest at room temperature for 30 minutes.
2. Meanwhile, in a large bowl, mix together the black beans, cilantro, cabbage, Monterey Jack cheese, and salsa.
3. On a floured surface, cut the dough in half; then form a ball and cut each ball into 6 equal pieces, totaling 12 equal pieces. Work with one piece at a time, and cover the remaining dough with a towel.
4. Roll out a piece of dough into a 6-inch round, much like a tortilla, ¼ inch thick. Place 4 tablespoons of filling in the center of the round, and fold over to form a half-circle. Using a fork, crimp the edges together and pierce the top for air holes. Repeat with the remaining dough and filling.
5. Preheat the air fryer to 350°F.
6. Working in batches, place 3 to 4 empanadas in the air fryer basket and spray with cooking spray. Cook for 4 minutes, flip over the empanadas and spray with cooking spray, and cook another 4 minutes.

Quinoa & Black Bean Stuffed Peppers

Servings: 4
Cooking Time: 30 Minutes
Ingredients:
- ½ cup vegetable broth
- ½ cup quinoa
- 1 can black beans
- ½ cup diced red onion
- 1 garlic clove, minced
- ½ tsp salt
- ½ tsp ground cumin
- ¼ tsp paprika
- ¼ tsp ancho chili powder
- 4 bell peppers, any color
- ½ cup grated cheddar
- ¼ cup chopped cilantro
- ½ cup red enchilada sauce

Directions:
1. Add vegetable broth and quinoa to a small saucepan over medium heat. Bring to a boil, then cover and let it simmer for 5 minutes. Turn off the heat.
2. Preheat air fryer to 350°F. Transfer quinoa to a medium bowl and stir in black beans, onion, red enchilada sauce, ancho chili powder, garlic, salt, cumin, and paprika. Cut the top ¼-inch off the bell peppers. Remove seeds and membranes. Scoop quinoa filling into each pepper and top with cheddar cheese. Transfer peppers to the frying basket and bake for 10 minutes until peppers are soft and filling is heated through. Garnish with cilantro. Serve warm along with salsa. Enjoy!

Sushi-style Deviled Eggs

Servings: 4
Cooking Time: 20 Minutes
Ingredients:
- ¼ cup crabmeat, shells discarded
- 4 eggs
- 2 tbsp mayonnaise
- ½ tsp soy sauce
- ¼ avocado, diced
- ¼ tsp wasabi powder
- 2 tbsp diced cucumber
- 1 sheet nori, sliced
- 8 jarred pickled ginger slices
- 1 tsp toasted sesame seeds
- 2 spring onions, sliced

Directions:
1. Preheat air fryer to 260°F. Place the eggs in muffin cups to avoid bumping around and cracking during the cooking process. Add silicone cups to the frying basket and Air Fry for 15 minutes. Remove and plunge the eggs immediately into an ice bath to cool, about 5 minutes. Carefully peel and slice them in half lengthwise. Spoon yolks into a separate medium bowl and arrange white halves on a large plate. Mash the yolks with a fork. Stir in mayonnaise, soy sauce, avocado, and wasabi powder until smooth. Mix in cucumber and spoon into white halves. Scatter eggs with crabmeat, nori, pickled ginger, spring onions and sesame seeds to serve.

Mushroom And Fried Onion Quesadilla

Servings: 2
Cooking Time: 33 Minutes
Ingredients:
- 1 onion, sliced
- 2 tablespoons butter, melted
- 10 ounces button mushrooms, sliced
- 2 tablespoons Worcestershire sauce
- salt and freshly ground black pepper
- 4 (8-inch) flour tortillas
- 2 cups grated Fontina cheese
- vegetable or olive oil

Directions:
1. Preheat the air fryer to 400°F.
2. Toss the onion slices with the melted butter and transfer them to the air fryer basket. Air-fry at 400°F for 15 minutes, shaking the basket several times during the cooking process. Add the mushrooms and Worcestershire sauce to the onions and stir to combine. Air-fry at 400°F for an additional 10 minutes. Season with salt and freshly ground black pepper.
3. Lay two of the tortillas on a cutting board. Top each tortilla with ½ cup of the grated cheese, half of the onion and mushroom mixture and then finally another ½ cup of the cheese. Place the remaining tortillas on top of the cheese and press down firmly.
4. Brush the air fryer basket with a little oil. Place a quesadilla in the basket and brush the top with a little oil. Secure the top tortilla to the bottom with three toothpicks and air-fry at 400°F for 5 minutes. Flip the quesadilla over by inverting it onto a plate and sliding it back into the basket. Remove the toothpicks and brush the other side with oil. Air-fry for an additional 3 minutes.
5. Invert the quesadilla onto a cutting board and cut it into 4 or 6 triangles. Serve immediately.

Cheesy Eggplant Rounds

Servings: 4
Cooking Time: 35 Minutes
Ingredients:
- 1 eggplant, peeled
- 2 eggs
- ½ cup all-purpose flour
- ¾ cup bread crumbs
- 2 tbsp grated Swiss cheese
- Salt and pepper to taste
- ¾ cup tomato passata
- ½ cup shredded Parmesan
- ½ cup shredded mozzarella

Directions:
1. Preheat air fryer to 400°F. Slice the eggplant into ½-inch rounds. Set aside. Set out three small bowls. In the first bowl, add flour. In the second bowl, beat the eggs. In the third bowl, mix the crumbs, 2 tbsp of grated Swiss cheese, salt, and pepper. Dip each eggplant in the flour, then dredge in egg, then coat with bread crumb mixture. Arrange the eggplant rounds on the greased frying basket and spray with cooking oil. Bake for 7 minutes. Top each eggplant round with 1 tsp passata and ½ tbsp each of shredded Parmesan and mozzarella. Cook until the cheese melts, 2-3 minutes. Serve warm and enjoy!

Quinoa Green Pizza

Servings: 2
Cooking Time: 25 Minutes
Ingredients:
- ¾ cup quinoa flour
- ½ tsp dried basil
- ½ tsp dried oregano
- 1 tbsp apple cider vinegar
- 1/3 cup ricotta cheese
- 2/3 cup chopped broccoli
- ½ tsp garlic powder

Directions:
1. Preheat air fryer to 350°F. Whisk quinoa flour, basil, oregano, apple cider vinegar, and ½ cup of water until smooth. Set aside. Cut 2 pieces of parchment paper. Place the quinoa mixture on one paper, top with another piece, and flatten to create a crust. Discard the top piece of paper. Bake for 5 minutes, turn and discard the other piece of paper. Spread the ricotta cheese over the crust, scatter with broccoli, and sprinkle with garlic. Grill at 400°F for 5 minutes until golden brown. Serve warm.

Hearty Salad

Servings: 2
Cooking Time: 15 Minutes
Ingredients:
- 5 oz cauliflower, cut into florets
- 2 grated carrots
- 1 tbsp olive oil
- 1 tbsp lemon juice
- 2 tbsp raisins
- 2 tbsp roasted pepitas
- 2 tbsp diced red onion
- ¼ cup mayonnaise
- 1/8 tsp black pepper
- 1 tsp cumin
- ½ tsp chia seeds
- ½ tsp sesame seeds

Directions:
1. Preheat air fryer at 350°F. Combine the cauliflower, cumin, olive oil, black pepper and lemon juice in a bowl, place it in the frying basket, and Bake for 5 minutes. Transfer it to a serving dish. Toss in the remaining ingredients. Let chill covered in the fridge until ready to use. Serve sprinkled with sesame and chia seeds.

Pineapple & Veggie Souvlaki

Servings: 4
Cooking Time: 35 Minutes
Ingredients:
- 1 can pineapple rings in pineapple juice
- 1 red bell pepper, stemmed and seeded
- 1/3 cup butter
- 2 tbsp apple cider vinegar
- 2 tbsp hot sauce
- 1 tbsp allspice
- 1 tsp ground nutmeg
- 16 oz feta cheese
- 1 red onion, peeled
- 8 mushrooms, quartered

Directions:
1. Preheat air fryer to 400°F. Whisk the butter, pineapple juice, apple vinegar, hot sauce, allspice, and nutmeg until smooth. Set aside. Slice feta cheese into 16 cubes, then the bell pepper into 16 chunks, and finally red onion into 8 wedges, separating each wedge into 2 pieces.
2. Cut pineapple ring into quarters. Place veggie cubes and feta into the butter bowl and toss to coat. Thread the veggies, tofu, and pineapple onto 8 skewers, alternating 16 pieces on each skewer. Grill for 15 minutes until golden brown and cooked. Serve warm.

Roasted Vegetable Lasagna

Servings: 6
Cooking Time: 55 Minutes
Ingredients:
- 1 zucchini, sliced
- 1 yellow squash, sliced
- 8 ounces mushrooms, sliced
- 1 red bell pepper, cut into 2-inch strips
- 1 tablespoon olive oil
- 2 cups ricotta cheese
- 2 cups grated mozzarella cheese, divided
- 1 egg
- 1 teaspoon salt
- freshly ground black pepper
- ¼ cup shredded carrots
- ½ cup chopped fresh spinach
- 8 lasagna noodles, cooked
- Béchamel Sauce:
- 3 tablespoons butter
- 3 tablespoons flour
- 2½ cups milk
- ½ cup grated Parmesan cheese
- ½ teaspoon salt
- freshly ground black pepper
- pinch of ground nutmeg

Directions:
1. Preheat the air fryer to 400°F.
2. Toss the zucchini, yellow squash, mushrooms and red pepper in a large bowl with the olive oil and season with salt and pepper. Air-fry for 10 minutes, shaking the basket once or twice while the vegetables cook.
3. While the vegetables are cooking, make the béchamel sauce and cheese filling. Melt the butter in a medium saucepan over medium-high heat on the stovetop. Add the flour and whisk, cooking for a couple of minutes. Add the milk and whisk vigorously until smooth. Bring the mixture to a boil and simmer until the sauce thickens. Stir in the Parmesan cheese and season with the salt, pepper and nutmeg. Set the sauce aside.
4. Combine the ricotta cheese, 1¼ cups of the mozzarella cheese, egg, salt and pepper in a large bowl and stir until combined. Fold in the carrots and spinach.
5. When the vegetables have finished cooking, build the lasagna. Use a baking dish that is 6 inches in diameter and 4 inches high. Cover the bottom of the baking dish with a little béchamel sauce. Top with two lasagna noodles, cut to fit the dish and overlapping each other a little. Spoon a third of the ricotta cheese mixture and then a third of the roasted veggies on top of the noodles. Pour ½ cup of béchamel sauce on top and then repeat these layers two more times: noodles – cheese mixture – vegetables – béchamel sauce. Sprinkle the remaining mozzarella cheese over the top. Cover the dish with aluminum foil, tenting it loosely so the aluminum doesn't touch the cheese.
6. Lower the dish into the air fryer basket using an aluminum foil sling (fold a piece of aluminum foil into a strip about 2-inches wide by 24-inches long). Fold the ends of the aluminum foil over the top of the dish before returning the basket to the air fryer. Air-fry for 45 minutes, removing the foil for the last 2 minutes, to slightly brown the cheese on top.
7. Let the lasagna rest for at least 20 minutes to set up a little before slicing into it and serving.

Party Giant Nachos

Servings: 2
Cooking Time: 20 Minutes
Ingredients:
- 2 tbsp sour cream
- ½ tsp chili powder
- Salt to taste
- 2 soft corn tortillas
- 2 tsp avocado oil
- ½ cup refried beans
- ¼ cup cheddar cheese shreds
- 2 tbsp Parmesan cheese
- 2 tbsp sliced black olives
- ¼ cup torn iceberg lettuce
- ¼ cup baby spinach
- ½ sliced avocado
- 1 tomato, diced
- 2 lime wedges

Directions:
1. Preheat air fryer at 400°F. Whisk the sour cream, chili powder, and salt in a small bowl. Brush tortillas with avocado

oil and season one side with salt. Place tortillas in the frying basket and Bake for 3 minutes. Set aside.

2. Layer the refried beans, Parmesan and cheddar cheeses in the tortillas. Place them back into the basket and Bake for 2 minutes. Divide tortillas into 2 serving plates. Top each tortilla with black olives, baby spinach, lettuce, and tomatoes. Dollop sour cream mixture on each. Serve with lime and avocado wedges on the side.

Two-cheese Grilled Sandwiches

Servings: 2
Cooking Time: 30 Minutes
Ingredients:
- 4 sourdough bread slices
- 2 cheddar cheese slices
- 2 Swiss cheese slices
- 1 tbsp butter
- 2 dill pickles, sliced

Directions:
1. Preheat air fryer to 360°F. Smear both sides of the sourdough bread with butter and place them in the frying basket. Toast the bread for 6 minutes, flipping once.
2. Divide the cheddar cheese between 2 of the bread slices. Cover the remaining 2 bread slices with Swiss cheese slices. Bake for 10 more minutes until the cheeses have melted and lightly bubbled and the bread has golden brown. Set the cheddar-covered bread slices on a serving plate, cover with pickles, and top each with the Swiss-covered slices. Serve and enjoy!

Vegetarian Shepherd's Pie

Servings: 4
Cooking Time: 40 Minutes
Ingredients:
- 1 russet potato, peeled and diced
- 1 tbsp olive oil
- 2 tbsp balsamic vinegar
- ¼ cup cheddar shreds
- 2 tbsp milk
- Salt and pepper to taste
- 2 tsp avocado oil
- 1 cup beefless grounds
- ½ onion, diced
- 3 cloves garlic
- 1 carrot, diced
- ¼ diced green bell peppers
- 1 celery stalk, diced
- 2/3 cup tomato sauce
- 1 tsp chopped rosemary
- 1 tbsp sesame seeds
- 1 tsp thyme leaves
- 1 lemon

Directions:
1. Add salted water to a pot over high heat and bring it to a boil. Add in diced potatoes and cook for 5 minutes until fork tender. Drain and transfer it to a bowl. Add in the olive oil cheddar shreds, milk, salt, and pepper and mash it until smooth. Set the potato topping aside.

2. Preheat air fryer at 350ºF. Place avocado oil, beefless grounds, garlic, onion, carrot, bell pepper, and celery in a skillet over medium heat and cook for 4 minutes until the veggies are tender. Stir in the remaining ingredients and turn the heat off. Spoon the filling into a greased cake pan. Top with the potato topping.

3. Using tines of a fork, create shallow lines along the top of mashed potatoes. Place cake pan in the frying basket and Bake for 12 minutes. Let rest for 10 minutes before serving sprinkled with sesame seeds and squeezed lemon.

Tandoori Paneer Naan Pizza

Servings: 4
Cooking Time: 10 Minutes
Ingredients:
- 6 tablespoons plain Greek yogurt, divided
- 1¼ teaspoons garam marsala, divided
- ½ teaspoon turmeric, divided
- ¼ teaspoon garlic powder
- ½ teaspoon paprika, divided
- ½ teaspoon black pepper, divided
- 3 ounces paneer, cut into small cubes
- 1 tablespoon extra-virgin olive oil
- 2 teaspoons minced garlic
- 4 cups baby spinach
- 2 tablespoons marinara sauce
- ¼ teaspoon salt
- 2 plain naan breads (approximately 6 inches in diameter)
- ½ cup shredded part-skim mozzarella cheese

Directions:
1. Preheat the air fryer to 350°F.
2. In a small bowl, mix 2 tablespoons of the yogurt, ½ teaspoon of the garam marsala, ¼ teaspoon of the turmeric, the garlic powder, ¼ teaspoon of the paprika, and ¼ teaspoon of the black pepper. Toss the paneer cubes in the mixture and let marinate for at least an hour.
3. Meanwhile, in a pan, heat the olive oil over medium heat. Add in the minced garlic and sauté for 1 minute. Stir in the spinach and begin to cook until it wilts. Add in the remaining 4 tablespoons of yogurt and the marinara sauce. Stir in the remaining ¾ teaspoon of garam marsala, the remaining ¼ teaspoon of turmeric, the remaining ¼ teaspoon of paprika, the remaining ¼ teaspoon of black pepper, and the salt. Let simmer a minute or two, and then remove from the heat.
4. Equally divide the spinach mixture amongst the two naan breads. Place 1½ ounces of the marinated paneer on each naan.
5. Liberally spray the air fryer basket with olive oil mist.
6. Use a spatula to pick up one naan and place it in the air fryer basket.
7. Cook for 4 minutes, open the basket and sprinkle ¼ cup of mozzarella cheese on top, and cook another 4 minutes.
8. Remove from the air fryer and repeat with the remaining naan.
9. Serve warm.

Mushroom Lasagna

Servings: 4
Cooking Time: 40 Minutes
Ingredients:
- 2 tbsp olive oil
- 1 zucchini, diced
- ½ cup diced mushrooms
- ¼ cup diced onion
- 1 cup marinara sauce
- 1 cup ricotta cheese
- 1/3 cup grated Parmesan
- 1 egg
- 2 tsp Italian seasoning
- 2 tbsp fresh basil, chopped
- ½ tsp thyme
- 1 tbsp red pepper flakes
- ½ tsp salt
- 5 lasagna noodle sheets
- 1 cup grated mozzarella

Directions:
1. Heat the oil in a skillet over medium heat. Add zucchini, mushrooms, 1 tbsp of basil, thyme, red pepper flakes and onion and cook for 4 minutes until the veggies are tender. Toss in marinara sauce, and bring it to a bowl. Then, low the heat and simmer for 3 minutes.
2. Preheat air fryer at 375°F. Combine ricotta cheese, Parmesan cheese, egg, Italian seasoning, and salt in a bowl. Spoon ¼ of the veggie mixture into a cake pan. Add a layer of lasagna noodles on top, breaking apart noodles first to fit pan. Then, top with 1/3 of ricotta mixture and ¼ of mozzarella cheese. Repeat the layer 2 more times, finishing with mozzarella cheese on top. Cover cake pan with aluminum foil.
3. Place cake pan in the frying basket and Bake for 12 minutes. Remove the foil and cook for 3 more minutes. Let rest for 10 minutes before slicing. Serve immediately sprinkled with the remaining fresh basil.

Golden Breaded Mushrooms

Servings: 2
Cooking Time: 20 Minutes
Ingredients:
- 2 cups crispy rice cereal
- 1 tsp nutritional yeast
- 2 tsp garlic powder
- 1tsp dried oregano
- 1 tsp dried basil
- Salt to taste
- 1 tbsp Dijon mustard
- 1 tbsp mayonnaise
- ¼ cup milk
- 8 oz whole mushrooms
- 4 tbsp chili sauce
- 3 tbsp mayonnaise

Directions:
1. Preheat air fryer at 350°F. Blend rice cereal, garlic powder, oregano, basil, nutritional yeast, and salt in a food processor until it gets a breadcrumb consistency. Set aside in a bowl. Mix the mustard, mayonnaise, and milk in a bowl. Dip mushrooms in the mustard mixture; shake off any excess. Then, dredge them in the breadcrumbs; shake off any excess. Places mushrooms in the greased frying basket and Air Fry for 7 minutes, shaking once. Mix the mayonnaise with chili sauce in a small bowl. Serve the mushrooms with the dipping sauce on the side.

Crunchy Rice Paper Samosas

Servings: 2
Cooking Time: 20 Minutes
Ingredients:
- 1 boiled potato, mashed
- ¼ cup green peas
- 1 tsp garam masala powder
- ½ tsp ginger garlic paste
- ½ tsp cayenne pepper
- ½ tsp turmeric powder
- Salt and pepper to taste
- 3 rice paper wrappers

Directions:
1. Preheat air fryer to 350°F. Place the mashed potatoes in a bowl. Add the peas, garam masala powder, ginger garlic paste, cayenne pepper, turmeric powder, salt, and pepper and stir until ingredients are evenly blended.
2. Lay the rice paper wrappers out on a lightly floured surface. Divide the potato mixture between the wrappers and fold the top edges over to seal. Transfer the samosas to the greased frying basket and Air Fry for 12 minutes, flipping once until the samosas are crispy and flaky. Remove and leave to cool for 5 minutes. Serve and enjoy!

Harissa Veggie Fries

Servings: 4
Cooking Time: 55 Minutes
Ingredients:
- 1 pound red potatoes, cut into rounds
- 1 onion, diced
- 1 green bell pepper, diced
- 1 red bell pepper, diced
- 2 tbsp olive oil
- Salt and pepper to taste
- ¾ tsp garlic powder
- ¾ tsp harissa seasoning

Directions:
1. Combine all ingredients in a large bowl and mix until potatoes are well coated and seasoned. Preheat air fryer to 350°F. Pour all of the contents in the bowl into the frying basket. Bake for 35 minutes, shaking every 10 minutes, until golden brown and soft. Serve hot.

Tropical Salsa

Servings: 4
Cooking Time: 15 Minutes
Ingredients:
- 1 cup pineapple cubes
- ½ apple, cubed
- Salt to taste
- ¼ tsp olive oil
- 2 tomatoes, diced
- 1 avocado, diced
- 3-4 strawberries, diced
- ¼ cup diced red onion
- 1 tbsp chopped cilantro
- 1 tbsp chopped parsley
- 2 cloves garlic, minced
- ½ tsp granulated sugar
- ½ lime, juiced

Directions:
1. Preheat air fryer at 400ºF. Combine pineapple cubes, apples, olive oil, and salt in a bowl. Place pineapple in the greased frying basket, and Air Fry for 8 minutes, shaking once. Transfer it to a bowl. Toss in tomatoes, avocado, strawberries, onion, cilantro, parsley, garlic, sugar, lime juice, and salt. Let chill in the fridge before using.

Rainbow Quinoa Patties

Servings: 4
Cooking Time: 20 Minutes
Ingredients:
- 1 cup canned tri-bean blend, drained and rinsed
- 2 tbsp olive oil
- ½ tsp ground cumin
- ½ tsp garlic salt
- 1 tbsp paprika
- 1/3 cup uncooked quinoa
- 2 tbsp chopped onion
- ¼ cup shredded carrot
- 2 tbsp chopped cilantro
- 1 tsp chili powder
- ½ tsp salt
- 2 tbsp mascarpone cheese

Directions:
1. Place 1/3 cup of water, 1 tbsp of olive oil, cumin, and salt in a saucepan over medium heat and bring it to a boil. Remove from the heat and stir in quinoa. Let rest covered for 5 minutes.
2. Preheat air fryer at 350ºF. Using the back of a fork, mash beans until smooth. Toss in cooked quinoa and the remaining ingredients. Form mixture into 4 patties. Place patties in the greased frying basket and Air Fry for 6 minutes, turning once, and brush with the remaining olive oil. Serve immediately.

Stuffed Portobellos

Servings: 4
Cooking Time: 45 Minutes
Ingredients:
- 1 cup cherry tomatoes
- 2 ¼ tsp olive oil
- 3 tbsp grated mozzarella
- 1 cup chopped baby spinach
- 1 garlic clove, minced
- ¼ tsp dried oregano
- ¼ tsp dried thyme
- Salt and pepper to taste
- ¼ cup bread crumbs
- 4 portobello mushrooms, stemmed and gills removed
- 1 tbsp chopped parsley

Directions:
1. Preheat air fryer to 360°F. Combine tomatoes, ¼ teaspoon olive oil, and salt in a small bowl. Arrange in a single layer in the parchment-lined frying basket and Air Fry for 10 minutes. Stir and flatten the tomatoes with the back of a spoon, then Air Fry for another 6-8 minutes. Transfer the tomatoes to a medium bowl and combine with spinach, garlic, oregano, thyme, pepper, bread crumbs, and the rest of the olive oil.
2. Place the mushrooms on a work surface with the gills facing up. Spoon tomato mixture and mozzarella cheese equally into the mushroom caps and transfer the mushrooms to the frying basket. Air Fry for 8-10 minutes until the mushrooms have softened and the tops are golden. Garnish with chopped parsley and serve.

Sweet Corn Bread

Servings: 6
Cooking Time: 35 Minutes
Ingredients:
- 2 eggs, beaten
- ½ cup cornmeal
- ½ cup pastry flour
- 1/3 cup sugar
- 1 tsp lemon zest
- ½ tbsp baking powder
- ¼ tsp salt
- ¼ tsp baking soda
- ½ tbsp lemon juice
- ½ cup milk
- ¼ cup sunflower oil

Directions:
1. Preheat air fryer to 350°F. Add the cornmeal, flour, sugar, lemon zest, baking powder, salt, and baking soda in a bowl. Stir with a whisk until combined. Add the eggs, lemon juice, milk, and oil to another bowl and stir well. Add the wet mixture to the dry mixture and stir gently until combined. Spray a baking pan with oil. Pour the batter in and Bake in the fryer for 25 minutes or until golden and a knife inserted in the center comes out clean. Cut into wedges and serve.

Cheddar-bean Flautas

Servings: 4
Cooking Time: 15 Minutes
Ingredients:
- 8 corn tortillas
- 1 can refried beans
- 1 cup shredded cheddar
- 1 cup guacamole

Directions:
1. Preheat air fryer to 390°F. Wet the tortillas with water. Spray the frying basket with oil and stack the tortillas inside. Air Fry for 1 minute. Remove to a flat surface, laying them out individually. Scoop an equal amount of beans in a line down the center of each tortilla. Top with cheddar cheese. Roll the tortilla sides over the filling and put seam-side down in the greased frying basket. Air Fry for 7 minutes or until the tortillas are golden and crispy. Serve immediately topped with guacamole.

Easy Zucchini Lasagna Roll-ups

Servings: 2
Cooking Time: 40 Minutes
Ingredients:
- 2 medium zucchini
- 2 tbsp lemon juice
- 1 ½ cups ricotta cheese
- 1 tbsp allspice
- 2 cups marinara sauce
- 1/3 cup mozzarella cheese

Directions:
1. Preheat air fryer to 400°F. Cut the ends of each zucchini, then slice into 1/4-inch thick pieces and drizzle with lemon juice. Roast for 5 minutes until slightly tender. Let cool slightly. Combine ricotta cheese and allspice in a bowl; set aside. Spread 2 tbsp of marinara sauce on the bottom of a baking pan. Spoon 1-2 tbsp of the ricotta mixture onto each slice, roll up each slice and place them spiral-side up in the pan. Scatter with the remaining ricotta mixture and drizzle with marinara sauce. Top with mozzarella cheese and Bake at 360°F for 20 minutes until the cheese is bubbly and golden brown. Serve warm.

Stuffed Zucchini Boats

Servings: 2
Cooking Time: 20 Minutes
Ingredients:
- olive oil
- ½ cup onion, finely chopped
- 1 clove garlic, finely minced
- ½ teaspoon dried oregano
- ¼ teaspoon dried thyme
- ¾ cup couscous
- 1½ cups chicken stock, divided
- 1 tomato, seeds removed and finely chopped
- ½ cup coarsely chopped Kalamata olives
- ½ cup grated Romano cheese
- ¼ cup pine nuts, toasted
- 1 tablespoon chopped fresh parsley
- 1 teaspoon salt
- freshly ground black pepper
- 1 egg, beaten
- 1 cup grated mozzarella cheese, divided
- 2 thick zucchini

Directions:
1. Preheat a sauté pan on the stovetop over medium-high heat. Add the olive oil and sauté the onion until it just starts to soften–about 4 minutes. Stir in the garlic, dried oregano and thyme. Add the couscous and sauté for just a minute. Add 1¼ cups of the chicken stock and simmer over low heat for 3 to 5 minutes, until liquid has been absorbed and the couscous is soft. Remove the pan from heat and set it aside to cool slightly.
2. Fluff the couscous and add the tomato, Kalamata olives, Romano cheese, pine nuts, parsley, salt and pepper. Mix well. Add the remaining chicken stock, the egg and ½ cup of the mozzarella cheese. Stir to ensure everything is combined.
3. Cut each zucchini in half lengthwise. Then, trim each half of the zucchini into four 5-inch lengths. (Save the trimmed ends of the zucchini for another use.) Use a spoon to scoop out the center of the zucchini, leaving some flesh around the sides. Brush both sides of the zucchini with olive oil and season the cut side with salt and pepper.
4. Preheat the air fryer to 380°F.
5. Divide the couscous filling between the four zucchini boats. Use your hands to press the filling together and fill the inside of the zucchini. The filling should be mounded into the boats and rounded on top.
6. Transfer the zucchini boats to the air fryer basket and drizzle the stuffed zucchini boats with olive oil. Air-fry for 19 minutes. Then, sprinkle the remaining mozzarella cheese on top of the zucchini, pressing it down onto the filling lightly to prevent it from blowing around in the air fryer. Air-fry for one more minute to melt the cheese. Transfer the finished zucchini boats to a serving platter and garnish with the chopped parsley.

Veggie Burgers

Servings: 4
Cooking Time: 15 Minutes
Ingredients:
- 2 cans black beans, rinsed and drained
- ½ cup cooked quinoa
- ½ cup shredded raw sweet potato
- ¼ cup diced red onion
- 2 teaspoons ground cumin
- 1 teaspoon coriander powder
- ½ teaspoon salt
- oil for misting or cooking spray
- 8 slices bread
- suggested toppings: lettuce, tomato, red onion, Pepper Jack cheese, guacamole

Directions:
1. In a medium bowl, mash the beans with a fork.

2. Add the quinoa, sweet potato, onion, cumin, coriander, and salt and mix well with the fork.
3. Shape into 4 patties, each ¾-inch thick.
4. Mist both sides with oil or cooking spray and also mist the basket.
5. Cook at 390°F for 15minutes.
6. Follow the recipe for Toast, Plain & Simple.
7. Pop the veggie burgers back in the air fryer for a minute or two to reheat if necessary.
8. Serve on the toast with your favorite burger toppings.

Curried Potato, Cauliflower And Pea Turnovers

Servings: 4
Cooking Time: 40 Minutes
Ingredients:
- Dough:
- 2 cups all-purpose flour
- ½ teaspoon baking powder
- 1 teaspoon salt
- freshly ground black pepper
- ¼ teaspoon dried thyme
- ¼ cup canola oil
- ½ to ⅔ cup water
- Turnover Filling:
- 1 tablespoon canola or vegetable oil
- 1 onion, finely chopped
- 1 clove garlic, minced
- 1 tablespoon grated fresh ginger
- ½ teaspoon cumin seeds
- ½ teaspoon fennel seeds
- 1 teaspoon curry powder
- 2 russet potatoes, diced
- 2 cups cauliflower florets
- ½ cup frozen peas
- 2 tablespoons chopped fresh cilantro
- salt and freshly ground black pepper
- 2 tablespoons butter, melted
- mango chutney, for serving

Directions:
1. Start by making the dough. Combine the flour, baking powder, salt, pepper and dried thyme in a mixing bowl or the bowl of a stand mixer. Drizzle in the canola oil and pinch it together with your fingers to turn the flour into a crumby mixture. Stir in the water (enough to bring the dough together). Knead the dough for 5 minutes or so until it is smooth. Add a little more water or flour as needed. Let the dough rest while you make the turnover filling.
2. Preheat a large skillet on the stovetop over medium-high heat. Add the oil and sauté the onion until it starts to become tender – about 4 minutes. Add the garlic and ginger and continue to cook for another minute. Add the dried spices and toss everything to coat. Add the potatoes and cauliflower to the skillet and pour in 1½ cups of water. Simmer everything together for 20 to 25 minutes, or until the potatoes are soft and most of the water has evaporated. If the water has evaporated and the vegetables still need more time, just add a little water and continue to simmer until everything is tender. Stir well, crushing the potatoes and cauliflower a little as you do so. Stir in the peas and cilantro, season to taste with salt and freshly ground black pepper and set aside to cool.
3. Divide the dough into 4 balls. Roll the dough balls out into ¼-inch thick circles. Divide the cooled potato filling between the dough circles, placing a mound of the filling on one side of each piece of dough, leaving an empty border around the edge of the dough. Brush the edges of the dough with a little water and fold one edge of circle over the filling to meet the other edge of the circle, creating a half moon. Pinch the edges together with your fingers and then press the edge with the tines of a fork to decorate and seal.
4. Preheat the air fryer to 380°F.
5. Spray or brush the air fryer basket with oil. Brush the turnovers with the melted butter and place 2 turnovers into the air fryer basket. Air-fry for 15 minutes. Flip the turnovers over and air-fry for another 5 minutes. Repeat with the remaining 2 turnovers.
6. These will be very hot when they come out of the air fryer. Let them cool for at least 20 minutes before serving warm with mango chutney.

Roasted Veggie Bowls

Servings:4
Cooking Time: 30 Minutes
Ingredients:
- 1 cup Brussels sprouts, trimmed and quartered
- ½ onion, cut into half-moons
- ½ cup green beans, chopped
- 1 cup broccoli florets
- 1 red bell pepper, sliced
- 1 yellow bell pepper, sliced
- 1 tbsp olive oil
- ½ tsp chili powder
- ¼ tsp ground cumin
- ¼ tsp ground coriander

Directions:
1. Preheat air fryer to 350ºF. Combine all ingredients in a bowl. Place veggie mixture in the frying basket and Air Fry for 15 minutes, tossing every 5 minutes. Divide between 4 medium bowls and serve.

Lentil Burritos With Cilantro Chutney

Servings: 4
Cooking Time: 30 Minutes
Ingredients:
- 1 cup cilantro chutney
- 1 lb cooked potatoes, mashed
- 2 tsp sunflower oil
- 3 garlic cloves, minced
- 1 ½ tbsp fresh lime juice
- 1 ½ tsp cumin powder
- 1 tsp onion powder

- 1 tsp coriander powder
- Salt to taste
- ½ tsp turmeric
- ¼ tsp cayenne powder
- 4 large flour tortillas
- 1 cup cooked lentils
- ½ cup shredded cabbage
- ¼ cup minced red onions

Directions:

1. Preheat air fryer to 390°F. Place the mashed potatoes, sunflower oil, garlic, lime, cumin, onion powder, coriander, salt, turmeric, and cayenne in a large bowl. Stir well until combined. Lay the tortillas out flat on the counter. In the middle of each, distribute the potato filling. Add some of the lentils, cabbage, and red onions on top of the potatoes. Close the wraps by folding the bottom of the tortillas up and over the filling, then folding the sides in, then roll the bottom up to form a burrito. Place the wraps in the greased frying basket, seam side down. Air Fry for 6-8 minutes, flipping once until golden and crispy. Serve topped with cilantro chutney.

Arancini With Marinara

Servings: 6
Cooking Time: 15 Minutes
Ingredients:

- 2 cups cooked rice
- 1 cup grated Parmesan cheese
- 1 egg, whisked
- ¼ teaspoon dried thyme
- ½ teaspoon dried oregano
- ½ teaspoon dried basil
- ½ teaspoon dried parsley
- 1 teaspoon salt
- ¼ teaspoon paprika
- 1 cup breadcrumbs
- 4 ounces mozzarella, cut into 24 cubes
- 2 cups marinara sauce

Directions:

1. In a large bowl, mix together the rice, Parmesan cheese, and egg.
2. In another bowl, mix together the thyme, oregano, basil, parsley, salt, paprika, and breadcrumbs.
3. Form 24 rice balls with the rice mixture. Use your thumb to make an indentation in the center and stuff 1 cube of mozzarella in the center of the rice; close the ball around the cheese.
4. Roll the rice balls in the seasoned breadcrumbs until all are coated.
5. Preheat the air fryer to 400°F.
6. Place the rice balls in the air fryer basket and coat with cooking spray. Cook for 8 minutes, shake the basket, and cook another 7 minutes.
7. Heat the marinara sauce in a saucepan until warm. Serve sauce as a dip for arancini.

Colorful Vegetable Medley

Servings: 4
Cooking Time: 20 Minutes
Ingredients:

- 1 lb green beans, chopped
- 2 carrots, cubed
- Salt and pepper to taste
- 1 zucchini, cut into chunks
- 1 red bell pepper, sliced

Directions:

1. Preheat air fryer to 390°F. Combine green beans, carrots, salt and pepper in a large bowl. Spray with cooking oil and transfer to the frying basket. Roast for 6 minutes.
2. Combine zucchini and red pepper in a bowl. Season to taste and spray with cooking oil; set aside. When the cooking time is up, add the zucchini and red pepper to the basket. Cook for another 6 minutes. Serve and enjoy.

Cheese & Bean Burgers

Servings: 2
Cooking Time: 35 Minutes
Ingredients:

- 1 cup cooked black beans
- ½ cup shredded cheddar
- 1 egg, beaten
- Salt and pepper to taste
- 1 cup bread crumbs
- ½ cup grated carrots

Directions:

1. Preheat air fryer to 350°F. Mash the beans with a fork in a bowl. Mix in the cheese, salt, and pepper until evenly combined. Stir in half of the bread crumbs and egg. Shape the mixture into 2 patties. Coat each patty with the remaining bread crumbs and spray with cooking oil. Air Fry for 14-16 minutes, turning once. When ready, removeto a plate. Top with grated carrots and serve.

Garlic Okra Chips

Servings: 4
Cooking Time: 20 Minutes
Ingredients:

- 2 cups okra, cut into rounds
- 1 ½ tbsp. melted butter
- 1 garlic clove, minced
- 1 tsp powdered paprika
- Salt and pepper to taste

Directions:

1. Preheat air fryer to 350°F. Toss okra, melted butter, paprika, garlic, salt and pepper in a medium bowl until okra is coated. Place okra in the frying basket and Air Fry for 5 minutes. Shake the basket and Air Fry for another 5 minutes. Shake one more time and Air Fry for 2 minutes until crispy. Serve warm and enjoy.

Spaghetti Squash And Kale Fritters With Pomodoro Sauce

Servings: 3
Cooking Time: 45 Minutes
Ingredients:
- 1½-pound spaghetti squash (about half a large or a whole small squash)
- olive oil
- ½ onion, diced
- ½ red bell pepper, diced
- 2 cloves garlic, minced
- 4 cups coarsely chopped kale
- salt and freshly ground black pepper
- 1 egg
- ⅓ cup breadcrumbs, divided*
- ⅓ cup grated Parmesan cheese
- ½ teaspoon dried rubbed sage
- pinch nutmeg
- Pomodoro Sauce:
- 2 tablespoons olive oil
- ½ onion, chopped
- 1 to 2 cloves garlic, minced
- 1 (28-ounce) can peeled tomatoes
- ¼ cup red wine
- 1 teaspoon Italian seasoning
- 2 tablespoons chopped fresh basil, plus more for garnish
- salt and freshly ground black pepper
- ½ teaspoon sugar (optional)

Directions:
1. Preheat the air fryer to 370°F.
2. Cut the spaghetti squash in half lengthwise and remove the seeds. Rub the inside of the squash with olive oil and season with salt and pepper. Place the squash, cut side up, into the air fryer basket and air-fry for 30 minutes, flipping the squash over halfway through the cooking process.
3. While the squash is cooking, Preheat a large sauté pan over medium heat on the stovetop. Add a little olive oil and sauté the onions for 3 minutes, until they start to soften. Add the red pepper and garlic and continue to sauté for an additional 4 minutes. Add the kale and season with salt and pepper. Cook for 2 more minutes, or until the kale is soft. Transfer the mixture to a large bowl and let it cool.
4. While the squash continues to cook, make the Pomodoro sauce. Preheat the large sauté pan again over medium heat on the stovetop. Add the olive oil and sauté the onion and garlic for 2 to 3 minutes, until the onion begins to soften. Crush the canned tomatoes with your hands and add them to the pan along with the red wine and Italian seasoning and simmer for 20 minutes. Add the basil and season to taste with salt, pepper and sugar (if using).
5. When the spaghetti squash has finished cooking, use a fork to scrape the inside flesh of the squash onto a sheet pan. Spread the squash out and let it cool.
6. Once cool, add the spaghetti squash to the kale mixture, along with the egg, breadcrumbs, Parmesan cheese, sage, nutmeg, salt and freshly ground black pepper. Stir to combine well and then divide the mixture into 6 thick portions. You can shape the portions into patties, but I prefer to keep them a little random and unique in shape. Spray or brush the fritters with olive oil.
7. Preheat the air fryer to 370°F.
8. Brush the air fryer basket with a little olive oil and transfer the fritters to the basket. Air-fry the squash and kale fritters at 370°F for 15 minutes, flipping them over halfway through the cooking process.
9. Serve the fritters warm with the Pomodoro sauce spooned over the top or pooled on your plate. Garnish with the fresh basil leaves.

Meatless Kimchi Bowls

Servings: 4
Cooking Time: 20 Minutes
Ingredients:
- 2 cups canned chickpeas
- 1 carrot, julienned
- 6 scallions, sliced
- 1 zucchini, diced
- 2 tbsp coconut aminos
- 2 tsp sesame oil
- 1 tsp rice vinegar
- 2 tsp granulated sugar
- 1 tbsp gochujang
- ¼ tsp salt
- ½ cup kimchi
- 2 tsp roasted sesame seeds

Directions:
1. Preheat air fryer to 350°F. Combine all ingredients, except for the kimchi, 2 scallions, and sesame seeds, in a baking pan. Place the pan in the frying basket and Air Fry for 6 minutes. Toss in kimchi and cook for 2 more minutes. Divide between 2 bowls and garnish with the remaining scallions and sesame seeds. Serve immediately.

Bell Pepper & Lentil Tacos

Servings: 2
Cooking Time: 40 Minutes
Ingredients:
- 2 corn tortilla shells
- ½ cup cooked lentils
- ½ white onion, sliced
- ½ red pepper, sliced
- ½ green pepper, sliced
- ½ yellow pepper, sliced
- ½ cup shredded mozzarella
- ½ tsp Tabasco sauce

Directions:
1. Preheat air fryer to 320°F. Sprinkle half of the mozzarella cheese over one of the tortillas, then top with lentils, Tabasco sauce, onion, and peppers. Scatter the remaining mozzarella cheese, cover with the other tortilla and place in the frying

basket. Bake for 6 minutes, flipping halfway through cooking. Serve and enjoy!

Falafels

Servings: 12
Cooking Time: 10 Minutes
Ingredients:
- 1 pouch falafel mix
- 2–3 tablespoons plain breadcrumbs
- oil for misting or cooking spray

Directions:
1. Prepare falafel mix according to package directions.
2. Preheat air fryer to 390°F.
3. Place breadcrumbs in shallow dish or on wax paper.
4. Shape falafel mixture into 12 balls and flatten slightly. Roll in breadcrumbs to coat all sides and mist with oil or cooking spray.
5. Place falafels in air fryer basket in single layer and cook for 5minutes. Shake basket, and continue cooking for 5minutes, until they brown and are crispy.

Curried Cauliflower

Servings: 2
Cooking Time: 30 Minutes
Ingredients:
- 1 cup canned diced tomatoes
- 2 cups milk
- 2 tbsp lime juice
- 1 tbsp allspice
- 1 tbsp curry powder
- 1 tsp ground ginger
- ½ tsp ground cumin
- 12 oz frozen cauliflower
- 16 oz cheddar cheese, cubed
- ¼ cup chopped cilantro

Directions:
1. Preheat air fryer to 375°F. Combine the tomatoes and their juices, milk, lime juice, allspice, curry powder, ginger, and cumin in a baking pan. Toss in cauliflower and cheddar cheese until coated. Roast for 15 minutes, stir and Roast for another 10 minutes until bubbly. Scatter with cilantro before serving.

Effortless Mac `n´ Cheese

Servings: 4
Cooking Time: 15 Minutes
Ingredients:
- 1 cup heavy cream
- 1 cup milk
- ½ cup mozzarella cheese
- 2 tsp grated Parmesan cheese
- 16 oz cooked elbow macaroni

Directions:
1. Preheat air fryer to 400°F. Whisk the heavy cream, milk, mozzarella cheese, and Parmesan cheese until smooth in a bowl. Stir in the macaroni and pour into a baking dish. Cover with foil and Bake in the air fryer for 6 minutes. Remove foil and Bake until cooked through and bubbly, 3-5 minutes. Serve warm.

Tex-mex Potatoes With Avocado Dressing

Servings: 2
Cooking Time: 60 Minutes
Ingredients:
- ¼ cup chopped parsley, dill, cilantro, chives
- ¼ cup yogurt
- ½ avocado, diced
- 2 tbsp milk
- 2 tsp lemon juice
- ½ tsp lemon zest
- 1 green onion, chopped
- 2 cloves garlic, quartered
- Salt and pepper to taste
- 2 tsp olive oil
- 2 russet potatoes, scrubbed and perforated with a fork
- 1 cup steamed broccoli florets
- ½ cup canned white beans

Directions:
1. In a food processor, blend the yogurt, avocado, milk, lemon juice, lemon zest, green onion, garlic, parsley, dill, cilantro, chives, salt and pepper until smooth. Transfer it to a small bowl and let chill the dressing covered in the fridge until ready to use.
2. Preheat air fryer at 400ºF. Rub olive oil over both potatoes and sprinkle with salt and pepper. Place them in the frying basket and Bake for 45 minutes, flipping at 30 minutes mark. Let cool onto a cutting board for 5 minutes until cool enough to handle. Cut each potato lengthwise into slices and pinch ends together to open up each slice. Stuff broccoli and beans into potatoes and put them back into the basket, and cook for 3 more minutes. Drizzle avocado dressing over and serve.

Cheesy Veggie Frittata

Servings: 2
Cooking Time: 65 Minutes
Ingredients:
- 4 oz Bella mushrooms, chopped
- ¼ cup halved grape tomatoes
- 1 cup baby spinach
- 1/3 cup chopped leeks
- 1 baby carrot, chopped
- 4 eggs
- ½ cup grated cheddar
- 1 tbsp milk
- ¼ tsp garlic powder
- ¼ tsp dried oregano
- Salt and pepper to taste

Directions:
1. Preheat air fryer to 300°F. Crack the eggs into a bowl and beat them with a fork or whisk. Mix in the remaining ingredients until well combined. Pour into a greased cake pan.

Put the pan into the frying basket and Bake for 20-23 minutes or until eggs are set in the center. Remove from the fryer. Cut into halves and serve.

Tofu & Spinach Lasagna

Servings: 4
Cooking Time: 30 Minutes
Ingredients:
- 8 oz cooked lasagne noodles
- 1 tbsp olive oil
- 2 cups crumbled tofu
- 2 cups fresh spinach
- 2 tbsp cornstarch
- 1 tsp onion powder
- Salt and pepper to taste
- 2 garlic cloves, minced
- 2 cups marinara sauce
- ½ cup shredded mozzarella

Directions:
1. Warm the olive oil in a large pan over medium heat. Add the tofu and spinach and stir-fry for a minute. Add the cornstarch, onion powder, salt, pepper, and garlic. Stir until the spinach wilts. Remove from heat.
2. Preheat air fryer to 390°F. Pour a thin layer of pasta sauce in a baking pan. Layer 2-3 lasagne noodles on top of the marinara sauce. Top with a little more sauce and some of the tofu mix. Add another 2-3 noodles on top, then another layer of sauce, then another layer of tofu. Finish with a layer of noodles and a final layer of sauce. Sprinkle with mozzarella cheese on top. Place the pan in the air fryer and Bake for 15 minutes or until the noodle edges are browned and the cheese is melted. Cut and serve.

Spinach And Cheese Calzone

Servings: 2
Cooking Time: 10 Minutes
Ingredients:
- ⅔ cup frozen chopped spinach, thawed
- 1 cup grated mozzarella cheese
- 1 cup ricotta cheese
- ½ teaspoon Italian seasoning
- ½ teaspoon salt
- freshly ground black pepper
- 1 store-bought or homemade pizza dough* (about 12 to 16 ounces)
- 2 tablespoons olive oil
- pizza or marinara sauce (optional)

Directions:
1. Drain and squeeze all the water out of the thawed spinach and set it aside. Mix the mozzarella cheese, ricotta cheese, Italian seasoning, salt and freshly ground black pepper together in a bowl. Stir in the chopped spinach.
2. Divide the dough in half. With floured hands or on a floured surface, stretch or roll one half of the dough into a 10-inch circle. Spread half of the cheese and spinach mixture on half of the dough, leaving about one inch of dough empty around the edge.
3. Fold the other half of the dough over the cheese mixture, almost to the edge of the bottom dough to form a half moon. Fold the bottom edge of dough up over the top edge and crimp the dough around the edges in order to make the crust and seal the calzone. Brush the dough with olive oil. Repeat with the second half of dough to make the second calzone.
4. Preheat the air fryer to 360°F.
5. Brush or spray the air fryer basket with olive oil. Air-fry the calzones one at a time for 10 minutes, flipping the calzone over half way through. Serve with warm pizza or marinara sauce if desired.

Honey Pear Chips

Servings: 4
Cooking Time: 30 Minutes
Ingredients:
- 2 firm pears, thinly sliced
- 1 tbsp lemon juice
- ½ tsp ground cinnamon
- 1 tsp honey

Directions:
1. Preheat air fryer to 380°F. Arrange the pear slices on the parchment-lined cooking basket. Drizzle with lemon juice and honey and sprinkle with cinnamon. Air Fry for 6-8 minutes, shaking the basket once, until golden. Leave to cool. Serve immediately or save for later in an airtight container. Good for 2 days.

Crispy Apple Fries With Caramel Sauce

Servings: 4
Cooking Time: 15 Minutes
Ingredients:
- 4 medium apples, cored
- ¼ tsp cinnamon
- ¼ tsp nutmeg
- 1 cup caramel sauce

Directions:
1. Preheat air fryer to 350°F. Slice the apples to a 1/3-inch thickness for a crunchy chip. Place in a large bowl and sprinkle with cinnamon and nutmeg. Place the slices in the air fryer basket. Bake for 6 minutes. Shake the basket, then cook for another 4 minutes or until crunchy. Serve drizzled with caramel sauce and enjoy!

Spinach & Brie Frittata

Servings: 4
Cooking Time: 25 Minutes
Ingredients:
- 5 eggs
- Salt and pepper to taste
- ½ cup baby spinach
- 1 shallot, diced
- 4 oz brie cheese, cubed

- 1 tomato, sliced

Directions:

1. Preheat air fryer to 320°F. Whisk all ingredients, except for the tomato slices, in a bowl. Transfer to a baking pan greased with olive oil and top with tomato slices. Place the pan in the frying basket and Bake for 14 minutes. Let cool for 5 minutes before slicing. Serve and enjoy!

Healthy Living Mushroom Enchiladas

Servings: 4
Cooking Time: 40 Minutes
Ingredients:

- 2 cups sliced mushrooms
- ½ onion, thinly sliced
- 2 garlic cloves, minced
- 1 tbsp olive oil
- 10 oz spinach, chopped
- ½ tsp ground cumin
- 1 tbsp dried oregano
- 1 tsp chili powder
- ¼ cup grated feta cheese
- ¼ tsp red pepper flakes
- 1 cup grated mozzarella cheese
- 1 cup sour cream
- 2 tbsp mayonnaise
- Juice of 1 lime
- Salt and pepper to taste
- 8 corn tortillas
- 1 jalapeño pepper, diced
- ¼ cup chopped cilantro

Directions:

1. Preheat air fryer to 400°F. Combine mushrooms, onion, oregano, garlic, chili powder, olive oil, and salt in a small bowl until well coated. Transfer to the greased frying basket. Cook for 5 minutes, then shake the basket. Cook for another 3 to 4 minutes, then transfer to a medium bowl. Wipe out the frying basket. Take the garlic cloves from the mushroom mixture and finely mince them. Return half of the garlic to the bowl with the mushrooms. Stir in spinach, cumin, red pepper flakes, and ½ cup of mozzarella. Place the other half of the minced garlic in a small bowl along with sour cream, mayonnaise, feta, the rest of the mozzarella, lime juice, and black pepper.
2. To prepare the enchiladas, spoon 2 tablespoons of mushroom mixture in the center of each tortilla. Roll the tortilla and place it seam-side down in the baking dish. Repeat for the rest of the tortillas. Top with sour cream mixture and garnish with jalapenos. Place the dish in the frying basket and bake for 20 minutes until heated through and just brown on top. Top with cilantro. Serve.

Fried Potatoes With Bell Peppers

Servings: 4
Cooking Time: 30 Minutes
Ingredients:

- 3 russet potatoes, cubed
- 1 tbsp canola oil
- 1 tbsp olive oil
- 1 tsp paprika
- Salt and pepper to taste
- 1 chopped shallot
- ½ chopped red bell peppers
- ½ diced yellow bell peppers

Directions:

1. Preheat air fryer to 370°F. Whisk the canola oil, olive oil, paprika, salt, and pepper in a bowl. Toss in the potatoes to coat. Place the potatoes in the air fryer and Bake for 20 minutes, shaking the basket periodically. Top the potatoes with shallot and bell peppers and cook for an additional 3-4 minutes or until the potatoes are cooked through and the peppers are soft. Serve warm.

Spring Veggie Empanadas

Servings: 4
Cooking Time: 75 Minutes
Ingredients:

- 10 empanada pastry discs
- 1 tbsp olive oil
- 1 shallot, minced
- 1 garlic clove, minced
- ½ cup whole milk
- 1 cup chopped broccoli
- ½ cup chopped cauliflower
- ½ cup diced carrots
- ¼ cup diced celery
- ⅛ tsp ground nutmeg
- 1 tsp cumin powder
- 1 tsp minced ginger
- 1 egg

Directions:

1. Melt the olive oil in a pot over medium heat. Stir in shallot and garlic and cook through for 1 minute. Next, add 1 tablespoon of flour and continue stirring. Whisk in milk, then lower the heat. After that, add broccoli, cauliflower, carrots, celery, cumin powder, pepper, ginger, and nutmeg. Cook for 2 minutes then remove from the heat. Allow to cool for 5 minutes.
2. Preheat air fryer to 350°F. Lightly flour a flat work surface and turn out the pastry discs. Scoop ¼ of the vegetables in the center of each circle. Whisk the egg and 1 teaspoon of water in a small bowl and brush the entire edge of the circle with the egg wash and fold the dough over the filling into a half-moon shape. Crimp the edge with a fork to seal. Arrange the patties in a single layer in the frying basket and bake for 12 minutes. Flip the patties and bake for another 10 to 12 minutes until the outside crust is golden. Serve immediately and enjoy.

Mexican Twice Air-fried Sweet Potatoes

Servings: 2
Cooking Time: 42 Minutes
Ingredients:
- 2 large sweet potatoes
- olive oil
- salt and freshly ground black pepper
- ⅓ cup diced red onion
- ⅓ cup diced red bell pepper
- ½ cup canned black beans, drained and rinsed
- ½ cup corn kernels, fresh or frozen
- ½ teaspoon chili powder
- 1½ cups grated pepper jack cheese, divided
- Jalapeño peppers, sliced

Directions:
1. Preheat the air fryer to 400°F.
2. Rub the outside of the sweet potatoes with olive oil and season with salt and freshly ground black pepper. Transfer the potatoes into the air fryer basket and air-fry at 400°F for 30 minutes, rotating the potatoes a few times during the cooking process.
3. While the potatoes are air-frying, start the potato filling. Preheat a large sauté pan over medium heat on the stovetop. Add the onion and pepper and sauté for a few minutes, until the vegetables start to soften. Add the black beans, corn, and chili powder and sauté for another 3 minutes. Set the mixture aside.
4. Remove the sweet potatoes from the air fryer and let them rest for 5 minutes. Slice off one inch of the flattest side of both potatoes. Scrape the potato flesh out of the potatoes, leaving half an inch of potato flesh around the edge of the potato. Place all the potato flesh into a large bowl and mash it with a fork. Add the black bean mixture and 1 cup of the pepper jack cheese to the mashed sweet potatoes. Season with salt and freshly ground black pepper and mix well. Stuff the hollowed out potato shells with the black bean and sweet potato mixture, mounding the filling high in the potatoes.
5. Transfer the stuffed potatoes back into the air fryer basket and air-fry at 370°F for 10 minutes. Sprinkle the remaining cheese on top of each stuffed potato, lower the heat to 340°F and air-fry for an additional 2 minutes to melt the cheese. Top with a couple slices of Jalapeño pepper and serve warm with a green salad.

Chicano Rice Bowls

Servings: 4
Cooking Time: 10 Minutes
Ingredients:
- 1 cup sour cream
- 2 tbsp milk
- 1 tsp ground cumin
- 1 tsp chili powder
- 1/8 tsp cayenne pepper
- 1 tbsp tomato paste
- 1 white onion, chopped
- 1 clove garlic, minced
- ½ tsp ground turmeric
- ½ tsp salt
- 1 cup canned black beans
- 1 cup canned corn kernels
- 1 tsp olive oil
- 4 cups cooked brown rice
- 3 tomatoes, diced
- 1 avocado, diced

Directions:
1. Whisk the sour cream, milk, cumin, ground turmeric, chili powder, cayenne pepper, and salt in a bowl. Let chill covered in the fridge until ready to use.
2. Preheat air fryer at 350ºF. Combine beans, white onion, tomato paste, garlic, corn, and olive oil in a bowl. Transfer it into the frying basket and Air Fry for 5 minutes. Divide cooked rice into 4 serving bowls. Top each with bean mixture, tomatoes, and avocado and drizzle with sour cream mixture over. Serve immediately.

Pine Nut Eggplant Dip

Servings: 4
Cooking Time: 35 Minutes
Ingredients:
- 2 ½ tsp olive oil
- 1 eggplant, halved lengthwise
- 1/2 cup Parmesan cheese
- 2 tsp pine nuts
- 1 tbsp chopped walnuts
- ¼ cup tahini
- 1 tbsp lemon juice
- 2 cloves garlic, minced
- 1/8 tsp ground cumin
- 1 tsp smoked paprika
- Salt and pepper to taste
- 1 tbsp chopped parsley

Directions:
1. Preheat air fryer at 375ºF. Rub olive oil over eggplant and pierce the eggplant flesh 3 times with a fork. Place eggplant, flat side down, in the frying basket and Bake for 25 minutes. Let cool onto a cutting board for 5 minutes until cool enough to handle. Scoop out eggplant flesh. Add pine nuts and walnuts to the basket and Air Fry for 2 minutes, shaking every 30 seconds to ensure they don´t burn. Set aside in a bowl.
2. In a food processor, blend eggplant flesh, tahini, lemon juice, garlic, smoked paprika, cumin, salt, and pepper until smooth. Transfer to a bowl. Scatter with the roasted pine nuts, Parmesan cheese, and parsley. Drizzle the dip with the remaining olive oil. Serve and enjoy!

Garlicky Roasted Mushrooms

Servings: 4
Cooking Time: 30 Minutes
Ingredients:
- 16 garlic cloves, peeled
- 2 tsp olive oil
- 16 button mushrooms
- 2 tbsp fresh chives, snipped
- Salt and pepper to taste
- 1 tbsp white wine

Directions:
1. Preheat air fryer to 350°F. Coat the garlic with some olive oil in a baking pan, then Roast in the air fryer for 12 minutes. When done, take the pan out and stir in the mushrooms, salt, and pepper. Then add the remaining olive oil and white wine. Put the pan back into the fryer and Bake for 10-15 minutes until the mushrooms and garlic soften. Sprinkle with chives and serve warm.

Mushroom, Zucchini And Black Bean Burgers

Servings: 4
Cooking Time: 18 Minutes
Ingredients:
- 1 cup diced zucchini, (about ½ medium zucchini)
- 1 tablespoon olive oil
- salt and freshly ground black pepper
- 1 cup chopped brown mushrooms (about 3 ounces)
- 1 small clove garlic
- 1 (15-ounce) can black beans, drained and rinsed
- 1 teaspoon lemon zest
- 1 tablespoon chopped fresh cilantro
- ½ cup plain breadcrumbs
- 1 egg, beaten
- ½ teaspoon salt
- freshly ground black pepper
- whole-wheat pita bread, burger buns or brioche buns
- mayonnaise, tomato, avocado and lettuce, for serving

Directions:
1. Preheat the air fryer to 400°F.
2. Toss the zucchini with the olive oil, season with salt and freshly ground black pepper and air-fry for 6 minutes, shaking the basket once or twice while it cooks.
3. Transfer the zucchini to a food processor with the mushrooms, garlic and black beans and process until still a little chunky but broken down and pasty. Transfer the mixture to a bowl. Add the lemon zest, cilantro, breadcrumbs and egg and mix well. Season again with salt and freshly ground black pepper. Shape the mixture into four burger patties and refrigerate for at least 15 minutes.
4. Preheat the air fryer to 370°F. Transfer two of the veggie burgers to the air fryer basket and air-fry for 12 minutes, flipping the burgers gently halfway through the cooking time. Keep the burgers warm by loosely tenting them with foil while you cook the remaining two burgers. Return the first batch of burgers back into the air fryer with the second batch for the last two minutes of cooking to re-heat.
5. Serve on toasted whole-wheat pita bread, burger buns or brioche buns with some mayonnaise, tomato, avocado and lettuce.

Roasted Vegetable Pita Pizza

Servings: 4
Cooking Time: 20 Minutes
Ingredients:
- 1 medium red bell pepper, seeded and cut into quarters
- 1 teaspoon extra-virgin olive oil
- ⅛ teaspoon black pepper
- ⅛ teaspoon salt
- Two 6-inch whole-grain pita breads
- 6 tablespoons pesto sauce
- ¼ small red onion, thinly sliced
- ½ cup shredded part-skim mozzarella cheese

Directions:
1. Preheat the air fryer to 400°F.
2. In a small bowl, toss the bell peppers with the olive oil, pepper, and salt.
3. Place the bell peppers in the air fryer and cook for 15 minutes, shaking every 5 minutes to prevent burning.
4. Remove the peppers and set aside. Turn the air fryer temperature down to 350°F.
5. Lay the pita bread on a flat surface. Cover each with half the pesto sauce; then top with even portions of the red bell peppers and onions. Sprinkle cheese over the top. Spray the air fryer basket with olive oil mist.
6. Carefully lift the pita bread into the air fryer basket with a spatula.
7. Cook for 5 to 8 minutes, or until the outer edges begin to brown and the cheese is melted.
8. Serve warm with desired sides.

Creamy Broccoli & Mushroom Casserole

Servings: 4
Cooking Time: 30 Minutes
Ingredients:
- 4 cups broccoli florets, chopped
- 1 cup crushed cheddar cheese crisps
- ¼ cup diced onion
- ¼ tsp dried thyme
- ¼ tsp dried marjoram
- ¼ tsp dried oregano
- ½ cup diced mushrooms
- 1 egg
- 2 tbsp sour cream
- ¼ cup mayonnaise
- Salt and pepper to taste

Directions:
1. Preheat air fryer to 350ºF. Combine all ingredients, except for the cheese crisps, in a bowl. Spoon mixture into a round cake pan. Place cake pan in the frying basket and Bake for 14 minutes. Let sit for 10 minutes. Distribute crushed cheddar cheese crisps over the top and serve.

Chapter 8 Vegetable Side Dishes Recipes

Speedy Baked Caprese With Avocado

Servings:4
Cooking Time: 15 Minutes
Ingredients:
- 4 oz fresh mozzarella
- 8 cherry tomatoes
- 2 tsp olive oil
- 2 halved avocados, pitted
- ¼ tsp salt
- 2 tbsp basil, torn

Directions:
1. Preheat air fryer to 375°F. In a bowl, combine tomatoes and olive oil. Set aside. Add avocado halves, cut sides up, in the frying basket, scatter tomatoes around halves, and Bake for 7 minutes. Divide avocado halves between 4 small plates, top each with 2 tomatoes and sprinkle with salt. Cut mozzarella cheese and evenly distribute over tomatoes. Scatter with the basil to serve.

Green Dip With Pine Nuts

Servings: 3
Cooking Time: 30 Minutes
Ingredients:
- 10 oz canned artichokes, chopped
- 2 tsp grated Parmesan cheese
- 10 oz spinach, chopped
- 2 scallions, finely chopped
- ½ cup pine nuts
- ½ cup milk
- 3 tbsp lemon juice
- 2 tsp tapioca flour
- 1 tsp allspice

Directions:
1. Preheat air fryer to 360°F. Arrange spinach, artichokes, and scallions in a pan. Set aside. In a food processor, blitz the pine nuts, milk, lemon juice, Parmesan cheese, flour, and allspice on high until smooth. Pour it over the veggies and Bake for 20 minutes, stirring every 5 minutes. Serve.

Tuna Platter

Servings: 4
Cooking Time: 9 Minutes
Ingredients:
- 4 new potatoes, boiled in their jackets
- ½ cup vinaigrette dressing, plus 2 tablespoons
- ½ pound fresh green beans, cut in half-inch pieces and steamed
- 1 tablespoon Herbes de Provence
- 1 tablespoon minced shallots
- 1½ tablespoons tarragon vinegar
- 4 tuna steaks, each ¾-inch thick, about 1 pound
- salt and pepper
- Salad
- 8 cups chopped romaine lettuce
- 12 grape tomatoes, halved lengthwise
- ½ cup pitted olives (black, green, nicoise, or combination)
- 2 boiled eggs, peeled and halved lengthwise

Directions:
1. Quarter potatoes and toss with 1 tablespoon salad dressing.
2. Toss the warm beans with the other tablespoon of salad dressing. Set both aside while you prepare the tuna.
3. Mix together the herbs, shallots, and vinegar and rub into all sides of tuna. Season fish to taste with salt and pepper.
4. Cook tuna at 390°F for 7minutes and check. If needed, cook 2 minutes longer, until tuna is barely pink in the center.
5. Spread the lettuce over a large platter.
6. Slice the tuna steaks in ½-inch pieces and arrange them in the center of the lettuce.
7. Place the remaining ingredients around the tuna. Diners create their own plates by selecting what they want from the platter. Pass remainder of salad dressing at the table.

Dijon Artichoke Hearts

Servings:4
Cooking Time: 25 Minutes
Ingredients:
- 1 jar artichoke hearts in water, drained
- 1 egg
- 1 tbsp Dijon mustard
- ½ cup bread crumbs
- ¼ cup flour
- 6 basil leaves

Directions:
1. Preheat air fryer to 350°F. Beat egg and mustard in a bowl. In another bowl, combine bread crumbs and flour. Dip artichoke hearts in egg mixture, then dredge in crumb mixture. Place artichoke hearts in the greased frying basket and Air Fry for 7-10 minutes until crispy. Serve topped with basil. Enjoy!

Tofu & Broccoli Salad

Servings: 4
Cooking Time: 17 Minutes
Ingredients:
- Broccoli Salad
- 4 cups fresh broccoli, cut into bite-size pieces
- ½ cup red onion, chopped
- ⅓ cup raisins or dried cherries
- ¾ cup sliced almonds
- ½ cup Asian-style salad dressing
- Tofu
- 4 ounces extra firm tofu
- 1 teaspoon smoked paprika
- 1 teaspoon onion powder
- ¼ teaspoon salt

- 2 tablespoons cornstarch
- 1 tablespoon extra virgin olive oil

Directions:
1. Place several folded paper towels on a plate and set tofu on top. Cover tofu with another folded paper towel, put another plate on top, and add heavy items such as canned goods to weigh it down. Press tofu for 30minutes.
2. While tofu is draining, combine all salad ingredients in a large bowl. Toss together well, cover, and chill until ready to serve.
3. Cut the tofu into small cubes, about ¼-inch thick. Sprinkle the cubes top and bottom with the paprika, onion powder, and salt.
4. Place cornstarch in small plastic bag, add tofu, and shake until cubes are well coated.
5. Place olive oil in another small plastic bag, add coated tofu, and shake to coat well.
6. Cook at 330°F for 17 minutes or until as crispy as you like.
7. To serve, stir chilled salad well, divide among 4 plates, and top with fried tofu.

Blistered Green Beans

Servings: 3
Cooking Time: 10 Minutes
Ingredients:
- ¾ pound Green beans, trimmed on both ends
- 1½ tablespoons Olive oil
- 3 tablespoons Pine nuts
- 1½ tablespoons Balsamic vinegar
- 1½ teaspoons Minced garlic
- ¾ teaspoon Table salt
- ¾ teaspoon Ground black pepper

Directions:
1. Preheat the air fryer to 400°F.
2. Toss the green beans and oil in a large bowl until all the green beans are glistening.
3. When the machine is at temperature, pile the green beans into the basket. Air-fry for 10 minutes, tossing often to rearrange the green beans in the basket, or until blistered and tender.
4. Dump the contents of the basket into a serving bowl. Add the pine nuts, vinegar, garlic, salt, and pepper. Toss well to coat and combine. Serve warm or at room temperature.

Parmesan Asparagus

Servings: 2
Cooking Time: 5 Minutes
Ingredients:
- 1 bunch asparagus, stems trimmed
- 1 teaspoon olive oil
- salt and freshly ground black pepper
- ¼ cup coarsely grated Parmesan cheese
- ½ lemon

Directions:
1. Preheat the air fryer to 400°F.
2. Toss the asparagus with the oil and season with salt and freshly ground black pepper.
3. Transfer the asparagus to the air fryer basket and air-fry at 400°F for 5 minutes, shaking the basket to turn the asparagus once or twice during the cooking process.
4. When the asparagus is cooked to your liking, sprinkle the asparagus generously with the Parmesan cheese and close the air fryer drawer again. Let the asparagus sit for 1 minute in the turned-off air fryer. Then, remove the asparagus, transfer it to a serving dish and finish with a grind of black pepper and a squeeze of lemon juice.

Okra

Servings: 4
Cooking Time: 12 Minutes
Ingredients:
- 7–8 ounces fresh okra
- 1 egg
- 1 cup milk
- 1 cup breadcrumbs
- ½ teaspoon salt
- oil for misting or cooking spray

Directions:
1. Remove stem ends from okra and cut in ½-inch slices.
2. In a medium bowl, beat together egg and milk. Add okra slices and stir to coat.
3. In a sealable plastic bag or container with lid, mix together the breadcrumbs and salt.
4. Remove okra from egg mixture, letting excess drip off, and transfer into bag with breadcrumbs.
5. Shake okra in crumbs to coat well.
6. Place all of the coated okra into the air fryer basket and mist with oil or cooking spray. Okra doesn't need to cook in a single layer, nor is it necessary to spray all sides at this point. A good spritz on top will do.
7. Cook at 390°F for 5minutes. Shake basket to redistribute and give it another spritz as you shake.
8. Cook 5 more minutes. Shake and spray again. Cook for 2 minutes longer or until golden brown and crispy.

Latkes

Servings: 12
Cooking Time: 13 Minutes
Ingredients:
- 1 russet potato
- ¼ onion
- 2 eggs, lightly beaten
- ⅓ cup flour*
- ½ teaspoon baking powder
- 1 teaspoon salt
- freshly ground black pepper
- canola or vegetable oil, in a spray bottle
- chopped chives, for garnish
- apple sauce
- sour cream

Directions:

1. Shred the potato and onion with a coarse box grater or a food processor with the shredding blade. Place the shredded vegetables into a colander or mesh strainer and squeeze or press down firmly to remove the excess water.
2. Transfer the onion and potato to a large bowl and add the eggs, flour, baking powder, salt and black pepper. Mix to combine and then shape the mixture into patties, about ¼-cup of mixture each. Brush or spray both sides of the latkes with oil.
3. Preheat the air fryer to 400°F.
4. Air-fry the latkes in batches. Transfer one layer of the latkes to the air fryer basket and air-fry at 400°F for 12 to 13 minutes, flipping them over halfway through the cooking time. Transfer the finished latkes to a platter and cover with aluminum foil, or place them in a warm oven to keep warm.
5. Garnish the latkes with chopped chives and serve with sour cream and applesauce.

Zucchini Fries

Servings: 3
Cooking Time: 12 Minutes
Ingredients:
- 1 large Zucchini
- ½ cup All-purpose flour or tapioca flour
- 2 Large egg(s), well beaten
- 1 cup Seasoned Italian-style dried bread crumbs (gluten-free, if a concern)
- Olive oil spray

Directions:
1. Preheat the air fryer to 400°F.
2. Trim the zucchini into a long rectangular block, taking off the ends and four "sides" to make this shape. Cut the block lengthwise into ½-inch-thick slices. Lay these slices flat and cut in half widthwise. Slice each of these pieces into ½-inch-thick batons.
3. Set up and fill three shallow soup plates or small pie plates on your counter: one for the flour, one for the beaten egg(s), and one for the bread crumbs.
4. Set a zucchini baton in the flour and turn it several times to coat all sides. Gently shake off any excess flour, then dip it in the egg(s), turning it to coat. Let any excess egg slip back into the rest, then set the baton in the bread crumbs and turn it several times, pressing gently to coat all sides, even the ends. Set aside on a cutting board and continue coating the remainder of the batons in the same way.
5. Lightly coat the batons on all sides with olive oil spray. Set them in two flat layers in the basket, the top layer at a 90-degree angle to the bottom one, with a little air space between the batons in each layer. In the end, the whole thing will look like a crosshatch pattern. Air-fry undisturbed for 6 minutes.
6. Use kitchen tongs to gently rearrange the batons so that any covered parts are now uncovered. The batons no longer need to be in a crosshatch pattern. Continue air-frying undisturbed for 6 minutes, or until lightly browned and crisp.
7. Gently pour the contents of the basket onto a wire rack. Spread the batons out and cool for only a minute or two before serving.

Herbed Zucchini Poppers

Servings: 4
Cooking Time: 30 Minutes
Ingredients:
- 1 tbsp grated Parmesan cheese
- 2 zucchini, sliced
- 1 cup breadcrumbs
- 2 eggs, beaten
- Salt and pepper to taste
- 1 tsp dry tarragon
- 1 tsp dry dill

Directions:
1. Preheat air fryer to 390°F. Place the breadcrumbs, Parmesan, tarragon, dill, salt, and pepper in a bowl and stir to combine. Dip the zucchini into the beaten eggs, then coat with Parmesan-crumb mixture. Lay the zucchini slices on the greased frying basket in an even layer. Air Fry for 14-16 minutes, shaking the basket several times during cooking. When ready, the zucchini will be crispy and golden brown. Serve hot and enjoy!

Sweet Roasted Pumpkin Rounds

Servings: 4
Cooking Time: 35 Minutes
Ingredients:
- 1 pumpkin
- 1 tbsp honey
- 1 tbsp melted butter
- ¼ tsp cardamom
- ¼ tsp sea salt

Directions:
1. Preheat the air fryer to 370°F. Cut the pumpkin in half lengthwise and remove the seeds. Slice each half crosswise into 1-inch-wide half-circles, then cut each half-circle in half again to make quarter rounds. Combine the honey, butter, cardamom, and salt in a bowl and mix well. Toss the pumpkin in the mixture until coated, then put into the frying basket. Bake for 15-20 minutes, shaking once during cooking until the edges start to brown and the squash is tender.

Simple Zucchini Ribbons

Servings: 4
Cooking Time: 15 Minutes
Ingredients:
- 2 zucchini
- 2 tsp butter, melted
- ¼ tsp garlic powder
- ¼ tsp chili flakes
- 8 cherry tomatoes, halved
- Salt and pepper to taste

Directions:
1. Preheat air fryer to 275°F. Cut the zucchini into ribbons with a vegetable peeler. Mix them with butter, garlic, chili flakes, salt, and pepper in a bowl. Transfer to the frying basket and Air Fry for 2 minutes. Toss and add the cherry tomatoes. Cook for another 2 minutes. Serve.

Butternut Medallions With Honey Butter And Sage

Servings: 2
Cooking Time: 15 Minutes
Ingredients:
- 1 butternut squash, peeled
- olive oil, in a spray bottle
- salt and freshly ground black pepper
- 2 tablespoons butter, softened
- 2 tablespoons honey
- pinch ground cinnamon
- pinch ground nutmeg
- chopped fresh sage

Directions:
1. Preheat the air fryer to 370°F.
2. Cut the neck of the butternut squash into disks about ½-inch thick. (Use the base of the butternut squash for another use.) Brush or spray the disks with oil and season with salt and freshly ground black pepper.
3. Transfer the butternut disks to the air fryer in one layer (or just ever so slightly overlapping). Air-fry at 370°F for 5 minutes.
4. While the butternut squash is cooking, combine the butter, honey, cinnamon and nutmeg in a small bowl. Brush this mixture on the butternut squash, flip the disks over and brush the other side as well. Continue to air-fry at 370°F for another 5 minutes. Flip the disks once more, brush with more of the honey butter and air-fry for another 5 minutes. The butternut should be browning nicely around the edges.
5. Remove the butternut squash from the air-fryer and repeat with additional batches if necessary. Transfer to a serving platter, sprinkle with the fresh sage and serve.

Steakhouse Baked Potatoes

Servings: 3
Cooking Time: 55 Minutes
Ingredients:
- 3 10-ounce russet potatoes
- 2 tablespoons Olive oil
- 1 teaspoon Table salt

Directions:
1. Preheat the air fryer to 375°F.
2. Poke holes all over each potato with a fork. Rub the skin of each potato with 2 teaspoons of the olive oil, then sprinkle ¼ teaspoon salt all over each potato.
3. When the machine is at temperature, set the potatoes in the basket in one layer with as much air space between them as possible. Air-fry for 50 minutes, turning once, or until soft to the touch but with crunchy skins. If the machine is at 360°F, you may need to add up to 5 minutes to the cooking time.
4. Use kitchen tongs to gently transfer the baked potatoes to a wire rack. Cool for 5 or 10 minutes before serving.

Sesame Carrots And Sugar Snap Peas

Cooking Time: 16 Minutes
Servings: 4
Ingredients:
- 1 pound carrots, peeled sliced on the bias (½-inch slices)
- 1 teaspoon olive oil
- salt and freshly ground black pepper
- ⅓ cup honey
- 1 tablespoon sesame oil
- 1 tablespoon soy sauce
- ½ teaspoon minced fresh ginger
- 4 ounces sugar snap peas (about 1 cup)
- 1½ teaspoons sesame seeds

Directions:
1. Preheat the air fryer to 360°F.
2. Toss the carrots with the olive oil, season with salt and pepper and air-fry for 10 minutes, shaking the basket once or twice during the cooking process.
3. Combine the honey, sesame oil, soy sauce and minced ginger in a large bowl. Add the sugar snap peas and the air-fried carrots to the honey mixture, toss to coat and return everything to the air fryer basket.
4. Turn up the temperature to 400°F and air-fry for an additional 6 minutes, shaking the basket once during the cooking process.
5. Transfer the carrots and sugar snap peas to a serving bowl. Pour the sauce from the bottom of the cooker over the vegetables and sprinkle sesame seeds over top. Serve immediately.

Glazed Carrots

Servings: 4
Cooking Time: 10 Minutes
Ingredients:
- 2 teaspoons honey
- 1 teaspoon orange juice
- ½ teaspoon grated orange rind
- ⅛ teaspoon ginger
- 1 pound baby carrots
- 2 teaspoons olive oil
- ¼ teaspoon salt

Directions:
1. Combine honey, orange juice, grated rind, and ginger in a small bowl and set aside.
2. Toss the carrots, oil, and salt together to coat well and pour them into the air fryer basket.
3. Cook at 390°F for 5 minutes. Shake basket to stir a little and cook for 4 minutes more, until carrots are barely tender.
4. Pour carrots into air fryer baking pan.
5. Stir the honey mixture to combine well, pour glaze over carrots, and stir to coat.
6. Cook at 360°F for 1 minute or just until heated through.

Creole Potato Wedges

Servings: 4
Cooking Time: 10 Minutes
Ingredients:
- 1 pound medium Yukon gold potatoes
- ½ teaspoon cayenne pepper
- ½ teaspoon thyme
- ½ teaspoon garlic powder
- ½ teaspoon salt
- ½ teaspoon smoked paprika
- 1 cup dry breadcrumbs
- oil for misting or cooking spray

Directions:
1. Wash potatoes, cut into thick wedges, and drop wedges into a bowl of water to prevent browning.
2. Mix together the cayenne pepper, thyme, garlic powder, salt, paprika, and breadcrumbs and spread on a sheet of wax paper.
3. Remove potatoes from water and, without drying them, roll in the breadcrumb mixture.
4. Spray air fryer basket with oil or cooking spray and pile potato wedges into basket. It's okay if they form more than a single layer.
5. Cook at 390°F for 8minutes. Shake basket, then continue cooking for 2 minutes longer, until coating is crisp and potato centers are soft. Total cooking time will vary, depending on thickness of potato wedges.

Asiago Broccoli

Servings: 4
Cooking Time: 14 Minutes
Ingredients:
- 1 head broccoli, cut into florets
- 1 tablespoon extra-virgin olive oil
- 1 teaspoon minced garlic
- ¼ teaspoon ground black pepper
- ¼ teaspoon salt
- ¼ cup asiago cheese

Directions:
1. Preheat the air fryer to 360°F.
2. In a medium bowl, toss the broccoli florets with the olive oil, garlic, pepper, and salt. Lightly spray the air fryer basket with olive oil spray.
3. Place the broccoli florets into the basket and cook for 7 minutes. Shake the basket and sprinkle the broccoli with cheese. Cook another 7 minutes.
4. Remove from the basket and serve warm.

Salt And Pepper Baked Potatoes

Cooking Time: 40 Minutes
Servings: 4
Ingredients:
- 1 to 2 tablespoons olive oil
- 4 medium russet potatoes (about 9 to 10 ounces each)
- salt and coarsely ground black pepper
- butter, sour cream, chopped fresh chives, scallions or bacon bits (optional)

Directions:
1. Preheat the air fryer to 400°F.
2. Rub the olive oil all over the potatoes and season them generously with salt and coarsely ground black pepper. Pierce all sides of the potatoes several times with the tines of a fork.
3. Air-fry for 40 minutes, turning the potatoes over halfway through the cooking time.
4. Serve the potatoes, split open with butter, sour cream, fresh chives, scallions or bacon bits.

Stuffed Onions

Servings: 6
Cooking Time: 27 Minutes
Ingredients:
- 6 Small 3½- to 4-ounce yellow or white onions
- Olive oil spray
- 6 ounces Bulk sweet Italian sausage meat (gluten-free, if a concern)
- 9 Cherry tomatoes, chopped
- 3 tablespoons Seasoned Italian-style dried bread crumbs (gluten-free, if a concern)
- 3 tablespoons (about ½ ounce) Finely grated Parmesan cheese

Directions:
1. Preheat the air fryer to 325°F (or 330°F, if that's the closest setting).
2. Cut just enough off the root ends of the onions so they will stand up on a cutting board when this end is turned down. Carefully peel off just the brown, papery skin. Now cut the top quarter off each and place the onion back on the cutting board with this end facing up. Use a flatware spoon (preferably a serrated grapefruit spoon) or a melon baller to scoop out the "insides" (interior layers) of the onion, leaving enough of the bottom and side walls so that the onion does not collapse. Depending on the thickness of the layers in the onion, this may be one or two of those layers—or even three, if they're very thin.
3. Coat the insides and outsides of the onions with olive oil spray. Set the onion "shells" in the basket and air-fry for 15 minutes.
4. Meanwhile, make the filling. Set a medium skillet over medium heat for a couple of minutes, then crumble in the sausage meat. Cook, stirring often, until browned, about 4 minutes. Transfer the contents of the skillet to a medium bowl (leave the fat behind in the skillet or add it to the bowl, depending on your cross-trainer regimen). Stir in the tomatoes, bread crumbs, and cheese until well combined.
5. When the onions are ready, use a nonstick-safe spatula to gently transfer them to a cutting board. Increase the air fryer's temperature to 350°F.
6. Pack the sausage mixture into the onion shells, gently compacting the filling and mounding it up at the top.
7. When the machine is at temperature, set the onions stuffing side up in the basket with at least ¼ inch between them. Air-fry for 12 minutes, or until lightly browned and sizzling hot.

8. Use a nonstick-safe spatula, and perhaps a flatware fork for balance, to transfer the onions to a cutting board or serving platter. Cool for 5 minutes before serving.

Crispy Noodle Salad

Servings: 3
Cooking Time: 22 Minutes
Ingredients:
- 6 ounces Fresh Chinese-style stir-fry or lo mein wheat noodles
- 1½ tablespoons Cornstarch
- ¾ cup Chopped stemmed and cored red bell pepper
- 2 Medium scallion(s), trimmed and thinly sliced
- 2 teaspoons Sambal oelek or other pulpy hot red pepper sauce (see here)
- 2 teaspoons Thai sweet chili sauce or red ketchup-like chili sauce, such as Heinz
- 2 teaspoons Regular or low-sodium soy sauce or tamari sauce
- 2 teaspoons Unseasoned rice vinegar (see here)
- 1 tablespoon White or black sesame seeds

Directions:
1. Bring a large saucepan of water to a boil over high heat. Add the noodles and boil for 2 minutes. Drain in a colander set in the sink. Rinse several times with cold water, shaking the colander to drain the noodles very well. Spread the noodles out on a large cutting board and air-dry for 10 minutes.
2. Preheat the air fryer to 400°F.
3. Toss the noodles in a bowl with the cornstarch until well coated. Spread them out across the entire basket (although they will be touching and overlapping a bit). Air-fry for 6 minutes, then turn the solid mass of noodles over as one piece. If it cracks in half or smaller pieces, just fit these back together after turning. Continue air-frying for 6 minutes, or until golden brown and crisp.
4. As the noodles cook, stir the bell pepper, scallion(s), sambal oelek, red chili sauce, soy sauce, vinegar, and sesame seeds in a serving bowl until well combined.
5. Turn the basket of noodles out onto a cutting board and cool for a minute or two. Break the mass of noodles into individual noodles and/or small chunks and add to the dressing in the serving bowl. Toss well to serve.

Goat Cheese Stuffed Portobellos

Servings: 4
Cooking Time: 35 Minutes
Ingredients:
- 1 cup baby spinach
- ¾ cup crumbled goat cheese
- 2 tsp grated Parmesan cheese
- 4 portobello caps, cleaned
- Salt and pepper to taste
- 2 tomatoes, chopped
- 1 leek, chopped
- 1 garlic clove, minced
- ¼ cup chopped parsley
- 2 tbsp panko bread crumbs
- 1 tbsp chopped oregano
- 1 tbsp olive oil
- Balsamic glaze for drizzling

Directions:
1. Brush the mushrooms with olive oil and sprinkle with salt. Mix the remaining ingredients, excluding the balsamic glaze, in a bowl. Fill each mushroom cap with the mixture. Preheat air fryer to 370°F. Place the mushroom caps in the greased frying basket and Bake for 10-12 minutes or until the top is golden and the mushrooms are tender. Carefully transfer them to a serving dish. Drizzle with balsamic glaze and serve warm. Enjoy!

Fried Pearl Onions With Balsamic Vinegar And Basil

Servings: 2
Cooking Time: 10 Minutes
Ingredients:
- 1 pound fresh pearl onions
- 1 tablespoon olive oil
- salt and freshly ground black pepper
- 1 teaspoon high quality aged balsamic vinegar
- 1 tablespoon chopped fresh basil leaves (or mint)

Directions:
1. Preheat the air fryer to 400°F.
2. Decide whether you want to peel the onions before or after they cook. Peeling them ahead of time is a little more laborious. Peeling after they cook is easier, but a little messier since the onions are hot and you may discard more of the onion than you'd like to. If you opt to peel them first, trim the tiny root of the onions off and pinch off any loose papery skins. (It's ok if there are some skins left on the onions.) Toss the pearl onions with the olive oil, salt and freshly ground black pepper.
3. Air-fry for 10 minutes, shaking the basket a couple of times during the cooking process. (If your pearl onions are very large, you may need to add a couple of minutes to this cooking time.)
4. Let the onions cool slightly and then slip off any remaining skins.
5. Toss the onions with the balsamic vinegar and basil and serve.

Fried Eggplant Slices

Servings: 3
Cooking Time: 12 Minutes
Ingredients:
- 1½ sleeves (about 60 saltines) Saltine crackers
- ¾ cup Cornstarch
- 2 Large egg(s), well beaten
- 1 medium (about ¾ pound) Eggplant, stemmed, peeled, and cut into ¼-inch-thick rounds
- Olive oil spray

Directions:
1. Preheat the air fryer to 400°F. Also, position the rack in the center of the oven and heat the oven to 175°F.

2. Grind the saltines, in batches if necessary, in a food processor, pulsing the machine and rearranging the saltine pieces every few pulses. Or pulverize the saltines in a large, heavy zip-closed plastic bag with the bottom of a heavy saucepan. In either case, you want small bits of saltines, not just crumbs.

3. Set up and fill three shallow soup plates or small pie plates on your counter: one for the cornstarch, one for the beaten egg(s), and one for the pulverized saltines.

4. Set an eggplant slice in the cornstarch and turn it to coat on both sides. Use a brush to lightly remove any excess. Dip it into the beaten egg(s) and turn to coat both sides. Let any excess egg slip back into the rest, then set the slice in the saltines. Turn several times, pressing gently to coat both sides evenly but not heavily. Coat both sides of the slice with olive oil spray and set it aside. Continue dipping and coating the remaining slices.

5. Set one, two, or maybe three slices in the basket. There should be at least ½ inch between them for proper air flow. Air-fry undisturbed for 12 minutes, or until crisp and browned.

6. Use a nonstick-safe spatula to transfer the slice(s) to a large baking sheet. Slip it into the oven to keep the slices warm as you air-fry more batches, as needed, always transferring the slices to the baking sheet to stay warm.

Perfect Broccolini

Servings: 4
Cooking Time: 15 Minutes
Ingredients:
- 1 pound Broccolini
- Olive oil spray
- Coarse sea salt or kosher salt

Directions:
1. Preheat the air fryer to 375°F.
2. Place the broccolini on a cutting board. Generously coat it with olive oil spray, turning the vegetables and rearranging them before spraying a couple of times more, to make sure everything's well coated, even the flowery bits in their heads.
3. When the machine is at temperature, pile the broccolini in the basket, spreading it into as close to one layer as you can. Air-fry for 5 minutes, tossing once to get any covered or touching parts exposed to the air currents, until the leaves begin to get brown and even crisp. Watch carefully and use this visual cue to know the moment to stop the cooking.
4. Transfer the broccolini to a platter. Spread out the pieces and sprinkle them with salt to taste.

Succulent Roasted Peppers

Servings: 2
Cooking Time: 35 Minutes
Ingredients:
- 2 red bell peppers
- 2 tbsp olive oil
- Salt to taste
- 1 tsp dill, chopped

Directions:
1. Preheat air fryer to 400°F. Remove the tops and bottoms of the peppers. Cut along rib sections and discard the seeds. Combine the bell peppers and olive oil in a bowl. Place bell peppers in the frying basket. Roast for 24 minutes, flipping once. Transfer the roasted peppers to a small bowl and cover for 15 minutes. Then, peel and discard the skins. Sprinkle with salt and dill and serve.

Cheesy Potato Pot

Servings: 4
Cooking Time: 13 Minutes
Ingredients:
- 3 cups cubed red potatoes (unpeeled, cut into ½-inch cubes)
- ½ teaspoon garlic powder
- salt and pepper
- 1 tablespoon oil
- chopped chives for garnish (optional)
- Sauce
- 2 tablespoons milk
- 1 tablespoon butter
- 2 ounces sharp Cheddar cheese, grated
- 1 tablespoon sour cream

Directions:
1. Place potato cubes in large bowl and sprinkle with garlic, salt, and pepper. Add oil and stir to coat well.
2. Cook at 390°F for 13 minutes or until potatoes are tender. Stir every 4 or 5 minutes during cooking time.
3. While potatoes are cooking, combine milk and butter in a small saucepan. Warm over medium-low heat to melt butter. Add cheese and stir until it melts. The melted cheese will remain separated from the milk mixture. Remove from heat until potatoes are done.
4. When ready to serve, add sour cream to cheese mixture and stir over medium-low heat just until warmed. Place cooked potatoes in serving bowl. Pour sauce over potatoes and stir to combine.
5. Garnish with chives if desired.

Simple Green Bake

Servings: 4
Cooking Time: 15 Minutes
Ingredients:
- 1 cup asparagus, chopped
- 2 cups broccoli florets
- 1 tbsp olive oil
- 1 tbsp lemon juice
- 1 cup green peas
- 2 tbsp honey mustard
- Salt and pepper to taste

Directions:
1. Preheat air fryer to 330°F. Add asparagus and broccoli to the frying basket. Drizzle with olive oil and lemon juice and toss. Bake for 6 minutes. Remove the basket and add peas. Steam for another 3 minutes or until the vegetables are hot and tender. Pour the vegetables into a serving dish. Drizzle with honey mustard and season with salt and pepper. Toss and serve warm.

Green Beans

Servings: 4
Cooking Time: 12 Minutes
Ingredients:
- 1 pound fresh green beans
- 2 tablespoons Italian salad dressing
- salt and pepper

Directions:
1. Wash beans and snap off stem ends.
2. In a large bowl, toss beans with Italian dressing.
3. Cook at 330°F for 5minutes. Shake basket or stir and cook 5minutes longer. Shake basket again and, if needed, continue cooking for 2 minutes, until as tender as you like. Beans should shrivel slightly and brown in places.
4. Sprinkle with salt and pepper to taste.

Spiced Pumpkin Wedges

Servings: 4
Cooking Time: 35 Minutes
Ingredients:
- 2 ½ cups pumpkin, cubed
- 2 tbsp olive oil
- Salt and pepper to taste
- ¼ tsp pumpkin pie spice
- 1 tbsp thyme
- ¼ cup grated Parmesan

Directions:
1. Preheat air fryer to 360°F. Put the cubed pumpkin with olive oil, salt, pumpkin pie spice, black pepper, and thyme in a bowl and stir until the pumpkin is well coated. Pour this mixture into the frying basket and Roast for 18-20 minutes, stirring once. Sprinkle the pumpkin with grated Parmesan. Serve and enjoy!

Jerk Rubbed Corn On The Cob

Servings: 4
Cooking Time: 6 Minutes
Ingredients:
- 1 teaspoon ground allspice
- 1 teaspoon dried thyme
- ½ teaspoon ground ginger
- ½ teaspoon ground cinnamon
- ¼ teaspoon ground nutmeg
- ⅛ teaspoon ground cayenne pepper
- 1 teaspoon salt
- 2 tablespoons butter, melted
- 4 ears of corn, husked

Directions:
1. Preheat the air fryer to 380°F.
2. Combine all the spices in a bowl. Brush the corn with the melted butter and then sprinkle the spices generously on all sides of each ear of corn.
3. Transfer the ears of corn to the air fryer basket. It's ok if they are crisscrossed on top of each other. Air-fry at 380°F for 6 minutes, rotating the ears as they cook.
4. Brush more butter on at the end and sprinkle with any remaining spice mixture.

Summer Vegetables With Balsamic Drizzle, Goat Cheese And Basil

Servings: 2
Cooking Time: 17 Minutes
Ingredients:
- 1 cup balsamic vinegar
- 1 zucchini, sliced
- 1 yellow squash, sliced
- 2 tablespoons olive oil
- 1 clove garlic, minced
- ½ teaspoon Italian seasoning
- salt and freshly ground black pepper
- ½ cup cherry tomatoes, halved
- 2 ounces crumbled goat cheese
- 2 tablespoons chopped fresh basil, plus more leaves for garnish

Directions:
1. Place the balsamic vinegar in a small saucepot on the stovetop. Bring the vinegar to a boil, lower the heat and simmer uncovered for 20 minutes, until the mixture reduces and thickens. Set aside to cool.
2. Preheat the air fryer to 390°F.
3. Combine the zucchini and yellow squash in a large bowl. Add the olive oil, minced garlic, Italian seasoning, salt and pepper and toss to coat.
4. Air-fry the vegetables at 390°F for 10 minutes, shaking the basket several times during the cooking process. Add the cherry tomatoes and continue to air-fry for another 5 minutes. Sprinkle the goat cheese over the vegetables and air-fry for 2 more minutes.
5. Transfer the vegetables to a serving dish, drizzle with the balsamic reduction and season with freshly ground black pepper. Garnish with the fresh basil leaves.

Ajillo Mushrooms

Servings: 4
Cooking Time: 30 Minutes
Ingredients:
- 2/3 cup panko bread crumbs
- 1 cup cremini mushrooms
- 1/3 cup all-purpose flour
- 1 egg, beaten
- ½ tsp smoked paprika
- 3 garlic cloves, minced
- Salt and pepper to taste

Directions:
1. Preheat the air fryer to 400°F. Put the flour on a plate. Mix the egg and garlic in a shallow bowl. On a separate plate, combine the panko, smoked paprika, salt, and pepper and mix well. Cut the mushrooms through the stems into quarters. Dip the mushrooms in flour, then the egg, then in the panko mix. Press to coat, then put on a wire rack and set aside. Add the mushrooms to the frying basket in a single layer and spray with

cooking oil. Air Fry for 6-8 minutes, flipping them once until crisp. Serve warm.

Curried Cauliflower With Cashews And Yogurt

Servings: 2
Cooking Time: 12 Minutes
Ingredients:
- 4 cups cauliflower florets (about half a large head)
- 1 tablespoon olive oil
- salt
- 1 teaspoon curry powder
- ½ cup toasted, chopped cashews
- Cool Yogurt Drizzle
- ¼ cup plain yogurt
- 2 tablespoons sour cream
- 1 teaspoon lemon juice
- pinch cayenne pepper
- salt
- 1 teaspoon honey
- 1 tablespoon chopped fresh cilantro, plus leaves for garnish

Directions:
1. Preheat the air fryer to 400°F.
2. Toss the cauliflower florets with the olive oil, salt and curry powder, coating evenly.
3. Transfer the cauliflower to the air fryer basket and air-fry at 400°F for 12 minutes, shaking the basket a couple of times during the cooking process.
4. While the cauliflower is cooking, make the cool yogurt drizzle by combining all ingredients in a bowl.
5. When the cauliflower is cooked to your liking, serve it warm with the cool yogurt either underneath or drizzled over the top. Scatter the cashews and cilantro leaves around.

Smooth & Silky Cauliflower Purée

Servings: 4
Cooking Time: 25 Minutes
Ingredients:
- 1 head cauliflower, cut into florets
- 1 rutabaga, diced
- 4 tbsp butter, divided
- Salt and pepper to taste
- 3 cloves garlic, peeled
- 2 oz cream cheese, softened
- ½ cup milk
- 1 tsp dried thyme

Directions:
1. Preheat air fryer to 350°F. Combine cauliflower, rutabaga, 2 tbsp of butter, and salt to taste in a bowl. Add veggie mixture to the frying basket and Air Fry for 10 minutes, tossing once. Put in garlic and Air Fry for 5 more minutes. Let them cool a bit, then transfer them to a blender. Blend them along with 2 tbsp of butter, salt, black pepper, cream cheese, thyme and milk until smooth. Serve immediately.

Broccoli Au Gratin

Servings: 2
Cooking Time: 25 Minutes
Ingredients:
- 2 cups broccoli florets, chopped
- 6 tbsp grated Gruyère cheese
- 1 tbsp grated Pecorino cheese
- ½ tbsp olive oil
- 1 tbsp flour
- 1/3 cup milk
- ½ tsp ground coriander
- Salt and black pepper
- 2 tbsp panko bread crumbs

Directions:
1. Whisk the olive oil, flour, milk, coriander, salt, and pepper in a bowl. Incorporate broccoli, Gruyere cheese, panko bread crumbs, and Pecorino cheese until well combined. Pour in a greased baking dish.
2. Preheat air fryer to 330°F. Put the baking dish into the frying basket. Bake until the broccoli is crisp-tender and the top is golden, or about 12-15 minutes. Serve warm.

Sticky Broccoli Florets

Servings: 4
Cooking Time: 20 Minutes
Ingredients:
- 4 cups broccoli florets
- 2 tbsp olive oil
- ½ tsp salt
- ½ cup grapefruit juice
- 1 tbsp raw honey
- 4-6 grapefruit wedges

Directions:
1. Preheat air fryer to 360°F. Add the broccoli, olive oil, salt, grapefruit juice, and honey to a bowl. Toss the broccoli in the liquid until well coated. Pour the broccoli mixture into the frying basket and Roast for 12 minutes, stirring once. Serve with grapefruit wedges.

Roasted Brussels Sprouts

Servings: 4
Cooking Time: 25 Minutes
Ingredients:
- ½ cup balsamic vinegar
- 2 tablespoons honey
- 1 pound Brussels sprouts, halved lengthwise
- 2 slices bacon, chopped
- ½ teaspoon garlic powder
- 1 teaspoon salt
- 1 tablespoon extra-virgin olive oil
- ¼ cup grated Parmesan cheese

Directions:
1. Preheat the air fryer to 370°F.

2. In a small saucepan, heat the vinegar and honey for 8 to 10 minutes over medium-low heat, or until the balsamic vinegar reduces by half to create a thick balsamic glazing sauce.
3. While the balsamic glaze is reducing, in a large bowl, toss together the Brussels sprouts, bacon, garlic powder, salt, and olive oil. Pour the mixture into the air fryer basket and cook for 10 minutes; check for doneness. Cook another 2 to 5 minutes or until slightly crispy and tender.
4. Pour the balsamic glaze into a serving bowl and add the cooked Brussels sprouts to the dish, stirring to coat. Top with grated Parmesan cheese and serve.

Almond-crusted Zucchini Fries

Servings: 2
Cooking Time: 30 Minutes
Ingredients:
- ½ cup grated Pecorino cheese
- 1 zucchini, cut into fries
- 1 tsp salt
- 1 egg
- 1 tbsp almond milk
- ½ cup almond flour

Directions:
1. Preheat air fryer to 370ºF. Distribute zucchini fries evenly over a paper towel, sprinkle with salt, and let sit for 10 minutes to pull out moisture. Pat them dry with paper towels. In a bowl, beat egg and almond milk. In another bowl, combine almond flour and Pecorino cheese. Dip fries in egg mixture and then dredge them in flour mixture. Place zucchini fries in the lightly greased frying basket and Air Fry for 10 minutes, flipping once. Serve.

Roasted Fennel Salad

Servings: 3
Cooking Time: 20 Minutes
Ingredients:
- 3 cups (about ¾ pound) Trimmed fennel (see the headnote), roughly chopped
- 1½ tablespoons Olive oil
- ¼ teaspoon Table salt
- ¼ teaspoon Ground black pepper
- 1½ tablespoons White balsamic vinegar (see here)

Directions:
1. Preheat the air fryer to 400°F.
2. Toss the fennel, olive oil, salt, and pepper in a large bowl until the fennel is well coated in the oil.
3. When the machine is at temperature, pour the fennel into the basket, spreading it out into as close to one layer as possible. Air-fry for 20 minutes, tossing and rearranging the fennel pieces twice so that any covered or touching parts get exposed to the air currents, until golden at the edges and softened.
4. Pour the fennel into a serving bowl. Add the vinegar while hot. Toss well, then cool a couple of minutes before serving. Or serve at room temperature.

Basic Corn On The Cob

Servings: 4
Cooking Time: 15 Minutes
Ingredients:
- 3 ears of corn, shucked and halved
- 2 tbsp butter, melted
- Salt and pepper to taste
- 1 tsp minced garlic
- 1 tsp paprika

Directions:
1. Preheat air fryer at 400ºF. Toss all ingredients in a bowl. Place corn in the frying basket and Bake for 7 minutes, turning once. Serve immediately.

Hasselback Garlic-and-butter Potatoes

Servings: 3
Cooking Time: 48 Minutes
Ingredients:
- 3 8-ounce russet potatoes
- 6 Brown button or Baby Bella mushrooms, very thinly sliced
- Olive oil spray
- 3 tablespoons Butter, melted and cooled
- 1 tablespoon Minced garlic
- ¾ teaspoon Table salt
- 3 tablespoons (about ½ ounce) Finely grated Parmesan cheese

Directions:
1. Preheat the air fryer to 350°F.
2. Cut slits down the length of each potato, about three-quarters down into the potato and spaced about ¼ inch apart. Wedge a thin mushroom slice in each slit. Generously coat the potatoes on all sides with olive oil spray.
3. When the machine is at temperature, set the potatoes mushroom side up in the basket with as much air space between them as possible. Air-fry undisturbed for 45 minutes, or tender when pricked with a fork.
4. Increase the machine's temperature to 400°F. Use kitchen tongs, and perhaps a flatware fork for balance, to gently transfer the potatoes to a cutting board. Brush each evenly with butter, then sprinkle the minced garlic and salt over them. Sprinkle the cheese evenly over the potatoes.
5. Use those same tongs to gently transfer the potatoes cheese side up to the basket in one layer with some space for air flow between them. Air-fry undisturbed for 3 minutes, or until the cheese has melted and begun to brown.
6. Use those same tongs to gently transfer the potatoes back to the wire rack. Cool for 5 minutes before serving.

Beet Fries

Servings: 3
Cooking Time: 22 Minutes
Ingredients:
- 3 6-ounce red beets
- Vegetable oil spray
- To taste Coarse sea salt or kosher salt

Directions:
1. Preheat the air fryer to 375°F.
2. Remove the stems from the beets and peel them with a knife or vegetable peeler. Slice them into ½-inch-thick circles. Lay these flat on a cutting board and slice them into ½-inch-thick sticks. Generously coat the sticks on all sides with vegetable oil spray.
3. When the machine is at temperature, drop them into the basket, shake the basket to even the sticks out into as close to one layer as possible, and air-fry for 20 minutes, tossing and rearranging the beet matchsticks every 5 minutes, or until brown and even crisp at the ends. If the machine is at 360°F, you may need to add 2 minutes to the cooking time.
4. Pour the fries into a big bowl, add the salt, toss well, and serve warm.

Mom´s Potatoes Au Gratin

Servings: 4
Cooking Time: 50 Minutes
Ingredients:
- 4 Yukon Gold potatoes, peeled
- 1 cup shredded cheddar cheese
- 2 tbsp grated Parmesan cheese
- 2 garlic cloves, minced
- 1/3 cup heavy cream
- 1/3 cup whole milk
- ½ tsp dried marjoram
- Salt and pepper to taste

Directions:
1. Preheat the air fryer to 350°F. Spray a 7-inch round pan thoroughly with cooking oil. Cut the potatoes into ⅛-inch-thick slices and layer the potatoes inside the pan along with cheddar cheese and garlic. Mix the cream, milk, marjoram, salt, and pepper in a bowl, then slowly pour the mix over the potatoes. Sprinkle with Parmesan and put the pan in the fryer. Bake for 25-35 minutes or until the potatoes are tender, the sauce is bubbling, and the top is golden. Serve warm.

Honey-roasted Parsnips

Servings: 3
Cooking Time: 23 Minutes
Ingredients:
- 1½ pounds Medium parsnips, peeled
- Olive oil spray
- 1 tablespoon Honey
- 1½ teaspoons Water
- ¼ teaspoon Table salt

Directions:
1. Preheat the air fryer to 350°F.
2. If the thick end of a parsnip is more than ½ inch in diameter, cut the parsnip just below where it swells to its large end, then slice the large section in half lengthwise. If the parsnips are larger than the basket (or basket attachment), trim off the thin end so the parsnips will fit. Generously coat the parsnips on all sides with olive oil spray.
3. When the machine is at temperature, set the parsnips in the basket with as much air space between them as possible. Air-fry undisturbed for 20 minutes.
4. Whisk the honey, water, and salt in a small bowl until smooth. Brush this mixture over the parsnips. Air-fry undisturbed for 3 minutes more, or until the glaze is lightly browned.
5. Use kitchen tongs to transfer the parsnips to a wire rack or a serving platter. Cool for a couple of minutes before serving.

Roasted Eggplant Halves With Herbed Ricotta

Servings: 3
Cooking Time: 20 Minutes
Ingredients:
- 3 5- to 6-ounce small eggplants, stemmed
- Olive oil spray
- ¼ teaspoon Table salt
- ¼ teaspoon Ground black pepper
- ½ cup Regular or low-fat ricotta
- 1½ tablespoons Minced fresh basil leaves
- 1¼ teaspoons Minced fresh oregano leaves
- Honey

Directions:
1. Preheat the air fryer to 325°F (or 330°F, if that's the closest setting).
2. Cut the eggplants in half lengthwise. Set them cut side up on your work surface. Using the tip of a paring knife, make a series of slits about three-quarters down into the flesh of each eggplant half; work at a 45-degree angle to the (former) stem across the vegetable and make the slits about ½ inch apart. Make a second set of equidistant slits at a 90-degree angle to the first slits, thus creating a crosshatch pattern in the vegetable.
3. Generously coat the cut sides of the eggplants with olive oil spray. Sprinkle the salt and pepper over the cut surfaces.
4. Set the eggplant halves cut side up in the basket with as much air space between them as possible. Air-fry undisturbed for 20 minutes, or until soft and golden.
5. Use kitchen tongs to gently transfer the eggplant halves to serving plates or a platter. Cool for 5 minutes.
6. Whisk the ricotta, basil, and oregano in a small bowl until well combined. Top the eggplant halves with this mixture. Drizzle the halves with honey to taste before serving warm.

Tomato Candy

Servings: 12
Cooking Time: 120 Minutes
Ingredients:
- 6 Small Roma or plum tomatoes, halved lengthwise
- 1½ teaspoons Coarse sea salt or kosher salt

Directions:
1. Before you turn the machine on, set the tomatoes cut side up in a single layer in the basket (or the basket attachment). They can touch each other, but try to leave at least a fraction of an inch between them (depending, of course, on the size of the basket or basket attachment). Sprinkle the cut sides of the tomatoes with the salt.
2. Set the machine to cook at 225°F (or 230°F, if that's the closest setting). Put the basket in the machine and air-fry for 2 hours, or until the tomatoes are dry but pliable, with a little moisture down in their centers.
3. Remove the basket from the machine and cool the tomatoes in it for 10 minutes before gently transferring them to a plate for serving, or to a shallow dish that you can cover and store in the refrigerator for up to 1 week.

Hasselbacks

Servings: 4
Cooking Time: 41 Minutes
Ingredients:
- 2 large potatoes (approx. 1 pound each)
- oil for misting or cooking spray
- salt, pepper, and garlic powder
- 1½ ounces sharp Cheddar cheese, sliced very thin
- ¼ cup chopped green onions
- 2 strips turkey bacon, cooked and crumbled
- light sour cream for serving (optional)

Directions:
1. Preheat air fryer to 390°F.
2. Scrub potatoes. Cut thin vertical slices ¼-inch thick crosswise about three-quarters of the way down so that bottom of potato remains intact.
3. Fan potatoes slightly to separate slices. Mist with oil and sprinkle with salt, pepper, and garlic powder to taste. Potatoes will be very stiff, but try to get some of the oil and seasoning between the slices.
4. Place potatoes in air fryer basket and cook for 40 minutes or until centers test done when pierced with a fork.
5. Top potatoes with cheese slices and cook for 30 seconds to 1 minute to melt cheese.
6. Cut each potato in half crosswise, and sprinkle with green onions and crumbled bacon. If you like, add a dollop of sour cream before serving.

Fried Okra

Servings: 4
Cooking Time: 8 Minutes
Ingredients:
- 1 pound okra
- 1 large egg
- 1 tablespoon milk
- 1 teaspoon salt, divided
- ½ teaspoon black pepper, divided
- ¼ teaspoon paprika
- ¼ teaspoon thyme
- ½ cup cornmeal
- ½ cup all-purpose flour

Directions:
1. Preheat the air fryer to 400°F.
2. Cut the okra into ½-inch rounds.
3. In a medium bowl, whisk together the egg, milk, ½ teaspoon of the salt, and ¼ teaspoon of black pepper. Place the okra into the egg mixture and toss until well coated.
4. In a separate bowl, mix together the remaining ½ teaspoon of salt, the remaining ¼ teaspoon of black pepper, the paprika, the thyme, the cornmeal, and the flour. Working in small batches, dredge the egg-coated okra in the cornmeal mixture until all the okra has been breaded.
5. Place a single layer of okra in the air fryer basket and spray with cooking spray. Cook for 4 minutes, toss to check for crispness, and cook another 4 minutes. Repeat in batches, as needed.

Crispy Herbed Potatoes

Servings: 6
Cooking Time: 20 Minutes
Ingredients:
- 3 medium baking potatoes, washed and cubed
- ½ teaspoon dried thyme
- 1 teaspoon minced dried rosemary
- ½ teaspoon garlic powder
- 1 teaspoon sea salt
- ½ teaspoon black pepper
- 2 tablespoons extra-virgin olive oil
- ¼ cup chopped parsley

Directions:
1. Preheat the air fryer to 390°F.
2. Pat the potatoes dry. In a large bowl, mix together the cubed potatoes, thyme, rosemary, garlic powder, sea salt, and pepper. Drizzle and toss with olive oil.
3. Pour the herbed potatoes into the air fryer basket. Cook for 20 minutes, stirring every 5 minutes.
4. Toss the cooked potatoes with chopped parsley and serve immediately.
5. VARY IT! Potatoes are versatile — add any spice or seasoning mixture you prefer and create your own favorite side dish.

Sriracha Green Beans

Servings: 4
Cooking Time: 30 Minutes
Ingredients:
- ½ tbsp toasted sesame seeds
- 1 tbsp tamari
- ½ tbsp Sriracha sauce
- 4 tsp canola oil
- 12 oz trimmed green beans
- 1 tbsp cilantro, chopped

Directions:
1. Mix the tamari, sriracha, and 1 tsp of canola oil in a small bowl. In a large bowl, toss green beans with the remaining oil. Preheat air fryer to 375°F. Place the green beans in the frying basket and Air Fry for 8 minutes, shaking the basket once until the beans are charred and tender. Toss the beans with sauce, cilantro, and sesame seeds. Serve.

Parsnip Fries With Romesco Sauce

Servings: 2
Cooking Time: 24 Minutes
Ingredients:
- Romesco Sauce:
- 1 red bell pepper, halved and seeded
- 1 (1-inch) thick slice of Italian bread, torn into pieces (about 1 to 1½ cups)
- 1 cup almonds, toasted
- olive oil
- ½ Jalapeño pepper, seeded
- 1 tablespoon fresh parsley leaves
- 1 clove garlic
- 2 Roma tomatoes, peeled and seeded (or ⅓ cup canned crushed tomatoes)
- 1 tablespoon red wine vinegar
- ¼ teaspoon smoked paprika
- ½ teaspoon salt
- ¾ cup olive oil
- 3 parsnips, peeled and cut into long strips
- 2 teaspoons olive oil
- salt and freshly ground black pepper

Directions:
1. Preheat the air fryer to 400°F.
2. Place the red pepper halves, cut side down, in the air fryer basket and air-fry for 10 minutes, or until the skin turns black all over. Remove the pepper from the air fryer and let it cool. When it is cool enough to handle, peel the pepper.
3. Toss the torn bread and almonds with a little olive oil and air-fry for 4 minutes, shaking the basket a couple times throughout the cooking time. When the bread and almonds are nicely toasted, remove them from the air fryer and let them cool for just a minute or two.
4. Combine the toasted bread, almonds, roasted red pepper, Jalapeño pepper, parsley, garlic, tomatoes, vinegar, smoked paprika and salt in a food processor or blender. Process until smooth. With the processor running, add the olive oil through the feed tube until the sauce comes together in a smooth paste that is barely pourable.
5. Toss the parsnip strips with the olive oil, salt and freshly ground black pepper and air-fry at 400°F for 10 minutes, shaking the basket a couple times during the cooking process so they brown and cook evenly. Serve the parsnip fries warm with the Romesco sauce to dip into.

Lemony Green Bean Sautée

Servings: 6
Cooking Time: 15 Minutes
Ingredients:
- 1 tbsp cilantro, chopped
- 1 lb green beans, trimmed
- ½ red onion, sliced
- 2 tbsp olive oil
- Salt and pepper to taste
- 1 tbsp grapefruit juice
- 6 lemon wedges

Directions:
1. Preheat air fryer to 360°F. Coat the green beans, red onion, olive oil, salt, pepper, cilantro and grapefruit juice in a bowl. Pour the mixture into the air fryer and Bake for 5 minutes. Stir well and cook for 5 minutes more. Serve with lemon wedges. Enjoy!

Roasted Broccoli And Red Bean Salad

Servings: 3
Cooking Time: 14 Minutes
Ingredients:
- 3 cups (about 1 pound) 1- to 1½-inch fresh broccoli florets (not frozen)
- 1½ tablespoons Olive oil spray
- 1¼ cups Canned red kidney beans, drained and rinsed
- 3 tablespoons Minced yellow or white onion
- 2 tablespoons plus 1 teaspoon Red wine vinegar
- ¾ teaspoon Dried oregano
- ¼ teaspoon Table salt
- ¼ teaspoon Ground black pepper

Directions:
1. Preheat the air fryer to 375°F.
2. Put the broccoli florets in a big bowl, coat them generously with olive oil spray, then toss to coat all surfaces, even down into the crannies, spraying them a couple of times more.
3. Pour the florets into the basket, spreading them into as close to one layer as you can. Air-fry for 12 minutes, tossing and rearranging the florets twice so that any touching or covered parts are eventually exposed to the air currents, until light browned but still a bit firm. (If the machine is at 360°F, you may need to add 2 minutes to the cooking time.)
4. Dump the contents of the basket onto a large cutting board. Cool for a minute or two, then chop the florets into small bits. Scrape these into a bowl and add the kidney beans, onion, vinegar, oregano, salt, and pepper. Toss well and serve warm or at room temperature.

Sea Salt Radishes

Servings: 4
Cooking Time: 25 Minutes
Ingredients:
- 1 lb radishes
- 2 tbsp olive oil
- ½ tsp sea salt
- ½ tsp garlic powder

Directions:
1. Preheat air fryer to 360°F. Toss the radishes with olive oil, garlic powder, and salt in a bowl. Pour them into the air fryer. Air Fry for 18 minutes, turning once. Serve.

Balsamic Stuffed Mushrooms

Servings: 4
Cooking Time: 30 Minutes
Ingredients:
- ¼ cup chopped roasted red peppers
- 12 portobello mushroom caps
- 2 tsp grated Parmesan cheese
- 10 oz spinach, chopped
- 3 scallions, chopped
- ¼ cup chickpea flour
- 1 tsp garlic powder
- 1 tbsp balsamic vinegar
- ½ lemon

Directions:
1. Preheat air fryer to 360°F. In a bowl, squeeze any excess water from the spinach; discard the water. Stir in scallions, red pepper, chickpea flour, Parmesan cheese, garlic, and balsamic vinegar until well combined. Fill each mushroom cap with spinach mixture until covering the tops, pressing down slightly. Bake for 12 minutes until crispy. Drizzle with lemon juice before serving.

Thyme Sweet Potato Wedges

Servings: 4
Cooking Time: 30 Minutes
Ingredients:
- 2 peeled sweet potatoes, cubed
- ¼ cup grated Parmesan
- 1 tbsp olive oil
- Salt and pepper to taste
- ½ tsp dried thyme
- ½ tsp ground cumin

Directions:
1. Preheat air fryer to 330°F. Add sweet potato cubes to the frying basket, then drizzle with oil. Toss to gently coat. Season with salt, pepper, thyme, and cumin. Roast the potatoes for about 10 minutes. Shake the basket and continue roasting for another 10 minutes. Shake the basket again, this time adding Parmesan cheese. Shake and return to the air fryer. Roast until the potatoes are tender, 4-6 minutes. Serve and enjoy!

Home Fries

Servings: 4
Cooking Time: 20 Minutes
Ingredients:
- 3 pounds potatoes, cut into 1-inch cubes
- ½ teaspoon oil
- salt and pepper

Directions:
1. In a large bowl, mix the potatoes and oil thoroughly.
2. Cook at 390°F for 10minutes and shake the basket to redistribute potatoes.
3. Cook for an additional 10 minutes, until brown and crisp.
4. Season with salt and pepper to taste.

Turkish Mutabal (eggplant Dip)

Servings: 2
Cooking Time: 40 Minutes
Ingredients:
- 1 medium eggplant
- 2 tbsp tahini
- 2 tbsp lemon juice
- 1 tsp garlic powder
- ¼ tsp sumac
- 1 tsp chopped parsley

Directions:
1. Preheat air fryer to 400°F. Place the eggplant in a pan and Roast for 30 minutes, turning once. Let cool for 5-10 minutes. Scoop out the flesh and place it in a bowl. Squeeze any excess water; discard the water. Mix the flesh, tahini, lemon juice, garlic, and sumac until well combined. Scatter with parsley and serve.

Curried Fruit

Servings: 6
Cooking Time: 20 Minutes
Ingredients:
- 1 cup cubed fresh pineapple
- 1 cup cubed fresh pear (firm, not overly ripe)
- 8 ounces frozen peaches, thawed
- 1 15-ounce can dark, sweet, pitted cherries with juice
- 2 tablespoons brown sugar
- 1 teaspoon curry powder

Directions:
1. Combine all ingredients in large bowl. Stir gently to mix in the sugar and curry.
2. Pour into air fryer baking pan and cook at 360°F for 10minutes.
3. Stir fruit and cook 10 more minutes.
4. Serve hot.

Pecorino Dill Muffins

Servings: 4
Cooking Time: 25 Minutes
Ingredients:
- ¼ cup grated Pecorino cheese
- 1 cup flour
- 1 tsp dried dill
- ⅛ tsp salt
- ¼ tsp onion powder
- 2 tsp baking powder
- 1 egg
- ¼ cup Greek yogurt

Directions:
1. Preheat air fryer to 350ºF. In a bowl, combine dry the ingredients. Set aside. In another bowl, whisk the wet ingredients. Add the wet ingredients to the dry ingredients and combine until blended.
2. Transfer the batter to 6 silicone muffin cups lightly greased with olive oil. Place muffin cups in the frying basket and Bake for 12 minutes. Serve right away.

Herb Roasted Jicama

Servings: 6
Cooking Time: 25 Minutes
Ingredients:
- 1 lb jicama, cut into fries
- ¼ cup olive oil
- Salt and pepper to taste
- 1 garlic clove, minced
- 4 thyme sprigs

Directions:
1. Preheat air fryer to 360°F. Coat the jicamas with olive oil, salt, pepper, and garlic in a bowl. Pour the jicama fries into the frying basket and top with the thyme sprigs. Roast for 20 minutes, stirring twice. Remove the rosemary sprigs. Serve and enjoy!

Veggie Fritters

Servings: 4
Cooking Time: 35 Minutes
Ingredients:
- ¼ cup crumbled feta cheese
- 1 grated zucchini
- ¼ cup Parmesan cheese
- 2 tbsp minced onion
- 1 tbs powder garlic
- 1 tbsp flour
- 1 tbsp cornmeal
- 1 tbsp butter, melted
- 1 egg
- 2 tsp chopped dill
- 2 tsp chopped parsley
- Salt and pepper to taste
- 1 cup bread crumbs

Directions:
1. Preheat air fryer at 350ºF. Squeeze grated zucchini between paper towels to remove excess moisture. In a bowl, combine all ingredients except breadcrumbs. Form mixture into 12 balls, about 2 tbsp each. In a shallow bowl, add breadcrumbs. Roll each ball in breadcrumbs, covering all sides. Place fritters on an ungreased pizza pan. Place in the frying basket and Air Fry for 11 minutes, flipping once. Serve.

Dijon Roasted Purple Potatoes

Servings: 4
Cooking Time: 25 Minutes
Ingredients:
- 1 lb purple potatoes, scrubbed and halved
- 1 tbsp olive oil
- 1 tsp Dijon mustard
- 1 tsp lemon juice
- 2 cloves garlic, minced
- Salt and pepper to taste
- 2 tbsp butter, melted
- 1 tbsp chopped cilantro
- 1 tsp fresh rosemary

Directions:
1. Mix the olive oil, mustard, garlic, lemon juice, pepper, salt and rosemary in a bowl. Let chill covered in the fridge until ready to use.
2. Preheat air fryer at 350ºF. Toss the potatoes, salt, pepper, and butter in a bowl, place the potatoes in the frying basket, and Roast for 18-20 minutes, tossing once. Transfer them into a bowl. Drizzle potatoes with the dressing and toss to coat. Garnish with cilantro to serve.

Tasty Brussels Sprouts With Guanciale

Servings: 4
Cooking Time: 50 Minutes
Ingredients:
- 3 guanciale slices, halved
- 1 lb Brussels sprouts, halved
- 2 tbsp olive oil
- ¼ tsp salt
- ¼ tsp dried thyme

Directions:
1. Preheat air fryer to 350°F. Air Fry Lay the guanciale in the air fryer, until crispy, 10 minutes. Remove and drain on a paper towel. Give the guanciale a rough chop and Set aside. Coat Brussels sprouts with olive oil in a large bowl. Add salt and thyme, then toss. Place the sprouts in the frying basket. Air Fry for about 12-15 minutes, shake the basket once until the sprouts are golden and tender. Top with guanciale and serve.

Fried Cauliflower with Parmesan Lemon Dressing

Servings: 2
Cooking Time: 12 Minutes
Ingredients:
- 4 cups cauliflower florets (about half a large head)
- 1 tablespoon olive oil
- salt and freshly ground black pepper
- 1 teaspoon finely chopped lemon zest
- 1 tablespoon fresh lemon juice (about half a lemon)
- ¼ cup grated Parmigiano-Reggiano cheese
- 4 tablespoons extra virgin olive oil
- ¼ teaspoon salt
- lots of freshly ground black pepper
- 1 tablespoon chopped fresh parsley

Directions:
1. Preheat the air fryer to 400°F.
2. Toss the cauliflower florets with the olive oil, salt and freshly ground black pepper. Air-fry for 12 minutes, shaking the basket a couple of times during the cooking process.
3. While the cauliflower is frying, make the dressing. Combine the lemon zest, lemon juice, Parmigiano-Reggiano cheese and olive oil in a small bowl. Season with salt and lots of freshly ground black pepper. Stir in the parsley.
4. Turn the fried cauliflower out onto a serving platter and drizzle the dressing over the top.

Cheese-rice Stuffed Bell Peppers

Servings: 4
Cooking Time: 30 Minutes
Ingredients:
- 2 red bell peppers, halved and seeds and stem removed
- 1 cup cooked brown rice
- 2 tomatoes, diced
- 1 garlic clove, minced
- Salt and pepper to taste
- 4 oz goat cheese
- 3 tbsp basil, chopped
- 3 tbsp oregano, chopped
- 1 tbsp parsley, chopped
- ¼ cup grated Parmesan

Directions:
1. Preheat air fryer to 360°F. Place the brown rice, tomatoes, garlic, salt, and pepper in a bowl and stir. Divide the rice filling evenly among the bell pepper halves. Combine the goat cheese, basil, parsley and oregano in a small bowl. Sprinkle each bell pepper with the herbed cheese. Arrange the bell peppers on the air fryer and Bake for 20 minutes. Serve topped with grated Parmesan and parsley.

Chapter 9 Desserts And Sweets Recipes

Nutty Cookies

Servings: 6
Cooking Time: 25 Minutes
Ingredients:
- ¼ cup pistachios
- ¼ cup evaporated cane sugar
- ¼ cup raw almonds
- ½ cup almond flour
- 1 tsp pure vanilla extract
- 1 egg white

Directions:
1. Preheat air fryer to 375°F. Add ¼ cup of pistachios and almonds into a food processor. Pulse until they resemble crumbles. Roughly chop the rest of the pistachios with a sharp knife. Combine all ingredients in a large bowl until completely incorporated. Form 6 equally-sized balls and transfer to the parchment-lined frying basket. Allow for 1 inch between each portion. Bake for 7 minutes. Cool on a wire rack for 5 minutes. Serve and enjoy.

Banana-almond Delights

Servings: 4
Cooking Time: 30 Minutes
Ingredients:
- 1 ripe banana, mashed
- 1 tbsp almond liqueur
- ½ tsp ground cinnamon
- 2 tbsp coconut sugar
- 1 cup almond flour
- ¼ tsp baking soda
- 8 raw almonds

Directions:
1. Preheat air fryer to 300°F. Add the banana to a bowl and stir in almond liqueur, cinnamon, and coconut sugar until well combined. Toss in almond flour and baking soda until smooth. Make 8 balls out of the mixture. Place the balls onto the parchment-lined frying basket, flatten each into ½-inch thick, and press 1 almond into the center. Bake for 12 minutes, turn and Bake for 6 more minutes. Let cool slightly before serving.

Cinnamon Canned Biscuit Donuts

Servings: 4
Cooking Time: 25 Minutes
Ingredients:
- 1 can jumbo biscuits
- 1 cup cinnamon sugar

Directions:
1. Preheat air fryer to 360°F. Divide biscuit dough into 8 biscuits and place on a flat work surface. Cut a small circle in the center of the biscuit with a small cookie cutter. Place a batch of 4 donuts in the air fryer. Spray with oil and Bake for 8 minutes, flipping once. Drizzle the cinnamon sugar over the donuts and serve.

Cheese Blintzes

Servings: 6
Cooking Time: 10 Minutes
Ingredients:
- 1½ 7½-ounce package(s) farmer cheese
- 3 tablespoons Regular or low-fat cream cheese (not fat-free)
- 3 tablespoons Granulated white sugar
- ¼ teaspoon Vanilla extract
- 6 Egg roll wrappers
- 3 tablespoons Butter, melted and cooled

Directions:
1. Preheat the air fryer to 375°F.
2. Use a flatware fork to mash the farmer cheese, cream cheese, sugar, and vanilla in a small bowl until smooth.
3. Set one egg roll wrapper on a clean, dry work surface. Place ¼ cup of the filling at the edge closest to you, leaving a ½-inch gap before the edge of the wrapper. Dip your clean finger in water and wet the edges of the wrapper. Fold the perpendicular sides over the filling, then roll the wrapper closed with the filling inside. Set it aside seam side down and continue filling the remainder of the wrappers.
4. Brush the wrappers on all sides with the melted butter. Be generous. Set them seam side down in the basket with as much space between them as possible. Air-fry undisturbed for 10 minutes, or until lightly browned.
5. Use a nonstick-safe spatula to transfer the blintzes to a wire rack. Cool for at least 5 minutes or up to 20 minutes before serving.

Sweet Potato Donut Holes

Servings: 18
Cooking Time: 4 Minutes Per Batch
Ingredients:
- 1 cup flour
- ⅓ cup sugar
- ¼ teaspoon baking soda
- 1 teaspoon baking powder
- ⅛ teaspoon salt
- ½ cup cooked mashed purple sweet potatoes
- 1 egg, beaten
- 2 tablespoons butter, melted
- 1 teaspoon pure vanilla extract
- oil for misting or cooking spray

Directions:
1. Preheat air fryer to 390°F.
2. In a large bowl, stir together the flour, sugar, baking soda, baking powder, and salt.
3. In a separate bowl, combine the potatoes, egg, butter, and vanilla and mix well.
4. Add potato mixture to dry ingredients and stir into a soft dough.
5. Shape dough into 1½-inch balls. Mist lightly with oil or cooking spray.
6. Place 9 donut holes in air fryer basket, leaving a little space in between. Cook for 4 minutes, until done in center and lightly browned outside.
7. Repeat step 6 to cook remaining donut holes.

Honey-roasted Mixed Nuts

Servings: 8
Cooking Time: 15 Minutes
Ingredients:
- ½ cup raw, shelled pistachios
- ½ cup raw almonds
- 1 cup raw walnuts
- 2 tablespoons filtered water
- 2 tablespoons honey
- 1 tablespoon vegetable oil
- 2 tablespoons sugar
- ½ teaspoon salt

Directions:
1. Preheat the air fryer to 300°F.
2. Lightly spray an air-fryer-safe pan with olive oil; then place the pistachios, almonds, and walnuts inside the pan and place the pan inside the air fryer basket.
3. Cook for 15 minutes, shaking the basket every 5 minutes to rotate the nuts.
4. While the nuts are roasting, boil the water in a small pan and stir in the honey and oil. Continue to stir while cooking until the water begins to evaporate and a thick sauce is formed. Note: The sauce should stick to the back of a wooden spoon when mixed. Turn off the heat.
5. Remove the nuts from the air fryer (cooking should have just completed) and spoon the nuts into the stovetop pan. Use a spatula to coat the nuts with the honey syrup.
6. Line a baking sheet with parchment paper and spoon the nuts onto the sheet. Lightly sprinkle the sugar and salt over the nuts and let cool in the refrigerator for at least 2 hours.
7. When the honey and sugar have hardened, store the nuts in an airtight container in the refrigerator.

Nutty Banana Bread

Servings: 6
Cooking Time: 30 Minutes
Ingredients:
- 2 bananas
- 2 tbsp ground flaxseed
- ¼ cup milk
- 1 tbsp apple cider vinegar
- 1 tbsp vanilla extract
- ½ tsp ground cinnamon
- 2 tbsp honey
- ½ cup oat flour
- ½ tsp baking soda
- 3 tbsp butter

Directions:
1. Preheat air fryer to 320°F. Using a fork, mash the bananas until chunky. Mix in flaxseed, milk, apple vinegar, vanilla extract, cinnamon, and honey. Finally, toss in oat flour and baking soda until smooth but still chunky. Divide the batter between 6 cupcake molds. Top with one and a half teaspoons of butter each and swirl it a little. Bake for 18 minutes until golden brown and puffy. Let cool completely before serving.

Giant Buttery Chocolate Chip Cookie

Servings: 4
Cooking Time: 16 Minutes
Ingredients:
- ⅔ cup plus 1 tablespoon All-purpose flour
- ¼ teaspoon Baking soda
- ¼ teaspoon Table salt
- Baking spray (see the headnote)
- 4 tablespoons (¼ cup/½ stick) plus 1 teaspoon Butter, at room temperature
- ¼ cup plus 1 teaspoon Packed dark brown sugar
- 3 tablespoons plus 1 teaspoon Granulated white sugar
- 2½ tablespoons Pasteurized egg substitute, such as Egg Beaters
- ½ teaspoon Vanilla extract
- ¾ cup plus 1 tablespoon Semisweet or bittersweet chocolate chips

Directions:
1. Preheat the air fryer to 350°F.
2. Whisk the flour, baking soda, and salt in a bowl until well combined.
3. For a small air fryer, coat the inside of a 6-inch round cake pan with baking spray. For a medium air fryer, coat the inside of a 7-inch round cake pan with baking spray. And for a large air fryer, coat the inside of an 8-inch round cake pan with baking spray.
4. Using a hand electric mixer at medium speed, beat the butter, brown sugar, and granulated white sugar in a bowl until smooth and thick, about 3 minutes, scraping down the inside of the bowl several times.
5. Beat in the pasteurized egg substitute or egg (as applicable) and vanilla until uniform. Scrape down and remove the beaters. Fold in the flour mixture and chocolate chips with a rubber spatula, just until combined. Scrape and gently press this dough into the prepared pan, getting it even across the pan to the perimeter.
6. Set the pan in the basket and air-fry undisturbed for 16 minutes, or until the cookie is puffed, browned, and feels set to the touch.
7. Transfer the pan to a wire rack and cool for 10 minutes. Loosen the cookie from the perimeter with a spatula, then invert the pan onto a cutting board and let the cookie come free. Remove the pan and reinvert the cookie onto the wire rack. Cool for 5 minutes more before slicing into wedges to serve.

Peanut Butter Cup Doughnut Holes

Servings: 24
Cooking Time: 4 Minutes
Ingredients:
- 1½ cups bread flour
- 1 teaspoon active dry yeast
- 1 tablespoon sugar
- ¼ teaspoon salt
- ½ cup warm milk
- ½ teaspoon vanilla extract
- 2 egg yolks
- 2 tablespoons melted butter
- 24 miniature peanut butter cups, plus a few more for garnish
- vegetable oil, in a spray bottle
- Doughnut Topping
- 1 cup chocolate chips
- 2 tablespoons milk

Directions:
1. Combine the flour, yeast, sugar and salt in a bowl. Add the milk, vanilla, egg yolks and butter. Mix well until the dough starts to come together. Transfer the dough to a floured surface and knead by hand for 2 minutes. Shape the dough into a ball and transfer it to a large oiled bowl. Cover the bowl with a towel and let the dough rise in a warm place for 1 to 1½ hours, until the dough has doubled in size.
2. When the dough has risen, punch it down and roll it into a 24-inch long log. Cut the dough into 24 pieces. Push a peanut butter cup into the center of each piece of dough, pinch the dough shut and roll it into a ball. Place the dough balls on a cookie sheet and let them rise in a warm place for 30 minutes.
3. Preheat the air fryer to 400°F.
4. Spray or brush the dough balls lightly with vegetable oil. Air-fry eight at a time, at 400°F for 4 minutes, turning them over halfway through the cooking process.
5. While the doughnuts are air frying, prepare the topping. Place the chocolate chips and milk in a microwave safe bowl. Microwave on high for 1 minute. Stir and microwave for an additional 30 seconds if necessary to get all the chips to melt. Stir until the chips are melted and smooth.
6. Dip the top half of the doughnut holes into the melted chocolate. Place them on a rack to set up for just a few minutes and watch them disappear.

Maple Cinnamon Cheesecake

Servings: 4
Cooking Time: 12 Minutes
Ingredients:
- 6 sheets of cinnamon graham crackers
- 2 tablespoons butter
- 8 ounces Neufchâtel cream cheese
- 3 tablespoons pure maple syrup
- 1 large egg
- ½ teaspoon ground cinnamon
- ¼ teaspoon salt

Directions:
1. Preheat the air fryer to 350°F.
2. Place the graham crackers in a food processor and process until crushed into a flour. Mix with the butter and press into a mini air-fryer-safe pan lined at the bottom with parchment paper. Place in the air fryer and cook for 4 minutes.
3. In a large bowl, place the cream cheese and maple syrup. Use a hand mixer or stand mixer and beat together until smooth. Add in the egg, cinnamon, and salt and mix on medium speed until combined.
4. Remove the graham cracker crust from the air fryer and pour the batter into the pan.
5. Place the pan back in the air fryer, adjusting the temperature to 315°F. Cook for 18 minutes. Carefully remove when cooking completes. The top should be lightly browned and firm.
6. Keep the cheesecake in the pan and place in the refrigerator for 3 or more hours to firm up before serving.

Giant Buttery Oatmeal Cookie

Servings: 4
Cooking Time: 16 Minutes
Ingredients:
- 1 cup Rolled oats (not quick-cooking or steel-cut oats)
- ½ cup All-purpose flour
- ½ teaspoon Baking soda
- ½ teaspoon Ground cinnamon
- ½ teaspoon Table salt
- 3½ tablespoons Butter, at room temperature
- ⅓ cup Packed dark brown sugar
- 1½ tablespoons Granulated white sugar
- 3 tablespoons (or 1 medium egg, well beaten) Pasteurized egg substitute, such as Egg Beaters
- ¾ teaspoon Vanilla extract
- ⅓ cup Chopped pecans
- Baking spray

Directions:
1. Preheat the air fryer to 350°F.
2. Stir the oats, flour, baking soda, cinnamon, and salt in a bowl until well combined.
3. Using an electric hand mixer at medium speed, beat the butter, brown sugar, and granulated white sugar until creamy and thick, about 3 minutes, scraping down the inside of the bowl occasionally. Beat in the egg substitute or egg (as applicable) and vanilla until uniform.
4. Scrape down and remove the beaters. Fold in the flour mixture and pecans with a rubber spatula just until all the flour is moistened and the nuts are even throughout the dough.
5. For a small air fryer, coat the inside of a 6-inch round cake pan with baking spray. For a medium air fryer, coat the inside of a 7-inch round cake pan with baking spray. And for a large air fryer, coat the inside of an 8-inch round cake pan with baking spray. Scrape and gently press the dough into the prepared pan, spreading it into an even layer to the perimeter.
6. Set the pan in the basket and air-fry undisturbed for 16 minutes, or until puffed and browned.
7. Transfer the pan to a wire rack and cool for 10 minutes. Loosen the cookie from the perimeter with a spatula, then invert the pan onto a cutting board and let the cookie come free. Remove the pan and reinvert the cookie onto the wire rack. Cool for 5 minutes more before slicing into wedges to serve.

Fluffy Orange Cake

Servings: 6
Cooking Time: 30 Minutes
Ingredients:
- 1/3 cup cornmeal
- 1 ¼ cups flour
- ¾ cup white sugar
- 1 tsp baking soda
- ¼ cup safflower oil
- 1 ¼ cups orange juice
- 1 tsp orange zest
- ¼ cup powdered sugar

Directions:
1. Preheat air fryer to 340°F. Mix cornmeal, flour, sugar, baking soda, safflower oil, 1 cup of orange juice, and orange zest in a medium bowl. Mix until combined.
2. Pour the batter into a greased baking pan and set into the air fryer. Bake until a toothpick in the center of the cake comes out clean. Remove the cake and place it on a cooling rack. Use the toothpick to make 20 holes in the cake. Meanwhile, combine the rest of the juice with the powdered sugar in a small bowl. Drizzle the glaze over the hot cake and allow it to absorb. Leave to cool completely, then cut into pieces. Serve and enjoy!

Sea-salted Caramel Cookie Cups

Servings: 12
Cooking Time: 12 Minutes
Ingredients:
- ⅓ cup butter
- ¼ cup brown sugar
- 1 teaspoon vanilla extract
- 1 large egg
- 1 cup all-purpose flour
- ½ cup old-fashioned oats
- ½ teaspoon baking soda
- ¼ teaspoon salt
- ⅓ cup sea-salted caramel chips

Directions:
1. Preheat the air fryer to 300°F.
2. In a large bowl, cream the butter with the brown sugar and vanilla. Whisk in the egg and set aside.
3. In a separate bowl, mix the flour, oats, baking soda, and salt. Then gently mix the dry ingredients into the wet. Fold in the caramel chips.
4. Divide the batter into 12 silicon muffin liners. Place the cookie cups into the air fryer basket and cook for 12 minutes or until a toothpick inserted in the center comes out clean.
5. Remove and let cool 5 minutes before serving.

Homemade Chips Ahoy

Servings: 4
Cooking Time: 20 Minutes
Ingredients:
- 1 tbsp coconut oil, melted
- 1 tbsp honey
- 1 tbsp milk
- ½ tsp vanilla extract
- ¼ cup oat flour
- 2 tbsp coconut sugar
- ¼ tsp salt
- ¼ tsp baking powder
- 2 tbsp chocolate chips

Directions:
1. Combine the coconut oil, honey, milk, and vanilla in a bowl. Add the oat flour, coconut sugar, salt, and baking powder. Stir until combined. Add the chocolate chips and stir. Preheat air fryer to 350°F. Pour the batter into a greased baking pan, leaving a little room in between. Bake for 7 minutes or until golden. Do not overcook. Move to a cooling rack and serve chilled.

Strawberry Pastry Rolls

Servings: 4
Cooking Time: 6 Minutes
Ingredients:
- 3 ounces low-fat cream cheese
- 2 tablespoons plain yogurt
- 2 teaspoons sugar
- ¼ teaspoon pure vanilla extract
- 8 ounces fresh strawberries
- 8 sheets phyllo dough
- butter-flavored cooking spray
- ¼–½ cup dark chocolate chips (optional)

Directions:
1. In a medium bowl, combine the cream cheese, yogurt, sugar, and vanilla. Beat with hand mixer at high speed until smooth, about 1 minute.
2. Wash strawberries and destem. Chop enough of them to measure ½ cup. Stir into cheese mixture.
3. Preheat air fryer to 330°F.
4. Phyllo dough dries out quickly, so cover your stack of phyllo sheets with waxed paper and then place a damp dish towel on top of that. Remove only one sheet at a time as you work.
5. To create one pastry roll, lay out a single sheet of phyllo. Spray lightly with butter-flavored spray, top with a second sheet of phyllo, and spray the second sheet lightly.
6. Place a quarter of the filling (about 3 tablespoons) about ½ inch from the edge of one short side. Fold the end of the phyllo over the filling and keep rolling a turn or two. Fold in both the left and right sides so that the edges meet in the middle of your roll. Then roll up completely. Spray outside of pastry roll with butter spray.
7. When you have 4 rolls, place them in the air fryer basket, seam side down, leaving some space in between each. Cook at 330°F for 6 minutes, until they turn a delicate golden brown.
8. Repeat step 7 for remaining rolls.
9. Allow pastries to cool to room temperature.
10. When ready to serve, slice the remaining strawberries. If desired, melt the chocolate chips in microwave or double boiler. Place 1 pastry on each dessert plate, and top with sliced strawberries. Drizzle melted chocolate over strawberries and onto plate.

Healthy Chickpea Cookies

Servings: 6
Cooking Time: 25 Minutes
Ingredients:
- 1 cup canned chickpeas
- 2 tsp vanilla extract
- 1 tsp lemon juice
- 1/3 cup date paste
- 2 tbsp butter, melted
- 1/3 cup flour
- ½ tsp baking powder
- ¼ cup dark chocolate chips

Directions:
1. Preheat air fryer to 320°F. Line the basket with parchment paper. In a blender, blitz chickpeas, vanilla extract, and lemon juice until smooth. Remove it to a bowl. Stir in date paste and butter until well combined. Then mix in flour, baking powder, chocolate chips. Make 2-tablespoon balls out of the mixture. Place the balls onto the paper, flatten them into a cookie shape. Bake for 13 minutes until golden brown. Let cool slightly. Serve.

Honeyed Tortilla Fritters

Servings: 8
Cooking Time: 10 Minutes
Ingredients:
- 2 tbsp granulated sugar
- ½ tsp ground cinnamon
- 1 tsp vanilla powder
- Salt to taste
- 8 flour tortillas, quartered
- 2 tbsp butter, melted
- 4 tsp honey
- 1 tbsp almond flakes

Directions:
1. Preheat air fryer at 400ºF. Combine the sugar, cinnamon, vanilla powder, and salt in a bowl. Set aside. Brush tortilla quarters with melted butter and sprinkle with sugar mixture. Place tortilla quarters in the frying basket and Air Fry for 4 minutes, turning once. Let cool on a large plate for 5 minutes until hardened. Drizzle with honey and scatter with almond flakes to serve.

Mango Cobbler With Raspberries

Servings: 4
Cooking Time: 30 Minutes
Ingredients:
- 1 ½ cups chopped mango
- 1 cup raspberries
- 1 tbsp brown sugar
- 2 tsp cornstarch
- 1 tsp lemon juice
- 2 tbsp sunflower oil
- 1 tbsp maple syrup
- 1 tsp vanilla
- ½ cup rolled oats
- 1/3 cup flour
- 3 tbsp coconut sugar
- 1 tsp cinnamon
- ¼ tsp nutmeg
- ⅛ tsp salt

Directions:
1. Place the mango, raspberries, brown sugar, cornstarch, and lemon juice in a baking pan. Stir with a rubber spatula until combined. Set aside.
2. In a separate bowl, add the oil, maple syrup, and vanilla and stir well. Toss in the oats, flour, coconut sugar, cinnamon, nutmeg, and salt. Stir until combined. Sprinkle evenly over the mango-raspberry filling. Preheat air fryer to 320°F. Bake for 20 minutes or until the topping is crispy and golden. Enjoy warm.

Honey-pecan Yogurt Cake

Servings: 6
Cooking Time: 18-24 Minutes
Ingredients:
- 1 cup plus 3½ tablespoons All-purpose flour
- ¼ teaspoon Baking powder
- ¼ teaspoon Baking soda
- ¼ teaspoon Table salt
- 5 tablespoons Plain full-fat, low-fat, or fat-free Greek yogurt
- 5 tablespoons Honey
- 5 tablespoons Pasteurized egg substitute, such as Egg Beaters
- 2 teaspoons Vanilla extract
- ⅔ cup Chopped pecans
- Baking spray (see here)

Directions:
1. Preheat the air fryer to 325°F (or 330°F, if the closest setting).
2. Mix the flour, baking powder, baking soda, and salt in a small bowl until well combined.
3. Using an electric hand mixer at medium speed, beat the yogurt, honey, egg substitute or egg, and vanilla in a medium bowl until smooth, about 2 minutes, scraping down the inside of the bowl once or twice.
4. Turn off the mixer; scrape down and remove the beaters. Fold in the flour mixture with a rubber spatula, just until all of the flour has been moistened. Fold in the pecans until they are evenly distributed in the mixture.
5. Use the baking spray to generously coat the inside of a 6-inch round cake pan for a small batch, a 7-inch round cake pan for a medium batch, or an 8-inch round cake pan for a large batch. Scrape and spread the batter into the pan, smoothing the batter out to an even layer.
6. Set the pan in the basket and air-fry for 18 minutes for a 6-inch layer, 22 minutes for a 7-inch layer, or 24 minutes for an 8-inch layer, or until a toothpick or cake tester inserted into the center of the cake comes out clean. Start checking it at the 15-minute mark to know where you are.
7. Use hot pads or silicone baking mitts to transfer the cake pan to a wire rack. Cool for 5 minutes. To unmold, set a cutting board over the baking pan and invert both the board and the pan. Lift the still-warm pan off the cake layer. Set the wire rack on top of that layer and invert all of it with the cutting board so that the cake layer is now right side up on the wire rack. Remove the cutting board and continue cooling the cake for at least 10 minutes or to room temperature, about 30 minutes, before slicing into wedges.

Coconut Cream Roll-ups

Servings: 4
Cooking Time: 20 Minutes
Ingredients:
- ½ cup cream cheese, softened
- 1 cup fresh raspberries
- ¼ cup brown sugar
- ¼ cup coconut cream
- 1 egg
- 1 tsp corn starch
- 6 spring roll wrappers

Directions:
1. Preheat air fryer to 350°F. Add the cream cheese, brown sugar, coconut cream, cornstarch, and egg to a bowl and whisk until all ingredients are completely mixed and fluffy, thick and stiff. Spoon even amounts of the creamy filling into each spring roll wrapper, then top each dollop of filling with several raspberries. Roll up the wraps around the creamy raspberry filling, and seal the seams with a few dabs of water.
2. Place each roll on the foil-lined frying basket, seams facing down. Bake for 10 minutes, flipping them once until golden brown and perfect on the outside, while the raspberries and cream filling will have cooked together in a glorious fusion. Remove with tongs and serve hot or cold. Serve and enjoy!

Berry Streusel Cake

Servings: 6
Cooking Time: 60 Minutes
Ingredients:
- 2 tbsp demerara sugar
- 2 tbsp sunflower oil
- ¼ cup almond flour
- 1 cup pastry flour
- ½ cup brown sugar
- 1 tsp baking powder
- 1 tbsp lemon zest
- ¼ tsp salt
- ¾ cup milk
- 2 tbsp olive oil
- 1 tsp vanilla
- 1 cup blueberries
- ½ cup powdered sugar
- 1 tbsp lemon juice
- ⅛ tsp salt

Directions:
1. Mix the demerara sugar, sunflower oil, and almond flour in a bowl and put it in the refrigerator. Whisk the pastry flour, brown sugar, baking powder, lemon zest, and salt in another bowl. Add the milk, olive oil, and vanilla and stir with a rubber spatula until combined. Add the blueberries and stir slowly. Coat the inside of a baking pan with oil and pour the batter into the pan.
2. Preheat air fryer to 310°F. Remove the almond mix from the fridge and spread it over the cake batter. Put the cake in the air fryer and Bake for 45 minutes or until a knife inserted in the center comes out clean and the top is golden. Combine the powdered sugar, lemon juice and salt in a bowl. Once the cake has cooled, slice it into 4 pieces and drizzle each with icing. Serve.

Orange Gooey Butter Cake

Servings: 6
Cooking Time: 85 Minutes
Ingredients:
- Crust Layer:
- ½ cup flour
- ¼ cup sugar
- ½ teaspoon baking powder
- ⅛ teaspoon salt
- 2 ounces (½ stick) unsalted European style butter, melted
- 1 egg
- 1 teaspoon orange extract
- 2 tablespoons orange zest
- Gooey Butter Layer:
- 8 ounces cream cheese, softened
- 4 ounces (1 stick) unsalted European style butter, melted
- 2 eggs
- 2 teaspoons orange extract
- 2 tablespoons orange zest
- 4 cups powdered sugar
- Garnish:
- powdered sugar
- orange slices

Directions:
1. Preheat the air fryer to 350°F.
2. Grease a 7-inch cake pan and line the bottom with parchment paper. Combine the flour, sugar, baking powder and salt in a bowl. Add the melted butter, egg, orange extract and orange zest. Mix well and press this mixture into the bottom of the greased cake pan. Lower the pan into the basket using an aluminum foil sling (fold a piece of aluminum foil into a strip about 2-inches wide by 24-inches long). Fold the ends of the aluminum foil over the top of the dish before returning the basket to the air fryer. Air-fry uncovered for 8 minutes.
3. To make the gooey butter layer, beat the cream cheese, melted butter, eggs, orange extract and orange zest in a large bowl using an electric hand mixer. Add the powdered sugar in stages, beat until smooth with each addition. Pour this mixture on top of the baked crust in the cake pan. Wrap the pan with a piece of greased aluminum foil, tenting the top of the foil to leave a little room for the cake to rise.
4. Air-fry for 60 minutes at 350°F. Remove the aluminum foil and air-fry for an additional 17 minutes.
5. Let the cake cool inside the pan for at least 10 minutes. Then, run a butter knife around the cake and let the cake cool completely in the pan. When cooled, run the butter knife around the edges of the cake again and invert it onto a plate and then back onto a serving platter. Sprinkle the powdered sugar over the top of the cake and garnish with orange slices.

Mixed Berry Pie

Servings: 4
Cooking Time: 25 Minutes
Ingredients:
- 2/3 cup blackberries, cut into thirds
- ¼ cup sugar
- 2 tbsp cornstarch
- ¼ tsp vanilla extract
- ¼ tsp peppermint extract
- ½ tsp lemon zest
- 1 cup sliced strawberries
- 1 cup raspberries
- 1 refrigerated piecrust
- 1 large egg

Directions:
1. Mix the sugar, cornstarch, vanilla, peppermint extract, and lemon zest in a bowl. Toss in all berries gently until combined. Pour into a greased dish. On a clean workspace, lay out the dough and cut into a 7-inch diameter round. Cover the baking dish with the round and crimp the edges. With a knife, cut 4 slits in the top to vent.
2. Beat 1 egg and 1 tbsp of water to make an egg wash. Brush the egg wash over the crust. Preheat air fryer to 350°F. Put the baking dish into the frying basket. Bake for 15 minutes or until the crust is golden and the berries are bubbling through the

vents. Remove from the air fryer and let cool for 15 minutes. Serve warm.

Vanilla-strawberry Muffins

Servings: 4
Cooking Time: 25 Minutes
Ingredients:
- ¼ cup diced strawberries
- 2 tbsp powdered sugar
- 1 cup flour
- ½ tsp baking soda
- 1/3 cup granulated sugar
- ¼ tsp salt
- 1 tsp vanilla extract
- 1 egg
- 1 tbsp butter, melted
- ½ cup diced strawberries
- 2 tbsp chopped walnuts
- 6 tbsp butter, softened
- 1 ½ cups powdered sugar
- 1/8 tsp peppermint extract

Directions:
1. Preheat air fryer at 375ºF. Combine flour, baking soda, granulated sugar, and salt in a bowl. In another bowl, combine the vanilla, egg, walnuts and melted butter. Pour wet ingredients into dry ingredients and toss to combine. Fold in half of the strawberries and spoon mixture into 8 greased silicone cupcake liners.
2. Place cupcakes in the frying basket and Bake for 6-8 minutes. Let cool onto a cooling rack for 10 minutes. Blend the remaining strawberries in a food processor until smooth. Slowly add powdered sugar to softened butter while beating in a bowl. Stir in peppermint extract and puréed strawberries until blended. Spread over cooled cupcakes. Serve sprinkled with powdered sugar

Brownies With White Chocolate

Servings: 6
Cooking Time: 30 Minutes
Ingredients:
- ¼ cup white chocolate chips
- ¼ cup muscovado sugar
- 1 egg
- 2 tbsp white sugar
- 2 tbsp canola oil
- 1 tsp vanilla
- ¼ cup cocoa powder
- 1/3 cup flour

Directions:
1. Preheat air fryer to 340°F. Beat the egg with muscovado sugar and white sugar in a bowl. Mix in the canola oil and vanilla. Next, stir in cocoa powder and flour until just combined. Gently fold in white chocolate chips. Spoon the batter into a lightly pan. Bake until the brownies are set when lightly touched on top, about 20 minutes. Let to cool completely before slicing.

Giant Oatmeal–peanut Butter Cookie

Servings: 4
Cooking Time: 18 Minutes
Ingredients:
- 1 cup Rolled oats (not quick-cooking or steel-cut oats)
- ½ cup All-purpose flour
- ½ teaspoon Ground cinnamon
- ½ teaspoon Baking soda
- 1/3 cup Packed light brown sugar
- ¼ cup Solid vegetable shortening
- 2 tablespoons Natural-style creamy peanut butter
- 3 tablespoons Granulated white sugar
- 2 tablespoons (or 1 small egg, well beaten) Pasteurized egg substitute, such as Egg Beaters
- 1/3 cup Roasted, salted peanuts, chopped
- Baking spray

Directions:
1. Preheat the air fryer to 350°F.
2. Stir the oats, flour, cinnamon, and baking soda in a bowl until well combined.
3. Using an electric hand mixer at medium speed, beat the brown sugar, shortening, peanut butter, granulated white sugar, and egg substitute or egg (as applicable) until smooth and creamy, about 3 minutes, scraping down the inside of the bowl occasionally.
4. Scrape down and remove the beaters. Fold in the flour mixture and peanuts with a rubber spatula just until all the flour is moistened and the peanut bits are evenly distributed in the dough.
5. For a small air fryer, coat the inside of a 6-inch round cake pan with baking spray. For a medium air fryer, coat the inside of a 7-inch round cake pan with baking spray. And for a large air fryer, coat the inside of an 8-inch round cake pan with baking spray. Scrape and gently press the dough into the prepared pan, spreading it into an even layer to the perimeter.
6. Set the pan in the basket and air-fry undisturbed for 18 minutes, or until well browned.
7. Transfer the pan to a wire rack and cool for 15 minutes. Loosen the cookie from the perimeter with a spatula, then invert the pan onto a cutting board and let the cookie come free. Remove the pan and reinvert the cookie onto the wire rack. Cool for 5 minutes more before slicing into wedges to serve.

Famous Chocolate Lava Cake

Servings: 4
Cooking Time: 15 Minutes
Ingredients:
- ¼ cup flour
- 1 tbsp cocoa powder
- 1/8 tsp salt
- ½ tsp baking powder
- 1 tsp vanilla extract
- ¼ cup raw honey
- 1 egg, beaten
- 2 tbsp olive oil

- 2 tbsp icing sugar, to dust

Directions:
1. Preheat air fryer to 380°F. Sift the flour, cocoa powder, salt, vanilla, and baking powder in a bowl. Add in honey, egg, and olive oil and stir to combine. Divide the batter evenly among greased ramekins. Put the filled ramekins inside the air fryer and Bake for 10 minutes. Remove the lava cakes from the fryer and slide a knife around the outside edge of each cake. Turn each ramekin upside down on a saucer and serve dusted with icing sugar.

One-bowl Chocolate Buttermilk Cake

Servings: 6
Cooking Time: 16-20 Minutes
Ingredients:
- ¾ cup All-purpose flour
- ½ cup Granulated white sugar
- 3 tablespoons Unsweetened cocoa powder
- ½ teaspoon Baking soda
- ¼ teaspoon Table salt
- ½ cup Buttermilk
- 2 tablespoons Vegetable oil
- ¾ teaspoon Vanilla extract
- Baking spray (see here)

Directions:
1. Preheat the air fryer to 325°F (or 330°F, if that's the closest setting).
2. Stir the flour, sugar, cocoa powder, baking soda, and salt in a large bowl until well combined. Add the buttermilk, oil, and vanilla. Stir just until a thick, grainy batter forms.
3. Use the baking spray to generously coat the inside of a 6-inch round cake pan for a small batch, a 7-inch round cake pan for a medium batch, or an 8-inch round cake pan for a large batch. Scrape and spread the chocolate batter into this pan, smoothing the batter out to an even layer.
4. Set the pan in the basket and air-fry undisturbed for 16 minutes for a 6-inch layer, 18 minutes for a 7-inch layer, or 20 minutes for an 8-inch layer, or until a toothpick or cake tester inserted into the center of the cake comes out clean. Start checking it at the 14-minute mark to know where you are.
5. Use hot pads or silicone baking mitts to transfer the cake pan to a wire rack. Cool for 5 minutes. To unmold, set a cutting board over the baking pan and invert both the board and the pan. Lift the still-warm pan off the cake layer. Set the wire rack on top of the cake layer and invert all of it with the cutting board so that the cake layer is now right side up on the wire rack. Remove the cutting board and continue cooling the cake for at least 10 minutes or to room temperature, about 30 minutes, before slicing into wedges.

Apple & Blueberry Crumble

Servings: 4
Cooking Time: 20 Minutes
Ingredients:
- 5 apples, peeled and diced
- ½ lemon, zested and juiced
- ½ cup blueberries
- 1 cup brown sugar
- 1 tsp cinnamon
- ½ cup butter
- ½ cup flour

Directions:
1. Preheat air fryer to 340°F. Place the apple chunks, blueberries, lemon juice and zest, half of the butter, half of the brown sugar, and cinnamon in a greased baking dish. Combine thoroughly until all is well mixed. Combine the flour with the remaining butter and brown sugar in a separate bowl. Stir until it forms a crumbly consistency. Spread the mixture over the fruit. Bake in the air fryer for 10-15 minutes until golden and bubbling. Serve and enjoy!

Baked Caramelized Peaches

Servings: 6
Cooking Time: 25 Minutes
Ingredients:
- 3 pitted peaches, halved
- 2 tbsp brown sugar
- 1 cup heavy cream
- 1 tsp vanilla extract
- ¼ tsp ground cinnamon
- 1 cup fresh blueberries

Directions:
1. Preheat air fryer to 380°F. Lay the peaches in the frying basket with the cut side up, then top them with brown sugar. Bake for 7-11 minutes, allowing the peaches to brown around the edges. In a mixing bowl, whisk heavy cream, vanilla, and cinnamon until stiff peaks form. Fold the peaches into a plate. Spoon the cream mixture into the peach cups, top with blueberries, and serve.

Pear And Almond Biscotti Crumble

Servings: 6
Cooking Time: 65 Minutes
Ingredients:
- 7-inch cake pan or ceramic dish
- 3 pears, peeled, cored and sliced
- ½ cup brown sugar
- ¼ teaspoon ground ginger
- 1 teaspoon ground cinnamon
- ⅛ teaspoon ground nutmeg
- 2 tablespoons cornstarch
- 1¼ cups (4 to 5) almond biscotti, coarsely crushed
- ¼ cup all-purpose flour
- ¼ cup sliced almonds
- ¼ cup butter, melted

Directions:
1. Combine the pears, brown sugar, ginger, cinnamon, nutmeg and cornstarch in a bowl. Toss to combine and then pour the pear mixture into a greased 7-inch cake pan or ceramic dish.
2. Combine the crushed biscotti, flour, almonds and melted butter in a medium bowl. Toss with a fork until the mixture

resembles large crumbles. Sprinkle the biscotti crumble over the pears and cover the pan with aluminum foil.
3. Preheat the air fryer to 350°F.
4. Air-fry at 350°F for 60 minutes. Remove the aluminum foil and air-fry for an additional 5 minutes to brown the crumble layer.
5. Serve warm.

Dark Chocolate Cream Galette

Servings: 4
Cooking Time: 55 Minutes + Cooling Time
Ingredients:
- 16 oz cream cheese, softened
- 1 cup crumbled graham crackers
- 1 cup dark cocoa powder
- ½ cup white sugar
- 1 tsp peppermint extract
- 1 tsp ground cinnamon
- 1 egg
- 1 cup condensed milk
- 2 tbsp muscovado sugar
- 1 ½ tsp butter, melted

Directions:
1. Preheat air fryer to 350°F. Place the crumbled graham crackers in a large bowl and stir in the muscovado sugar and melted butter. Spread the mixture into a greased pie pan, pressing down to form the galette base. Place the pan into the air fryer and Bake for 5 minutes. Remove the pan and set aside.
2. Place the cocoa powder, cream cheese, peppermint extract, white sugar, cinnamon, condensed milk, and egg in a large bowl and whip thoroughly to combine. Spoon the chocolate mixture over the graham cracker crust and level the top with a spatula. Put in the air fryer and Bake for 40 minutes until firm. Transfer the cookies to a wire rack to cool. Serve and enjoy!

Nutella Torte

Servings: 6
Cooking Time: 55 Minutes
Ingredients:
- ¼ cup unsalted butter, softened
- ½ cup sugar
- 2 eggs
- 1 teaspoon vanilla
- 1¼ cups Nutella® (or other chocolate hazelnut spread), divided
- ¼ cup flour
- 1 teaspoon baking powder
- ¼ teaspoon salt
- dark chocolate fudge topping
- coarsely chopped toasted hazelnuts

Directions:
1. Cream the butter and sugar together with an electric hand mixer until light and fluffy. Add the eggs, vanilla, and ¾ cup of the Nutella® and mix until combined. Combine the flour, baking powder and salt together, and add these dry ingredients to the butter mixture, beating for 1 minute.
2. Preheat the air fryer to 350°F.
3. Grease a 7-inch cake pan with butter and then line the bottom of the pan with a circle of parchment paper. Grease the parchment paper circle as well. Pour the batter into the prepared cake pan and wrap the pan completely with aluminum foil. Lower the pan into the air fryer basket with an aluminum sling (fold a piece of aluminum foil into a strip about 2-inches wide by 24-inches long). Fold the ends of the aluminum foil over the top of the dish before returning the basket to the air fryer. Air-fry for 30 minutes. Remove the foil and air-fry for another 25 minutes.
4. Remove the cake from air fryer and let it cool for 10 minutes. Invert the cake onto a plate, remove the parchment paper and invert the cake back onto a serving platter. While the cake is still warm, spread the remaining ½ cup of Nutella® over the top of the cake. Melt the dark chocolate fudge in the microwave for about 10 seconds so it melts enough to be pourable. Drizzle the sauce on top of the cake in a zigzag motion. Turn the cake 90 degrees and drizzle more sauce in zigzags perpendicular to the first zigzags. Garnish the edges of the torte with the toasted hazelnuts and serve.

British Bread Pudding

Servings: 4
Cooking Time: 30 Minutes
Ingredients:
- 4 bread slices
- 1 cup milk
- ¼ cup sugar
- 2 eggs, beaten
- 1 tbsp vanilla extract
- ½ tsp ground cinnamon

Directions:
1. Preheat air fryer to 320°F. Slice bread into bite-size pieces. Set aside in a small cake pan. Mix the milk, sugar, eggs, vanilla extract, and cinnamon in a bowl until well combined. Pour over the bread and toss to coat. Bake for 20 minutes until crispy and all liquid is absorbed. Slice into 4 pieces. Serve and enjoy!

Rich Blueberry Biscuit Shortcakes

Servings: 4
Cooking Time: 35 Minutes
Ingredients:
- 1 lb blueberries, halved
- ¼ cup granulated sugar
- 1 tsp orange zest
- 1 cup heavy cream
- 1 tbsp orange juice
- 2 tbsp powdered sugar
- ¼ tsp cinnamon
- ¼ tsp nutmeg
- 2 cups flour
- 1 egg yolk
- 1 tbsp baking powder
- ½ tsp baking soda
- ½ tsp cornstarch

- ½ tsp salt
- ½ tsp vanilla extract
- ½ tsp honey
- 4 tbsp cold butter, cubed
- 1 ¼ cups buttermilk

Directions:
1. Combine blueberries, granulated sugar, and orange zest in a bowl. Let chill the topping covered in the fridge until ready to use. Beat heavy cream, orange juice, egg yolk, vanilla extract and powdered sugar in a metal bowl until peaks form. Let chill the whipped cream covered in the fridge until ready to use.
2. Preheat air fryer at 350°F. Combine flour, cinnamon, nutmeg, baking powder, baking soda, cornstarch, honey, butter cubes, and buttermilk in a bowl until a sticky dough forms. Flour your hands and form dough into 8 balls. Place them on a lightly greased pizza pan. Place pizza pan in the frying basket and Air Fry for 8 minutes. Transfer biscuits to serving plates and cut them in half. Spread blueberry mixture to each biscuit bottom and place tops of biscuits. Garnish with whipped cream and serve.

Apple Crisp

Servings: 4
Cooking Time: 16 Minutes
Ingredients:
- Filling
- 3 Granny Smith apples, thinly sliced (about 4 cups)
- ¼ teaspoon ground cinnamon
- ⅛ teaspoon salt
- 1½ teaspoons lemon juice
- 2 tablespoons honey
- 1 tablespoon brown sugar
- cooking spray
- Crumb Topping
- 2 tablespoons oats
- 2 tablespoons oat bran
- 2 tablespoons cooked quinoa
- 2 tablespoons chopped walnuts
- 2 tablespoons brown sugar
- 2 teaspoons coconut oil

Directions:
1. Combine all filling ingredients and stir well so that apples are evenly coated.
2. Spray air fryer baking pan with nonstick cooking spray and spoon in the apple mixture.
3. Cook at 360°F for 5minutes. Stir well, scooping up from the bottom to mix apples and sauce.
4. At this point, the apples should be crisp-tender. Continue cooking in 3-minute intervals until apples are as soft as you like.
5. While apples are cooking, combine all topping ingredients in a small bowl. Stir until coconut oil mixes in well and distributes evenly. If your coconut oil is cold, it may be easier to mix in by hand.
6. When apples are cooked to your liking, sprinkle crumb mixture on top. Cook at 360°F for 8 minutes or until crumb topping is golden brown and crispy.

Fruity Oatmeal Crisp

Servings: 6
Cooking Time: 25 Minutes
Ingredients:
- 2 peeled nectarines, chopped
- 1 peeled apple, chopped
- 1/3 cup raisins
- 2 tbsp honey
- 1/3 cup brown sugar
- ¼ cup flour
- ½ cup oatmeal
- 3 tbsp softened butter

Directions:
1. Preheat air fryer to 380°F. Mix together nectarines, apple, raisins, and honey in a baking pan. Set aside. Mix brown sugar, flour, oatmeal and butter in a medium bowl until crumbly. Top the fruit in a greased pan with the crumble. Bake until bubbly and the topping is golden, 10-12 minutes. Serve warm and top with vanilla ice cream if desired.

Cheese & Honey Stuffed Figs

Servings: 4
Cooking Time: 15 Minutes
Ingredients:
- 8 figs, stem off
- 2 oz cottage cheese
- ¼ tsp ground cinnamon
- ¼ tsp orange zest
- ¼ tsp vanilla extract
- 2 tbsp honey
- 1 tbsp olive oil

Directions:
1. Preheat air fryer to 360°F. Cut an "X" in the top of each fig 1/3 way through, leaving intact the base. Mix together the cottage cheese, cinnamon, orange zest, vanilla extract and 1 tbsp of honey in a bowl. Spoon the cheese mixture into the cavity of each fig. Put the figs in a single layer in the frying basket. Drizzle the olive oil over the top of the figs and Roast for 10 minutes. Drizzle with the remaining honey. Serve and enjoy!

Air-fried Beignets

Servings: 24
Cooking Time: 5 Minutes
Ingredients:
- ¾ cup lukewarm water (about 90°F)
- ¼ cup sugar
- 1 generous teaspoon active dry yeast (½ envelope)
- 3½ to 4 cups all-purpose flour
- ½ teaspoon salt
- 2 tablespoons unsalted butter, room temperature and cut into small pieces
- 1 egg, lightly beaten
- ½ cup evaporated milk
- ¼ cup melted butter

- 1 cup confectioners' sugar
- chocolate sauce or raspberry sauce, to dip

Directions:
1. Combine the lukewarm water, a pinch of the sugar and the yeast in a bowl and let it proof for 5 minutes. It should froth a little. If it doesn't froth, your yeast is not active and you should start again with new yeast.
2. Combine 3½ cups of the flour, salt, 2 tablespoons of butter and the remaining sugar in a large bowl, or in the bowl of a stand mixer. Add the egg, evaporated milk and yeast mixture to the bowl and mix with a wooden spoon (or the paddle attachment of the stand mixer) until the dough comes together in a sticky ball. Add a little more flour if necessary to get the dough to form. Transfer the dough to an oiled bowl, cover with plastic wrap or a clean kitchen towel and let it rise in a warm place for at least 2 hours or until it has doubled in size. Longer is better for flavor development and you can even let the dough rest in the refrigerator overnight (just remember to bring it to room temperature before proceeding with the recipe).
3. Roll the dough out to ½-inch thickness. Cut the dough into rectangular or diamond-shaped pieces. You can make the beignets any size you like, but this recipe will give you 24 (2-inch x 3-inch) rectangles.
4. Preheat the air fryer to 350°F.
5. Brush the beignets on both sides with some of the melted butter and air-fry in batches at 350°F for 5 minutes, turning them over halfway through if desired. (They will brown on all sides without being flipped, but flipping them will brown them more evenly.)
6. As soon as the beignets are finished, transfer them to a plate or baking sheet and dust with the confectioners' sugar. Serve warm with a chocolate or raspberry sauce.

Fried Banana S'mores

Servings: 4
Cooking Time: 6 Minutes
Ingredients:
- 4 bananas
- 3 tablespoons mini semi-sweet chocolate chips
- 3 tablespoons mini peanut butter chips
- 3 tablespoons mini marshmallows
- 3 tablespoons graham cracker cereal

Directions:
1. Preheat the air fryer to 400°F.
2. Slice into the un-peeled bananas lengthwise along the inside of the curve, but do not slice through the bottom of the peel. Open the banana slightly to form a pocket.
3. Fill each pocket with chocolate chips, peanut butter chips and marshmallows. Poke the graham cracker cereal into the filling.
4. Place the bananas in the air fryer basket, resting them on the side of the basket and each other to keep them upright with the filling facing up. Air-fry for 6 minutes, or until the bananas are soft to the touch, the peels have blackened and the chocolate and marshmallows have melted and toasted.
5. Let them cool for a couple of minutes and then simply serve with a spoon to scoop out the filling.

Pumpkin Brownies

Servings: 4
Cooking Time: 30 Minutes
Ingredients:
- ¼ cup canned pumpkin
- ½ cup maple syrup
- 2 eggs, beaten
- 1 tbsp vanilla extract
- ¼ cup tapioca flour
- ¼ cup flour
- ½ tsp baking powder

Directions:
1. Preheat air fryer to 320°F. Mix the pumpkin, maple syrup, eggs, and vanilla extract in a bowl. Toss in tapioca flour, flour, and baking powder until smooth. Pour the batter into a small round cake pan and Bake for 20 minutes until a toothpick comes out clean. Let cool completely before slicing into 4 brownies. Serve and enjoy!

Strawberry Donuts

Servings: 4
Cooking Time: 55 Minutes
Ingredients:
- ¾ cup Greek yogurt
- 2 tbsp maple syrup
- 1 tbsp vanilla extract
- 2 tsp active dry yeast
- 1 ½ cups all-purpose flour
- 3 tbsp milk
- ½ cup strawberry jam

Directions:
1. Preheat air fryer to 350°F. Whisk the Greek yogurt, maple syrup, vanilla extract, and yeast until well combined. Then toss in flour until you get a sticky dough. Let rest covered for 10 minutes. Flour a parchment paper on a flat surface, lay the dough, sprinkle with some flour, and flatten to ½-inch thick with a rolling pin.
2. Using a 3-inch cookie cutter, cut the donuts. Repeat the process until no dough is left. Place the donuts in the basket and let rise for 15-20 minutes. Spread some milk on top of each donut and Air Fry for 4 minutes. Turn the donuts, spread more milk, and Air Fry for 4 more minutes until golden brown. Let cool for 15 minutes. Using a knife, cut the donuts 3/4 lengthwise, brush 1 tbsp of strawberry jam on each and close them. Serve.

Mini Carrot Cakes

Servings: 6
Cooking Time: 25 Minutes
Ingredients:
- 1 cup grated carrots
- ¼ cup raw honey
- ¼ cup olive oil
- ½ tsp vanilla extract
- ½ tsp lemon zest
- 1 egg

- ¼ cup applesauce
- 1 1/3 cups flour
- ¾ tsp baking powder
- ½ tsp baking soda
- ½ tsp ground cinnamon
- ¼ tsp ground nutmeg
- ⅛ tsp ground ginger
- ⅛ tsp salt
- ¼ cup chopped hazelnuts
- 2 tbsp chopped sultanas

Directions:
1. Preheat air fryer to 380°F. Combine the carrots, honey, olive oil, vanilla extract, lemon zest, egg, and applesauce in a bowl. Sift the flour, baking powder, baking soda, cinnamon, nutmeg, ginger, and salt in a separate bowl. Add the wet ingredients to the dry ingredients, mixing until just combined. Fold in the hazelnuts and sultanas. Fill greased muffin cups three-quarters full with the batter, and place them in the frying basket. Bake for 10-12 minutes until a toothpick inserted in the center of a cupcake comes out clean. Serve and enjoy!

Spiced Fruit Skewers

Servings: 4
Cooking Time: 15 Minutes
Ingredients:
- 2 peeled peaches, thickly sliced
- 3 plums, halved and pitted
- 3 peeled kiwi, quartered
- 1 tbsp honey
- ½ tsp ground cinnamon
- ¼ tsp ground allspice
- ¼ tsp cayenne pepper

Directions:
1. Preheat air fryer to 400°F. Combine the honey, cinnamon, allspice, and cayenne and set aside. Alternate fruits on 8 bamboo skewers, then brush the fruit with the honey mix. Lay the skewers in the air fryer and Air Fry for 3-5 minutes. Allow to chill for 5 minutes before serving.

Easy Churros

Servings: 12
Cooking Time: 10 Minutes
Ingredients:
- ½ cup Water
- 4 tablespoons (¼ cup/½ stick) Butter
- ¼ teaspoon Table salt
- ½ cup All-purpose flour
- 2 Large egg(s)
- ¼ cup Granulated white sugar
- 2 teaspoons Ground cinnamon

Directions:
1. Bring the water, butter, and salt to a boil in a small saucepan set over high heat, stirring occasionally.
2. When the butter has fully melted, reduce the heat to medium and stir in the flour to form a dough. Continue cooking, stirring constantly, to dry out the dough until it coats the bottom and sides of the pan with a film, even a crust. Remove the pan from the heat, scrape the dough into a bowl, and cool for 15 minutes.
3. Using an electric hand mixer at medium speed, beat in the egg, or eggs one at a time, until the dough is smooth and firm enough to hold its shape.
4. Mix the sugar and cinnamon in a small bowl. Scoop up 1 tablespoon of the dough and roll it in the sugar mixture to form a small, coated tube about ½ inch in diameter and 2 inches long. Set it aside and make 5 more tubes for the small batch or 11 more for the large one.
5. Set the tubes on a plate and freeze for 20 minutes. Meanwhile, Preheat the air fryer to 375°F.
6. Set 3 frozen tubes in the basket for a small batch or 6 for a large one with as much air space between them as possible. Air-fry undisturbed for 10 minutes, or until puffed, brown, and set.
7. Use kitchen tongs to transfer the churros to a wire rack to cool for at least 5 minutes. Meanwhile, air-fry and cool the second batch of churros in the same way.

Sugared Pizza Dough Dippers With Raspberry Cream Cheese Dip

Servings: 10
Cooking Time: 8 Minutes
Ingredients:
- 1 pound pizza dough*
- ½ cup butter, melted
- ¾ to 1 cup sugar
- Raspberry Cream Cheese Dip
- 4 ounces cream cheese, softened
- 2 tablespoons powdered sugar
- ½ teaspoon almond extract or almond paste
- 1½ tablespoons milk
- ¼ cup raspberry preserves
- fresh raspberries

Directions:
1. Cut the ingredients in half or save half of the dough for another recipe.
2. When you're ready to make your sugared dough dippers, remove your pizza dough from the refrigerator at least 1 hour prior to baking and let it sit on the counter, covered gently with plastic wrap.
3. Roll the dough into two 15-inch logs. Cut each log into 20 slices and roll each slice so that it is 3- to 3½-inches long. Cut each slice in half and twist the dough halves together 3 to 4 times. Place the twisted dough on a cookie sheet, brush with melted butter and sprinkle sugar over the dough twists.
4. Preheat the air fryer to 350°F.
5. Brush the bottom of the air fryer basket with a little melted butter. Air-fry the dough twists in batches. Place 8 to 12 (depending on the size of your air fryer) in the air fryer basket.
6. Air-fry for 6 minutes. Turn the dough strips over and brush the other side with butter. Air-fry for an additional 2 minutes.
7. While the dough twists are cooking, make the cream cheese and raspberry dip. Whip the cream cheese with a hand

mixer until fluffy. Add the powdered sugar, almond extract and milk, and beat until smooth. Fold in the raspberry preserves and transfer to a serving dish.

8. As the batches of dough twists are complete, place them into a shallow dish. Brush with more melted butter and generously coat with sugar, shaking the dish to cover both sides. Serve the sugared dough dippers warm with the raspberry cream cheese dip on the side. Garnish with fresh raspberries.

Banana Fritters

Servings: 6
Cooking Time: 20 Minutes
Ingredients:
- 1 egg
- ¼ cup cornstarch
- ¼ cup bread crumbs
- 3 bananas, halved crosswise
- ¼ cup caramel sauce

Directions:
1. Preheat air fryer to 350°F. Set up three small bowls. In the first bowl, add cornstarch. In the second bowl, beat the egg. In the third bowl, add bread crumbs. Dip the bananas in the cornstarch first, then the egg, and then dredge in bread crumbs. Put the bananas in the greased frying basket and spray with oil. Air Fry for 8 minutes, flipping once around minute 5. Remove to a serving plate and drizzle with caramel sauce. Serve warm and enjoy.

Mom's Amaretto Cheesecake

Servings: 6
Cooking Time: 35 Minutes
Ingredients:
- 2/3 cup slivered almonds
- ½ cup Corn Chex
- 1 tbsp light brown sugar
- 3 tbsp butter, melted
- 14 oz cream cheese
- 2 tbsp sour cream
- ½ cup granulated sugar
- ½ cup Amaretto liqueur
- ½ tsp lemon juice
- 2 tbsp almond flakes

Directions:
1. In a food processor, pulse corn Chex, almonds, and brown sugar until it has a powdered consistency. Transfer it to a bowl. Stir in melted butter with a fork until butter is well distributed. Press mixture into a greased cake pan.
2. Preheat air fryer at 400°F. In a bowl, combine cream cheese, sour cream, granulated sugar, Amaretto liqueur, and lemon juice until smooth. Pour it over the crust and cover with aluminum foil. Place springform pan in the frying basket and Bake for 16 minutes. Remove the foil and cook for 6 more minutes until a little jiggly in the center. Let sit covered in the fridge for at least 2 hours. Release side pan and serve sprinkled with almond flakes.

Fried Pineapple Chunks

Servings: 3
Cooking Time: 10 Minutes
Ingredients:
- 3 tablespoons Cornstarch
- 1 Large egg white, beaten until foamy
- 1 cup (4 ounces) Ground vanilla wafer cookies (not low-fat cookies)
- ¼ teaspoon Ground dried ginger
- 18 (about 2¼ cups) Fresh 1-inch chunks peeled and cored pineapple

Directions:
1. Preheat the air fryer to 400°F.
2. Put the cornstarch in a medium or large bowl. Put the beaten egg white in a small bowl. Pour the cookie crumbs and ground dried ginger into a large zip-closed plastic bag, shaking it a bit to combine them.
3. Dump the pineapple chunks into the bowl with the cornstarch. Toss and stir until well coated. Use your cleaned fingers or a large fork like a shovel to pick up a few pineapple chunks, shake off any excess cornstarch, and put them in the bowl with the egg white. Stir gently, then pick them up and let any excess egg white slip back into the rest. Put them in the bag with the crumb mixture. Repeat the cornstarch-then-egg process until all the pineapple chunks are in the bag. Seal the bag and shake gently, turning the bag this way and that, to coat the pieces well.
4. Set the coated pineapple chunks in the basket with as much air space between them as possible. Even a fraction of an inch will work, but they should not touch. Air-fry undisturbed for 10 minutes, or until golden brown and crisp.
5. Gently dump the contents of the basket onto a wire rack. Cool for at least 5 minutes or up to 15 minutes before serving.

Blueberry Cheesecake Tartlets

Servings: 9
Cooking Time: 6 Minutes
Ingredients:
- 8 ounces cream cheese, softened
- ¼ cup sugar
- 1 egg
- ½ teaspoon vanilla extract
- zest of 2 lemons, divided
- 9 mini graham cracker tartlet shells*
- 2 cups blueberries
- ½ teaspoon ground cinnamon
- juice of ½ lemon
- ¼ cup apricot preserves

Directions:
1. Preheat the air fryer to 330°F.
2. Combine the cream cheese, sugar, egg, vanilla and the zest of one lemon in a medium bowl and blend until smooth by hand or with an electric hand mixer. Pour the cream cheese mixture into the tartlet shells.
3. Air-fry 3 tartlets at a time at 330°F for 6 minutes, rotating them in the air fryer basket halfway through the cooking time.

4. Combine the blueberries, cinnamon, zest of one lemon and juice of half a lemon in a bowl. Melt the apricot preserves in the microwave or over low heat in a saucepan. Pour the apricot preserves over the blueberries and gently toss to coat.
5. Allow the cheesecakes to cool completely and then top each one with some of the blueberry mixture. Garnish the tartlets with a little sugared lemon peel and refrigerate until you are ready to serve.

Peanut Butter S'mores

Servings: 10
Cooking Time: 1 Minute
Ingredients:
- 10 Graham crackers (full, double-square cookies as they come out of the package)
- 5 tablespoons Natural-style creamy or crunchy peanut butter
- ½ cup Milk chocolate chips
- 10 Standard-size marshmallows (not minis and not jumbo campfire ones)

Directions:
1. Preheat the air fryer to 350°F.
2. Break the graham crackers in half widthwise at the marked place, so the rectangle is now in two squares. Set half of the squares flat side up on your work surface. Spread each with about 1½ teaspoons peanut butter, then set 10 to 12 chocolate chips point side up into the peanut butter on each, pressing gently so the chips stick.
3. Flatten a marshmallow between your clean, dry hands and set it atop the chips. Do the same with the remaining marshmallows on the other coated graham crackers. Do not set the other half of the graham crackers on top of these coated graham crackers.
4. When the machine is at temperature, set the treats graham cracker side down in a single layer in the basket. They may touch, but even a fraction of an inch between them will provide better air flow. Air-fry undisturbed for 45 seconds.
5. Use a nonstick-safe spatula to transfer the topped graham crackers to a wire rack. Set the other graham cracker squares flat side down over the marshmallows. Cool for a couple of minutes before serving.

Fried Cannoli Wontons

Servings: 10
Cooking Time: 8 Minutes
Ingredients:
- 8 ounces Neufchâtel cream cheese
- ¼ cup powdered sugar
- 1 teaspoon vanilla extract
- ¼ teaspoon salt
- ¼ cup mini chocolate chips
- 2 tablespoons chopped pecans (optional)
- 20 wonton wrappers
- ¼ cup filtered water

Directions:
1. Preheat the air fryer to 370°F.
2. In a large bowl, use a hand mixer to combine the cream cheese with the powdered sugar, vanilla, and salt. Fold in the chocolate chips and pecans. Set aside.
3. Lay the wonton wrappers out on a flat, smooth surface and place a bowl with the filtered water next to them.
4. Use a teaspoon to evenly divide the cream cheese mixture among the 20 wonton wrappers, placing the batter in the center of the wontons.
5. Wet the tip of your index finger, and gently moisten the outer edges of the wrapper. Then fold each wrapper until it creates a secure pocket.
6. Liberally spray the air fryer basket with olive oil mist.
7. Place the wontons into the basket, and cook for 5 to 8 minutes. When the outer edges begin to brown, remove the wontons from the air fryer basket. Repeat cooking with remaining wontons.
8. Serve warm.

Oreo-coated Peanut Butter Cups

Servings: 8
Cooking Time: 4 Minutes
Ingredients:
- 8 Standard ¾-ounce peanut butter cups, frozen
- ⅓ cup All-purpose flour
- 2 Large egg white(s), beaten until foamy
- 16 Oreos or other creme-filled chocolate sandwich cookies, ground to crumbs in a food processor
- Vegetable oil spray

Directions:
1. Set up and fill three shallow soup plates or small pie plates on your counter: one for the flour, one for the beaten egg white(s), and one for the cookie crumbs.
2. Dip a frozen peanut butter cup in the flour, turning it to coat all sides. Shake off any excess, then set it in the beaten egg white(s). Turn it to coat all sides, then let any excess egg white slip back into the rest. Set the candy bar in the cookie crumbs. Turn to coat on all parts, even the sides. Dip the peanut butter cup back in the egg white(s) as before, then into the cookie crumbs as before, making sure you have a solid, even coating all around the cup. Set aside while you dip and coat the remaining cups.
3. When all the peanut butter cups are dipped and coated, lightly coat them on all sides with the vegetable oil spray. Set them on a plate and freeze while the air fryer heats.
4. Preheat the air fryer to 400°F.
5. Set the dipped cups wider side up in the basket with as much air space between them as possible. Air-fry undisturbed for 4 minutes, or until they feel soft but the coating is set.
6. Turn off the machine and remove the basket from it. Set aside the basket with the fried cups for 10 minutes. Use a nonstick-safe spatula to transfer the fried cups to a wire rack. Cool for at least another 5 minutes before serving.

Chewy Coconut Cake

Servings: 6
Cooking Time: 18-22 Minutes
Ingredients:
- ¾ cup plus 2½ tablespoons All-purpose flour
- ¾ teaspoon Baking powder
- ⅛ teaspoon Table salt
- 7½ tablespoons (1 stick minus ½ tablespoon) Butter, at room temperature
- ⅓ cup plus 1 tablespoon Granulated white sugar
- 5 tablespoons Packed light brown sugar
- 5 tablespoons Pasteurized egg substitute, such as Egg Beaters
- 2 teaspoons Vanilla extract
- ½ cup Unsweetened shredded coconut (see here)
- Baking spray

Directions:
1. Preheat the air fryer to 325°F (or 330°F, if that's the closest setting).
2. Mix the flour, baking powder, and salt in a small bowl until well combined.
3. Using an electric hand mixer at medium speed, beat the butter, granulated white sugar, and brown sugar in a medium bowl until creamy and smooth, about 3 minutes, occasionally scraping down the inside of the bowl. Beat in the egg substitute or egg and vanilla until smooth.
4. Scrape down and remove the beaters. Fold in the flour mixture with a rubber spatula just until all the flour is moistened. Fold in the coconut until the mixture is a uniform color.
5. Use the baking spray to generously coat the inside of a 6-inch round cake pan for a small batch, a 7-inch round cake pan for a medium batch, or an 8-inch round cake pan for a large batch. Scrape and spread the batter into the pan, smoothing the batter out to an even layer.
6. Set the pan in the basket and air-fry for 18 minutes for a 6-inch layer, 20 minutes for a 7-inch layer, or 22 minutes for an 8-inch layer, or until the cake is well browned and set even if there's a little soft give right at the center. Start checking it at the 16-minute mark to know where you are.
7. Use hot pads or silicone baking mitts to transfer the cake pan to a wire rack. Cool for at least 1 hour or up to 4 hours. Use a nonstick-safe knife to slice the cake into wedges right in the pan, lifting them out one by one.

Chocolate Cake

Servings: 8
Cooking Time: 20 Minutes
Ingredients:
- ½ cup sugar
- ¼ cup flour, plus 3 tablespoons
- 3 tablespoons cocoa
- ½ teaspoon baking powder
- ½ teaspoon baking soda
- ¼ teaspoon salt
- 1 egg
- 2 tablespoons oil
- ½ cup milk
- ½ teaspoon vanilla extract

Directions:
1. Preheat air fryer to 330°F.
2. Grease and flour a 6 x 6-inch baking pan.
3. In a medium bowl, stir together the sugar, flour, cocoa, baking powder, baking soda, and salt.
4. Add all other ingredients and beat with a wire whisk until smooth.
5. Pour batter into prepared pan and bake at 330°F for 20 minutes, until toothpick inserted in center comes out clean or with crumbs clinging to it.

Tortilla Fried Pies

Servings: 12
Cooking Time: 5 Minutes
Ingredients:
- 12 small flour tortillas (4-inch diameter)
- ½ cup fig preserves
- ¼ cup sliced almonds
- 2 tablespoons shredded, unsweetened coconut
- oil for misting or cooking spray

Directions:
1. Wrap refrigerated tortillas in damp paper towels and heat in microwave 30 seconds to warm.
2. Working with one tortilla at a time, place 2 teaspoons fig preserves, 1 teaspoon sliced almonds, and ½ teaspoon coconut in the center of each.
3. Moisten outer edges of tortilla all around.
4. Fold one side of tortilla over filling to make a half-moon shape and press down lightly on center. Using the tines of a fork, press down firmly on edges of tortilla to seal in filling.
5. Mist both sides with oil or cooking spray.
6. Place hand pies in air fryer basket close but not overlapping. It's fine to lean some against the sides and corners of the basket. You may need to cook in 2 batches.
7. Cook at 390°F for 5minutes or until lightly browned. Serve hot.
8. Refrigerate any leftover pies in a closed container. To serve later, toss them back in the air fryer basket and cook for 2 or 3minutes to reheat.

Mango-chocolate Custard

Servings: 4
Cooking Time: 40 Minutes
Ingredients:
- 4 egg yolks
- 2 tbsp granulated sugar
- 1/8 tsp almond extract
- 1 ½ cups half-and-half
- 3/4 cup chocolate chips
- 1 mango, pureed
- 1 mango, chopped
- 1 tsp fresh mint, chopped

Directions:

1. Beat the egg yolks, sugar, and almond extract in a bowl. Set aside. Place half-and-half in a saucepan over low heat and bring it to a low simmer. Whisk a spoonful of heated half-and-half into egg mixture, then slowly whisk egg mixture into saucepan. Stir in chocolate chips and mango purée for 10 minutes until chocolate melts. Divide between 4 ramekins.

2. Preheat air fryer at 350°F. Place ramekins in the frying basket and Bake for 6-8 minutes. Let cool onto a cooling rack for 15 minutes, then let chill covered in the fridge for at least 2 hours or up to 2 days. Serve with chopped mangoes and mint on top.

Custard

Servings: 4
Cooking Time: 45 Minutes
Ingredients:
- 2 cups whole milk
- 2 eggs
- ¼ cup sugar
- ⅛ teaspoon salt
- ¼ teaspoon vanilla
- cooking spray
- ⅛ teaspoon nutmeg

Directions:
1. In a blender, process milk, egg, sugar, salt, and vanilla until smooth.
2. Spray a 6 x 6-inch baking pan with nonstick spray and pour the custard into it.
3. Cook at 300°F for 45 minutes. Custard is done when the center sets.
4. Sprinkle top with the nutmeg.
5. Allow custard to cool slightly.
6. Serve it warm, at room temperature, or chilled.

Cherry Cheesecake Rolls

Servings: 6
Cooking Time: 30 Minutes
Ingredients:
- 1 can crescent rolls
- 4 oz cream cheese
- 1 tbsp cherry preserves
- 1/3 cup sliced fresh cherries

Directions:
1. Roll out the dough into a large rectangle on a flat work surface. Cut the dough into 12 rectangles by cutting 3 cuts across and 2 cuts down. In a microwave-safe bowl, soften cream cheese for 15 seconds. Stir together with cherry preserves. Mound 2 tsp of the cherries-cheese mix on each piece of dough. Carefully spread the mixture but not on the edges. Top with 2 tsp of cherries each. Roll each triangle to make a cylinder.
2. Preheat air fryer to 350°F. Place the first batch of the rolls in the greased air fryer. Spray the rolls with cooking oil and Bake for 8 minutes. Let cool in the air fryer for 2-3 minutes before removing. Serve.

Chocolate Soufflés

Servings: 2
Cooking Time: 14 Minutes
Ingredients:
- butter and sugar for greasing the ramekins
- 3 ounces semi-sweet chocolate, chopped
- ¼ cup unsalted butter
- 2 eggs, yolks and white separated
- 3 tablespoons sugar
- ½ teaspoon pure vanilla extract
- 2 tablespoons all-purpose flour
- powdered sugar, for dusting the finished soufflés
- heavy cream, for serving

Directions:
1. Butter and sugar two 6-ounce ramekins. (Butter the ramekins and then coat the butter with sugar by shaking it around in the ramekin and dumping out any excess.)
2. Melt the chocolate and butter together, either in the microwave or in a double boiler. In a separate bowl, beat the egg yolks vigorously. Add the sugar and the vanilla extract and beat well again. Drizzle in the chocolate and butter, mixing well. Stir in the flour, combining until there are no lumps.
3. Preheat the air fryer to 330°F.
4. In a separate bowl, whisk the egg whites to soft peak stage (the point at which the whites can almost stand up on the end of your whisk). Fold the whipped egg whites into the chocolate mixture gently and in stages.
5. Transfer the batter carefully to the buttered ramekins, leaving about ½-inch at the top. (You may have a little extra batter, depending on how airy the batter is, so you might be able to squeeze out a third soufflé if you want to.) Place the ramekins into the air fryer basket and air-fry for 14 minutes. The soufflés should have risen nicely and be brown on top. (Don't worry if the top gets a little dark – you'll be covering it with powdered sugar in the next step.)
6. Dust with powdered sugar and serve immediately with heavy cream to pour over the top at the table.
1.

Black And Blue Clafoutis

Servings: 2
Cooking Time: 15minutes
Ingredients:
- 6-inch pie pan
- 3 large eggs
- ½ cup sugar
- 1 teaspoon vanilla extract
- 2 tablespoons butter, melted 1 cup milk
- ½ cup all-purpose flour
- 1 cup blackberries
- 1 cup blueberries
- 2 tablespoons confectioners' sugar

Directions:
1. Preheat the air fryer to 320°F.

2. Combine the eggs and sugar in a bowl and whisk vigorously until smooth, lighter in color and well combined. Add the vanilla extract, butter and milk and whisk together well. Add the flour and whisk just until no lumps or streaks of white remain.

3. Scatter half the blueberries and blackberries in a greased (6-inch) pie pan or cake pan. Pour half of the batter (about 1¼ cups) on top of the berries and transfer the tart pan to the air fryer basket. You can use an aluminum foil sling to help with this by taking a long piece of aluminum foil, folding it in half lengthwise twice until it is roughly 26-inches by 3-inches. Place this under the pie dish and hold the ends of the foil to move the pie dish in and out of the air fryer basket. Tuck the ends of the foil beside the pie dish while it cooks in the air fryer.

4. Air-fry at 320°F for 15 minutes or until the clafoutis has puffed up and is still a little jiggly in the center. Remove the clafoutis from the air fryer, invert it onto a plate and let it cool while you bake the second batch. Serve the clafoutis warm, dusted with confectioners' sugar on top.

Fast Brownies

Servings: 4
Cooking Time: 25 Minutes
Ingredients:
- ½ cup flour
- 2 tbsp cocoa
- 1/3 cup granulated sugar
- ¼ tsp baking soda
- 3 tbsp butter, melted
- 1 egg
- ¼ tsp salt
- ½ cup chocolate chips
- ¼ cup chopped hazelnuts
- 1 tbsp powdered sugar
- 1 tsp vanilla extract

Directions:

1. Preheat air fryer at 350°F. Combine all ingredients, except chocolate chips, hazelnuts, and powdered sugar, in a bowl. Fold in chocolate chips and pecans. Press mixture into a greased cake pan. Place cake pan in the frying basket and Bake for 12 minutes. Let cool for 10 minutes before slicing into 9 brownies. Scatter with powdered sugar and serve.

Caramel Blondies With Macadamia Nuts

Servings: 4
Cooking Time: 35 Minutes + Cooling Time
Ingredients:
- 1/3 cup ground macadamia
- ½ cup unsalted butter
- 1 cup white sugar
- 1 tsp vanilla extract
- 2 eggs
- ½ cup all-purpose flour
- ½ cup caramel chips
- ¼ tsp baking powder
- A pinch of salt

Directions:

1. Preheat air fryer to 340°F. Whisk the eggs in a bowl. Add the melted butter and vanilla extract and whip thoroughly until slightly fluffy. Combine the flour, sugar, ground macadamia, caramel chips, salt, and baking powder in another bowl. Slowly pour the dry ingredients into the wet ingredients, stirring until thoroughly blended and until there are no lumps in the batter. Spoon the batter into a greased cake pan. Place the pan in the air fryer. Bake for 20 minutes until a knife comes out dry and clean. Let cool for a few minutes before cutting and serving.

RECIPES INDEX

A

Air-fried Beignets 135
Air-fried Roast Beef With Rosemary Roasted Potatoes 61
Air-fried Turkey Breast With Cherry Glaze 66
Ajillo Mushrooms 117
Almond-crusted Zucchini Fries 119
Antipasto-stuffed Cherry Tomatoes 33
Apple & Blueberry Crumble 133
Apple & Turkey Breakfast Sausages 28
Apple Crisp 135
Apple-cinnamon-walnut Muffins 24
Arancini With Marinara 103
Aromatic Pork Tenderloin 59
Artichoke-spinach Dip 31
Asiago Broccoli 114
Asian Five-spice Wings 39
Asian-style Flank Steak 58
Asian-style Orange Chicken 81
Asian-style Salmon Fillets 94
Authentic Country-style Pork Ribs 58
Avocado Egg Rolls 37
Avocado Fries 36
Avocado Fries With Quick Salsa Fresca 43
Avocado Fries, Vegan 35
Avocado Toasts With Poached Eggs 22

B

Baba Ghanouj 43
Bacon, Broccoli And Swiss Cheese Bread Pudding 25
Baked Caramelized Peaches 133
Balsamic Beef & Veggie Skewers 52
Balsamic Grape Dip 36
Balsamic Stuffed Mushrooms 123
Banana Fritters 138
Banana Muffins With Chocolate Chips 16
Banana-almond Delights 125
Banana-blackberry Muffins 25
Banana-strawberry Cakecups 14
Basic Corn On The Cob 119
Basil Cheese & Ham Stromboli 59
Beef Short Ribs 54
Beet Fries 120
Bell Pepper & Lentil Tacos 104
Berry Streusel Cake 131
Berry-glazed Turkey Breast 72
Black And Blue Clafoutis 141
Black Bean Empanadas 95
Blackberry Bbq Glazed Country-style Ribs 54
Blistered Green Beans 111
Blueberry Cheesecake Tartlets 138
Blueberry French Toast Sticks 23
Blueberry Pannenkoek (dutch Pancake) 15
Boneless Ribeyes 55
Breaded Mozzarella Sticks 45
Breakfast Burrito With Sausage 17
Breakfast Frittata 19
Breakfast Pot Pies 19
British Bread Pudding 134
Broccoli Au Gratin 118
Broccoli Cornbread 25
Brownies With White Chocolate 132
Buffalo Egg Rolls 68
Buttermilk-fried Drumsticks 72
Butternut Medallions With Honey Butter And Sage 113
Buttery Chicken Legs 75

C

Cajun Flounder Fillets 86
Cajun-spiced Pickle Chips 42
Calf's Liver 64
Cal-mex Chimichangas 56
Cal-mex Turkey Patties 66
Canadian-inspired Waffle Poutine 41
Cantonese Chicken Drumsticks 77
Caramel Blondies With Macadamia Nuts 142
Caribbean Jerk Cod Fillets 90
Carne Asada 56
Carrot Orange Muffins 20
Cauliflower "tater" Tots 40

Cheddar Cheese Biscuits 19

Cheddar Stuffed Jalapeños 47

Cheddar-bean Flautas 101

Cheese & Bean Burgers 103

Cheese & Crab Stuffed Mushrooms 91

Cheese & Honey Stuffed Figs 135

Cheese Blintzes 126

Cheese-rice Stuffed Bell Peppers 125

Cheesy Chicken Tenders 80

Cheesy Chicken-avocado Paninis 76

Cheesy Eggplant Rounds 96

Cheesy Mushroom-stuffed Pork Loins 49

Cheesy Pigs In A Blanket 35

Cheesy Potato Canapés With Bacon 48

Cheesy Potato Pot 116

Cheesy Salmon-stuffed Avocados 82

Cheesy Tortellini Bites 48

Cheesy Veggie Frittata 105

Cherry Beignets 17

Cherry Cheesecake Rolls 141

Chewy Coconut Cake 140

Chia Seed Banana Bread 22

Chicano Rice Bowls 108

Chicken Breasts Wrapped In Bacon 76

Chicken Chimichangas 68

Chicken Cordon Bleu 70

Chicken Fried Steak With Gravy 69

Chicken Pigs In Blankets 67

Chicken Scotch Eggs 15

Chicken Thighs In Salsa Verde 80

Chicken Wellington 81

Chinese-style Potstickers 44

Chocolate Cake 140

Chocolate Soufflés 141

Chorizo Sausage & Cheese Balls 30

Christmas Eggnog Bread 17

Cinnamon Canned Biscuit Donuts 126

Cinnamon Pear Oat Muffins 28

Cinnamon Sweet Potato Fries 41

Cinnamon-coconut Doughnuts 20

Cinnamon-stick Kofta Skewers 62

Citrus Pork Lettuce Wraps 50

Classic Chicken Wings 48

Classic Salisbury Steak Burgers 59

Coconut & Peanut Rice Cereal 28

Coconut Chicken With Apricot-ginger Sauce 79

Coconut Cream Roll-ups 130

Coconut-shrimp Po' Boys 93

Coffee-rubbed Pork Tenderloin 61

Collard Green & Cod Packets 86

Colorful Vegetable Medley 103

Corn Dog Bites 33

Cornflake Chicken Nuggets 81

Cornish Hens With Honey-lime Glaze 75

Country Chicken Hoagies 80

Crab Cakes 83

Crab Rangoon Dip With Wonton Chips 44

Crabmeat-stuffed Flounder 89

Crab-stuffed Mushrooms 46

Cream Cheese Deviled Eggs 22

Creamy Broccoli & Mushroom Casserole 109

Creamy Horseradish Roast Beef 60

Creole Potato Wedges 114

Creole Tilapia With Garlic Mayo 82

Crispy "fried" Chicken 74

Crispy Apple Fries With Caramel Sauce 106

Crispy Curried Sweet Potato Fries 46

Crispy Duck With Cherry Sauce 71

Crispy Fish Sandwiches 85

Crispy Five-spice Pork Belly 62

Crispy Ham And Eggs 49

Crispy Herbed Potatoes 121

Crispy Lamb Shoulder Chops 54

Crispy Noodle Salad 115

Crispy Pierogi With Kielbasa And Onions 51

Crispy Pork Pork Escalopes 50

Crispy Ravioli Bites 34

Crispy Tofu Bites 42

Crunchy Chicken Strips 70

Crunchy Granola Muffins 29

Crunchy Rice Paper Samosas 99

Cuban Sliders 33

Curried Cauliflower 105

Curried Cauliflower With Cashews And Yogurt 118

Curried Fruit 123

Curried Potato, Cauliflower And Pea Turnovers 102

Curried Sweet-and-spicy Scallops 94
Custard 141

D

Daadi Chicken Salad 70
Dark Chocolate Cream Galette 134
Dijon Artichoke Hearts 110
Dijon Roasted Purple Potatoes 124

E

Easy Caprese Flatbread 15
Easy Carnitas 52
Easy Churros 137
Easy Corn Dog Cupcakes 16
Easy Crab Cakes 47
Easy Scallops With Lemon Butter 83
Easy Zucchini Lasagna Roll-ups 101
Easy-peasy Beef Sliders 65
Effortless Mac 'n' Cheese 105
Egg & Bacon Toasts 15
Egg And Sausage Crescent Rolls 26
Eggs In Avocado Halves 35
English Scones 21

F

Falafels 105
Famous Chocolate Lava Cake 132
Fancy Chicken Piccata 78
Farmer's Fried Chicken 79
Farmers Market Quiche 23
Fast Brownies 142
Fennel & Chicken Ratatouille 73
Fiery Sweet Chicken Wings 47
Fish Cakes 90
Fish Nuggets With Broccoli Dip 85
Fish Sticks For Grown-ups 83
Fish Tacos With Jalapeño-lime Sauce 93
Flank Steak With Chimichurri Sauce 63
Flounder Fillets 92
Fluffy Orange Cake 128
French Toast Sticks 27
French-style Pork Medallions 60
French-style Steak Salad 50
Fried Banana S'mores 136

Fried Bananas 30
Fried Cannoli Wontons 139
Fried Cauliflower with Parmesan Lemon Dressing 125
Fried Dill Pickle Chips 42
Fried Eggplant Slices 115
Fried Okra 121
Fried Peaches 37
Fried Pearl Onions With Balsamic Vinegar And Basil 115
Fried Pineapple Chunks 138
Fried Potatoes With Bell Peppers 107
Fried String Beans With Greek Sauce 37
Fried Wontons 31
Fruity Oatmeal Crisp 135

G

Garlic Okra Chips 103
Garlic Parmesan Bread Ring 15
Garlic-butter Lobster Tails 82
Garlic-herb Pita Chips 45
Garlicky Roasted Mushrooms 109
Garlic-lemon Steamer Clams 87
German Chicken Frikadellen 76
Giant Buttery Chocolate Chip Cookie 127
Giant Buttery Oatmeal Cookie 128
Giant Oatmeal–peanut Butter Cookie 132
Glazed Carrots 113
Goat Cheese Stuffed Portobellos 115
Goat Cheese Stuffed Turkey Roulade 73
Golden Breaded Mushrooms 99
Greek Gyros With Chicken & Rice 77
Green Beans 117
Green Dip With Pine Nuts 110
Green Egg Quiche 14
Green Onion Pancakes 20
Grilled Cheese Sandwich Deluxe 30

H

Ham And Cheddar Gritters 26
Harissa Veggie Fries 99
Hasselback Garlic-and-butter Potatoes 119
Hasselbacks 121
Hawaiian Ahi Tuna Bowls 38
Healthy Chickpea Cookies 129
Healthy Granola 14

Healthy Living Mushroom Enchiladas 107
Hearty Salad 96
Herb Roasted Jicama 124
Herbed Zucchini Poppers 112
Herb-rubbed Salmon With Avocado 88
Herby Parmesan Pita 29
Home Fries 123
Homemade Chips Ahoy 129
Honey Lemon Thyme Glazed Cornish Hen 80
Honey Oatmeal 26
Honey Pear Chips 106
Honeyed Tortilla Fritters 129
Honey-mustard Chicken Wings 40
Honey-pecan Yogurt Cake 130
Honey-roasted Mixed Nuts 126
Honey-roasted Parsnips 120
Horseradish Crusted Salmon 85
Hot Calamari Rings 87
Huevos Rancheros 22

I

Indian Chicken Tandoori 78
Indian Fry Bread Tacos 58
Indian-inspired Chicken Skewers 76
Intense Buffalo Chicken Wings 75
Italian-style Fried Olives 44

J

Jalapeño Poppers 40
Jerk Rubbed Corn On The Cob 117

K

Kawaii Pork Roast 55
Kielbasa Sausage With Pierogies And Caramelized Onions 51
King Prawns Al Ajillo 87
Kochukaru Pork Lettuce Cups 55

L

Lamb Meatballs With Quick Tomato Sauce 53
Latkes 111
Lazy Mexican Meat Pizza 65
Leftover Roast Beef Risotto 56
Lemon Pork Escalopes 58

Lemon-blueberry Morning Bread 28
Lemon-garlic Strip Steak 57
Lemony Green Bean Sautée 122
Lentil Burritos With Cilantro Chutney 102
Lightened-up Breaded Fish Filets 86
Lime Muffins 19

M

Maewoon Chicken Legs 78
Mango Cobbler With Raspberries 130
Mango-chocolate Custard 140
Maple Bacon Wrapped Chicken Breasts 73
Maple Cinnamon Cheesecake 128
Marinated Rib-eye Steak With Herb Roasted Mushrooms 63
Mascarpone Iced Cinnamon Rolls 24
Meatless Kimchi Bowls 104
Mediterranean Granola 23
Mediterranean Potato Skins 41
Mediterranean Salmon Cakes 88
Mexican Twice Air-fried Sweet Potatoes 108
Mexican-style Salmon Stir-fry 87
Mini Bacon Egg Quiches 21
Mini Carrot Cakes 136
Mini Everything Bagels 16
Mini Meatloaves With Pancetta 49
Mini Pita Breads 27
Miso-rubbed Salmon Fillets 83
Mixed Berry Pie 131
Mom's Amaretto Cheesecake 138
Mom's Potatoes Au Gratin 120
Mongolian Beef 52
Moroccan-style Chicken Strips 68
Mozzarella En Carrozza With Puttanesca Sauce 38
Mumbai Chicken Nuggets 77
Mushroom & Turkey Bread Pizza 76
Mushroom And Fried Onion Quesadilla 96
Mushroom Lasagna 99
Mushroom, Zucchini And Black Bean Burgers 109

N

Nacho Chicken Fries 69
Natchitoches Meat Pies 64
Nutella Torte 134
Nutty Banana Bread 127

Nutty Cookies 125

O

Okra 111
Okra Chips 35
Old Bay Lobster Tails 87
Olive & Pepper Tapenade 39
One-bowl Chocolate Buttermilk Cake 133
Onion Puffs 39
Onion Ring Nachos 34
Orange Glazed Pork Tenderloin 55
Orange Gooey Butter Cake 131
Orange Trail Oatmeal 23
Oreo-coated Peanut Butter Cups 139
Original Köttbullar 61
Oyster Shrimp With Fried Rice 90

P

Paprika Fried Beef 64
Paprika Onion Blossom 46
Parmesan Asparagus 111
Parmesan Chicken Meatloaf 70
Parmesan Fish Bites 91
Parsley Egg Scramble With Cottage Cheese 17
Parsnip Fries With Romesco Sauce 122
Party Buffalo Chicken Drumettes 77
Party Giant Nachos 97
Peach Fritters 18
Peachy Chicken Chunks With Cherries 74
Peanut Butter Cup Doughnut Holes 127
Peanut Butter S'mores 139
Pear And Almond Biscotti Crumble 133
Pecorino Dill Muffins 124
Pepper Steak 65
Peppered Steak Bites 50
Pepperoni Bagel Pizzas 64
Pepperoni Pizza Bread 24
Perfect Broccolini 116
Pesto Egg & Ham Sandwiches 17
Piña Colada Shrimp 92
Pine Nut Eggplant Dip 108
Pineapple & Veggie Souvlaki 97
Piri Piri Chicken Wings 37
Plantain Chips 32

Poppy Seed Mini Hot Dog Rolls 38
Pork Chops With Cereal Crust 54
Pork Cutlets With Almond-lemon Crust 59
Pork Schnitzel With Dill Sauce 57
Poutine 32
Provençal Grilled Rib-eye 55
Pumpkin Brownies 136

Q

Quick Tuna Tacos 89
Quinoa & Black Bean Stuffed Peppers 95
Quinoa Green Pizza 96

R

Rainbow Quinoa Patties 100
Ranch Chicken Tortillas 75
Ranch Chips 42
Red Potato Chips With Mexican Dip 36
Rich Blueberry Biscuit Shortcakes 134
Rich Clam Spread 35
Rich Salmon Burgers With Broccoli Slaw 84
Rich Turkey Burgers 78
Roasted Broccoli And Red Bean Salad 122
Roasted Brussels Sprouts 118
Roasted Eggplant Halves With Herbed Ricotta 120
Roasted Fennel Salad 119
Roasted Tomatillo Salsa 31
Roasted Tomato And Cheddar Rolls 21
Roasted Vegetable Lasagna 97
Roasted Vegetable Pita Pizza 109
Roasted Veggie Bowls 102
Root Vegetable Crisps 36
Rumaki 39
Russian Pierogi With Cheese Dip 42

S

Sage Pork With Potatoes 59
Salmon Croquettes 84
Salmon Puttanesca En Papillotte With Zucchini 84
Salt And Pepper Baked Potatoes 114
Salty German-style Shrimp Pancakes 85
Satay Chicken Skewers 79
Saucy Shrimp 91
Sausage-cheese Calzone 61

Savory Sausage Balls 31

Sea Salt Radishes 123

Seafood Egg Rolls 30

Sea-salted Caramel Cookie Cups 128

Sesame Carrots And Sugar Snap Peas 113

Sesame Orange Chicken 66

Shakshuka Cups 26

Shrimp Egg Rolls 32

Shrimp Patties 86

Shrimp Sliders With Avocado 92

Shrimp, Chorizo And Fingerling Potatoes 89

Simple Green Bake 116

Simple Zucchini Ribbons 112

Sinaloa Fish Fajitas 89

Skirt Steak Fajitas 60

Smoked Paprika Cod Goujons 93

Smooth & Silky Cauliflower Purée 118

Smooth Walnut-banana Loaf 29

Southern Shrimp With Cocktail Sauce 91

Spaghetti Squash And Kale Fritters With Pomodoro Sauce 104

Speedy Baked Caprese With Avocado 110

Spiced Beef Empanadas 63

Spiced Fruit Skewers 137

Spiced Mexican Stir-fried Chicken 74

Spiced Parsnip Chips 48

Spiced Pumpkin Wedges 117

Spiced Roasted Pepitas 47

Spiced Shrimp Empanadas 88

Spicy Black Bean Turkey Burgers With Cumin-avocado Spread 72

Spicy Hoisin Bbq Pork Chops 53

Spicy Sweet Potato Tater-tots 41

Spinach & Brie Frittata 106

Spinach And Cheese Calzone 106

Spinach And Feta Stuffed Chicken Breasts 74

Spring Chicken Salad 73

Spring Veggie Empanadas 107

Sriracha Green Beans 122

Steakhouse Baked Potatoes 113

Sticky Broccoli Florets 118

Strawberry Donuts 136

Strawberry Pastry Rolls 129

String Bean Fries 34

Stuffed Onions 114

Stuffed Pork Chops 65

Stuffed Portobellos 100

Stuffed Zucchini Boats 101

Succulent Roasted Peppers 116

Sugar-dusted Beignets 28

Sugared Pizza Dough Dippers With Raspberry Cream Cheese Dip 137

Summer Sea Scallops 86

Summer Vegetables With Balsamic Drizzle, Goat Cheese And Basil 117

Super-simple Herby Turkey 82

Sushi-style Deviled Eggs 95

Suwon Pork Meatballs 51

Sweet Chili Peanuts 46

Sweet Corn Bread 100

Sweet Nutty Chicken Breasts 75

Sweet Plantain Chips 45

Sweet Potato Donut Holes 126

Sweet Potato–wrapped Shrimp 88

Sweet Roasted Pumpkin Rounds 112

Sweet-hot Pepperoni Pizza 25

T

Tandoori Paneer Naan Pizza 98

Taquito Quesadillas 45

Taquitos 71

Tasty Brussels Sprouts With Guanciale 124

T-bone Steak With Roasted Tomato, Corn And Asparagus Salsa 57

Tender Steak With Salsa Verde 56

Teriyaki Chicken Drumsticks 67

Tex-mex Beef Carnitas 51

Tex-mex Potatoes With Avocado Dressing 105

Thai Turkey Sausage Patties 16

Thyme Beef & Eggs 29

Thyme Sweet Potato Wedges 123

Tilapia Al Pesto 90

Tofu & Broccoli Salad 110

Tofu & Spinach Lasagna 106

Tomato & Garlic Roasted Potatoes 33

Tomato Candy 121

Tortilla Fried Pies 140

Tri-color Frittata 14

Tropical Salsa 100

Tuna Nuggets In Hoisin Sauce 94

Tuna Platter 110

Turkey Burger Sliders 39

Turkey Burgers 66

Turkey Scotch Eggs 67

Turkey Spring Rolls 45

Turkey Tenderloin With A Lemon Touch 80

Turkey-hummus Wraps 71

Turkish Mutabal (eggplant Dip) 123

Tuscan Chimichangas 52

Tuscan Stuffed Chicken 78

Two-cheese Grilled Sandwiches 98

V

Vanilla-strawberry Muffins 132

Vegetarian Fritters With Green Dip 47

Vegetarian Shepherd's Pie 98

Veggie Burgers 101

Veggie Fritters 124

Vip's Club Sandwiches 69

Vodka Basil Muffins With Strawberries 21

W

Walnut Pancake 27

Wasabi-coated Pork Loin Chops 49

Western Frittata 18

Wiener Schnitzel 50

Y

Yogurt-marinated Chicken Legs 81

Z

Zucchini Boats With Bacon 33

Zucchini Fries 112

Zucchini Fritters 43

Printed in Great Britain
by Amazon

23864391R00084